ISLAMIC
GUNPOWDER
EMPIRES

ISLAMIC GUNPOWDER EMPIRES

Ottomans, Safavids, and Mughals

Douglas E. Streusand

Marine Corps Command and Staff College

WESTVIEW PRESS

A Member of the Perseus Books Group

About the Cover
The cover image is a detail from a painting produced 1590–1595 in opaque watercolor and gold on paper by the artist Tulsi Kalan depicting the 1577 battle that preceded the Mughal capture of the Fort at Bundi in Rajasthan. This folio (IS.2:103-1896) is from a copy of the *Akbarnama* (*Book of Akbar*), the official biography of Akbar, the third Mughal Emperor (r. 1556–1605) in the collection of the Victoria and Albert Museum, London. Cover image © Stapleton Collection/Corbis.

Published by Westview Press,
A Member of the Perseus Books Group

Find us on the World Wide Web at www.westviewpress.com.

Every effort has been made to secure required permissions to use all images, maps, and other art included in this volume.

Interior illustration credits are provided on p. 371.

Westview Press books are available at special discounts for bulk purchases in the United States by corporations, institutions, and other organizations. For more information, please contact the Special Markets Department at the Perseus Books Group, 2300 Chestnut Street, Suite 200, Philadelphia, PA 19103, or call (800) 810-4145, ext. 5000, or e-mail special.markets@perseusbooks.com.

Designed by Brent Wilcox

Library of Congress Cataloging-in-Publication Data
Streusand, Douglas E.
    Islamic gunpowder empires : Ottomans, Safavids, and Mughals / Douglas E. Streusand.
       p.   cm.
    Includes bibliographical references and index.
    ISBN 978-0-8133-1359-7 (alk. paper)
    1. Turkey—History—Ottoman Empire, 1288–1918.   2. Iran—History—Safavid dynasty, 1501–1736.   3. Mogul Empire.   I. Title.
    DR486.S77 2011
    909'.09767—dc22
                                        2010024984

10 9 8 7 6 5 4 3 2 1

Contents

Illustrations

Preface

I first conceived of this book as a graduate student in the early 1980s, began it as a project in 1990, and have taken twenty distracted years to complete it. Its purpose has remained constant: to provide a coherent, current, and accessible introduction to the Ottoman, Safavid, and Mughal empires, using comparison to illuminate their distinctive features. Within that general mission, I sought to accomplish the following objectives:

- to put the three empires in the context of their common background and political goals
- to incorporate current historiography into a new synthesis rather than recycle the findings of earlier general accounts
- to reevaluate the concept of the gunpowder empire and provide a more accurate and complete explanation of the growth and durability of the three empires
- to explain the complex, diverse, and dynamic political ideologies of the empires
- to present the empires as part of a connected Islamic world that was itself part of a more broadly connected global system in which commercial and cultural networks crossed political boundaries
- to assess the issue of the decline of the three empires without reference to the eventual global superiority of the West
- to depict the historiography of the empires as dynamic rather than static

Islamic Gunpowder Empires is not a comprehensive history of the Islamic world in the early modern era; it is both spatially and topically incomplete. It excludes Morocco, sub-Saharan Africa, central Asia, and Southeast Asia and pays insufficient attention to social, cultural, and intellectual history. As a study of power and political order, it focuses on political, military, and economic history, on the problems of power and the burdens of power holders. It does not ignore social and cultural history entirely but seeks to place those topics in political context.

Although a history of power, this volume developed in the light of a history of conscience, Marshall G. S. Hodgson's *The Venture of Islam: Conscience and History in a World Civilization.* Though Hodgson died more than forty years ago, *The Venture of Islam* remains the greatest study of Islamic civilization. Book 5, in which Hodgson propounds his conception of gunpowder empires, suffers more from the incompleteness caused by his sudden death than any other part of the book. I undertook this project in hope of providing a current and coherent alternative to that section of Hodgson.

In doing so, I sought to continue Hodgson's enterprise of presenting the complexity and diversity of Islamic civilization. Like Western civilization, Islamic civilization is, and has been, a composite of different elements in tension. The equation of Islamic civilization with Islam and of Islam with the Shariah obscures, distorts, and oversimplifies complex realities. The emphasis on the wide variety of principles of political legitimacy operating in the three empires draws attention to this complexity. I intend this book as "history-minded" history," as J. H. Hexter explains the concept in his well-known essay "The Historian and His Day," but history-minded history inevitably illuminates the present.[1]

The target audience for the book is upper-level undergraduates, who have taken a world history survey. The book will fit into an Islamic civilization survey course, the original venue for which Hodgson produced *Venture,* or serve as the nucleus for a course on the three empires. It differs from most undergraduate texts in that it encompasses historiographic controversy. I believe that students will benefit from knowing that historians disagree and interpretations change.

In the two decades since I began the project, the historians of all three empires have been extremely productive. I have been hard put to keep pace with them and have tried to do so systematically only with works published up to 2006; I have consulted later works for clarification of particular problems or simple convenience.

Because I have completed the book while on the faculty of the Marine Corps Command & Staff College, a unit of Marine Corps University, I must include the mandatory disclaimer that it does not speak for Marine Corps University or for any agency of the U.S. government. I have, in fact, the same, if not greater, academic freedom here as at a civilian university. The college and university leadership has been strongly supportive of my research but expressed little interest in its content.

Although at various times I have studied original sources, both documents and texts, on all three empires, I have conducted extensive research only on the Mughals. The Mughal chapter is derived in great part from my *Formation of the Mughal Empire* and from further research that I hope will appear in a later book on the Mughals. The Ottoman and Safavid chapters depend on the work of other historians. Some of the interpretation is original, but none of the research is. My many professional colleagues who have spent untold hours deciphering Ottoman archival documents may resent my intrusion into their field; I can only respond that if my book succeeds in its purpose, its readers will swiftly progress from my work to theirs. Like most general works, it is likely to satisfy its readers in its treatment of everything but their own specialties.

The introduction explains the historiographic setting and interpretive themes of the book. The second chapter, "Common Heritage, Common Dilemma" explains the shared political traditions and structures and the political impasse in the Islamic world that the Ottoman, Safavid, and Mughal polities overcame. The three substantive chapters begin with a brief description of the history and institutions of each empire, followed by chronological summaries and sections on the military political institutions, economies, societies, and cultural forms. The conclusion deals with overall interpretive issues.

Notes

1. J. H. Hexter, "The Historian and His Day," in *Reappraisals in History: New Views on History and Society in Early Modern Europe*, with a foreword by Peter Laslett (Evanston, IL: Northwestern Univesity Press, 1961), 1. Multiple reprints. Hexter attributes the concept to R. L. Schuyler.

Author's Note and Acknowledgments

Twenty years have passed since Peter Kracht, the original editor for the project at Westview, called me about writing this book. The reader may have no interest in the circumstances that caused the long delay but is at least entitled to an explanation. For my part, I received no outside funding to support the project and spent most of those years engaged in child rearing as well as other professional pursuits. I have had a full-time university affiliation only since 2005 and never had ready access to a major research library. The only form of institutional support I have received has come from the Institute of World Politics (IWP), where I have taught as an adjunct professor since 2006, which provided me with research assistance in the summers of 2008 and 2009.

Much has changed over those two decades. My parents, Jane and Alan Streusand, who were enormously supportive of my aspirations in general and of this project in particular, have passed from the scene. My daughters, Deb and Rachel, have grown from cute little girls into formidable young women. I do not rue the time I spent nurturing them rather than this book. My wife, Esther, has been the constant; I hope she shares in the satisfaction of the project's completion.

Quite a number of people have provided concrete assistance over the years. I take great pleasure in acknowledging the contribution of my dear friend Rochelle Kessler, who is responsible for the selection of the illustrations, their captions, and the note on the cover. Ernest Tucker of the U.S. Naval Academy has read multiple versions of the manuscript and given me unflagging support from beginning to end. Michael O'Neal, my former student at the IWP, read most of the text and provided valuable, detailed feedback and numerous corrections. Linda Darling commented on the Ottoman chapter and provided invaluable assistance. William R. (Vijay) Pinch, Cornell Fleisher, and John Woods spared me time. Alexander P. Cohen, Mart-Stewart Smith, and Margaret Harley, my research assistants from IWP, saved me many hours of moving electrons around. Some of the reviewers for Westview Press were more anonymous than others; I thank Ernest Tucker and Colin Mitchell by name and the others with equal sincerity. Cornell Fleisher and John Woods also provided valuable assistance and encouragement. My Quantico colleague Paul Gelpi read the introduction and preface. David Wurmser and Ian Snyder read and commented upon early drafts. Sholeh Quinn, Fariba Zarinbaf, Madeline Zilfi, and Sara Nur Yıldız offered insight and encouragement.

Because of the overlap between the research for this book and my graduate training, my intellectual acknowledgments must include my teachers. John Woods taught me Iranian, including Safavid, history. His understanding of the politics in the greater Iranian world during the era of Turko-Mongol dominance underlies much of my interpretation of the three empires. Halil Inalcık, the greatest historian of the Ottoman Empire, taught me Ottoman history and encouraged me to take a comparative approach to the Ottomans and their contemporaries. The late Bernard S. Cohn supervised my study of the Mughal Empire and, with Ronald Inden, taught me of Indian society and culture. Messrs. Woods, Inden, and Cohn encouraged me to focus on doctrines of kingship. Susanne H. Rudolph and Lloyd Rudolph encouraged my use of comparative methodology in approaching problems of state formation. William McNeill contributed to the work in several ways. At the University of Chicago, he encouraged my interest in military organization and steadily directed my attention to crucial questions and variables I had missed. As editor, with Ross Dunn of the University of California, San Diego, of the Essays in World History series, he developed the concept of the book. Lastly, when it became clear that my work did not fit the original profile, he supported the completion of the project as I envisioned it. My other professors at the University of Chicago, Richard Chambers, Walter Kaegi, Heshmat Moayyad, C. M. Naim, and John R. Perry; R. Stephen Humphreys, now of the University of California, Santa Barbara; Bruce Lawrence of Duke University; and Richard Eaton of the University of Arizona also assisted in the development of my ideas.

Of course, none of these worthy scholars is responsible for any errors of commission or omission.

At Marine Corps University (MCU), I am grateful to Maj. Gen. Donald R. Gardner, USMC (Ret.), president emeritus; Maj. Gen. Robert B. Neller, USMC, current president; Dr. Jerre Wilson, vice president for academic affairs; Maj. Gen. John A. Toolan, USMC, and Col. Tom Greenwood, USMC (Ret.), past directors of the Command & Staff College (C&SC); Col. Ray Damm, the current director; and especially Dr. Charles D. (Doug) McKenna, the dean of academics, for making MCU and C&SC a wonderful and nurturing place to work. I also appreciate the assistance of Rachel Kingcade and Cynthia Evans of the university's Gray Research Center.

A community of others, old friends and new, sustained me through the project In alphabetical order, they are Erica Anaya, Bruce Bechtol, Marcy Bixby, Patrick Clawson, Linda Feldman, Jocelyn Gebhardt, Paul Gelpi, Kit Goldman, Bill Gordon, the late William C. Green, John Gregory, Richard Horowitz, Ken Katzman, Rochelle Kessler, Andy and Julie Klingenstein, Barbara Lane, Chris Lay, John Lenczowski, Michael and Claudia Lewis, Mark Mandeles, Frank Mavlo, Mark Moyar, Jim Phillips, Daniel Pipes, Robert Schadler, the late Lt. Gen. Robert L. Schweitzer, USA (Ret), Jack Tierney, Alan Tonelson, Dalton West, and John Zucker. To my friends at Congregation Or Chadash, this book provides a partial resolution to the mystery of what I do every day. My office mates at C&SC, CDR Joe Arleth, USN, and Lt. Col. Loretta Vandenberg, USMC, have been wonderful company. My students at C&SC have been a tremendous source of inspiration and pleasure. I will name one from each category of students— each of the U.S. services, interagency, and international—to stand for all the others: Lt. Col. Robert E. McCarthy, USMC; Maj. Eric M. Johnson, USA; CDR Alexander R. Mackenzie, USN; Maj. Matthew R. Modarelli, USAF; Mr. Curt Klun of the Drug Enforcement Agency; and Lt. Col. Per Olav Vaagland, Norwegian Army.

At Westview Press, Peter Kracht brought the project to life, Steve Catalano revived it, and Karl Yambert saw it to completion. Michelle Welsh-Horst ably saw it through production, and Jennifer Kelland Fagan did a superb job of copyediting an extremely demanding text.

Tim McCranor helped me review the page proofs.

David Audley and Richard Sharpe have marched with me through the completion of the project. I am grateful to Anthony Price and Bernard Cornwell for their company.

Note on
Transliteration and Dating

There is no standard system of representing Arabic, Persian, and Turkish words in English, and even if there were, it would not solve the problem of transliteration for this book. The Safavids and Mughals used Modern Persian as the language of politics, administration, and high culture. The Ottomans used Ottoman Turkish, a form of Western Turkish written in Arabic script with many Persian words and expressions. Most academic writers use one of the scholarly systems of transliteration for Persian and use Modern Turkish, which began as a phonetic transliteration of Ottoman, for Ottoman. But most students find the diacritical marks used in scholarly transliteration confusing, and Modern Turkish uses a variety of characters unfamiliar to English readers. Using different transliteration systems for the two languages would obscure the essential similarity of the vocabularies the empires used. For this reason I have employed a simplified form of the *International Journal of Middle East Studies* system of transliteration, omitting diacritical marks entirely, and transliterated all words of Arabic or Persian origin in the Persian form, with some minor exceptions, such as using the Turkish Mehmed rather than Muhammad. I have formed plurals with the English *s*, but put the *s* in roman, not italic, font, to indicate that it is not part of the foreign word. I have transliterated words of Turkish origin used only in Ottoman in a simplified Turkish form. But in order to facilitate further reading in Ottoman history, I have put the Modern Turkish forms of Ottoman words in parentheses after their use and in the glossary, unless the form is identical to my Persianate transliteration. The Modern Turkish transliterations are always given in the singular. Students must appreciate, however, that the absence of a standard transliteration system means that they will encounter different forms of the same words. Safavid is sometimes Safawid; Mughal is sometimes Moghul.

I have given dates only in the Gregorian calendar. Since most Hijri years straddle two Gregorian years, it is in some cases uncertain in which Gregorian year an event took place. I have joined the two Gregorian years with a dash in these cases.

Chapter 1

INTRODUCTION

There is no list of seven wonders of the early modern world. If there were, it would certainly include the Blue Mosque in Istanbul, Turkey, the royal complex in Isfahan, Iran, and the Taj Mahal in Agra, India. These architectural and artistic achievements alone would justify the study of the Ottoman, Safavid, and Mughal empires that produced them. The importance of the three empires, however, goes far beyond what they wrought in stone.

To a world historian, they were among the most powerful and influential polities of the sixteenth and seventeenth centuries and, in the case of the Ottomans, the fifteenth century as well. They dominated much of the environment that Europeans encountered in their first era of exploration and expansion; their history is inextricably intertwined with that expansion. The image and influence of these empires affected Western views of non-Western societies profoundly. To a historian of Islamic civilization, they represent an era of cultural achievement second, perhaps, only to the first flowering of Islamic civilization in the time of the Abbasid caliphate, as well as a new form of polity that produced a level of order and stability not achieved for some five centuries before. For political historians, the empires offer an example of the evolution of new political doctrines, institutions, and practices in response to continuing challenges. For military historians, they were among the first to use firearms effectively. Significant developments in popular piety and religious identity took place under their sponsorship. Their impact on the contemporary world also garners attention. Much of the disorder in the post–Cold War

1

world, in the former Yugoslavia and in Iraq, reflects the difficulty of replacing the Ottoman regional order. The Safavid dynasty set the pattern of modern Iran by combining the eastern and western parts of the Iranian plateau and establishing Shii Islam as the dominant faith. The idea of political unity in South Asia passed from the Mughals to the British and into the present. For all these reasons, the Ottoman, Safavid, and Mughal empires deserve and demand close attention.

This book offers a comprehensive introduction to the three empires, intended for students and other readers with some general familiarity with world history and Islamic civilization. It attempts to bridge the gap between general texts on world and Islamic history, such as Marshall G. S. Hodgson's *The Venture of Islam* and Ira Lapidus's *A History of Islamic Societies*, and the specialized literature on the three empires. As the title implies, this book is a study of empire, an analysis of power and order. It is not a comprehensive history of the early modern Islamic world or even of the areas ruled by the empires. I focus on political and military history, with economic history not far behind. Social, cultural, and intellectual history receive much less attention, except when they pertain to political matters, though I do not neglect them entirely. I do not pretend, however, to give all components of society equal attention; the inequality of my treatment reflects, I hope accurately, the inequalities of the time.

INTERPRETIVE THEMES

Comparison of the three empires began with the Western travelers that visited them. They form a natural unit for study because of the sharp disparity between them and their predecessors in the Islamic world. In the fourteenth and fifteenth centuries, with the exception of the steadily expanding Ottoman principality in Anatolia and the Balkans and the distinctive, nondynastic Mamluk kingdom of Egypt and Syria, most principalities lasted only a few generations. Their rulers—dynasties like the Aqquyunlu, the Qaraquyunlu, the Tughluq, the Lodi, and the Muzaffarid—have fallen into obscurity. No evidence of their fluid boundaries remains on modern maps. Instability was chronic. To paraphrase Hodgson, politics had reached an impasse. The extent, durability, and centralization of the Ottoman, Safavid, and Mughal empires show that their regimes broke that impasse.[1] Hodgson and his University of Chicago colleague William H. McNeill label them "gunpowder empires." Following the distinguished

Russian scholar V. V. Bartold, they attribute Ottoman, Safavid, and Mughal political success to their ability to use artillery to take stone fortresses. The term *gunpowder empire* has remained current, but as the book explains, the gunpowder-empires hypothesis, as Hodgson and McNeill articulate it, is not an adequate or accurate explanation. The phrase "gunpowder empires" in the title means "empires of the gunpowder era" not "empires created by gunpowder weapons."

The concept of gunpowder empire implies a fundamental similarity among the three polities. Despite immense geographic, social, and economic differences, the three empires faced similar political, military, and administrative problems and carried the same set of political and institutional traditions. Politically, the doctrine of collective sovereignty and the appanage system, established in the Islamic world by the Saljuqs in the eleventh century and a vital part of the political legacy of the Chingiz Khanid Mongols, prevented lasting political unity. The impossibility of the central collection and distribution of revenue in vast empires with incompletely monetarized economies made fiscal decentralization inevitable, thus fostering political disunity. In Anatolia, Iraq, and Iran, tribes of pastoral nomads dominated political life, and empires consisted of tribal confederations; the patrimony of such confederations affected politics elsewhere. The three empires overcame these common problems, but in different ways, under different conditions, and along different timelines. Gunpowder empire is a convenient classification that facilitates comparison and contrast, not an ideal type that the Ottomans, Safavids, and Mughals approximated.

The difference in timelines requires clarification. Because the reigns of the Ottoman sultan Sulayman I (1520–1566), known in the West as Sulayman the Magnificent and in the Islamic world as Qanuni-Sulayman (Sulayman the Lawgiver), the Safavid shah Abbas I (1588–1629), and the Mughal emperor Akbar (1556–1605) overlapped, many historians have seen them as comparable figures. But Akbar and Abbas did for their dynasties what the Ottoman sultans Murad II (1421–1451) and Fatih Mehmet (1451–1481) did for theirs. They gave Safavid and Mughal institutions mature form nearly a century after the Ottomans achieved it. The Mughal ruler most comparable to Sulayman I was Shah Jahan (1628–1658).

Explaining the Ottoman, Safavid, and Mughal success in maintaining larger, more centralized, and more enduring polities than their predecessors is the fundamental interpretive theme of the book. Three aspects receive particular attention: military organization, weapons, and tactics; political ideology and legitimacy; and provincial government. The gunpowder-empires hypothesis, though inadequate as Bartold, Hodgson, and McNeill present it, correctly draws attention to the significance of military superiority. Discussion of the military systems of these empires raises another question. For some fifty years, the concept of a European military revolution in the late sixteenth and early seventeenth centuries has dominated the study of warfare in this era. The three empires did not go through the same transition. This book addresses the question of why.

Success in battles and sieges could not, however, have won and held the loyalty and cooperation of the diverse populations that the three empires ruled. The Christian subjects of the Ottomans and Hindu subjects of the Mughals did not regard themselves as captive populations. The three empires had complex, multifaceted, and dynamic forms of legitimacy that reflected several separate political traditions and evolved over time. The implementation of the ideological programs of the three empires had a profound effect on the religious life of their populations and thus on religious affiliation and identity throughout the Islamic world today. This process resembles what European historians call confessionalization. In Susan Boettcher's words,

> Confessionalization describes the ways an alliance of church and state mediated through confessional statements and church ordinances facilitated and accelerated the political centralization underway after the fifteenth century—including the elimination of local privileges, the growth of state apparatuses and bureaucracies, the acceptance of Roman legal traditions and the origins of absolutist territorial states.[2]

The concept of confessionalization asserts that church and state efforts to enforce the Peace of Augsburg principle of *cuius region eius religio* (the religion of the ruler should be the religion of the ruled) led to the development of national and linguistic, as well as religious, identities. The Safavids, from the beginning, imposed a new religious identity on their general population; they did not seek to develop a national or linguistic identity, but their policy had that effect. The text develops this theme in analyzing all three empires.

In addition to explaining imperial consolidation, the book emphasizes two other themes: the place of the empires in a connected world and the nature and causes of the changes in the empires in the late seventeenth and early eighteenth centuries. Western historiography has generally defined the boundaries between the Ottoman Empire and Christian Europe on the west and the Safavid Empire on the east not only as zones of conflict but also as serious barriers to the movement of commerce, ideas, and individuals. The conflicts were not chronic; nor were the barriers impermeable. The Safavid imposition of Shiism fractured, but did not destroy, the cultural unity of the Islamic world. Even after the Portuguese established themselves in the Indian Ocean, most East Asian and South Asian products reached Europe through the Ottoman Empire and the Mediterranean. The Ottoman efforts to impose commercial blockades on the Safavids in the early sixteenth century had little lasting effect. There was a vast disparity between the cultural and intellectual lives of Renaissance and Reformation Europe and the Islamic world, but some ideas, especially those associated with esoteric learning, had influence in both regions.

A generation ago, the last of the interpretive themes would have been decline. Since the Safavid and Mughal empires effectively disappeared in the first third of the eighteenth centuries, the word "decline" is indubitably appropriate for them. But the Ottoman Empire survived, and Ottoman historiography has begun to emphasize transformation under stress, rather than decline, as the best categorization of the changes it underwent. Without question, Ottoman power and wealth declined relative to European rivals, but the current generation of historians emphasizes their resilience rather than degeneration. For most of the last century, historians paid more attention to the ends of these empires than to their establishment and consolidation. Some have done so simply because they could rely more heavily on materials in European languages.

In the nineteenth and early twentieth centuries, European colonial historians recounted imperial triumphs. A book title from the thirties, *Rise and Fulfillment of British Rule in India*, exemplifies this type of literature. As resistance to colonialism developed and colonies began to gain independence, nationalist historians looked back to the seventeenth and eighteenth centuries to explain their loss of independence and find lessons for the future.

Nationalist historiography has overlapped with Marxist historiography of varying levels of sophistication, which depicts European expansion as the spread of global capitalist exploitation. The most influential Marxist scholar of the early modern period in recent decades, Immanuel Wallerstein, depicts the development of a "modern world system," in which the capitalist economies of Europe form the capitalist center and reduce the rest of the world to an economic periphery.[3] In contrast to this approach, I emphasize the internal dynamics of the three empires. The political transformation of the Islamic world affected European overseas expansion more than European commercial and maritime activities contributed to the decline of the three empires.

HISTORIOGRAPHY

The three empires have spawned vast and disparate historiographies, which of course form the basis of this volume. This book rejects the postmodernist/deconstructionist assumption that objective scholarship is impossible because no one can escape the restrictions and compulsions of his personal, political, and cultural biases. In the specific case of Western studies of the non-Western world, deconstructionists contend that those biases have made such studies, especially of the Islamic world, the intellectual component of Western imperialism and neocolonialism. This rejection is not, however, a complete dismissal. Shorn of the political agenda, extreme claims, and shrillness that typify this type of scholarship, it can be a fruitful line of inquiry. Long before the bitter controversy over Edward Said's *Orientalism*, Martin Dickson demonstrated the fallacy of using cultural or civilizational degeneracy as a mode of historical explanation. Bernard Cohn's judicious studies of British intellectual attitudes toward India provide significant insights into the nature of British rule.

The literature on the Ottomans is far vaster and more diverse than the literatures on the Safavids and Mughals for several reasons. From the fifteenth century onward, the Ottoman Empire was an integral part of the European power structure and drew attention from European historians from the beginning. The depth and variety of sources on the Ottomans far exceed what is available on their contemporaries. An immense number of Ottoman archival documents exist in collections in Turkey and the Ottoman successor states in the Balkans and the Middle East. There are many European documents, diplomatic and commercial, in various collections. European travelers' accounts, the Ottoman chronicle tradition, and European accounts of the European wars with the Ottomans provide the narrative framework. Those narrative works formed the basis for the beginning of Ottoman studies in the West. Three massive histories, produced in the nineteenth and early twentieth centuries by Joseph Freiherr von Hammer-Purgstall, Johann Wilhelm Zinkeisen, and Nikolai Iorga, embody the fruits of this tradition. These works provide a more complete chronological framework than any narrative work on the Safavid or Mughal empires.

Even as the tradition of narrative history reached its height and the Ottoman Empire came to an end, a new school of Ottoman studies appeared. Mehmet Fuad Köprülü (1890–1966) brought the social and economic concerns of what became the French Annales School to Turkey in the twenties and thirties. He and his students, most importantly Halil Inalcık, have advanced the study of Ottoman history far beyond that of any other Islamic society and moved historical studies within Turkey far ahead of those in any other part of the Islamic world. The existence of the Ottoman archives made this school possible. Omer Lutfi Barkan began the exploitation of the archives in the 1940s and 1950s. In the half century since then, the use of the Ottoman archives has led to the development of an extensive scholarly literature on Ottoman social and economic, as well as political, history.

Halil Inalcık has been the most influential Ottoman historian for half a century. The Ottoman section of this book follows his studies in almost all areas, more because of his stature within the field than because he was my teacher. Three of his articles, "Ottoman Methods of Conquest," "The Socio-Political Effects of the Diffusion of Fire-arms in the Middle East," and "Military and Fiscal Transformation in the Ottoman Empire," inspired this book. In the last several decades, numerous historians, imitating the examples of Inalcık and Barkan and frequently instructed by them, have advanced every aspect of Ottoman historiography. Suraiya Faroqhi discusses this historiography at length in her *Approaching Ottoman History*.

To master Ottoman historiography is a lifework; Safavid historiography takes a year. There are still only four comprehensive accounts of the Safavids in English. Prior to 1993, literature on the Safavids was extremely sparse. There is much less Safavid history than Ottoman history—roughly two centuries compared with six—and the scarcity of documents makes much of the history of the dynasty inaccessible. The Pahlavi regime's exaltation of the pre-Islamic past, the disruption caused by the Iranian Revolution, and the diplomatic difficulties of the Islamic Republic have also hindered Safavid studies. Since 1993, however, a new generation of historians has transformed Safavid historiography. Because of the lack of archival documents, this literature differs significantly from most contemporary research on the Ottomans. These works either deal with the

Safavid regime and ruling class or with international trade, about which European documents provide much of the information.

Mughal historiography occupies an intermediate position. Though the Mughal Empire never challenged the European powers the way the Ottomans did, it was immensely important to the British, who explicitly perceived themselves as the imperial heirs to the Mughals in India. Their concern with the Mughals led them to produce a series of narrative histories, culminating in the *Cambridge History of India* dealing with the Mughals, studies of institutional and administrative history, and, perhaps most importantly, a massive series of editions and translations of chronicles.

Studies of Mughal history in the subcontinent developed in parallel with the Indian independence movement. In the twentieth century Indian authors produced a series of narrative works on the reigns of the major Mughal rulers. Sir Jadunath Sarkar, the most famous and accomplished of the Indian narrative historians, produced massive accounts of the reign of Aurangzeb (1658–1707) and later Mughal history. These authors view the principle of religious toleration, established by Akbar, as the key to the Mughals' success and Aurangzeb's abandonment of that principle as the step that doomed the empire. They see this understanding of Mughal history as a guide for the future politics of the subcontinent. Sarkar, for example, ends his work on Aurangzeb with a chapter called "Aurangzeb and Indian Nationality," with a final section headed "The Significance of Aurangzeb's Reign: How an Indian Nationality Can Be Formed."[4] Pakistani historians invert this interpretation, condemning Akbar for abandoning Islam and lauding Aurangzeb for returning to it, despite the political cost.

Since the independence of India and Pakistan, most work on the Mughals has taken place at Aligarh Muslim University, the leading Muslim educational institution in the subcontinent despite its location in India. The Aligarh historians, including K. A. Nizami, Irfan Habib, Iqtidar Hussein Siddiqui, Iqtidar Alam Khan, M. Athar Ali, Shirin Moosvi, and most recently Farhat Hasan, have produced a broad range of works on political, economic, and social history, focused primarily on Mughal decline. Satish Chandra, the one major Indian historian of the Mughals not affiliated with Aligarh, had been extremely productive. Not surprisingly, since most of these historians are Muslims with a secular orientation and many are Marxists, they absolve Aurangzeb—and thus Islam—of causing the fall of the empire and focus instead on economic factors. Some of the Aligarh historians have also focused on the study of the Mughal ruling class, collecting and classifying vast amounts of data. Two American historians, John F. Richards and I, have focused attention on the patterns of behavior of the ruling class. There is a steady flow of research on the Mughals, generally within the framework of the historiography already described, and several new general works on the topic have appeared recently. Richards's contribution to *The New Cambridge History of India*, however, remains the best comprehensive treatment of the Mughals.

This book, then, seeks to integrate these disparate historiographies in a form accessible to undergraduates and even, should they be so inclined, general readers. It consists of five chapters in addition to this introduction. The second chapter, "Common Heritage, Common Dilemma," describes the common heritage of political ideas and the governmental and military institutions and practices that the three empires shared. The next three chapters, the main body of the book, cover the three empires. They each provide a chronological narrative and discuss topics such as sovereignty, faith, and law; expansion and military organization; central and provincial administration; economy, society, and culture; and transformation or decline. The concluding chapter addresses major interpretive issues.

Although the three main chapters have the same structure, they do not correspond exactly. The Ottoman chapter is significantly longer than the other two, and the Mughal chapter longer than that for the Safavids. The Ottoman chapter deserves its length for several reasons. The history of the Ottoman principality dates to circa 1300, two hundred years before the Safavid and Mughal empires developed. Although both the Safavids and the Mughals had precursors dating from the late fourteenth century, the two empires did not develop directly from those roots, as the Ottoman Empire did. The Ottoman Empire survived beyond the third decade of the eighteenth century essentially intact because it evolved what amounted to a new regime: a new military organization, new tax system, and new provincial elite. Neither of the other empires underwent such a transformation. The Ottomans had a far more complex geopolitical environment than the others. In the first half of the sixteenth century, their grand strategic concerns extended from the eastern Mediterranean to Sumatra. Theirs was a global empire on interior lines. Only the Ottoman Empire had a significant navy. The Mughal chapter is longer than that for the Safavids because the empire was larger in area and population, more diverse, and wealthier. The Safavid Empire, unlike the other two, did not expand steadily through its history.

Notes

1. Cf. Marshall G. S. Hodgson, *The Venture of Islam: Conscience and History in a World Civilization*, 3 vols. (Chicago: University of Chicago Press, 1974), 3:3: "The pattern of society and culture that had been formed after the fall of the High Caliphal state had come to some crucial impasses."

2. Susan R. Boettcher, "Confessionalization: Reformation, Religion, Absolutism and Modernity," *History Compass* 2 (2004): 1.

3. Immanuel Wallerstein, *The Modern World System*, 3 vols. (New York: Academic Press, 1975–1988), is the centerpiece of an enormous literature. Immanuel Wallerstein, *World Systems Analysis: An Introduction* (Durham, NC: Duke University Press, 2004), does what its title implies. Wallerstein's work has spawned an enormous literature; his influence is difficult to overestimate.

4. Jadunath Sarkar, *History of Aurangzib*, 5 vols. as 4 (Delhi: Orient Longman, 1973), 5:362–378.

Chapter 2

COMMON HERITAGE, COMMON DILEMMA

The three empires shared a common heritage and a common dilemma. This chapter analyzes the heritage and explains the origin and nature of the dilemma. It has three sections: a description of the essential characteristics of the Abbasid Empire and the devolution of its power, an analysis of political theory and practice in the post-Abbasid environment, and a review of the concepts of the Shariah, Sufism, and jihad. The Abbasid regime defined and articulated a set of political norms and expectations that remained influential throughout the subsequent history of Islamic civilization; its collapse and ultimate disappearance defined the political landscape. Although two of three empires were mostly outside the territory that the Abbasids had ruled, the political challenges they overcame nonetheless reflect the post-Abbasid political, military, economic, and cultural matrix.

The Abbasids were imperial rulers from 750 to 945, imperial figureheads from 945 to 1180, and regional rulers with imperial pretensions from 1180 until the Mongol conquest of Baghdad in 1258. Although they used the title caliph rather than a word meaning "emperor," the Abbasid polity resembled the agrarian bureaucratic empires that had ruled Iraq, the Abbasid heartland, for more than two millennia. It was the third polity that caliphs had governed. The first, the caliphate of Medina (632–661), governed a confederation of tribes, united by Islam, that conquered Egypt and the Fertile Crescent and began penetration of the Iranian plateau. The second, the Umayyad Empire (661–750), with its capital at Damascus, occupied an intermediate position between the Medinan caliphate and the Abbasid Empire. It retained an Arab tribal army, but the regime had become an empire based on agricultural taxes and adopted the institutions and practices of bureaucratic empires.

The Abbasids eliminated the Arab ethnic and tribal basis of power and identity and established a cosmopolitan imperial regime. The political patterns and institutions of the Abbasids incorporated much of the theory and practice of the Sasanian Empire, which ruled both Iraq and the Iranian plateau for more than four centuries before the Arab conquest in the seventh century. The Abbasid caliphate was an Irano-Islamic empire. The regime reflected the legacy of millennia of imperial rule in the region, not of the caliphate of Medina in the seventh century or the legal conception of the caliphate. It was the last empire to draw its principle revenue from the Sawad, the heavily irrigated lands of the Tigris-Euphrates Valley, which had nourished empires from Sumerian times on. This concentrated agricultural wealth supported a centralized, bureaucratic regime and a salaried, subordinate army. The empire extended far beyond the Tigris-Euphrates Valley, of course, but the ultimate pattern of governance derived from there.

Traditional attitudes and scholarship, both Muslim and Western, regard the transformation of the caliphate into an imperial monarchy as a betrayal, a denial of Islamic political norms, and a corruption and distortion of the caliphate. More recent scholarship has altered this image considerably, although no new consensus has emerged. The word "caliph" is an Anglicization of the Arabic *khalifa*, which means "deputy" or "successor." Caliphate (*khilafa*) denotes both the office of caliph and the principality or empire ruled by him; thus, the term *Abbasid caliphate* refers both to the period during which the Abbasid dynasty held the office of caliph and to the area it ruled. The traditional view holds that *khalifa* was short for *khalifat rasulullah*, meaning "deputy" or "successor of the Prophet of God," and that it implied neither the religious status of prophet nor the political status of king. In this view, the authority of the caliph derived from the Muslim community's recognition of his position as the successor to the Prophet and was merely political and administrative. The use of the title *khalifatullah*, "deputy of God," beginning with the third caliph, Uthman, began, in this view, the corruption of Islamic politics.

More recent scholarship suggests that the rulers of the Muslim community used the title *khalifatullah* from the beginning. Though not prophets, they had religious as well as political authority, interpreting as well as enforcing divine decrees. This conception of the caliphate resembled the sacral kingship of ancient Middle Eastern imperial tradition. Though lacking the exaltation of the ruler's position, it included authority over questions of religious doctrine. This model of the caliphate resembles the Shii concept of the imamate more than it does the standard model of the Sunni caliphate. If it is accurate, the early caliphs had some of the attributes of what the later caliphs clearly were, sacral kings.

In his landmark work *Kingship and the Gods*, Henri Frankfort distinguishes between two forms of kingship in the ancient Near East, divine and sacral. Divine kingship, in which the king himself is a god, developed in Egypt. Sacral kingship, in which the king is an ordinary mortal who receives a divine mandate to rule, developed in Mesopotamia. The sovereignty of the ruler on earth mirrors that of the single or dominant deity in the universe. The common analogy of the king as the shepherd of his subjects reflects the concept of sacral kingship. The shepherd is responsible for, but not to, his flock; he answers not to the sheep but to the flock's owner—by analogy, God. Ancient Near Eastern conceptions of kingship reached Islamic civilization through Sasanian Iran. The Iranians used the term *farr* for sovereignty; their iconography frequently showed their monarchs receiving a winged disk, representing *farr*, from God. The concept of the circle of justice, which dates back at least to the time of Hammurabi, was an inherent part of the Near Eastern tradition of sacral kingship. It remains influential to this day. It is a model of how society and polity should function.

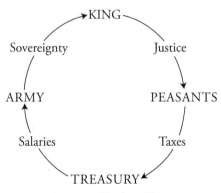

FIGURE 2.1 Circle of Justice

As Figure 2.1 shows, the king sits at the apex of the circle and maintains justice (primarily reasonable and predictable taxation and protection from oppressive officials). The peasants pay taxes into the treasury. The treasury pays the army. The army completes the circle by making the king secure and powerful. The proper functioning of the state protects the true religion, for the state and religion are brothers. The circle also assumes that there is a correspondence between the political and social order on earth and the natural order of the universe. Maintenance of the circle ensures the proper operation of the universe, meaning, most importantly, the right amount of rain at the right time to ensure agricultural productivity. Sacral kingship and the circle of justice explain the nature of the Abbasid regime far better than any concept of Islamic origin.

The circle of justice became a part of Arabic literature in the eighth century, when the process of translating Persian texts into Arabic began, but it became one of the functional norms in the seventh century when the caliph Umar took over the existing administrative systems of the newly conquered lands of Iraq and Syria. Many important Muslim writers incorporated the circle of justice into their work, including Abu Hamid Muhammad al-Ghazali (1058–1111), the most influential of all Sunni authors. He writes in this *Nasihat al-Muluk* (Advice for Kings), "The Religion depends on the monarchy, the monarchy on the army, the army on the suppliers, suppliers on prosperity, and prosperity upon justice."[1]

Most Western interpreters of Islam have regarded the transformation of the caliphate into an imperial monarchy as an abandonment of the egalitarian political program of Islam. H. A. R. Gibb, perhaps the most prominent Western student of Islamic civilization in the twentieth century, blamed Sasanian influence:

> The Sasanian strands which had been woven into the fabric of Muslim thought were, and remained, foreign to its native constitution. The ethical attitudes which they assumed were in open or latent opposition to the Islamic ethic, and the Sasanian tradition introduced into Islamic society a kernel of derangement, never wholly assimilated yet never wholly rejected.[2]

Recent scholarship, however, has demonstrated that the mainstream of Muslim thinkers embraced both sacral kingship and the circle of justice. The Irano-Islamic synthesis was in fact an Irano-Shari synthesis. The opposition to this synthesis took place on the fringes, in the form of pietist quietism, both Sunni and Shii, and revolutionary activism, usually but not always Shii.

The next significant religio-political transition, the bifurcation of the Prophet's legacy, took place in the middle of the ninth century. The caliphs retained the political leadership of the political community Muhammad had created but no longer acted as his spiritual successors. The ulama, the experts in Islamic law, became the primary exponents and interpreters of the Prophet's teaching. The basic conceptual and institutional patterns of the Shariah, *fiqh* (jurisprudence) and the schools of law (Arabic *madhab*, pl. *madhabib*; Persian sing., *mazhab*; Modern Turkish sing., *mezheb*; the meaning is closer to religious denomination than legal school), matured at this time. This division of authority became an enduring feature of Islamic societies. The degree of the ulama's political influence varied, but it was influence, not power.

The military and financial structure of the Abbasid Empire reflected that of its Sasanian predecessor. Iraq's agricultural productivity made a highly centralized administration, with a professional army paid directly from the central treasury, possible. The nature of the Abbasid army changed significantly in the early ninth century with the development of military slavery.

BOX 2.1 Military Slavery

Although their careers began as involuntary servitude and they had the legal status of slave, military slaves' status and function differ so dramatically from the common image of slavery that the term is misleading. In late childhood or early adolescence, military slaves, known in Arabic as *ghulam*s (young men) or *mamluk*s (owned), were acquired by rulers through purchase or capture; most were Turkic nomads from central Asia. They were well treated, often well educated, and given rigorous military training. They became highly capable soldiers, intensely loyal to their masters and to each other. Legal freedom, which most of the military slaves received in early adulthood, did not alter these relationships.

The systematic recruitment of military slaves began during the reign of the caliph al-Mamun (r. 813–833). It became a common feature of Muslim polities, surviving into the nineteenth century. Because of its frequency

(continues)

(continued)

in the Islamic world and extreme rarity outside it, the issue of a connection between military slavery and Islam has received much attention from scholars. Daniel Pipes, in the first systematic approach to the issue, summarizes his argument in the following four propositions:

> (1) that the impossibility of attaining Islamic public ideals caused Muslim subjects to relinquish their military role; (2) that marginal area soldiers filled this power vacuum; (3) that they rapidly became unreliable, creating the need for fresh marginal area soldiers and a way to bind them; (4) that military slavery supplied a way both to acquire and to control new marginal area soldiers.[1]

Hugh Kennedy, the leading Abbasid military historian, flatly disagrees with Pipes:

> The choice of men from these marginal areas to form the elite of armed forces was not because others refused to join up or because most Muslims disdained to serve a Caliphate which they felt had abandoned the ways of true Islam.[2]

He maintains that the caliphs hired outsiders because they lacked political baggage and outside loyalties and had significant military skills. But even if Kennedy's analysis is correct regarding the origin of military slavery in Abbasid times, there must be some explanation for the ubiquity of military slavery in the Islamic world and its virtual absence elsewhere.

In the post-Abbasid period, military slavery became one of the two standard forms of military organization, the other being tribal military armies. Rulers and ranking military and civilian officials (often former military slaves themselves) acquired contingents of slave soldiers. In northern India in the late twelfth and thirteenth centuries and in Egypt and Syria from the thirteenth through the early sixteenth centuries, military slaves ruled without a ruling dynasty. In the latter case, the Mamluk kingdom, multiple generations of military-slave elites ruled the principality, transmitting their status to slaves they had acquired rather than to their biological descendants.

NOTES

1. Daniel Pipes, *Slave Soldiers and Islam: The Genesis of a Military System* (New Haven, CT: Yale University Press, 1981), 193.

2. Hugh Kennedy, *The Army of the Caliphs: Military and Society in the Early Islamic State*. Warfare and History, ed. Jeremy Black (London: Routledge, 2001), 196.

As the discussion in Box 2.1 explains, historians do not agree on the reason for the evolution and persistence of this institution. Whatever the explanation, it clearly provided the Abbasids with a capable and cohesive army dependent on the central treasury and with no loyalty or connection to the general population. Military slavery became one of the two common forms of military organization in the Islamic world in the post-Abbasid period and remained a common feature in Islamic societies until the nineteenth century.

The highly centralized Abbasid regime, funded by agricultural taxes and maintained by a slave army paid from the central treasury, became the model of ideal government for the bureaucrats and administrators of later Islamic history. The Abbasids themselves could not maintain that ideal for long. The fratricidal struggle for the throne between al-Mamun and al-Amin (the fourth *fitna*, 809–813) marked the beginning of the loss of Abbasid authority in the outer provinces. The murder of the caliph al-Mutawakkil by his own military slaves in 861 began the process of political degeneration. The loss of control of the outer provinces and weakening of the regime at the center continued until the Abbasids became mere figureheads, under the tutelage of the Buyids (945–1055) and then the Saljuq Turks.

The explanation of Abbasid collapse begins with environmental change. The agricultural base of the Abbasid regime deteriorated due to erosion and rising soil salinity in the Sawad, the plain between the Tigris and the Euphrates. Given the economic conditions of the era, with taxes frequently paid in grain rather than currency and no economical method of transporting grain for long distances except over water, only a concentration of highly productive agricultural land could make fiscal centralization possible. The decline of Sawad agriculture changed the politics of the Middle East fundamentally. Except in Egypt, centralized government based on the concentrated collection of agricultural tax was no longer possible. Fiscal decentralization was inevitable; political decentralization soon followed. Fiscal decentralization generally took the form of the payment of soldiers, especially ranking officers, by land-revenue concessions rather than cash salary. Such concessions were not intended to include the grant of governing authority but in practice commonly did so. These revenue concessions, usually called *iqta*, resembled the Western fief only superficially, since such concessions were temporary, revocable, and did not imply governmental authority, though *iqta* holders frequently usurped it. Paying soldiers by revenue assignments inevitably weakened the government's control over both the territory assigned and the soldiers paid. The weakening of the regime at the center made holding the provinces difficult.

The decline in agricultural productivity extended beyond the Sawad. The climate of the entire region, which Marshall G. S. Hodgson calls the Arid Zone, apparently became dryer at this time. In much of what had been the Abbasid Empire, the ecological conditions became less favorable to agriculture and more favorable to pastoral nomadism. Agriculture required considerable investment, while pastoral nomadism was a profitable use of land. The Turks of the eleventh century and the Mongols of the thirteenth usually did not destroy intact irrigation systems; they wrecked, or simply ignored, works that offered little return on further investment. Their rule thus produced a decline in the cultivated area and an increase in the amount of land devoted to animal husbandry. There was less agricultural revenue to pay professional soldiers and more land suitable for the use of pastoral nomads, whose military skills, primarily as mounted archers, exceeded the capabilities of any soldiers other than professionals. In this circumstance, the military power of mounted archers gave them political dominance in most of the central Islamic lands, including the Iranian plateau, Iraq, and Syria. Mounted archers exercised their supremacy through confederations of tribes, ruled by dynasties that claimed a divine mandate to rule, including the Saljuqs, Chingiz Khanid Mongols, Timurids, and, ultimately, Safavids. The Saljuqs led a confederation of Turkic tribes known as the Oghuz. When the Oghuz settled in Anatolia, they became known as Turkmen (this word is transliterated or Anglicized in several ways, including "Turcoman," "Turkman," and "Türkmen").

The collapse of Abbasid authority and the growing nomad dominance altered the pattern of politics fundamentally. As Abbasid provinces became autonomous regional kingdoms, their rulers sought to justify their autonomy. The Shii Fatimids had conquered North Africa, Egypt, and part of Syria over the course of the ninth century; they rejected the Abbasid legacy entirely. In most of the rest of the empire, the regional rulers sought to maintain the pretext that they acted as Abbasid governors. There were exceptions; the Shii Buyids drew on the traditions of Iranian monarchy. But for the most part, the regional rulers sought to justify their positions within the Abbasid system, obtaining recognition of their positions from the caliph while simultaneously attempting to justify their rule on its own merits. Eventually the concept of the sultanate emerged. The title of sultan implied unrestricted sovereignty with caliphal certification, implying Sunni piety and Shari (the adjective for Shariah) rigor. Mahmud of Ghazna (r. 998–1030) was the first person to hold this title; the Saljuqs were the first dynasty of sultans. The Iranian titles *padishah* (protecting king) and *shahanshah* (king of kings) came back into use at this time. These terms expressed, however, the norms and mind-set of the Iranian tradition of monarchy.

The loss of political power naturally called the position of the Abbasids into question. Could a caliph be a caliph if he had no more than ritual power? An impotent figurehead could not be a sacral king, but he could form an essential link to the legacy of the Prophet, not as an interpreter of the message but as a symbol of the continuity of the Muslim community, the *umma*. As H. A. R. Gibb demonstrated half a century ago, the Sunni legal theory of the caliphate, expressed in Abu al-Hasan Ali al-Mawardi's (974–1058) *Al-Ahkam al-Sultaniyya* (Ordinances of Government) and the writings of Abu Hamid Muhammad al-Ghazali (1058–1111) on the subject, among other works, took form in response to this situation. That these theoretical writings define the caliph as something other than a sacral king makes sense given the circumstances.

The devolution of Abbasid authority meant the dispersion of Abbasid bureaucrats. The regional dynasties needed administrators, and those administrators carried and transmitted the norms and practices of Middle Eastern imperial bureaucracy. From Morocco to Bengal, and for nearly a millennium, the bureaucrats of the Islamic world sought to make governments conform to the Abbasid model of centralized, agrarian rule. Famous examples of this tradition, the *Siyasat-Nama* (Book of Government) or *Siyar al-Muluk* (Rules for Kings) of Nizam al-Mulk Tusi (1018–1092) and al-Ghazali's *Nasihat al-Muluk* (Advice for Kings), were written during the eleventh century. (Some scholars doubt that al-Ghazali wrote the entire *Nasihat*, but even if he did not, the attribution to him places it in the mainstream of Islamic thought.)

Both Nizam al-Mulk and al-Ghazali were pivotal figures in the development of Islam and Islamic civilization; one might describe the eleventh century as the axial age of Islamic civilization. Nizam al-Mulk, the vizier of the Saljuq sultans Alp Arslan (r. 1059–1063 in Khurasan and 1063–1073 as paramount ruler) and then Malikshah (r. 1073–1092), helped to set a pattern of government that persisted for perhaps a century; he also sponsored the establishment of the first madrasas, or religious colleges, which became the institutional bases of Sunni Islam. His political theory reflects the Iranian tradition of monarchy and government, including sacral kingship, the circle of justice, implying tight central supervision of provincial administration, and the interdependence of just government and right religion. His regime faced the revolutionary threat of the Nizari Ismailis (Sevener Shiis, better known as the Assassins), who sought to overthrow the Saljuq regime and the established political and social order through targeted assassination; his writing reflects the ubiquity and severity of this danger. He himself fell victim to the Assassins in 1092. The fundamental characteristics of the Saljuq polity, as well as of most other kingdoms of the middle periods of Islamic history, frustrated Nizam al-Mulk and the political agenda he represented. The Saljuq concept of kingship, fiscal decentralization, and nomad power made the Abbasid and Sasanian models impossible to emulate.

The Saljuqs, like other Turks and Mongols, also believed in sacral kingship, but their version included collective sovereignty. An origin myth or other portent demonstrated the validity of the claim to a divine mandate. The Saljuq dynastic myth included the story of the eponymous founder of the dynasty, Saljuq, urinating sparks that set the world on fire, graphically illustrating the idea that each of his descendants carried a spark of sovereignty. In the Chingiz Khanid case, *The Secret History of the Mongols*, a chronicle written shortly after Chingiz Khan's death, articulates his divine origin and sovereignty. The founders of these empires made the original distribution of appanages to their sons (and other male relatives if, as in the Saljuq case, the progenitor of the family did not actually begin the empire). After their deaths, family councils or, more often, internecine warfare settled the distribution of appanages and succession to the paramount throne. Continuing warfare over succession and appanage distribution led to the fragmentation of these polities into small, struggling principalities, usually by the third generation. Tribal chieftains frequently used princes as figureheads in their efforts to expand tribal and personal power. Collective sovereignty thus dovetailed with fiscal decentralization, creating a series of decentralized polities.

John E. Woods's study of the Aqquyunlu polity, a Turkmen tribal confederation that dominated eastern Anatolia and Azerbaijan in the second half of the fifteenth century, provides concepts and vocabulary for the description of such confederations. The ruling dynasty was the paramount clan. The Aqquyunlu confederation consisted of the relationship between the leaders of confederate tribes, numbering some fifty Turkish and Kurdish tribes in all. The men of these tribes furnished most of the military power of the confederation; their leaders had the most important military offices of the state. These offices included the chief of staff and president of the supreme administrative council (*amir-i divan* or *divan begi*; the council was called the *divan-i ala*), the commander in chief (*amir al-umara*), and other military administrators. To counterbalance the power of the confederate tribes, the rulers maintained personal military retinues, known as war bands. Their members were generally also Turks (or Mongols) who had abandoned their tribal affiliations to tie themselves to the ruler alone. Members of the war band filled court positions, such as chamberlain, reflecting their personal closeness to the ruler. In some cases, paramount rulers recruited military slaves for their war bands. The war band strengthened the ruler's position, but not enough to counterbalance the power of the confederate tribes. In some cases, rulers sought to reduce the nomads' influence by pushing them to the frontier, where they could continue to expand the empire without interfering with the central government.

The Saljuq use of this policy led to the Turkic occupation of Anatolia. After the Saljuq conquest of Iran, Iraq, and Syria, the rulers pushed the Turkmen to the Anatolian frontier. This steady movement led to constant pressure on the Byzantine frontier and eventually the conquest of major Byzantine cities. When the Byzantine emperor Romanus Diogenes led his army east against the Turkmen in 1071, the Saljuq sultan Alp Arslan brought the imperial Saljuq army against the Byzantines. The sultan's decisive victory at Malazgirt began the permanent Turkic conquest of eastern and central Anatolia. A branch of the Saljuq dynasty, known as the Saljuqs of Rum (Rome, Anatolia), ruled eastern and central Anatolia from their capital at Konya.

The Saljuq Empire gradually fragmented during the twelfth century, except for the Rum Saljuq kingdom. The most important successor state, the Khwarazm-Shah Empire, which briefly dominated the Iranian plateau in the late twelfth and early thirteenth centuries, is notable primarily because Ala al-Din Muhammad Khwarazam Shah provoked the first Mongol penetration of the Middle East. This incursion in 1219 led to a limited Mongol presence in the Middle East and ultimately to the Battle of Köse Dagh in 1243, in which the Mongol general Bayju defeated the Rum Saljuqs and established Mongol control over eastern Anatolia. The Mongols drove the Turks westward into Byzantine territory, thereby creating the frontier environment in which the principality that became the Ottoman Empire took root.

The Mongol invasion of the Middle East in the mid-thirteenth century led to the final destruction of the Abbasid caliphate in 1258 and the establishment of the Mongol Il-Khanid kingdom. The Il-Khans ruled the Iranian plateau, Iraq, and eastern Anatolia until the devolution of the empire in 1335. The Il-Khanate and its Mongol neighbor to the east, the Chaghatay khanate, created the environment in which the precursors of the three empires developed. Hodgson, following Martin Dickson, developed the concept of the military patronage state to describe the post-Mongol polities. He lists the distinctive characteristics of the military patronage state as follows:

> first, a legitimation of independent dynastic law; second, the conception of the whole state as a single military force; third, the attempt to exploit all economic and high cultural resources as appanages of the chief military families.[3]

In military patronage states, all the recipients of government salaries, be they soldiers, bureaucrats, or ulama, had military (*askari*) status. Taxpayers, whether they were peasants, artisans, merchants, or nomads, were *raya* (flock). This distinction cut across ethnic lines in concept, though in practice the Turkic and Mongol pastoral nomads were all *askari*, and the vast majority of the settled population was *raya*.

The Turko-Mongol dynasties could not govern without civilian ministers and bureaucrats, the Tajiks. The term *Tajik* literally means "ethnic Persian" but figuratively refers to the literate elites who staffed the financial administrative components of these regimes. Educated by their elders, these officials consistently strove to implement the policies of agrarian empire, notably centralized rule and direct payment of armies. The Turks filled executive and military officials; Tajiks held financial and administrative positions. The paramount rulers in tribal confederations naturally sought to maximize their own power. Their interests thus coincided with those of the Tajik bureaucrats. Robert Canfield and others have labeled the composite polities and societies that this circumstance produced Turko-Persia. The clash of political agendas was not a matter of mere ethnic tension or rivalry. There were ethnic tensions to be sure, but what mattered in politics was the clash of political cultures, expectations, and concepts of legitimacy. As time went on, Turkish speakers often took Tajik roles; not all ethnic Turks were political Turks.

The Turko-Mongol dynastic myths had limited appeal to the Tajik populations. Before the Mongol conquest of Baghdad, Sunni Muslim rulers generally relied on caliphal recognition and adherence to the standards of just government to maintain their legitimacy in the eyes of the sedentary Muslim population. The destruction of the Abbasid caliphate made the problem more complex. The Mamluk kingdom of Egypt and Syria maintained an Abbasid pretender in Cairo until the Ottoman conquest of Egypt in 1517, but Muslim rulers elsewhere rarely recognized his status. Even Mamluk legitimacy did not depend primarily on the shadow caliph. The caliphate had lost its central importance in Muslim politics. The effective disappearance of the caliphate as a source of political legitimacy and the enormous prestige of the Mongols transformed the politics of the Islamic world.

Two polities dominated the Islamic world after the fall of Baghdad, the Mongol Il-Khans and the Mamluk kingdom. The Il-Khanate became the model for the series of short-lived dynasties that dominated greater Iran after its collapse in 1335, the Jalayrids, Qaraquyunlu, Aqquyunlu, and Timurids. After the conversion of Ghazan Khan, the seventh Il-Khanid ruler, to Islam in 1295, the Il-Khans sought to articulate and justify their sovereignty in Muslim terms. Their status as descendants of Chingiz Khan and, more immediately, of Hulagu Khan, the founder of the Il-Khan line, however, provided their primary basis for legitimate sovereignty. The Il-Khanate was a tribal confederation that Tajik bureaucrats, such as the great vizier and historian Rashid al-Din Fazlullah, sought to reorient along traditional Irano-Islamic lines. This description fit the successor dynasties as well, all of which sought in some fashion to appropriate the Chingiz Khanid legacy, even though they were not themselves Chingiz Khanids. Timur, for example, ruled in the name of a Chingiz Khanid puppet and claimed to be recreating the Mongol empire as it should have been, though he also claimed sovereignty in his own right. His descendants later created a Timurid dynastic myth that paralleled the Chingiz Khanid original.

All of these dynasties expounded their sovereignty in Islamic terms as well. Woods's work on the Aqquyunlu ruler Uzun Hasan (r. 1467–1478) provides an excellent example. Uzun Hasan used the Turko-Mongol title *bahadur* (prince or monarch; literally, "hero") and the Irano-Islamic title *padishah*. He also claimed the Islamic title *mujadid* (renewer). This title comes from a hadith in which the Prophet foresees that in every century a person will appear to renew Islam. Muslim writers have generally designated religious teachers, such as al-Ghazali, as *mujadid*, but Uzun Hasan was not the only post-Abbasid ruler to claim the title—Shah Rukh, Timur's son and effective successor, did so as well—as it implied the intention to revivify

Islam and Muslim institutions. Uzun Hasan also claimed the title *ghazi* (discussed below) on the basis of his raids on the Christian Georgians, presumably to compete with his great Ottoman rival, Mehmed II. Uzun Hasan also sent a pilgrimage caravan from Iraq to Mecca including a *mahmil*, a ceremonial palanquin carried on a camel. Sending a *mahmil* on pilgrimage implied a claim to independent sovereignty.

The *Akhlaq-i Jalali* of Jalal al-Din Davani (d. 1503), written for Uzun Hasan, justifies his sovereignty in accord with the political expectations of the time. Davani offers three justifications for Uzun Hasan's rule: his divine mandate, demonstrated by his military victories and portents (generated through numerological analysis) in the Quran and hadith; the justice of his government, in accord with the Iranian kingship tradition; and his support for the Shariah. In Woods's words,

> It was Uzun Hasan's divine support evidenced first by his great military victories and buttressed by proofs from the Qur'an and the Prophetic Tradition, and secondarily by his respect for the twin ideals of the Sacred Law and secular justice that endowed his authority with unimpeachable legitimacy and universality.[4]

Davani also refers to Uzun Hasan's rule as a caliphate, which Woods explains meant no more than "Islamic administration," without any implication of his holding either the position of successor to the Prophet or universal sovereignty. In an official letter, Uzun Hasan asserted that his government met the standards of the Shariah and just kingship because of his suppression of immoral practices such as gambling, drinking, and prostitution, as well as of extreme Sufi movements (see the discussion of Sufism below), and his financial support of mosques and religious colleges. He also supported popular Sufi figures, including, as discussed in Chapter 4, the Safavids.

The Mamluk kingdom, which ruled Egypt and Syria from 1250 to 1517, had more prestige than any other Muslim dynasty in its time. The Abbasid figurehead contributed little to that status. The Mamluk polity came into existence when the military slaves of the Ayyubid dynasty took the throne for themselves. Military slaves dominated the army and administration and held the throne in a unique nondynastic, or quasi-dynastic, monarchy. Since there was no ruling family, there could be no claim of a dynastic divine mandate and no collective sovereignty. There were also, of course, no confederate tribes. The Mamluks won their eminence by prevailing against the Mongols, who defeated every other enemy they encountered north of the Hindu Kush and west of the Pacific Ocean, expelling the crusaders from Syria in 1291 and securing control of Mecca and Medina. Anne Broadridge discerns several different elements in Mamluk kingship. Before the conversion of the Il-Khans, the Mamluks emphasized their status as the guardians of Islam. After the Il-Khan conversion, the Mamluks claimed higher status as rulers because of their seniority as Muslims. They later focused on demonstrating their superiority as Muslims through their control of Mecca and Medina and the pilgrimage routes that led there. They took the title guardian of the two sanctuaries (*khadim al-haramayn al-sharifayn*) and ensured that their *mahmil* had precedence over those sent by other rulers. Mamluk diplomacy consistently subordinated other Muslim rulers, which they generally accepted as props to their own legitimacy. For the lack of a more elegant expression, I refer to the synthesis of Turko-Mongol, Iranian, and Islamic political ideas, practices, and institutions as Turko-Irano-Islamic statecraft.

Both the Aqquyunlu and the Mamluks based their claims to legitimacy, in part, on their military successes against non-Muslims. This issue—and more specifically the concepts of jihad (literally, "striving," with the expression *fisabillilah*, meaning "in the path of God," implied) and *ghaza* (raiding)—requires exploration. The contemporary significance of jihad and the proper use of the term have become bitterly controversial in the last decade. This discussion of jihad is entirely historical and refers only to jihad as warfare. Jihad, in this case meaning warfare to expand the area under Muslim government, had been a central activity of the early caliphs. Although in Abbasid times the frontiers of the empire had become stable, the caliphs still conducted campaigns on the Byzantine frontier into the second half of the ninth century. Jihad was no longer a primary concern of the regime or an essential element of legitimacy, though popular sentiment did support it. By the tenth century, however, it had receded in importance. Nizam al-Mulk, for example, does not mention jihad at all, even though his original patron, the Saljuq sultan Alp Arslan, won the great victory of Malazgirt. Neither the Saljuqs nor the Fatimids responded to the crusader conquest of Jerusalem in 1099 as a major emergency.

Nur al-Din ibn Zangi (r. 1146–1174) and his subordinate and then successor Salah al-Din (Saladin) Ayyubi (r. 1169–1193) restored jihad to prominence. Nur al-Din made the struggle to expel the crusaders a rallying cry to unify Mosul, Aleppo, and Damascus under his rule and a part of a pattern of ideal Islamic kingship that he projected. Salah al-Din and the dynasty that he founded continued that program. Their Mamluk successors did so as well. In practical policy, the Mamluks not only expelled the crusaders from Syria and fought off the Mongols but also developed a navy. They subjugated the crusader Kingdom of Cyprus in 1426 and also attacked Rhodes, held by the Knights of St. John. Jihad thus formed a major element of the Mamluk program and, by extension, a major source of legitimacy. Jihad in this context was a matter of government policy and ideology, not popular fervor. Other dynasties had less opportunity than the Mamluks to undertake jihad. When they did, it was rarely a major element of the regime's program. Uzun Hasan Aqquyunlu, for example, conducted raids on the Christian Georgians in 1458 and 1459, at the beginning of his career, and in 1476 and 1477, in an effort to restore his prestige after his shattering defeat at Bashkent at the hands of Mehmed II. Jihad clearly brought prestige, but it was neither a policy priority nor a primary source of legitimacy.

Although the terms *jihad* and *ghaza* were—and are—frequently used interchangeably, their connotations and associations differ significantly. Jihad was a matter of high politics, a prerogative of sovereigns. A policy of jihad generally implied a vigorous commitment to government in accord with the Shariah and condemnation of rival Muslim rulers for inadequate Islamic rigor, as in the Mamluk depiction of the Il-Khans after the conversion of Ghazan Khan. *Ghaza*, though itself an Arabic word, generally referred to frontier raiding, whether as a highly organized government activity (e.g., the Ghaznavid and Ghurid raids from the Afghan highlands into the Indo-Gangetic plain) or as the activity of autonomous frontier raiders (e.g., on the Anatolian frontier). Frontier *ghazi*s generally had more in common with their opponents in the frontier zone than with Muslim rulers in distant capitals. Their Islam reflected folk beliefs and popular Sufism, frequently with Muslim labels and concepts overlaying pre-Islamic beliefs and practices. Frontier raiders frequently formed alliances, temporary or durable, and marriage connections across confessional lines. The chieftains who developed followings in the frontier environment, such as Osman, the founder of the Ottoman dynasty, did not use jihad as the justification for their leadership.

Although the most elementary student of Islam is familiar with the terms *Sunni, Shii, Sufi,* and *Shariah*, the significance of these concepts during the period in which the three empires held sway requires elaboration. There was no simple opposition between either Sunni and Shii or Sufi and Shari in the post-Mongol era. As Hodgson states, there was no impermeable membrane between Sunni and Shii Islam in the middle periods of Islamic history. After the destruction of the Abbasid caliphate, the Sunnis had no center of political allegiance for the Shiis to challenge or for themselves to defend. The shadow caliphate in Cairo never served this purpose. Dynasties did not define themselves primarily by sectarian allegiance. The Sunni mainstream did not condemn even the exaltation of Ali above the first three caliphs as sectarian as long as it did not include active condemnation, or cursing, of the first three. In the words of H. R. Roemer, it was a time of "Sunni-Shii syncretism."[5] Mainstream Shiis, as well as Sunnis, condemned extremist (*ghulat*; the noun form is *ghuluww*, extremism) Shiism, in which the veneration of Ali and the imams went beyond regarding him as Muhammad's successor to endowing him with divine attributes. The extremism was in principle theological, not political, but some *ghulat* sects did engage in political extremism as well.

It is tempting to speak of a parallel Shari-Sufi syncretism, but the expression overstates the opposition between Shari and Sufi orientations. Though some extreme Shari groups opposed Sufism and some Sufi groups ignored some provisions of the Shariah, most Muslims accepted both, living in accord with the Shariah and pursuing spiritual insight in accord with the Sufi way as inherent and complementary components of being a Muslim. Al-Ghazali's spiritual and intellectual synthesis, which set the overall pattern of Muslim spirituality, incorporated both elements. Sufism did not necessarily imply political passivity; Sufis frequently participated in popular jihad on the central Asian and African frontiers. Only two major polities, the Almoravids and Almohads in the western extremities of the Islamic world, opposed Sufism in general as a matter of policy. Most others, including the Timurids, Aqquyunlu, and Mamluks, patronized Sufism.

Like Shiis, Sufis could go too far; the same terms, *ghulat* and *ghuluww*, applied. Not only Shariah-minded critics but many Sufis themselves regarded some Sufi doctrines and behaviors as deviating from Islamic norms. The most extreme Sufis asserted that through their spiritual exercises they could obtain not only intimate knowledge of, but unity with, God, eliminating the separation between creator and creation that mainstream Muslims regarded as fundamental. Such emphatic public utterances as al-Husayn ibn Mansur al-Hallaj's (d. 992) "I am the Truth," which led to his execution, deviated from general standards of propriety.

The doctrine of *wahdat al-wujud* (literally, "unity of existence"), first articulated by Muhyi al-Din ibn al-Arabi (1165–1240), put this concept in intellectual terms. Some mainstream Muslims also criticized the extent to which Sufism incorporated prior non-Muslim practices into local and regional Muslim piety. Sufi and Shii *ghuluww* overlapped and occasionally produced extremist movements, frequently among nomads whose religious practices and expectations reflected their pre-Islamic heritage.

Kathryn Babayan describes *ghuluww* in general as "a belief system that played a central role in the (trans)formation of Islamic identities . . . a repository for different traditions that with the cultural project of Islam came to be marginalized and cast as heretical."[6] It encompassed esoteric teachings from the Jewish, Christian, Zoroastrian, and other traditions and provided spiritual and ideological space for movements that sought to redress the grievances of groups that rejected the existing order, most commonly nomads on the margins of the Islamic societies. The leaders of these movements claimed prophetic or messianic status, sometimes on the basis of actual or fictional Alid descent. The Babai uprising in Anatolia, from roughly 1233 to 1243, was perhaps the first of these movements. The most famous, of course, led to the formation of the Safavid Empire. Nomad and frontier resistance to central authority was a major issue for all three empires.

The three empires thus shared the common heritage of Turko-Persia and the political dilemma inherent in its politics.

Notes

1. Abu Hamid Muhammad al-Ghazali, *Naṣīhat alMulūk*, trans. F. R. C. Bagley as *Ghazali's Book of Rules for Kings* (London: Oxford University Press, 1964), 19.

2. H. A. R. Gibb, "The Social Significance of the Shuubiya," in *Studia Orientalia Ioanni Pedersen septuagenario A.D. VII id. Nov. anno MCMLIII a colleges discipulis amicis dictate* (Hauniae [Copenhagen]: E. Munksgaard, 1953); reprinted as *Studies on the Civilization of Islam*, ed. Stanford J. Shaw and William R. Polk (Boston: Beacon, 1962), 72.

3. Marshall G. S. Hodgson, *The Venture of Islam: Conscience and History in a World Civilization*, 3 vols. (Chicago: University of Chicago Press, 1974), 2:405–406.

4. John E. Woods, *The Aqquyunlu: Clan, Confederation, Empire*, rev. ed. (Salt Lake City: University of Utah Press, 1999), 105–106.

5. H. R. Roemer, "The Safavid Period," in *The Cambridge History of Iran 6: The Timuri and Safavi Periods*, ed. Peter Jackson and Laurence Lockhart (Cambridge: Cambridge University Press, 1986), 110.

6. Kathryn Babayan, *Mystics, Monarchs, and Messiahs: Cultural Landscapes of Early Modern Iran*, Harvard Middle Eastern Monographs 35, ed. Habib Ladjevardi (Cambridge, MA: Harvard Univesity Press, 2002), xvii.

Chapter 3

THE OTTOMAN EMPIRE

The Ottoman Empire's long history, large size, and pivotal location offer multiple angles of approach to historians. Western historians have commonly seen the Ottomans as an alien threat, part of the Turkic third wave of Islamic aggression against Christendom. From the perspective of Islamic history, it was part of the second political and cultural flowering of the Islamic world. From a geographic perspective, it appears as a reassertion of the imperial pattern of the Eastern Roman (Byzantine) Empire. Fernand Braudel considers the Ottomans part of a unified and coherent Mediterranean region. Arab historians, like the Europeans, regard the Ottomans as intruding aliens. Each of these views of the Ottomans has an element of truth. The Ottomans carried the traditions and conflicts of the post-Abbasid Turko-Irano-Islamic political matrix into the fertile ground—literally and figuratively—of western Anatolia and the Balkans. Its geographic setting, the specific circumstances of its development, the quality of its leadership, its institutional development, and its military organization permitted the Ottoman polity to overcome the chronic weaknesses of post-Abbasid political formations and establish an enduring and extensive empire. The Ottomans integrated themselves into the political and economic environments of Europe and the Mediterranean.

For more than two generations, most historians have accepted the view of Paul Wittek that the Ottoman state, from beginning to end, had one

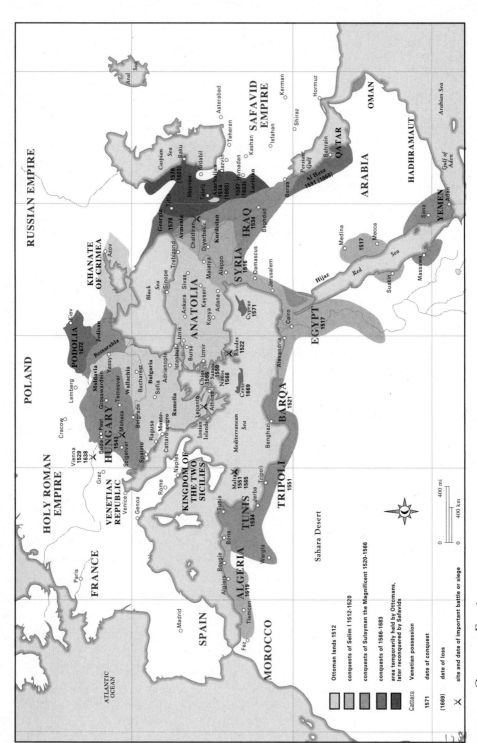

MAP 3.1 Ottoman Empire

primary reason for being: *ghaza*, which Wittek does not distinguish from jihad. Heath Lowry has recently demolished the Wittek thesis and discredited much of the scholarship behind it. As explained in chapter 2, frontier *ghaza* did not coincide with the legal concept of jihad. Even after a more formal and legal conception of *ghaza* as state expansion replaced the frontier conception, it did not dominate Ottoman political consciousness. The Ottomans articulated sovereignty and claimed legitimacy by multiple means, drawing on the entire legacy of Turko-Irano-Islamic kingship as well as their Byzantine heritage. Ottoman ideology won and held the loyalty of a vast and diverse population for centuries. Almost as importantly, the Ottomans avoided the worst of the consequences of collective sovereignty and the appanage system and eventually abandoned these concepts entirely.

The Ottoman regime conformed to the pattern of the military patronage state. The entire governmental machinery, civil administration and military forces, and even religious functionaries were treated as part of the military establishment. The Ottomans defined them as *askari* (*askeri*), literally meaning "military" though frequently translated as "ruling class." The subject population was the *raya* (flock). The *askari* received taxation, and the *raya* paid it. The circle of justice defined the proper relationship of the *askari* and the *raya*. Justice involved reasonable and predictable tax demands, the maintenance of order, and, for the Ottomans, the maintenance of the distinction between *askari* and *raya*, the most fundamental social division within the Ottoman Empire, though intermediate groups existed.

Within this overall structure, the Ottomans incorporated non-Muslims as *millet*s (literally, "community"), although the system did not become formal until the nineteenth century. Each *millet* had its own communal leadership, civil law, and legal system and provided its own social welfare and educational system. In the period under study, Ottomans recognized three *millet*s aside from Sunni Muslims: the Greek Orthodox, the Jews, and the Armenians. The Greek Orthodox *millet*, which included most of the subjects of the empire in the fifteenth century, united Slavic and Romanian, as well as Greek-speaking subjects of the empire. Mehmed II (r. 1451–1481) had brought all of these groups under the authority of the patriarch of Constantinople in return for his political support after the Ottoman conquest of that city. Practically but not formally, Mehmed incorporated the Greek Orthodox hierarchy into the Ottoman regime. The grand rabbi of

Constantinople received similar authority shortly thereafter. Mehmed II integrated the Armenian Church into the regime by classifying the Armenian bishop of Bursa as a patriarch with authority similar to that of the Orthodox patriarch. The absence of a Roman Catholic *millet*, even though the Ottomans had a substantial number of Catholic subjects, reflects the Ottoman perception of Catholics as the enemies of the empire; Catholic groups within its borders were treated as members of the Armenian *millet*. The empire's Orthodox and Armenian Christians were normally loyal subjects rather than resentful captives in the period under discussion. Orthodox Christians consistently preferred Ottoman to Catholic rule.

The economic basis of the Ottoman Empire evolved just as its military organization did. Agriculture and then commerce became major sources of wealth. Bursa, the first Ottoman capital, became a major center of international trade, especially as the destination for caravans carrying silk from Iran. The expansion of the empire brought more and more trade centers under control. After the conquests of Mehmed II and Bayazid II in the second half of the fifteenth century, the empire dominated the trade of the Black Sea and the eastern Mediterranean. The conquests of Selim and Sulayman gave the empire control of both of the traditional trade routes between the Indian Ocean and the Mediterranean Sea, the Euphrates River, and the Red Sea. Both Anatolian and European agriculture produced commodities for export as well as food and fibers for domestic consumption. In addition to exporting its own production, however, the Ottoman state consistently sought to gain control of long-distance trade routes, especially the major routes that connected the Indian Ocean to the Mediterranean. It was a commercial as well as an agricultural empire. Control of trade routes determined Ottoman grand strategy as much as the acquisition of agricultural land.

The constitutive principles of the Ottoman Empire thus included Islamic and Turko-Mongol ideological components; central, provincial, and frontier armies; extensive transit trade and agriculture; and the integration of civil, military, and religious authorities, including non-Muslims, into a single ruling class.

The remainder of this chapter consists of a narrative of Ottoman history from its beginning to 1730; discussions of Ottoman political ideology, military organization and methods of conquest, central and provincial administration, economy, society and popular religion, and cultural and intellectual history; an analysis of the transformation of the empire during the seventeenth and early eighteenth centuries; and concluding remarks.

CHRONOLOGY

Most historians have described Ottoman history as a gradual, linear rise—including both expansion and institutional development—to an imperial apogee in the reign of Qanuni Sulayman, Sulayman the Lawgiver, known in the West as Sulayman the Magnificent (1520–1566), followed by gradual degeneration to its status as the "sick man of Europe" in the nineteenth century. In this view, rise and decline each had one interruption. Bayazid I (1389–1402) deviated from the Ottoman policy of gradual expansion and met his nemesis in the form of Timur (Tamerlane) at the Battle of Ankara in 1402, and it took two decades for the empire to recover. In the seventeenth century, the Köprülü family of viziers temporarily restored Ottoman vigor before decline resumed. According to this model, Ottoman institutions evolved steadily toward the mature, classical form of the era of great Ottoman victories, from Mehmed II's conquest of Constantinople in 1453 to Sulayman the Lawgiver's conquest of Baghdad in 1534; change after that point was degeneration.

For the past several decades, historians have chipped away at this model. It now requires replacement. Ottoman growth and institutional development were not steady and linear; they reflected political tensions and clashes within the empire, the outcomes of which were not preordained. Changes after (and during) the reign of Sulayman I did not necessarily reflect decline or degeneration but responses to new internal and external challenges. The Ottoman regime changed profoundly between the reign of Sulayman and that of Ahmed III (1703–1730), one of the changes being a significant reduction in the power of the ruler and of the elites that had dominated the regime during the "classical period." But it survived, while the Safavid Empire disappeared entirely and the Mughal Empire became a symbolic shell. Historians and laymen alike have a tendency to equate the health of a monarchy with the power and effectiveness of the sovereign. By that standard, the Ottoman Empire of the late sixteenth and seventeenth centuries had clearly declined. But the status of the sovereign is not the measure of a government.

The framework of periodization, shorn of the implication of decline, remains useful. I divide Ottoman history into five periods: frontier principality, from Osman I's appearance in history through the Ottoman occupation of Gallipoli, the beginning of an enduring Ottoman presence in Europe (1300–1354); first empire, through Timur's crushing defeat of

Bayazid I at Ankara (1355–1402); reconstitution, through the accession of Mehmed II (1403–1451); mature empire, through the beginning of the Long War with the Hapsburgs (1451–1593); and stress and transformation, until the deposition of Ahmed III (1593–1730). The 1730 terminal date is convenient because it roughly coincides with the collapse of the Safavid and Mughal empires, but it has validity beyond that. The Treaty of Passarowitz (1719), the so-called Tulip Period under Ahmed III and his grand vizier Nevshehirli Damat Ibrahim Pasha from 1719 to 1730, and the deposition of Ahmed III marked a significant change in the nature and position of the Ottoman regime.

Frontier Principality

Two battles shaped the environment in which the Ottoman principality developed: (1) the victory of the Saljuq sultan Alp Arslan over the Byzantine emperor Romanus Diogenes at Malazgirt (Manzikert) in 1071, which opened Anatolia to Turkic settlement and led eventually to the establishment of the Rum Saljuq sultanate, and (2) the Mongol victory over the Rum Saljuqs at Köse Dagh in 1243, which fatally weakened the Rum Saljuq sultanate. Mongol pressure after the Battle of Köse Dagh drove many of the Turks of Anatolia to a new frontier in western Anatolia. In that frontier zone, Turks, Greeks, and others mingled. A series of new principalities appeared, receiving recognition from the Saljuqs and later the Mongols. The rulers of these states used the Turkish title bey (the word appears in various forms in Turkish; it may be translated as "chief," "lord," or "prince"); hence, they were called *beylik*s. The Ottoman Empire began as one *beylik* out of many.

These *beylik*s developed in the lands that the new leaders of the displaced Turks conquered from the weak Byzantine Empire. Mongol pressure had forced more people, primarily Turks but also Greeks, Armenians, and Jews, into the frontier regions than those disordered lands could support. The displaced peoples had no alternative to raiding for survival. Osman Bey (d. 1326), the first of the Ottomans, established a principality on the frontier of the remnant of the Byzantine Empire, which controlled only a small part of northwest Anatolia. Later accounts make Osman a member of the Qayi tribe of the Oghuz Turks, but his fame as a war leader, not his ancestry, won him followers. The word "Ottoman" is a Western form of the Turkish Osmanli; the -*li* suffix means "coming from" or "belonging to." Osman's followers thus took their identity from him. The Turks among them thus lost their previous tribal identities, which had depended in part on the patterns of seasonal migration, which the Mongol immigration had disrupted. The Ottoman principality, though predominantly Turkic in culture and origin, lacked the political patterns associated with confederations of pastoral nomadic tribes. Heath Lowry characterizes it as a "predatory confederacy," a commingling of frontier peoples, which served to bring together Muslim and Christian warriors in Bithynia (the Black Sea littoral of northwest Anatolia).[1] Osman's followers were known as *ghazi*s or *akinji*s (*akinci*), both words that mean "raider." Many *ghazi*s were either Christians or ethnic Greek converts to Islam.

Osman Bey entered history in 1301 as the victor the Battle of Bapheus. His forces had besieged the city of Nicea (later Iznik). Nicea had been the Byzantine capital during the era of Latin control of Constantinople (1204–1261) and was one of the few cities in Anatolia still under Byzantine control. When the Byzantine emperor Andronicus II Palaeologus sought to raise the siege, the Ottomans ambushed and defeated his army. Under Osman, the Ottomans established themselves in northwestern Anatolia, occupying the countryside around the major cities of Nicea (Iznik) and Bursa.

By the time Osman's son Orkhan Bey (r. 1326–1362) died, the Ottomans had evolved from the leaders of a raiding band into the rulers of a significant principality. They conquered substantial agricultural lands, which became productive because the Ottomans offered security and predictable taxation. Though the *akinji*s plundered on their own account, they did concede a fifth of their booty to their leader in accordance with Islamic law. Osman and Orkhan thus gradually became wealthy. They began to adopt the traditional agendas and institutions of Irano-Islamic government. They thus sought to reestablish flourishing agriculture, to create armies loyal and subordinate to them, and, eventually, to seek working diplomatic relationships with their neighbors. This change in ethos created a persistent tension between the nascent central government and the frontier raiders. In Osman Bey's time, the Ottomans were neither the largest nor the most prominent of the frontier *beylik*s. Umur Bey (d. 1348), for example, the ruler of the principality of Aydin further south on the west coast of Anatolia, did such damage in naval raids in the Aegean between 1330 and 1344 that he provoked a Venetian-Byzantine-Hospitaller expedition, which conquered his capital, Smyrna (Izmir). Orkhan brought the Ottomans to regional prominence.

Shortly after Osman's death, the Ottomans conquered Bursa, which became their capital. There, Orkhan first claimed sovereignty in the traditional Islamic manner, minting coins and having the *khutba* recited in his own name. Scholars and bureaucrats carried the political and administrative traditions of the central Islamic lands to the frontier. Their influence connected the nascent Ottoman polity to the political and administrative traditions and practices of the central Islamic lands. The symbolic articulation of sovereignty in Muslim terms, however, did not imply a rigid, sectarian political agenda. In 1328, Osman defeated the Byzantine emperor Andronicus III Paleologus at Maltepe. The victory ended Byzantine resistance in Anatolia. Between 1331 and 1338, the Ottoman forces occupied Nicea (Iznik), Nicomedia (Izmit), and Scutari (Uskudar). In 1331, Orkhan established the first Ottoman madrasa (Islamic religious college). In 1346 the Ottomans absorbed the neighboring *beylik* of Karesi, reaching the eastern shore of the Dardanelles.

The Ottomans entered Europe in 1352, as allies of John Catacuzenus, a contender for the Byzantine throne, against his rival, John V Palaeologus. Palaeologus had the support of the Serbian and Bulgarian kingdoms in the Balkans and the Venetians at sea. Genoa supported Catacuzenus. In 1352, Ottoman forces under Orkhan's son Sulayman crossed the Dardanelles in Genoese ships to support Catacuzenus. Sulayman defeated Palaeologus but refused to leave the Balkans. Two years later, an earthquake destroyed the walls of the fortresses on the Gallipoli Peninsula, permitting the Ottoman forces to occupy these strong points. Ottoman rule in Europe had begun. Ottoman forces apparently also occupied Ankara in Anatolia in 1354. The Ottoman principality had thus grown from one *beylik* out of many into a significant principality on both sides of the Straits.

First Empire, 1352–1402

The expanding Ottoman principality faced challengers in the east and the west. In the east, the Ottomans faced two main contenders for supremacy in Anatolia: the *beylik* of Karaman, which occupied the old Rum Saljuq capital of Konya, and that of Eretna, which held the old Mongol capital of Sivas. Eretna and Karaman allied against the Ottomans. In the west, the Ottomans had become a contender to succeed the Byzantine Empire as the dominant power in southeastern Europe. They confronted the rump of the Byzantine Empire and a shifting array of Balkan principalities, including

Hungary, Wallachia (between the Danube and the southern Carpathian mountains), and Moldavia (between the Carpathian mountains and the Dniester River north of the Danube) and Serbia, Bosnia, and Bulgaria south of the river. Under Stefan Dushan (r. 1345–1355) Serbia dominated the Balkans, but his empire fell apart after his death. Louis the Great, the Angevin king of Hungary (r. 1342–1382) and Poland (1370–1382), also sought to establish regional hegemony. The Italian city states of Venice and Genoa sought to dominate the Adriatic and Aegean littorals. The Ottomans had no navy, so communications between the European and Asian parts of the Ottoman principality were uncertain.

Orkhan's eldest son Sulayman, who had led the Ottomans in Europe, died in 1357. (Some historians place Sulayman in the line of Ottoman rulers as Sulayman I.) His brother Murad took over the offensive in Europe and ascended the throne when Orkhan died. Murad conquered Adrianople, the second city of the Byzantine Empire, in 1361; it became, as Edirne, the new Ottoman capital. As Murad pressed northward and westward, the Ottoman threat impelled John V Palaeologus, who had regained the Byzantine throne, to seek help from Latin Europe. Only Count Amadeos of Savoy responded. He took Gallipoli by sea in 1366 but could not hold it. His was the first of many expeditions against the Ottomans from Latin Europe.

Murad pressed northward along the Black Sea coast of Thrace, south toward the Aegean, and west toward the Adriatic. In 1371, the Ottoman forces won another major victory against a Serbian-Bulgarian coalition in the Battle of Chirmen on the Maritsa River. The Byzantine emperor and Bulgar king accepted Ottoman suzerainty in 1373 and 1376, respectively. In 1385 and 1386, the Ottomans occupied Nish and forced the Serbian ruler to submit. In Anatolia, Murad acquired territory through marriage and purchase rather than conquest, until the Ottoman frontier reached Karaman. He defeated the Karamanids in 1388. He then returned to the Balkans to face a coalition of the Serbs and Bulgar princes. At the decisive Battle of Kosovo in 1389, the Ottomans routed the Serb forces under Prince Lazar. Though it was a crushing defeat, this battle became the central tragedy of Serbian national identity; it still influences regional politics. Murad was assassinated on the field, and his son Bayazid succeeded him immediately.

Bayazid earned the epithet of Yildirim, the lightning bolt. Abandoning the policy of gradual expansion, he expanded the empire both east and west.

Bayazid established direct Ottoman rule in the former Balkan principalities south of the Danube, made major incursions into Hungary and Wallachia, and, in 1394, undertook the first Ottoman siege of Constantinople. King Sigismund of Hungary (r. 1387–1437; Holy Roman Emperor, 1433–1437), the Byzantine emperor Manuel II Paleologus, and Venice formed a coalition against the Ottomans and called for a crusade against them. A substantial force of French and Burgundian knights joined the coalition. Bayazid defeated them decisively at Nicopolis in 1396. He then turned eastward and by 1401 had conquered all the remaining *beylik*s, including Eretna and Karaman, reached the upper Euphrates Valley at Erzincan, and conquered the Mamluk outpost of Malatya.

Bayazid's rapid success, however, brought him to his nemesis. The ruling families of several of the *beylik*s that he had conquered in Anatolia took refuge with the great Turkic conqueror Timur and sought his support to regain their thrones. Timur led a major expedition into Anatolia. Many of the Anatolian Turkmen (Turkmen was the term used for Oghuz Turkic nomads of Anatolia, Syria, and Azerbaijan), who resented Ottoman authority rallied to his cause. He crushed the Ottoman army at the Battle of Ankara in 1402, taking Bayazid prisoner. The Ottoman Empire was shattered.

Recovery and Reestablishment

Although Timur's expeditions took him from Smyrna to Delhi and from the Gulf well into the Eurasian steppe, he did not attempt to establish direct control over the areas he conquered. He preferred to establish client rulers, generally from preexisting dynasties. His reordering of Ottoman territories reflected this practice. He reestablished the *beylik*s Bayazid had conquered and divided the remaining Ottoman territory among three of Bayazid's sons, thus implementing collective sovereignty and the appanage system. Sulayman ruled the European possessions and Isa and Mehmed divided the Ottoman possessions in Anatolia. Bayazid died in Timur's custody in 1403. A coalition of Western powers, including Venice, Genoa, and the Byzantine Empire, forced Sulayman to relinquish Salonica the same year.

The Ottoman Empire remained divided until 1413; the consequences of the division lasted decades longer. The pattern of events leading to the reunification is difficult to reconstruct in detail. The Balkan principalities sought advantage by backing different Ottoman contenders for the throne; there was no effective Christian solidarity. Mehmed defeated Isa, Sulayman, and a third brother, Musa, to reunite the empire. Mehmed I's final victory over Musa reflected the changing balance of power within the empire. Musa had allied himself with the *ghazi*s and their form of Islam, even making one of the popular Sufi *shaykh*s his chief religious official. His support for popular mysticism alienated the Ottoman religious establishment, and later efforts to assert control over the *ghazi*s turned them against him. The reunification did not end serious challenges to Mehmed's position. In Anatolia, Karaman was the principle threat; in Europe and the Adriatic, Venice backed yet another brother, Mustafa, against Mehmed. Mehmed also faced two *ghulat* uprisings, one under Shaykh Badr al-Din in Dobruja, on the Black Sea coast near the mouth of the Danube, and one in western Anatolia. Mehmed dealt effectively with all these challenges. By the time of his death in 1421, he had secured the empire against both Europe and Asia, though it was smaller than it had been in 1402.

Mehmed had designated his son Murad as his successor. Murad II faced two rivals, both named Mustafa. The elder Mustafa, his uncle, who had taken shelter in Constantinople after Mehmed defeated him, supported by the Byzantines, gained control of Rumelia (the Ottoman possessions in Europe) and invaded Anatolia in 1421. Mustafa received considerable support from the *ghazi*s of the Rumelian frontier as well as the Byzantines, but Murad had the support of the central administration, including the Janissaries. The *ghazi*s who supported Mustafa in the hope that he would give them a free hand in Europe would not support him in a campaign against Murad in Anatolia.

Murad defeated Mustafa in battle near Bursa and then besieged Constantinople because of the emperor's support for Mustafa. He raised the siege, however, to cope with the younger Mustafa, his own brother. Supported by the restored *beylik*s, Mustafa invaded Ottoman Anatolia in 1422. Murad defeated his brother in battle and between 1422 and 1428 reconquered all of the *beylik*s except Karaman and Jandar, which formed a buffer against Timur's son and successor, Shah Rukh. After this campaign, Murad sought stability rather than expansion in the east.

In Europe, Murad faced two major competitors for the Byzantine territorial legacy, Venice and Hungary, as well as the Byzantines themselves. The Ottomans had two major vassal states, Wallachia and Serbia. Venice sought to protect and expand its maritime possessions around the Adriatic and Aegean seas, most importantly the city of Salonica, which the Byzantines ceded to Venice in 1422. King Sigismund of Hungary sought to win suzerainty over Bosnia, Serbia, and Bulgaria, extending his power down the Danube, but was unable to do so and signed a truce with Murad in 1428. Hostilities between the Ottomans and Venice ended with the Ottoman conquest of Salonica in 1430. The year after King Sigismund died in 1437, Murad led his forces into Transylvania, demonstrating his ability to invade Hungary, and in 1439 the Ottomans occupied Serbia. In 1440, Murad made the first of many Ottoman attacks on the Hungarian fortress of Belgrade, which controlled the Danube.

Murad now met a formidable opponent in John Hunyadi, a Transylvanian nobleman who became the effective ruler of Hungary. Hunyadi defeated Ottoman expeditions in Transylvania in 1441 and 1442 and led an advance across the Danube in 1443. In 1444, faced with an attack from Karaman, Murad signed a treaty with Hunyadi at Edirne, accepting restoration of the Serbian monarchy in return for Hungarian guarantees not to cross the Danube. Murad made a similar arrangement with Karaman, making territorial concessions in return for a stable border.

Having stabilized frontiers east and west, Murad now sought to deliver his son and successor, Mehmed, from the successor disputes that had bedeviled his father and himself. He abdicated in Mehmed's favor and retired. Mehmed was then twelve. He immediately faced a major challenge in Rumelia. King Ladislas of Hungary and Poland renounced Hunyadi's treaty, and local dynasts throughout the Balkans took up arms against the Ottomans. These developments produced panic. Ladislas invaded Rumelia with a large army, including many crusaders from western Europe. The military commanders in Rumelia had no confidence in the young sultan and persuaded the grand vizier, Chandarli Khalil Pasha, to prevail upon Murad to return to the throne. Murad crossed the Straits to Rumelia and crushed the allied force at Varna on November 10, 1444. He attempted to retire again, but Mehmed still lacked the backing of the Turkish provincial elite and the Janissaries. From 1446 to 1451, Murad ruled, though Mehmed apparently continued to reign. When Murad finally died in 1451, Mehmed faced no opposition for the throne.

Murad established Ottoman rule in mainland Greece, though Venice, Genoa, and the Byzantines controlled most of the ports and islands. The Ottoman Empire also absorbed Bulgaria. John Hunyadi led another

IMAGE 3.1
Portrait of (Fatih) Mehmed II Smelling a Rose. Portraits of rulers holding flowers have been common since antiquity; they convey the subject's spiritual status or cultural refinement. This sensitive portrait of Mehmet II may reflect the influence of a contemporary portrait painted by Gentile Bellini who had visited the sultan as a representative of the Venetian government.

major expedition against Murad, meeting him in battle in 1448 at the old field of Kosovo. Murad, like his namesake sixty years earlier, won a great victory. Three years later, he died. He had maintained the unity of the Ottoman Empire and established its dominance in both Anatolia and the Balkans. The Byzantine Empire was now effectively reduced to the city of Constantinople, the natural capital of the Ottoman realm which surrounded it.

Apogee, 1451–1607

Mehmed II had no immediate challenger for the throne and secured his position completely by ordering the execution of his only surviving brother, an infant. He began his reign with one purpose: to take Constantinople. The city retained the geopolitical importance that had made it the natural capital of the Eastern Roman Empire; it had defied Muslim efforts to conquer it since the seventh century, and the notion of conquering it raised messianic expectations. He secured the eastern flank with an expedition against Karaman and turned his full attention to Constantinople. The siege lasted from April 6 to May 29, 1453. The Ottomans breached the walls, the strongest fortifications of the time, with artillery and crushed the final resistance of both the Byzantine garrison and the Venetian and Genoese contingents that supported it. Mehmed's victory made him one of the greatest rulers of his time.

In the ten years following the conquest of Constantinople, Mehmed II expanded his empire more rapidly than had any of his predecessors except Yildirim Bayazid. He failed to take the fortress of Belgrade in 1456 but established direct Ottoman rule in Serbia in 1459 and put an end to the Byzantine successor states of the Morea (the Peloponnese) in 1460 and Trebizond (Trabzond) in 1461. Between 1460 and 1463, the Ottomans occupied the Morea and Bosnia and began a sustained effort to subdue northern Albania. North of the Danube, the Ottomans invaded Wallachia in 1461 and replaced Vlad Dracul, a close ally of Hungary whose ferocity became the origin of the Dracula legend, with their own candidate as ruler. Elsewhere in the Balkans, Mehmed systematically eliminated the local dynasts. Further north, in 1475, the Ottomans took the former Genoese colony of Caffa (Feodosiya) in the Crimea. At this time, the Crimean Tatars, a predominantly Turkic nomad confederation ruled by a line of Chingiz Khanid princes, accepted Ottoman suzerainty. The Crimean Tatars became vital military auxiliaries to the Ottomans but also brought them to a new frontier, the Black Sea steppe.

In Rumelia, Mehmed's primary enemy was Hungary; in the east it was Karaman, and beyond that, the Aqquyunlu confederation, ruled by the great conqueror Uzun Hasan. The Ottomans absorbed Karaman in 1468, though they faced several Turkmen uprisings in favor of Karamanid contenders in later years. The Venetians attempted to make an alliance with Uzun Hasan against the Ottomans, involving the Knights of Rhodes as well as the king of Cyprus. In 1472 the Venetian fleet attacked the Ottoman coast, and Uzun Hasan advanced on Bursa from central Anatolia. Mehmed collected the largest possible army, advanced against Uzun Hasan, and crushed the Aqquyunlu forces at Bashkent on August 11, 1473. Bashkent ended the hopes of the coalition; Mehmed went on the offensive against Venice the next year in Albania. Venice signed a peace treaty in 1479, recognizing Ottoman territorial gains in the war, surrendering her own, and agreeing to pay an indemnity. In return, Mehmed granted the Venetians permission to trade in the empire.

The Ottoman borders now extended from the Euphrates in Anatolia to the Adriatic Sea, with the Danube as the northern border from Belgrade to the Black Sea. Venice still occupied some fortresses in Greece and Albania, Hungary held Belgrade and northern Bosnia, and Moldavia north of the Danube remained hostile to the Ottomans. In 1480, Mehmed sent expeditions by sea against Rhodes, the headquarters of the Knights of St. John, and across the Adriatic to Otranto in Italy. The attack on Rhodes failed, but Otranto fell to the Ottomans. Mehmed planned further expansion in Italy and eastward but died in 1481. In his three decades of rule, he made the Ottoman Empire one of the most powerful states in the world, dominating Anatolia, the Black Sea littoral, the Balkans, the Aegean, and the Adriatic and poised for further expansion in Europe. He deserved the epithet Fatih (the Conqueror), by which he is known to history.

Mehmed also gave the Ottoman regime its mature form, dominated by the *qapiqullar* (literally, "slaves of the gate"; imperial servants recruited as slaves). Many of his subjects, however, found Fatih Mehmed's rule harsh and repressive. By continuing his campaigns into the winter months, he exhausted his troops. To finance expansion, Fatih Mehmed had raised taxes and transferred revenue from the religious classes to the armed forces, causing significant discontent.

Though more a consolidator than a conqueror, Mehmed II's son and successor, Bayazid II, was hardly inactive. He won the throne, with the support of the Janissaries, in a contest with his brother Jem, who had the support of the Turkic provincial military elite. Jem survived, however, fleeing to the Mamluk kingdom and then to Europe. Until Jem's death in 1495, Bayazid could never ignore the threat of his return. In Rumelia, his policy was cautious. He allowed Otranto to fall but completed the subjugation of Bosnia in 1483 and secured the Black Sea ports of Kilia and Akkerman from Moldavia in 1484, confirming Ottoman domination of the Black Sea littoral. He paid subsidies to the Knights of St. John of Rhodes, where Jem fled in 1483, and then to the papacy, which gained custody of the prince in 1489, to keep him in custody, and he made diplomatic agreements with Venice and Hungary to prevent them from using Jem against him.

Bayazid's policy in the east was more aggressive. The empire had an ill-defined frontier with the Mamluk kingdom; the Mamluks and Ottomans were natural rivals for prestige in the Islamic world. Jem had first fled to the Mamluk kingdom and had invaded Anatolia in 1482 with Mamluk support; he took refuge on Rhodes after Bayazid defeated him. Bayazid attacked the Mamluks in 1485; the two empires fought each other to a standstill over the next six years. After Jem's death in 1495, Bayazid became more active in Europe as well. In 1499, he began hostilities against Venice, which was supported by Hungary. Though it produced little change in boundaries, the Ottoman-Venetian War of 1499 to 1502 marked the establishment of Ottoman naval power and the pivotal role of the empire in European politics. The treaty that resolved the conflict provided stability on the European frontier until 1521.

The world, and more specifically the Ottoman geopolitical context, changed dramatically during the second half of Bayazid II's reign. Vasco da Gama's landing on the Malabar Coast in 1498 began the era of Portuguese maritime dominance in the Indian Ocean. The establishment of the Safavid Empire, a Turkmen confederation led by a Shii Sufi *shaykh* with messianic pretensions that dominated western Iran from 1501 and the entire Iranian plateau from 1510, transformed the situation on the empire's eastern frontier. The Portuguese threatened the Mediterranean trade system on which much of the prosperity of the Ottoman Empire, as well as of Venice and the Mamluks, depended. The Safavids menaced Ottoman power in Anatolia. Their program appealed to the Turkmen of Anatolia, who resented Ottoman authority. Many of them had still had loyalties to the Karamanids or the Aqquyunlu; all of them resented the Ottomans' centralizing agenda. The Safavid ideology promised redress of the Turkmen grievances, offering a positive alternative to Ottoman rule. Fortunately for the Ottomans, the Mamluks regarded themselves as guardians of Sunni Islam, so they had no inclination to ally with the Safavids.

The Portuguese intrusion into the Indian Ocean threatened the vital interests of the Mamluks, who controlled the Red Sea route by which many of the spices and other commodities of the Indian Ocean region reached the Mediterranean and thus Europe. Portuguese domination of the Indian Ocean and the opening of the Cape Route to commerce threatened the commercial prosperity of the Mediterranean, as did the weakness of the Mamluk regime. The Portuguese had a coherent geopolitical plan to dominate the Indian Ocean by controlling the same maritime choke points that concern today's strategists, the Straits of Malacca, Hormuz, and the Bab al-Mandeb, the entrance to the Red Sea. In response to requests from Indian Ocean merchants for protection from the Portuguese, the Mamluk sultan Qansuh al-Ghawri began to develop his naval forces in 1505. The Ottomans provided him with ordnance, matériel, and personnel. This policy served several purposes: discouraging the Mamluks from allying with the Safavids against the Ottomans, preventing the Portuguese from blocking further Ottoman expansion eastward, and putting the

Mamluks in the position of Ottoman clients. From this time onward, for at least a century, Ottoman grand strategy encompassed the Indian Ocean as well the Mediterranean and Black seas. The Mamluks allied themselves with the sultan of Gujarat, who governed Surat, the major trading port on the west coast of India, against the Portuguese, but they suffered a crushing naval defeat in 1509.

Bayazid reacted cautiously to the Safavid threat, ordering the deportation of Safavid sympathizers to Europe and sending armies to the eastern frontier in 1501 and 1507 but avoiding open warfare with the Safavids. In 1511 there was a massive Turkmen uprising throughout Anatolia. Bayazid, aged and ill, took no action. His three adult sons were all provincial governors with their own establishments, but only Selim, known to history as Yavuz (the Grim), had a good military reputation. He defeated his brothers and took the throne, deposing his father, in 1512. Bayazid died of natural causes shortly afterwards; within a year Selim had executed his surviving brothers and their sons.

In 1514, Selim I led a massive army into Anatolia, crushing the rebel Turkmen in Ottoman territory (some 40,000 were imprisoned or executed) and then proceeded east to challenge the Safavids under Shah Ismail. The persecution of the Turkmen was entirely political; it was neither religious persecution nor ethnic cleansing. The two sovereigns met in battle at Chaldiran on August 23, 1514. The Ottomans won decisively, ending the Safavid threat and securing Ottoman control of eastern Anatolia; the local dynasties and tribal chieftains there gradually accepted Ottoman authority. Selim occupied the Safavid capital Tabriz but could not maintain the army so far afield through the winter. The Ottomans withdrew from Tabriz and turned to solidifying their suzerainty in Kurdistan and, more importantly, absorbing the Zul Qadr principality in Cilicia, which formed a buffer between the Mamluk kingdom and the Ottoman Empire. The victory over the Zul Qadr forces at Turna Dağ on June 12, 1515, opened the way for another clash with the Mamluks. Even as Ottoman-Mamluk hostilities appeared imminent, however, naval cooperation between the two groups continued. The Portuguese viceroy in India, Don Afonso d'Albuquerque, had attacked Aden in 1513, threatening Mamluk control of pilgrim access to Mecca and Medina and thus Mamluk legitimacy. In 1515, even as Selim's army was approaching Syria, an Ottoman-Mamluk fleet departed Suez under the Ottoman admiral Salman Rais but achieved nothing.

IMAGE 3.2
Sulayman at the Battle of Rhodes in 1522: folio from the *Süleymanname*. The illustrations contained in the *Süleymanname* (a history of Sulayman's reign between 1520 and 1555) are among the most fascinating and exquisite paintings produced by Ottoman painters. Written by Arifi, Sulayman's official court biographer, the text describes imperial ceremonies, the visits of foreign dignitaries and, as illustrated here, his military triumphs.

In 1516, Selim again proceeded east, threatening both the Safavids and the Mamluks. The Mamluk sultan Qansuh al-Ghawri led his forces across the Euphrates into Ottoman territory. Selim smashed the Mamluk army at Marj Dabik near Aleppo on July 28, 1516, and occupied Syria by the end of September. Selim did not withdraw at the end of the campaigning season but pressed on to Egypt. He won another decisive victory at Raydaniyya (outside Cairo) on January 22, 1517, and resistance ended a few months later. The conquest of the Mamluk kingdom permitted the Ottomans to establish suzerainty over Mecca and Medina. The local ruler there, known as the sharif, became the Ottoman governor of the region. Selim's victories had secured the Ottoman Empire's position as the premier Muslim state, gaining both the prestige of ruling Mecca and Medina and a huge increase in commercial income. Salman Rais defended Jiddah, the port of Mecca, against a Portuguese attack in 1517.

Selim defeated another Turkmen uprising in Anatolia in 1520 and had begun a campaign in Rumelia in 1520 when he died suddenly. In eight years, he had transformed the Ottoman Empire from a peripheral into a central power in the Islamic world, making it perhaps the most powerful empire in the world in his time. No other Ottoman ruler assembled a chain of great victories comparable to his. His only son, Sulayman, succeeded him.

Sulayman, known as Qanuni (the Lawgiver) or, in the West, as the Magnificent, certainly ranks among the greatest rulers of the empire. Within two years of his accession, his forces had taken two places that had withstood the efforts of Fatih Mehmed: Belgrade, which fell on August 29, 1521, and Rhodes, which surrendered on January 21, 1522.

The conquest of Belgrade made the Ottomans central players in European politics. European politics at this time, at least in the view of most historians, entailed, above all, the struggle for dominance between Charles V, the Hapsburg ruler of Austria and Spain as well as Holy Roman Emperor, and Francis I, the Valois ruler of France. Since the Hapsburg domains separated them, France and the Ottoman Empire were natural allies. At first, the French alliance was tacit, as Sulayman took advantage of Charles's distraction in Italy to take Belgrade. But when the Hapsburg forces defeated and imprisoned Francis at Pavia in 1525, he had no recourse but to ask for Ottoman assistance. In the interim, a series of revolts in Syria and Egypt had distracted the sultan. The uprisings did not seriously threaten Ottoman authority, and new political and administrative arrangements erected after their suppression brought the provinces thoroughly under Ottoman control.

In 1526, Sulayman turned westward against King Louis of Hungary, who had married a Hapsburg princess. Neither the peasants nor the notables of his realm supported Louis strongly. On August 28, 1526, the Ottomans crushed the Hungarian army at Mohacs on the Danube, occupying Buda and Pest shortly thereafter. Sulayman sought to make Hungary a vassal state, like Moldavia and Wallachia further east, with John Zapolya, the leader of the notables, as its ruler. The Hapsburg party in Hungary gave the throne to Charles V's brother, Archduke Ferdinand. He expelled Zapolya, forcing another Ottoman expedition in 1529. Sulayman reinstalled Zapolya and proceeded up the Danube to besiege Vienna briefly before the limited campaign radius of his army compelled him to withdraw.

The next phase in the Ottoman-Hapsburg war occurred in 1531, when Ferdinand besieged Buda. Sulayman dislodged the besiegers the next year. The support of Genoa, which shifted alliance from the Valois to the Hapsburgs in 1528, permitted the Hapsburgs to take the offensive in the Mediterranean. In 1532, a Hapsburg and Genoese force under the Genoese admiral Andrea Doria occupied the fortresses of Coron (modern Koroni) and Modon on the Gulf of Messina in the Morea. To deal with the naval threat, Sulayman gave command of the Ottoman navy in the Mediterranean to a successful corsair, Khayr al-Din Barbarossa, and ordered him to cooperate with the French navy. The Ottoman peril, however, combined with the growth of the Lutheran movement in Germany, persuaded Charles V to seek compromise on both fronts. In 1533 the Ottomans signed a truce with the Archduke Ferdinand, who agreed to pay annual tribute to the Ottomans and relinquished claims to most of Hungary. In 1534, the Ottomans regained Coron and Modon and their fleet under Barbarossa took Tunis, which had been a major Hapsburg naval base. Sulayman, however, had already turned his attention east.

Selim's triumph at Chaldiran had ended the Safavid threat to the Ottoman Empire, but it left what is now Iraq—the region dominated by Mosul, Baghdad, and Basra, but not then a political unit—in Safavid hands. The Ottomans had ideological (because of Baghdad's historical significance), commercial (because one of the two direct routes between the Arabian Sea and the Indian Ocean came through the Gulf and up the Euphrates), and strategic (because access to the Gulf would challenge the Portuguese) reasons to conquer Iraq, not to mention their hope of destroying the Safavid Empire. Sulayman advanced deep into northern Iran but failed to lure the Safavids into battle, then turned south to occupy Baghdad without serious opposition.

Returning to the European and Mediterranean theaters, Sulayman concluded a major treaty with France in 1536. The public part of the treaty granted French merchants the right to trade throughout the empire, paying taxes and duties at the same rates as Ottoman subjects and with immunity from Ottoman law, the first granting of these privileges to a major European power. The treaty also included secret provisions for military cooperation. Sulayman invited the Venetians to join the alliance against the Hapsburgs, but Venice refused. The potential Hapsburg threat to Venice itself outweighed the Ottoman threat to Venetian commerce. The Ottomans and French planned a coordinated campaign against the Hapsburgs, but Sulayman attacked Venice instead. The Ottomans raided Venetian ports in Italy but failed to take the major Venetian fortress on Corfu. In 1538, Venice allied with the Hapsburgs, but Barbarossa defeated the combined Hapsburg-Venetian fleet, led by the Genoese admiral Andrea Doria, at Prevesa on the west coast of Greece. The Ottoman-Venetian War ended in 1540 with Venice surrendering all of its possessions on the Greek mainland and in the Adriatic, except Crete.

In the east, the Ottomans' expansion continued in 1538. The previously autonomous ruler of Basra submitted to Ottoman authority, bringing the Ottoman frontier to the Persian Gulf. Ottoman forces from Egypt took control of Yemen, and the Ottoman Red Sea fleet crossed the Arabian Sea to attack Diu, one of the Portuguese fortified ports on the west coast of India. The siege failed, but the Ottomans did secure control of the Red Sea. Also in 1538, the Ottomans extended their struggle against the Portuguese by providing military aid to the sultanate of Aceh on the western end of Sumatra. Aceh posed a significant challenge to the Portuguese, threatening their position at the Straits of Malacca and offering an alternative to the Portuguese station there as a trading center. The Ottoman connection to Aceh thus reveals a comprehensive geopolitical response to the Portuguese; the Ottomans or their allies attacked all of the key points in the Portuguese strategy.

Zapolya's death in 1541 led to the renewal of hostilities between the Ottomans and Hapsburgs. Archduke Ferdinand sought to take control of the part of Hungary Zapolya had ruled; Sulayman drove the Hapsburgs out and transformed the area into an Ottoman province. In 1543, Sulayman invaded Hapsburg Hungary and sent Barbarossa to assist the French in operations against Nice (part of the duchy of Savoy, an ally of the Hapsburgs), and a French artillery unit served with the Ottomans in Hungary. This cooperation did not, however, bear much fruit. In 1547, the Ottomans and Hapsburgs signed another treaty, confirming Hapsburg possession of western Hungary and the Hapsburg payment of tribute to Sulayman. Hostilities broke out again in 1550. The Ottomans conquered Temesvar and established a durable frontier in Hungary.

Sulayman also encountered a new threat from the north, the growing power of Muscovy. Ivan IV, known as the Terrible, extended Russian power down the Volga in the middle of the sixteenth century, absorbing the khanates of Kazan in 1552 and Astrakhan in 1556, reaching the northern Caucasus. These events began the extremely complex and violent struggle among the Ottomans, Poles, Muscovites, Cossacks, and Crimean Tatars, to mention only the major actors, in the immense region surrounding the Black Sea. In 1559, a Cossack force attacked Azov at the mouth of the Don, the northernmost Ottoman outpost. From this time onward, Muscovy and the Cossacks occupied an increasing amount of Ottoman attention.

The Ottomans remained active on the Iranian and Indian Ocean fronts. In 1547, Sulayman again sent support to Aceh. In 1548, Sulayman again attacked the Safavids, supporting the rebel prince Alqas Mirza against his brother, Shah Tahmasp. Hostilities continued for seven years without major result. In 1555, Sulayman concluded the first formal diplomatic agreement with the Safavids, the Treaty of Amasya, which left the frontier essentially unchanged. Further east, the Ottomans sent assistance to Aceh again in 1547. An Ottoman fleet from Basra attacked the Portuguese at Hormuz without success in 1552. In 1555, the Ottomans extended their control of the African littoral in 1555 with the conquest of Asmara in modern Eritrea. In 1559, the Ottomans made their last effort at expansion on the Indian Ocean, an unsuccessful attack on Bahrain, but they did not become inactive. They had begun a policy of naval commerce raiding in the Arabian Sea and beyond, which persisted throughout the sixteenth century.

Sulayman devoted considerable attention to internal administration, promulgating new regulations dealing primarily with finance and the administration of justice. Grand Vizier Lutfi Pasha (d. 1562) and Shaykh al-Islam Abu al-Suud (d. 1574) orchestrated the considerable tightening of administration to prevent official corruption and the reorganization of virtually all aspects of governmental activity, from frontier garrisons to all forms of governmental income and expenditure.

By 1552, Sulayman was almost sixty and clearly aging. Succession to the throne became a major issue. Sulayman had three capable sons, two of them, Selim and Bayazid, by his favorite and wife, Hurrem Sultan (Roxelana). He had a third, Mustafa, who was extremely popular, executed in 1553, probably at Hurrem's instigation. After she died in 1558, the rivalry between Bayazid and Selim became unrestrained. Ultimately, Sulayman backed Selim over Bayazid, and his support allowed Selim to defeat his brother in 1560.

Hostilities between the Hapsburgs and the Ottomans continued in the Mediterranean during this period. Ottoman naval forces raided the coast of North Africa west of Algiers and the island of Minorca. As soon as the 1559 Treaty of Cateau-Cambrésis ended hostilities between France and the Hapsburgs, Phillip II, who had taken the thrones of Spain and Naples on the abdication of his father, Charles V, in 1555, immediately organized a major naval expedition against the corsair base at the island of Jerba, off the coast of Tunisia. The Hapsburgs conquered the island, but in 1560 the Ottoman fleet under Piyale Pasha defeated the Hapsburg fleet there. In 1565, the Ottomans attempted to conquer Malta, which had become the base of the Knights of St. John after Sulayman drove them from Rhodes. The knights,

IMAGE 3.3
Sultan Sulayman I. Melchior
Lorck was a member of the
embassy sent to the Ottoman
court by the Hapsburg King
Ferdinand I. This insightful
portrait of the great sultan
toward the end of his life
captures the ruler's intent
gaze, perhaps reflecting
Sulayman's role as pious
guardian of the realm rather
than as ardent conquer.

under their grand master Jean Parisot de la Valette, won renown for the epic
defense. The Ottomans withdrew before a relief force arrived.

The next year, Grand Vizier Sokollu Mehmed Pasha, who had dominated the affairs of the empire for a decade, convinced Sulayman that
Hapsburg pressure required another campaign. The Ottomans expelled
the Hapsburgs from Hungary, but Sulayman died on campaign on September 7, 1566. The attack on Malta and the 1566 campaign in Hungary
ended Ottoman expansion westward. The loss of the French alliance after
the Treaty of Cateau-Cambrésis had weakened the Ottoman strategic position in Europe substantially.

Sulayman is known as the Magnificent; Selim II (1566–1574) is
known as the Sot. This seemingly abrupt change in the character of rulers
symbolized, for generations of historians, the beginning of the decline of
the Ottoman Empire. But there was no such dramatic transition. Sulayman had become a passive figure before he died; Sokollu Mehmed Pasha
continued to dominate policy. The preference of Selim and his successors
for life in the palace rather than the field altered the political dynamics at
the top but did not automatically or inevitably lead to decline, except in
the personal power of the rulers. Sokollu Mehmed's power outlasted
Selim's. Three events stand out in Selim II's time: the northern expedition

in 1570, the invasion of Cyprus in the same year, and the Battle of Lepanto in 1571. The northern expedition attempted to secure Ottoman dominance north and east of the Black Sea by digging a canal between the Don River, which flows into the Black Sea, and the Volga, which flows into the Caspian. Such a canal would have extended Ottoman naval dominance from the Black Sea to the Caspian, giving the Ottomans control of much of central Asian trade, considerable leverage against the Safavids, and a strong defense against Muscovy and the Cossacks. The expedition failed for a variety of reasons, logistic and political.

Cyprus, a Venetian possession, was the last base for Christian corsairs in the eastern Mediterranean. Venice obtained the support of Genoa and Spain against the Ottoman expedition, but the Ottomans landed in May 1570 and subdued the island entirely the next year. Following that success, the Ottoman fleet retired to Lepanto in the Gulf of Patras for the winter. A combined Hapsburg-Genoese-Venetian fleet under Don John of Austria (an illegitimate son of Charles V) was too late to assist Cyprus but caught the Ottoman force at anchorage and virtually annihilated it on October 7, 1571. Lepanto was one of the greatest victories in the history of naval warfare, a maritime Cannae. Although Western historians have frequently described it as a decisive battle that ended Ottoman expansion in the Mediterranean, like Cannae it did not win a war. In the winter of 1571 and 1572, the Ottomans replaced the entire fleet destroyed at Lepanto, an extraordinary feat that compelled Venice to accept peace in 1573 at the cost of surrendering Cyprus and paying a huge indemnity. Selim II died in 1574.

Murad III (r. 1574–1595) was Selim's only son old enough to serve as a provincial governor, so there was no possibility of a succession dispute. He reluctantly had all five of his brothers executed on the day of his accession. Murad devoted most of his energy to the harem, fathering some forty children. Sokollu Mehmed Pasha retained his dominance at first and pursued a policy of peace with the empire's major rivals. The empire renewed treaties of peace and commerce with Iran, Venice, and the Hapsburgs in 1574, 1575, and 1577, respectively. The peace policy did not last long. The weakness of the Safavids after the death of Shah Tahmasp in 1576 meant opportunity. Hostilities with the Safavids lasted from 1578 to 1590. The Ottomans won numerous victories, notably the Battle of the Torches in the Caucasus in 1583, and secured control of that region. A major Ottoman expedition again conquered Tabriz in 1585, putting Azerbaijan under direct Ottoman administration. Shah Abbas I accepted Ot-

IMAGE 3.4

Selim II receiving gifts from the Safavid Ambassador Shah Quli at Edirne in 1568: folio from a manuscript of the *Nüzhet el-Esrar el-Ahbar der Sefer-i Szigetvar.* To commemorate Selim II's accession to the throne, an embassy was sent with lavish gifts from Shah Tahmasp Safavi. Here, the Safavid ambassador (wearing the distinctive tall, pointed, Safavid headgear) is shown bowing before Selim with Ottoman courtiers who assist him in submitting to imperial court ritual and protocol.

toman peace terms in 1590. The last major Ottoman effort on the Indian Ocean littoral apparently took place in 1588, when the Ottoman corsair Mir Ali Beg sought to expel the Portuguese from the entire east African littoral. The expedition failed.

Empire Transformed, 1593–1730

The Long War against the Hapsburgs (1593–1606) strained the Ottoman regime severely. What historians have called classical Ottoman institutions and practices had to change. The use of the term *classical* suggests that these changes constituted decline. Without doubt, the Ottoman Empire lost the military supremacy that had marked two centuries of imperial expansion, but it remained a great power. Equally indubitably, the empire faced significant internal challenges and its institutions and patterns of governance changed significantly. But challenges and transformation do not necessarily mean degeneration and devolution. Leslie Peirce, in one of the most remarkable contributions to recent Ottoman historiography, has demonstrated that the palace women contributed to the survival of the dynasty. The Ottomans faced the determined Hapsburgs in the west, the *jalali* (*celâlî*) revolts in Anatolia, and a Safavid resurgence in the east. They surrendered no territory in the west and only the most distant provinces in the east. Indeed, the ability to face the variety of challenges and adapt to circumstances indicated resilience rather than weakness.

Border warfare had continued in Hungary even during the peace. Major raids on Hapsburg territory between 1590 and 1593 impelled the Hapsburgs to break the treaty and attack the Ottoman Empire. So began the Long War. In the first two years of the war, the Ottomans took some border forts in Croatia but made no further gains. In 1594, Prince Michael of Wallachia rebelled against the sultan, posing a serious challenge to the Ottomans by depriving them of the use of the Danube, vital for both war and commerce. The death of Murad III in 1595 distracted the Ottoman leadership for a time. His eldest son, Mehmed III (1595–1603), the last Ottoman prince to serve in the provinces, took the throne without opposition. The distraction permitted the Hapsburgs to take the offensive. Wallachian popular resistance prevented the Ottomans from holding the province and encouraged an uprising in neighboring Moldavia as well. In Anatolia, the *jalali* disorders, analyzed below, began in 1596 and continued until 1610.

This desperate situation impelled Mehmed to take the field himself; he was the first Ottoman sultan to do so since Sulayman's death. He had two remarkable successes, taking the strategic fortress of Erlau (Eger), and defeating the Hapsburgs in battle at Mezo-Keresztes (Haçova) on October 26, 1596. These double victories gave the Ottomans the initiative in the west for the remainder of the war. In 1598, internal disorders in the Ottoman Empire permitted the Hapsburgs to advance, taking Raab. The Ottomans finally regained control of Wallachia and Moldavia by forming an alliance with Poland and drove the Hapsburgs out of Transylvania in 1605. With the situation stabilized and other threats to face, the Ottomans had no incentive to continue fighting. The Hapsburgs had similar motivations for peace. The empires signed the Treaty of Zsitvatorok on November 11, 1606. The Ottomans gained two border fortresses but relinquished annual tribute from the Hapsburgs; they also agreed to address the Hapsburg rulers as emperors without relinquishing their own claims to precedence. In 1607, 1614, and 1615, the Ottomans signed treaties with Transylvania, Poland, and again the Hapsburgs, stabilizing their European frontier.

In the east, Shah Abbas had reorganized the Safavid army so that it could meet the Ottomans in the field. He drove them out of Azerbaijan and the Caucasus from 1603 to 1605. The Safavids won a major victory at Sufiyan, near Tabriz, on November 6, 1605. This battle ended the major action of the war, but sporadic combats and negotiations continued for some years, with a lull but no peace in 1616, until the two empires signed the Peace of Sarab in 1618.

Mehmed III died in 1603. He had executed his eldest son, Mahmud, shortly before his own death, apparently because of the prince's popularity with the Janissaries and other forces within the palace. Two sons survived: Ahmed, an adolescent who had not yet proven his ability to father children, and Mustafa, an infant. Ahmed took the throne, but in order to secure the survival of the dynasty, Mustafa was permitted to live. Ahmed was chiefly interested in religious scholarship and good works, financing the construction of the famous Blue Mosque in Istanbul and seeking to improve observance of the Shariah by his subjects. He did not govern actively.

When he died in 1617, Ahmed had sired five sons, but palace politics, discussed below, led to the enthronement of his brother, Mustafa (1617–1618), who was deposed as insane within a year. Ahmed's eldest son then took the throne as Osman II (1618–1622). He intended to transform the Ottoman political and military system fundamentally, eliminating the existing central army of military slaves and recruiting a new army of Turks from the provinces. The Janissaries responded to this fundamental threat to their interests by overthrowing and eventually assassinating him. The oldest of his brothers was only twelve, so the Janissaries reenthroned Mustafa (1622–1623). Entirely incapable of dealing with the situation, Mustafa and his advisors lost control of the armed forces; Istanbul fell into anarchy, and the governor of Erzurum, Abaza Mehmed Pasha, led what became a general military revolt in Anatolia. This crisis led to a Janissary uprising in Istanbul. Provincial governors refused to remit revenue to the capital, creating a financial crisis. At last, Mustafa was removed, and Murad IV (1623–1640), Ahmed's eldest surviving son, took the throne.

From his accession until 1632, the political situation changed little. Abaza Mehmed Pasha controlled eastern Anatolia until 1628; Murad's mother and other palace figures struggled for dominance of the empire. Shah Abbas took advantage of Ottoman weakness to invade and conquer Iraq; Baghdad fell on January 12, 1624. Other parts of the Ottoman Empire, most importantly Egypt, Yemen, and the Druse lands of Mount

Lebanon, escaped central control. A series of military revolts finally gave Murad the opportunity to take control of the regime. The Grand Vizier Khusrev Mehmed Pasha invited all the rebels and provincial garrisons to come to the capital and state their grievances. This military migration led to anarchy in the capital and the dismissal of all of the top officials, but the rebels could not agree on what regime they wanted. Their divisions permitted Murad to eliminate the rebels and to demand that all members of the military class take an oath of loyalty to the sultan.

Murad's reforms, unlike Osman's program, were essentially conservative. To put an end to the problem of rural disorder, he ordered a popular mobilization against the rebels. This action and military expedition led to a general massacre of the rebels. Murad purged the muster rolls of soldiers who did not serve on campaigns and was able to reduce corruption significantly. Murad devoted his energy to external campaigns as well. In addition to one against the Poles in the Ukraine, Murad led a major incursion into the Caucasus and Azerbaijan in 1634, retaking both Erivan and Tabriz but holding neither. Distractions in the Crimea and Transylvania prevented another eastern campaign until 1638, when the Ottoman forces recaptured Baghdad after a difficult siege. Murad wintered in Mosul, hoping to occupy Azerbaijan the next year, but Shah Safi sued for peace, offering to abandon fortresses in Azerbaijan and recognize Ottoman control of Iraq. The long series of wars between the Ottomans and Safavids ended with the Treaty of Qasr-i Shirin on May 17, 1639. Murad thus secured the political and commercial advantages of controlling Iraq and ended the Safavid threat to the eastern frontier. He died on February 8, 1640, having restored order and vigor to the empire and executed some 20,000 men to do so.

Sultan Ibrahim (1640–1648), Murad's younger brother, was weak and eccentric, if not insane. With Murad's strong hand gone, official corruption once again became rampant, and the fiscal mechanism of the empire broke down. For a time, Murad's vizier, Kara Mustafa Pasha, held the administration together, but he fell victim to court politics and was executed in 1644. The same year, war began with Venice over Crete, which had replaced Cyprus as the major base for Christian corsairs in Europe. A huge Ottoman force landed on the island in 1645 and quickly took Canea (Khaniá), Crete's major port, but the campaign degenerated into a siege of Candia (modern Heraklion), the capital of the island. The city held out until 1662. The resurgent Venetian fleet blockaded the Dardanelles in

1647 and again in 1648. The second blockade led to a panic in Istanbul and the deposition of the sultan, who had alienated the Janissaries and ulama with fiscal demands.

Ibrahim's son, Mehmed IV (1648–1687), ruled longer than any Ottoman sultan except Sulayman I, yet made little impression upon history. His reign is instead associated with another name, that of Köprülü. For the first eight years of his reign, until he reached the age of fourteen, Mehmed's rule entailed merely undoing the effects of his father's eccentricities. Bitter factional rivalries continued, with the leaders of the Janissaries, various grand viziers, and the sultan's mother and grandmother all jockeying for position. Tarhonju Ahmed Pasha governed the empire effectively in 1652 and 1653 by returning to the methods of Murad IV. His opponents turned the young sultan against him, however, and chaos returned after his execution. By 1656 renewed disorders in Anatolia, a major Venetian victory over the Ottoman fleet outside the Dardanelles, and food shortages led to panic in the capital, and Mehmed turned to Köprülü Mehmed Pasha to rescue the situation.

Köprülü Mehmed Pasha had spent his life in the sultan's service, holding a wide variety of posts in the palace, central and provincial administration, the Janissary corps, and on campaign. He was living in retirement, aged almost eighty, when his supporters at court persuaded Mehmed IV and his mother that he could succeed where all others had failed. He took office as grand vizier, with complete authority, on September 14, 1656. Essentially, Köprülü Mehmed Pasha, who remained in office until his death in 1661, and his son Fazil Ahmed Pasha, who served as grand vizier from 1661 until he died in 1676, reprised Murad IV's program. They made the system work by dismissing or executing those who abused it, tightly controlling expenditures, and increasing income. When the first effort by the Ottoman fleet failed to break the Venetian blockade, Köprülü Mehmed Pasha executed its commanders on the spot. Eventually, the blockade was ended, and a new Ottoman fleet took the offensive. On land, Köprülü Mehmed Pasha faced challenges in the east and the west.

In Europe, George Rakoczy, the vassal ruler of Transylvania (eastern Hungary, east of the Ottoman province of Temesvar and north of the vassal state of Wallachia), claimed autonomy. He allied with King Carl Gustav X of Sweden in the First Northern War, persuaded his fellow vassals in Moldavia and Wallachia to join him, and invaded Poland. In 1657, the Ottomans expelled Rakoczy, established direct Ottoman rule in Transylvania, and replaced the rulers of Wallachia and Moldavia with more cooperative relatives.

In Anatolia, the weakness at the center had spawned a new uprising, led by Abaza Hasan Pasha, who sought to become the ruler of an independent Anatolia. The grand vizier returned from the campaign in Transylvania, defeated the rebels, who had reached Bosporus in 1658, and drove Abaza Hasan Pasha eastward. The revolt ended when Köprülü Mehmed Pasha offered the rebel leaders a truce, invited them to a banquet, and had them slaughtered. Some 12,000 rebels and sympathizers were executed before the grand vizier returned to the capital in 1659.

Fazil Ahmed Pasha faced almost continuous warfare during his years in office. He finally completed the conquest of Crete in 1662. The continuing instability of the frontier in Hungary led to another war with the Hapsburgs. A drawn battle at St. Gotthard on August 1, 1664, led to a compromise peace, but the restoration of Ottoman power caused consternation in Europe.

The Ottomans now turned their attention to the complex situation in the Ukraine, where they and their vassals, the Crimean Tatars, confronted Muscovy, Poland, and the Cossacks. The Cossack populations had come into existence in the fifteenth and early sixteenth centuries as a mixture of Turkic nomads from the remnants of the Golden Horde, Slavs who had settled on Russia's steppe border, and assorted renegades and fugitives. By the early seventeenth century, the Don Cossack host dominated the lower reaches of the river. The Cossacks had only a rudimentary state organization but formidable military capability. They served as the steppe auxiliaries of Muscovy, as the Crimean Tatars did for the Ottomans, but both Tatars and Cossacks pursued their own interests. As in the Mediterranean theater, various projects for grand coalitions against the Muslim Ottomans and Tatars foundered on the specific interests of the Christian powers and the division between the Catholic Poles and the Orthodox Russians and Cossacks.

Between 1660 and 1665, Poland and Muscovy fought a war over the Ukraine with different Cossack factions on each side. In 1665, Peter Doroshenko took power as hetman (leader) of the Cossacks and allied with the Tatars and Ottomans to gain autonomy from both Russia and Poland. When Muscovy and Poland made peace in 1677 and partitioned the Ukraine, they defeated Doroshenko and thus drew the Ottomans into the conflict. The first expedition to Poland in 1672 gave the Ottomans control of Podolia, the valley of the Bug River. The Poles accepted this situation in the Treaty of Buczacz on October 18, 1672. John (Jan) Sobieski, who became king of Poland in 1673, signed the Treaty of Zorvano in 1676 reconfirming the arrangement. This agreement marked the apogee of Ottoman expansion in Europe. Fazil Ahmed Pasha died the same year. Mehmed IV appointed his foster brother Kara Mustafa Pasha as grand vizier.

Kara Mustafa Pasha continued the domestic politics of his predecessors and sought expansion in Europe. Doroshenko shifted his allegiance from the Ottomans to Muscovy, and Kara Mustafa sought to replace him with another hetman, Yuri Khmelnytskyi (not the Bogdan Khmelnytskyi who led a Cossack revolt against Polish rule in the late 1640s and was responsible for the slaughter of thousands of Jews), but the Ottomans were unable to enforce their choice and accepted the loss of suzerainty over the Cossacks in 1681 in order to focus on the Hapsburgs. Opposition to Hapsburg dominance on national (anti-Hapsburg), religious (anti-Catholic), and social (antinobility) grounds made Hungary chronically unstable. The leaders of the national movement sought Ottoman support, and Kara Mustafa invaded and conquered Hapsburg Hungary in 1682. The next year, Kara Mustafa besieged Vienna. The siege came close to succeeding, but a Polish and Bavarian relief force, led by John Sobieski, broke it. The Ottomans withdrew to Belgrade, and Mehmed IV had Kara Mustafa executed.

The condition of the empire degenerated rapidly. Most of Hungary fell to the Hapsburgs between 1683 and 1686. Venice went on the offensive in the Adriatic, drove the Ottomans out of the Morea, and took Athens. An Ottoman counterattack in 1687 led to a battle at Mohacs, which reversed the results of the Ottoman victory there in 1526. Financial chaos and food shortages led to mutinies in the Ottoman army and disorders in Anatolia. Polish forces invaded Moldavia. Mehmed IV's lack of attention to this crisis led to his deposition. His younger brother, Sulayman II (1687–1691), took the throne after forty years in seclusion. For five months after his accession, various military units ran loose in Istanbul. The Hapsburgs took Belgrade in 1688, breaking the Danube barrier. The Ottomans sought to achieve a peace the next year, but negotiations failed, and the Hapsburgs occupied Wallachia and Transylvania and took Nish as well. The expulsion of the Ottomans from Europe seemed imminent.

To retrieve this desperate situation, in 1689 Sulayman called on another Köprülü, Fazil Mustafa Pasha, Fazil Ahmed's younger brother. He returned to the harsh measures of his elders, reconstituted the provincial forces, and restored order to the empire's finances. Hapsburg efforts to establish Catholicism in their newly conquered territories had swiftly alienated the Orthodox and Protestant populations. The sultan received requests for assistance from Transylvania, Serbia, and Wallachia. The Ottomans retook Nish, Semendria, and Belgrade and restored the Danube defense line in 1690. Having ended the crisis, Fazil Mustafa turned his attention to internal and military reform. His efforts encompassed new administrative arrangements in the reconquered areas to win the support of the subject peoples, attempts to increase food production, and improved drill and military education.

Fazil Mustafa's efforts came to naught. Sulayman II died on June 22, 1691. Shortly afterwards, the Hapsburgs ambushed and routed the Ottoman army at Slankamen. Fazil Mustafa was killed. The Ottomans held the Danube barrier, but the Hapsburgs demanded that the Ottomans relinquish Transylvania, Temesvar, Wallachia, Moldavia, and Bessarabia and cede Podolia to Poland and the Morea to Venice. Ahmed II (1691–1695), the third son of Sultan Ibrahim to take the throne, would not accept those terms.

The Ottoman throne then passed to the next generation in the person of Mustafa II (1695–1703), the son of Mehmed IV. With his tutor, Fayzullah Effendi, he sought to return to the Köprülü model of administration. Mustafa took the field against the Hapsburgs in Hungary with some success but met a crushing defeat in the Battle of Zenta at the hands of Prince Eugene of Savoy on September 11, 1697. The Ottomans also faced a challenge from further north. Russia had allied with the Hapsburgs against the Ottomans in 1686 but had not made an effective contribution until Peter the Great became the effective ruler of Russia in 1695. The Russians conquered the Ottoman fortress of Azov on the Black Sea the next year. The Ottomans had lost their former monopoly of control over the Black Sea.

In 1697, the Treaty of Ryswick had ended the War of the League of Augsburg, freeing the Hapsburgs from war with France. With pressure from the Romanovs in the north and Venice in the Mediterranean, as well as domestic food shortages, economic chaos, and disorders, the Ottomans had no choice but to sue for peace. Mustafa turned to Amjazade Husayn Pasha, a nephew of Mehmed Köprülü, to retrieve the situation. He negotiated a peace agreement with the Hapsburgs and Venetians at the village of Carlowitz on the Danube in 1699; the British and Dutch ambassadors (both representing William of Orange, who took the throne of England as William III in 1688 as a result of the Glorious Revolution) acted as medi-

IMAGE 3.5
Sultan Ahmed III: folio from the *Kebir Musavver Silsilename*. The rulers of all the gunpowder empires used illustrated dynastic genealogies as an important visual component in their rhetoric of legitimacy. For at least a century after Levni presented the *Silsilename* to his royal patron Ahmed III, it continued to provide a model for subsequent Ottoman genealogical portrait sets.

ators. The Ottomans surrendered Hungary, except for the province of Temesvar, ceded Podolia and the Ukraine to Poland, abandoned claims to suzerainty over the Cossacks, and accepted some Venetian conquests. They signed a separate treaty with Peter the Great in 1700, surrendering Azov.

The Treaty of Carlowitz marked the end of an era for the Ottoman Empire. The empire had surrendered territories in Europe that it had held for nearly two hundred years and no longer dominated the Aegean and Black seas. Muscovy had changed from a distant to an immediate threat. The Ottomans had faced a coalition of European powers that they could not withstand and significant internal difficulties as well. Husayn Pasha sought to restore order to the Ottoman economy. He reduced taxes, sought to create incentives for the cultivation of land to improve food supplies, and tried to create industries that could compete with Western manufacturers. He also sought to reform the Ottoman army and navy. Had his efforts succeeded, he might have placed the empire on a new basis, but he challenged the existing power structure too directly. Frustrated, he retired in 1702 and died shortly thereafter. The empire's fiscal problems had become so severe that the salaries of some soldiers were several years in arrears. This situation, together with Mustafa's apparent apathy, led to a mutiny, known as the Edirne Event. Rebels, demanding back pay and further concessions, took control of Istanbul while Mustafa was in Edirne. He sent troops against the rebels, who countermarched. The sultan's troops then joined them, marched to Edirne, and forced Mustafa to abdicate in favor of his brother, Ahmed III (1703–1730).

Ahmed III bought off the rebels with enormous bribes (accession taxes), which immediately created demands for similar gifts from other troops. The rebels contemplated ending the Ottoman dynasty, replacing the sultan with either a prince of the family of Crimean khans or with a descendant of Sokollu Mehmed and the daughter of Selim II. Ahmed skillfully kept the opposition divided until he won general acceptance of his position, then retired from active politics. His viziers sought to return to the Köprülü program of traditional reform and did strengthen the Ottoman army considerably. The Ottoman Empire avoided involvement in the War of Spanish Succession (1701–1714) and, for a while, the Great Northern War between Russia and Sweden (1700–1721), despite the efforts of France and Sweden to bring them in. The flight of Charles XII of Sweden to Ottoman territory after his great defeat at Poltava in 1709 eventually made Ottoman involvement inevitable. The Ottomans supported the Crimean khanate and the Cossacks against Peter the Great and actually defeated the great Russian ruler in the Pruth campaign of 1711. The czar and his army had advanced into Moldavia and run short of supplies. The Ottomans surrounded the Russian force. The Treaty of Pruth permitted Peter to withdraw in return for surrendering what he had taken.

Emboldened by this success, the Ottoman war party now turned its attention to Venice. Venetian violations of the Treaty of Carlowitz and pleas of the Orthodox populations of the territories Venice had conquered for liberation from Catholic rule offered a suitable pretext. War began in 1714. The Ottomans swiftly reconquered the Morea. After the end of the War of Spanish Succession, however, the Hapsburgs joined the Venetians, and Prince Eugene again took the field. Eugene defeated the Ottoman army at Peterovaradin (or Peterwardein) on August 5, 1716, and took Temesvar and Belgrade. These defeats ended support for the war in Istanbul. Ahmed III appointed a new grand vizier, Nevshehirli Damat Ibrahim Pasha, and set out to make peace. The result was the Peace of Passarowitz, signed on July 21, 1718, again with British and Dutch mediation, although the two thrones were no longer combined. The Ottomans surrendered Belgrade and Smederevo—albeit only temporarily—to the Hapsburgs, who abandoned their Venetian allies.

The appointment of Nevshehirli Damat Ibrahim Pasha marked the beginning of more than a decade of peace and prosperity, known retrospectively as the Tulip Period. The tulip craze from which the name is derived "symbolized both conspicuous consumption and cross-cultural borrowings since it was an item of exchange between the Ottoman Empire, west Europe, and east Asia," in the words of Donald Quataert.[2] The Ottomans had never lacked curiosity or been unwilling to learn from their enemies, but the tone of their borrowing had changed. The Ottomans recognized that they could learn not only military technology and technique but broader lessons about industry, technology, and education. European products were in vogue. Tacitly at least, the Ottoman elite had recognized that the empire had become a peripheral power rather than a global political, economic, and cultural center. Beneath the glitter at the top, however, there was growing popular discontent in Istanbul, partially as a result of the flow of refugees from territories surrendered at Carlowitz and Passarowitz. The appearance of a new threat in the east shattered the tranquil surface.

The collapse of the Safavid Empire in 1722 permitted the Ottomans to occupy Azerbaijan, Safavid territory since the Treaty of Zuhab in 1639, sharing territorial gains in northwest Iran with Russia. After two years of hostilities between the Ottomans and the Afghans, who had overthrown the Safavids, the Ottomans signed a peace treaty in 1728. But Nadir Quli Khan Afshar expelled the Afghans from Iran and invaded Ottoman territory, taking Tabriz in 1730. Ahmed III and Nevshehirli Damat Ibrahim Pasha mobilized a huge army, but a popular uprising in Istanbul led to the execution of the vizier and the deposition of Ahmed III. Ahmed III's nephew took the throne as Mahmud I. The overthrow of Ahmed III ended the Indian summer of the Tulip Period, and it marks the end of this chronology.

ASPECTS OF EMPIRE: IDEOLOGY AND LAW

Ideology

> I am a slave of God and I am the master in this world. . . . God's virtue
> and Muhammed's miracles are my companions. I am Sülaymân and my
> name is being read in the prayers in the holy cities of Islam. I launched

fleets in the Mediterranean on the part of the Franks in Maghreb as well as in the Indian Ocean. I am the Shah of Baghdad and Iraq, the Caesar of the Roman land and the Sultan of Egypt.[3]

Thus Sulayman describes himself in a 1538 inscription on the walls of the fortress at Bender, on the Dniester River in modern Moldova. The inscription shows that the Ottoman conception of sovereignty had multiple facets. Sulayman claims a divine mandate for universal rule, associates himself with Muhammad, asserts his sovereignty over Mecca and Medina as a demonstration of his status, fights the western Europeans in both the Mediterranean and the Indian Ocean, and combines in his own person the sovereignties of Baghdad, the original capital of the Abbasid caliphate, and Egypt, formerly the center of the most prestigious Muslim state. But the Bender inscription is a snapshot of a moment in the complex and dynamic evolution of Ottoman ideology. As the empire grew and its subjects and ruling class changed and became more diverse, the Ottoman doctrine of kingship and its symbolic presentation became more comprehensive and multifaceted. The heterogeneity was more than religious and ethnic. The Ottomans ruled a series of provincial elites with different expectations and perceptions: peasants and nomads, merchants and artisans, ulama and bureaucrats. Ottoman sovereignty, as it developed over time, appeared legitimate in the eyes of almost all of these groups well into the eighteenth century.

Ottoman ideology had at least six elements, each of which had primacy at different times for different audiences: frontier *ghazi*, warrior Irano-Islamic, Turko-Mongol, Roman, millenarian, and sedentary Irano-Islamic. The frontier *ghazi* element was most important in the early decades. The early development of the Ottoman principality took place in the historical shade; the later Ottoman accounts are legend rather than history. It appears that Osman had no specific ideology or claim to sovereignty; his position as a clan chieftain in the Qayi clan of the Oghuz Turks, if it is not entirely a later fabrication, had little to do with the formation of the Ottoman *beylik*. He became a bey by military success, by winning the confidence and respect of the Turkmen, Greeks, and others who followed him, and by dealing mildly with former opponents who surrendered to him. *Ghaza*, in this context, appeared in legends of warrior-Sufis, in Colin Imber's words, as "an epic struggle against unbelievers, conceived in terms of popular religion and popular heroism, . . . an ideology far removed from the doctrines of the sharī`ah and the world view of orthodox Islam."[4]

Osman's marriage to the daughter of a Sufi *shaykh*, Edebali, whose ancestors were apparently among the leaders of the Babi revolt, fits into this pattern. Edebali represented the tradition of Turkmen resentment of central authority and practice of a religion laced with central Asian elements and mystical practices with little space for law and learning. The later sources report that Osman had dreamed that a moon rose from Edebali's chest and entered his own, and then a tree grew from his navel and shaded the entire world. Edebali interpreted the moon as his own daughter, and the tree foreshadowed Osman's universal sovereignty. This legend articulates the Ottoman claim to a divine mandate to rule; it resembles the myths about other Turko-Mongol conquerors such as Chingiz Khan, Timur, and Uzun Hasan Aqquyunlu. The frontier *ghazi* ethos remained significant in Ottoman politics for generations after Osman, but as the principality grew and developed, it became a divisive force.

The successes of Osman and Orkhan made them rulers as well as frontier chieftains. The Ottomans began to project themselves as established sovereigns. Many officials and ulama from the Rum Saljuq kingdom entered Ottoman service. They brought with them the agrarian, centralizing agenda of Irano-Islamic monarchy and, associated with it, support for the formal, legalistic side of Islam. After the conquest of Bursa, the Ottomans began to articulate their sovereignty in stone through the construction of monumental buildings, most notably mosques. This practice continued as the capital moved from Bursa to Edirne and then Istanbul, as the numerous imperial mosque complexes in that city demonstrate. The foundation of the first Ottoman madrasa in Bursa in 1331 was a physical manifestation of the transformation of the Ottoman polity. The Ottoman ideological agenda carried with it the political theory that Jalal al-Din Davani epitomized a century later. The ruler demonstrated his legitimacy through victory, just governance, and enforcement of the Shariah. Victories in this context differed from successful raiding. They implied the defeat of other rulers in battle. Justice derived from the circle of justice and thus entailed an agrarian, rather than a pastoral, context. The expansion of the empire meant a growing agrarian base and peasant subjects. This aspect of the Irano-Islamic tradition of kingship became a fundamental and enduring aspect of Ottoman government. Orkhan was the first Ottoman to use the title sultan, conveying his commitment to government in accord with Islamic norms. Murad I used the title *sultan-i azam* (exalted sultan). In the early decades, however, the agrarian/Shari agenda clashed with the culture of the frontier. The later Ottoman sources depict conflict between the frontier *ghazi*s, with their informal Sufi religious orientation and nomadic ethos, and the agrarian, bureaucratic Shari agenda of the regime. Although the settled Christian populations whom the Ottomans now ruled had no interest in the Islamic aspect of this ideology, they responded to the security and just government, meaning reasonable and predictable revenue demands, that the Ottomans brought. The movement toward the Irano-Islamic tradition of government included the development of a more formal, legalistic definition of *ghaza*, associated with government policy and law rather than frontier heroism and charisma. According to Colin Imber, the legalistic view of *ghaza* became part of the Ottoman "dynastic myth," which in turn became the Wittek thesis. One fifteenth-century writer, Neshri, depicted the Ottomans as heirs of the Prophet and the Rightly Guided caliphs in the conduct of *ghaza*, thus connecting the role of *ghazi* to the traditional leadership of the Muslim community.

Expansion eastward forced the Ottomans to appeal to the Turkmen of the other *beylik*s. They did so by claiming hereditary primacy among the Oghuz and thus legitimate global sovereignty. It held that God had designated the mythical Oghuz Khan, the eponymous ancestor of the Oghuz, as the legitimate ruler of the world. Though it was not entirely an imitation of the Chingiz Khanid doctrine, the Oghuz claim to sovereignty followed the same pattern. In the Ottoman case, however, the writers focused on Ottoman primacy among the Oghuz Turks, seeking to demonstrate the propriety of Ottoman rule over the Turks of Anatolia and beyond, which included exalting the Oghuz/Ottoman claim over the Mongol/Timurid claim. Bayazid I advanced this claim against Timur, who denigrated the Ottoman lineage. Ottoman writers claimed primacy for the clan to which Osman belonged, the Qayi, rather than the Qiniq, the tribe of the Saljuqs, who had dominated the Oghuz for three centuries. The Ottomans sought to make the Oghuz genealogy the basis of a claim to universal sovereignty equal to that of the Chingiz Khanids and Timurids. In the fifteenth century, Ottoman authors also articulated a claim to sovereignty in Anatolia as the legitimate heirs of the Rum Saljuqs. One version of the story asserts that the Rum Saljuq sultan Ala al-Din Kay Qubadh I had granted land in northwest Anatolia to Ertoghrul, Osman I's father, and Ala al-Din Kay Qubadh II, who died childless, had designated Osman I as his heir. This legend provided another justification for Ottoman primacy over the Turkmen.

Since Anatolia was known as Rum (Rome) and its Saljuq rulers as the Rum Saljuqs, the Ottoman principality developed in the ideological context of the Roman Empire as well as the Islamic world. The Ottomans called their Europeans possessions *Rumeli* (Rome land); Bayazid I called himself *sultan al-Rum* (sultan of Rome). But the Ottoman connection to Rome was more than geographic and historical. They regarded themselves as the heirs of the Roman Empire. The conquest of Constantinople gave them an unmistakable claim to the status of Roman emperor, which they communicated through the use of the title caesar (*qaisar*). Fatih Mehmed converted the Hagia Sophia, the imperial church of the Eastern Roman Empire, into Aya Sofia, the imperial mosque of the Ottomans. The construction of minarets for Aya Sofia articulated the new imperial status of the Ottomans in stone. The Conqueror made a massive commitment to the reconstruction and repopulation of Constantinople, the second Rome.

Although Orthodox Christianity lost its greatest shrine and its status as the imperial faith, it retained an exalted and protected position. In Halil Inalcık's words, "Even before the conquest of Constantinople, the Ottomans appeared as protectors of the Church and considered the Greek Orthodox ecclesiastical organization as part of their administrative system."[5] After the conquest, Fatih Mehmed oversaw the installation of a new patriarch of the Orthodox Church and granted the eastern Christians special protection for their structures and ceremonies. Christian services in the Ottoman Empire included the name of the ruler and prayer for him. The Ottomans received the support of most of their Christian subjects for most of the period in question because their governance brought order, predictability, and a modicum of justice, not to mention freedom from the oppression that Orthodox Christians frequently experienced under Roman Catholic rule. The conquest and restoration of Constantinople added to Ottoman prestige among both Muslims and Christians.

The position of the Ottomans as the heir of Rome may explain the willingness of many members of the ruling families of Christian principalities to convert to Islam and enter Ottoman service. At least two, and perhaps three, of the nephews of Constantine IX Paleologus, the last Byzantine emperor, converted to Islam and became high Ottoman officials, one as governor of the province of Rumeli (the Balkans) and, as such, commander of one of the wings of the Ottoman army, and one, perhaps two, as grand vizier under Bayazid II. Many other high officials came from the ruling families of Balkan principalities. Whatever the specific motivation, this pattern was too common to classify the individuals involved as renegades. Presumably their prestige and connections in their former principalities facilitated Ottoman absorption of those areas, but this proposition could be valid only if conversion to Islam did not eliminate that prestige. Ottoman expansion clearly meant something other than the simple triumph of Muslim over Christian.

For the Ottomans, however, the victory over the Mamluk kingdom, which, even after the conquest of Constantinople, remained the most prestigious of Muslim states, meant more than the conquest of Constantinople. With the great victory at Chaldiran, it eliminated any rival to the Ottomans, in power and prestige in the Islamic world. The destruction of the shadow Abbasid caliphate meant nothing. The story, often repeated, that Yavuz Selim received the caliphate from the last Abbasid claimant in a ceremony in Cairo in 1517 is a myth. There is no connection between later Ottoman claims to the caliphate and the dismissal of the pretender in Cairo. The Ottomans did take a new title after the conquest of Egypt gave them control over the Hejaz, that of servitor of the two holy sanctuaries (*khadim al-Haramayn al-Sharifayn*), which the Mamluks had employed. This title implied superiority over other Muslim rulers. The Ottoman reaction to the Mughal emperor Akbar's interest in Mecca shows how seriously the Ottomans took their position there. In 1578, Akbar made large donations to causes in Mecca, which might have permitted him to challenge the Ottoman position as the principal patron of the holy cities. Immediately upon receiving this information, Selim II prohibited acceptance of any further donations from Akbar and ordered the expulsion of pilgrims from the Hejaz.

The millenarian and esoteric aspect of Ottoman sovereignty requires significant background explanation. Ottoman millenarianism developed in the context of an array of overlapping traditions of esoteric knowledge that affected political and intellectual elites, Muslim and Christian, across the entire Mediterranean and throughout the rest of the Islamic world. The elements of the array included Sufism, Kabala (there were Christian as well as Jewish Kabalists), astrology, numerology, neo-Platonic philosophy, and the Muslim concept of the renewer (*mujadid*). This overlay of secret knowledge connected the Muslim and Christian worlds; Christian writers made use of Jewish and Muslim works and vice versa. At least one major Muslim work in this tradition circulated in pocket-sized versions, showing its popularity and importance to its readers. In the late fifteenth and early sixteenth centuries, events, historical and anticipated, led to a surge of speculation about the end of the world. The steady pace of Ottoman conquest from Constantinople in 1453 to Egypt in 1517 and then further into Europe, along with the Spanish conquest of Grenada in 1492, the approach of the rare conjunction between Jupiter and Saturn in 1552 and 1553, the millennium of the Muslim calendar in 1591, and a variety of textual evidence, encouraged the interpretation of current events in the light of the end of days. One Christian scenario, for example, asserted that corruption within Christendom would lead to a victory for the Turks, after which the Turkish emperor would convert to Christianity and rule the world as the perfect ruler. This view of the world affected the highest levels of society, including the rulers themselves. Bayazid II, Selim I, and Sulayman, at least, responded to this esoteric tradition and propounded their sovereignty in millenarian terms, as did their Christian rivals, the Valois Francis I of France and the Hapsburg Charles V of the Holy Roman Empire, Spain, and Naples, as well as Shah Ismail Safavi.

In addition to *mujadid*, the titles associated with this conception of sovereignty included *sahib-i zaman* (meaning "lord of the age," a title also given to the *mahdi* in Shii Islam) and *sahib-qiran* (most commonly translated as "lord of the fortunate conjunction"). The latter title, most commonly associated with Timur, apparently originally referred to an astronomical event but had come to imply universal sovereignty in the sixteenth century, at least in a specific intellectual context. The Ottomans never used these titles in official documents, but they appear in texts and letters. Ibrahim Pasha, Sulayman's grand vizier and brother-in-law, had a central role in developing the Ottoman messianic conception of universal sovereignty. In Cornell Fleischer's words,

> Süleymân and İbrâhîm Pasha had attempted, at least for their own purposes and those of Palace circles, to formulate a new understanding of sovereignty, one that could at once comprehend and transcend historical models, including those fashioned by established communalist conceptions of the nature of terrestrial power. The apocalyptic content of the concept of *ṣâhib-qirân*, then, was an essential element in the sacralization of Suleymanic sovereignty . . . [6]

Gülrû Necipoğlu has demonstrated that Sulayman gave his claims physical form in a distinctive crown:

Sülaymân's composite crown—with its combined elements from the pope's tiara, the emperor's mitre-crown, and Hapsburg parade helmets with Islamic motifs—was an intelligible statement of Ottoman imperial claims. This idiosyncratic helmet disputed both the Holy Roman emperor's title of Caesar and the sanctioning power of the pope.[7]

The work of Fleischer, Necipoğlu, and others demonstrates that Selim, Sulayman, and Charles V, as well as Shah Ismail, presented themselves as messianic figures, not merely representatives of their faith communities, when they struggled for supremacy in the first half of the sixteenth century. Selim's victory at Chaldiran ended Ismail's bid. By 1550, both Charles V and Sulayman had abandoned the "utopian ambition of bringing the whole Mediterranean basin under one power by reuniting Constantinople with Rome."[8] Despite major victories over both the Hapsburgs and the Safavids, the Ottomans could not eliminate either adversary. Their efforts to counter the Portuguese in the Indian Ocean had failed. Logistics had overcome ambition. Later Ottoman rulers emphasized piety and law rather than warfare and universal aspirations. Sulayman in his later years was not *sahib-qiran*, the messianic lord of the fortunate conjunction, but *padishah alam panah* (emperor, refuge of the world), the protector of the faith rather than the conqueror of the world. In the language of anthropologist A. M. Hocart's comparative analysis of kingship, the Ottomans became judge kings rather than warrior kings. What Leslie Peirce calls "the sedentary sultanate," in which the ruler remained in the capital rather than going on campaign, supplanted the image of the *ghazi* ruler. This change took place for a variety of reasons; the personality of the sultans, which historians have traditionally regarded as critical, was not the primary one. As Peirce states,

> The ideal sovereign of the post-Süleymanic Ottoman Empire was a sedentary monarch whose defense of the faith was manifested more in demonstrations of piety, support of the holy law and endowment of religious institutions than in personal participation in battle, and whose charisma was derived more from seclusion broken by ritual ceremony than from martial glory.[9]

Elsewhere, drawing on the language of Lutfi Pasha, Sulayman's grand vizier and son-in-law, she observes,

In sixteenth-century legitimating polemic centering on the Ottoman sultan's duty to defend Islam, it was less the extension of its borders that was emphasized than the defense of its holy law . . . less the "power" of the Sultan than the Imam's maintenance of the Faith and government of the king of Islam with equity.[10]

Later Ottoman rulers made their piety and patronage of Sunni Islam, in both its Shari and Sufi aspects, the basis of their sovereignty. Unlike their predecessors, they actively encouraged Jews and Christians to convert to Islam, though this encouragement did not amount to persecution. The expansion and systematization of the religious establishment under imperial patronage and the emphasis on piety as the basis of legitimacy led to a vast expansion of the political and administrative roles and influence of the ulama. The effect it had on popular piety fit the pattern of confessionalization. The Ottomans sought to confine religious discourse and observance within defined and acceptable patterns. The effects of this effort were far more subtle than in Safavid Iran, but must have been significant none the less.

The first articulation of a unique Ottoman claim to the caliphate took place in this context. As explained in the chapter 2, the title caliph had come to denote a legitimate Muslim ruler, without implying either unique or universal sovereignty or coinciding with the legal writings on the caliphate. Late in Sulayman's reign, Lutfi Pasha and Abu Suud Effendi, the *shaykh al-Islam* (for discussion of this title, see below), articulated an explicit Ottoman claim to the status of caliph. According to Colin Imber, "The main purpose of the Ottoman claim to the caliphate was to enhance the Sultan's authority over his subjects and to assert his primacy over other Islamic rulers."[11] The claim to the caliphate did not, however, become a central or consistent feature of Ottoman ideology until the late eighteenth century. The transition to from *sahib-qiran* to *padishah alam panah* included an effort to enforce religious uniformity and an expansion and systematization of the clerical establishment.

Although the Ottoman dynasty suffered from a number of succession disputes over the centuries, it clearly escaped the debilitating effects of collective sovereignty and the appanage system that shortened the life span of most Turko-Mongol dynasties. Ottoman practices evolved over the centuries, roughly in parallel with the general evolution of the conception of kingship. The obscurity of the early decades of Ottoman history conceals early dynastic developments. It may be no more than happenstance that prevented succession disputes from hindering the Ottoman principality's growth into an empire. Perhaps the small size of the family and the long lives of Osman, Orkhan, and Murad prevented collective sovereignty from dividing the principality or causing prolonged disputes. Bayazid I began what became the standard Ottoman solution by executing his brother Yaqub shortly after he took the throne upon the death of their father, Murad I, in 1389. For this reason, the Ottomans did not face a succession dispute until Timur imposed his own dynastic views on the empire by dividing it into appanages.

Timur's division of the empire affected Ottoman politics for twenty years after the defeat at Ankara. Mehmed I's decade of struggle to reunite the empire left him and his descendants determined to prevent any repetition; he asserted in a letter to Timur's son and successor, Shah Rukh, that the Ottomans rejected sharing government, meaning the division of the empire among brothers. The Ottomans, by this time if not much earlier, had thus abandoned collective sovereignty in its standard form. Only one member of the family could rule the empire in each generation, but each son of the sovereign had an equal claim to succeed and, as a potential future sovereign, the right to govern a province. The ruler could attempt to manipulate circumstances to favor one son, but he could not actually determine his own successor. Mehmed sought to ensure the succession of Murad, the eldest of his four sons, by excluding the other claimants from the capital; however, he failed to do so, leading to the struggle against the two Mustafas. A different constituency within the Ottoman Empire supported each candidate—the frontier beys supported the elder Mustafa, the Turkmen of Anatolia backed the younger Mustafa, and the central administration and army favored Murad. Murad II's victory reflected the trend of Ottoman politics.

Murad II abdicated the throne in 1444 in favor of his son Mehmed for a variety of reasons, both personal and political; avoiding a succession dispute must have one of them. His inability to stay off the throne reflected the political circumstances of the time but not resistance to Mehmed's ultimate succession. Mehmed faced a major challenge in Europe as soon as he took the throne, and the military leaders in Europe had no confidence in the nineteen-year-old sultan. They prevailed on Grand Vizier Chandarli Khalil Pasha to ask Murad II to return to the throne, which he did in time to win the victory at Varna. Murad attempted to retire again, but Mehmed still lacked the backing of the Turkish provincial elite and the Janissaries. From 1446 to 1451, Murad ruled, though Mehmed apparently continued to reign. When Murad actually died in 1451, Mehmed faced no opposition for the throne. The *qanunnamah* (dynastic law book, discussed below) attributed to him makes royal fratricide, the execution of each generation's losers in the contest for succession, an explicit policy. Ottoman dynastic theory thus envisioned a single sovereign in each generation, each of whose sons carried the dynastic sovereign gene. At the death of the sovereign, his sons settled the succession by contest, and the losers faced inevitable execution. This system remained in place for roughly a century.

During that time, succession contests affected the empire three times, after the death of Mehmed II and in the last decade of Sulayman's reign. Selim I had only one son, Sulayman; there may have been younger brothers executed earlier. Selim II had only one son old enough to become a provincial governor, the future Murad III, so there was no succession contest. Murad's eldest son, Mehmed III, was the last Ottoman prince to serve as a governor, whether as a matter of policy or happenstance, since he was significantly older than his brothers. Of the two succession disputes, the one between Bayazid II and Jem Sultan was the most serious. Mehmed II did not put either of his sons in a position of advantage. Bayazid gained the throne because he had the support of the Janissaries and central administration; the Turkish provincial aristocracy supported Jem. Bayazid II had three sons serving as provincial governors at the end of his reign: Ahmed closest to the capital at Amasya, Korkud at Manisa, and Selim farthest away at Trebizond. The location of Ahmed's appointment suggested that Bayazid favored him, but Selim's record of military competence won him broad support, especially among the Janissaries, and secured his succession. Selim and Bayazid differed over policy. The father wanted to avoid a confrontation with the Safavids; the son, as governor of a threatened frontier, had pursued an active policy. Selim secured the throne before Bayazid died, and Sulayman succeeded his father without dispute. Selim II's succession, described above in the chronology, entailed an interesting combination of court politics and military contest. It was also the last Ottoman succession to involve warfare between princes.

Succession by contest produced warrior rulers. Ahmed I, for example, though not a warrior like Selim I or an innovator like Bayazid II, had a reputation for piety, sought to promote it, and spent lavishly to support learning and to build mosques and other religious institutions. Though not regarded by historians as a great sultan, Ahmed I clearly reflected the new Ottoman model of sultan as defined by Peirce. But Peirce also argues that the survival of multiple princes served the interests of potential king-makers, the officials of the empire, male and female. The change in the practice of succession thus served the political interest of the *qapiqullu* establishment. Discontinuing princely governorships had the obvious benefit of preventing succession wars. If the princes had no independent establishments, they could take no active role in seeking the throne and became passive figures, dependent on the backing of other leading figures in the court. There is little indication, however, whether the change in the practice of succession occurred to prevent succession disputes and the execution of princes, which had become both routine and unpopular, or to enhance the power of the kingmakers. Selim II and Murad III sent only their eldest sons to the provinces, suggesting that their goal was to avoid succession wars. They succeeded, since Murad and his son Mehmed III took the throne without dispute. Mehmed III, however, sent none of his sons to the provinces, perhaps because he distrusted his eldest son, whom he had executed shortly before his own death. None of his younger sons was old enough to receive a provincial assignment. Their youth led to the next change in succession practice, the end of fratricide.

Mehmed III's execution of nineteen brothers and twenty sisters caused widespread revulsion. It was the last such mass fratricide, partially because of the emotional reaction and partially because Mehmed III had only two sons, neither of whom had had children, so the execution of either would have put the survival of the dynasty into question. Since the older son, Mustafa, was mentally disabled, there was no doubt that the young Ahmed should take the throne. His accession marked the movement of the process of succession inside the palace and the rise of court women to political prominence. The Ottoman dynastic policy toward marriage and the production of heirs thus requires explanation at this point.

Leslie Peirce has demonstrated that the Ottomans, from Osman's reign on, manipulated royal marriage and reproduction to preserve the stability and enhance the prestige of the dynasty. There is no explicit textual explanation of this policy, but it appears undeniable. With the exception of Edebali's daughter and of Theodora Catacuzenus, the daughter of the Byzantine emperor John VI Catacuzenus, who married Orkhan in 1326, the wives of the early Ottoman rulers receive little attention from the Ottoman sources. The practice of marrying the princesses of other dynasties continued until the reign of Mehmed II. Apparently, however, from the beginning of the dynasty, the mothers of sultans were concubines, rather than wives, because the sultans had sex with the concubines rather than their wives. The reason was political rather than erotic. According to Peirce, "The admission of female lineage, of nobly born women, compromised the integrity and autonomy of the sultanate."[12] Women who became the lovers of the sultan received the title *khasiki* (*haseki*, special one). Four of the *khasiki* received the additional title of *kadin* (literally, "woman"), with the number four reflecting the number of wives permitted in Islam though no legal marriage was involved. The mother of the sultan's first son became the *bash* (*baş*, head) *kadin*. In general, once a concubine bore a son to the sovereign, he no longer had contact with her; her role changed from that of concubine to the sultan to that of mother, often effectively guardian, of a prince. As Peirce points out, the postsexual status of these women permitted them to play a substantial public role. When princes governed provinces, their mothers accompanied them and ran their households. When princes were confined to the palace, their mothers continued to serve as guardians, protectors, and advisors. When a woman's son gained the throne, she became one of the most influential figures in the court and government, with the title *valide sultan* (queen mother). This position was neither merely honorific nor dependent on the ruler's closeness to his mother.

Two women, Hurrem Sultan and Kosem Sultan, the favorite concubine of Ahmed I, bore more than one son to a sultan. Kosem Sultan was the mother of Murad IV; and Ibrahim and played a central role in dynastic politics from the later part of Ahmed's reign until her own assassination in 1651, through the accessions of Mustafa (twice), Osman, Murad IV, Ibrahim, and Mehmed IV and the depositions of Mustafa (twice), Osman, and Ibrahim. Kosem Sultan sought to ensure the survival and accession of her two sons, Murad and Ibrahim; she regarded Ahmed's eldest son, Osman, as a threat to her interests. She used her influence as Ahmed's favorite concubine to have Osman's mother banished from the palace, thereby weakening Osman's position, and she also cultivated Osman herself. Nonetheless, when Ahmed died she used her position to arrange the accession of Mustafa, believing her mentally deficient brother-in-law less of a threat to her sons than their older half-brother. Mustafa's own mother acted as regent during his two reigns; Osman II's lack of powerful support within the harem contributed to his political failure, deposition, and execution.

But Kosem acted as a regent during the early years of Murad IV's reign and throughout Ibrahim's reign. During Murad IV's active years, she was virtually a coruler. When the young Mehmed IV took the throne, his mother, Turhan Sultan, was so young and inexperienced that the leading officers appointed Kosem Sultan to act as his regent. As Turhan gained maturity and political support, Kosem sought to maintain her position by substituting another son of Ibrahim by a different mother for Mehmed. This effort led to her murder at Turhan Sultan's behest in 1651. Turhan Sultan was the last of the powerful *valide sultans*. She was in great part responsible for the appointment of Köprülü Mehmed Pasha. The *valide sultans* remained prominent figures in palace ceremonies and in philanthropy, but they were no longer at the center of power.

Traditional historiography, both Western and Ottoman, has disparaged this period as the "sultanate of women." Carl Brockelmann, for example, refers to "the evils of indiscipline and female rule."[13] The tendency of traditional chroniclers to focus on the behavior and character of the rulers led them to attribute the stresses and difficulties that the empire experienced in the first half of the seventeenth century to the poor character of the rulers, and they attributed that character in great part to women's stepping outside their traditional domestic role and intruding into politics. Palace women, however, displayed statesmanship, and as the guardians and tutors of princes, dynastic matriarchs, and preservers of dynastic continuity, to borrow expressions from Peirce, they had a vital role in the survival of the empire.

Since the feminine component of the Ottoman slave system, described in the section on central administration below, produced the concubines, the concubines' dominance in the palace mirrored the *qapiqullar* dominance of the government. Historians and contemporary observers alike have treated the growing political importance of palace women after the reign of Sulayman I as a symptom of Ottoman decline. But the prominence of palace women did not imply moral degeneration. It was a part of the palace dominance of the Ottoman regime.

Law

The tension among the different justifications for Ottoman legitimacy manifested itself most clearly in the clash of Ottoman dynastic law, *urf* (*örf*) or *qanun* (*kanun*), with the Shariah. The Ottomans applied dynastic law more rigorously and systematically than any of their predecessors, recording it in *qanunnamah*s (*kanunname*, dynastic law books). There were at least two varieties of *qanunnamah*. Beginning in the reign of Bayazid II, dynastic law books formed the introduction of provincial tax registers and described revenue regulations. The provincial registers incorporated numerous levies, regulations, practices, and terms from earlier principalities, Muslim and Christian. Bayazid II also ordered the preparation of the first systematic and complete *qanunnamah* for the empire in the early sixteenth century. In general, *qanun* regulations covered taxation, land tenure, and criminal matters, leaving commercial and familial matters to the Shariah.

The *askari/raya* distinction was a basic principle of dynastic law. Dynastic law provided the working basis of Ottoman government, but government in accordance with *qanun* did not provide a justification for Ottoman rule. The status of legitimate sovereign had to precede the right to impose dynastic law, and for some audiences, reliance on dynastic rather than religious law put that legitimacy into question. Various Ottoman authors addressed this issue. The fifteenth-century historian Tursun Bey argues that *urf* is less than the Shariah but still vital. Shariah, divine law, offers happiness in this life and the next, but royal authority and regulation are necessary to deal with the mundane world. Abu Suud, the religious authority, presents Ottoman authority as an indispensable prerequisite to the regulation of society in accordance with the Shariah. He further attempts to incorporate *qanun* into Shariah, thus eliminating the conflict. The Ottomans gave *qazi*s (*kadı*, Shari judges) jurisdiction over both codes, contrary to the practice of some other dynasties. In the seventeenth and eighteenth centuries, the scope of *qanun* contracted and that of the Shariah expanded as the importance of Islam as the basis of Ottoman sovereignty and the power of the ulama, specifically the *shaykh al-Islam* (the chief religious official of the empire), grew. In 1696, an official decree banned the use of the word *qanun*.

The Ottomans supported Islamic legal and educational institutions from Orkhan's time. The religious, legal, and educational structures were known as the *ilmiye* (learned institution). By the time of Sulayman, the empire had an elaborate hierarchy of madrasas and a parallel structure of Shariah courts and judgeships. At the apex of the religio-legal hierarchy stood the *shaykh al-Islam*, or chief mufti, who had no administrative authority but immense prestige as the highest source of fatwas (*fetva*), rulings to resolve legal questions. Immediately below the *shaykh al-Islam* came the two *qazi-askar* (literally, "army judges") of Anatolia and Rumelia. Abu Suud combined the posts of *shaykh al-Islam* and *qazi-askar* of Rumelia. Below the *qazi-askar* came the chief *qazis* of Istanbul, Mecca, Cairo, Damascus, Edirne, and other leading cities, and then the provincial *qazis*. Ottoman *qazis*, unlike their predecessors in earlier Islamic history and their Safavid and Mughal contemporaries, had executive and administrative as well as judicial responsibilities. The professors of the leading madrasas came below the leading judges, passing up a madrasa hierarchy and from the top of it to the major judgeships. Below this central hierarchy was a provincial hierarchy of judges, muftis, and professors at provincial madrasas. There were also numerous religious supernumeraries, including the mosque preachers. The leading madrasas were associated with the great mosque complexes of Istanbul. By the eighteenth century, an aristocracy of learned families dominated the legal hierarchy.

The non-Muslim minorities had autonomy in civil matters, with their own court systems. Non-Muslims had, however, access to Shariah courts as well and frequently exercised it, even for resolution of disputes within their own communities.

STRATEGY, EXPANSION, AND MILITARY ORGANIZATION

Strategy

Until the transition to the sedentary sultanate, all of the different Ottoman ideologies justified expansion, as did the internal political dynamics of the empire, as the discussion of the *timar* system below explains. The historiography of the last two decades has made clear that the Ottomans, in Palmira Brummett's words, "[participated] in the contest for commercial hegemony in the economic space stretching from Venice to the Indian Ocean."[14] The Ottoman ruling elite took part in commerce as well as receiving income from the assignment of land revenue. Once the Ottoman principality had become more than one *beylik* among many, the Ottomans sought to secure for themselves the legacy of the Byzantine Empire, commercially as well as territorially and ideologically. Bayazid II completed that task. The advent of the Safavid Empire and the establishment of Portuguese power impelled Yavuz Selim and Sulayman to look eastward. The Ottomans could not destroy the Safavids or expel the Portuguese from the Indian Ocean, but they did establish control over the Persian Gulf and Red Sea routes between the Mediterranean and the Indian Ocean and kept both routes active.

Expansion

Nearly four centuries passed between the advent of the Ottoman principality and the end of expansion. The process of the conquest and incorporation of new territories naturally varied over this time, but the Ottomans had a standard approach. Halil Inalcık, in one of his many significant contributions to the field, divides the process into two phases: the establishment of suzerainty over neighboring principalities and their incorporation into the empire proper. Indirect Ottoman rule preceded direct Ottoman rule. Only Yildirim Bayazid deviated significantly from this pattern. Some principalities, notably Moldavia and Wallachia, never became part of the empire proper. In others, the process of incorporation took decades of movement backward and forward.

The case of Serbia offers an excellent example. Ottoman and Serbian forces first met in battle in 1349, when the Ottomans were serving as Byzantine auxiliaries. The process of the conquest of Serbia began in 1371, with the Ottoman victory over the Serbs at Chirmen. The Serbian rulers then began to pay tribute and contributed auxiliary forces to Ottoman campaigns. But this status did not mean an end to hostilities between the Ottomans and the Serbs. The Ottomans tightened the conditions of Serbian vassalage in 1385, then defeated the Serbs at Kosovo in 1389. Despite this series of victories, the Ottomans did not choose to absorb Serbia. Stephen Lazarevich, the ruler installed after Kosovo, supported Bayazid I at Nicopolis and remained loyal to the Ottomans during the interregnum. Before he died in 1427, he arranged for his nephew, George Brankovich, to succeed him and to shift his allegiance from the Ottomans to Hungary. An Ottoman expedition swiftly forced George to change his mind: He also had to cede some territory, pay a heavy tribute, and construct fortresses to guarantee the Ottomans' effective control of Serbia. A decade later Brankovich supported Venice and Hungary against the Ottomans, who absorbed Serbia in 1439. Brankovich received his principality back in 1444 as a part of the temporary peace settlement of that year and provided vital assistance to the Ottomans in the Varna campaign. The Ottomans did not finally annex Serbia until 1459, after Brankovich had died. An autonomous Serbia had strategic value as a buffer between the Ottoman Empire and the Kingdom of Hungary, but the policy of gradual incorporation had broader justification.

Leaving local rulers in place prevented the popular opposition that direct Ottoman rule might have provoked. Regimes with local roots could collect revenue and convert it into military force efficiently. The long process of incorporation gave the conquered populations a chance to recognize the Ottomans as tolerant and fair-minded rulers rather than alien oppressors. The Ottoman policy of *mudarra* (*müdarra*, moderation, friendship) had this purpose. Ottoman governance came to mean security, reasonable and predictable taxation, and the right to petition for relief from abuses. As the Ottoman frontier moved westward in Europe and eastward in Anatolia, former frontier areas were incorporated into the standard of Ottoman provincial administration, the *tahrir-timar* (*tahrir-tımar*) system. *Tahrir* denotes the detailed survey and recording of the revenue sources of the region; *timar* refers to the system of dividing the region into sections that paid their revenue to assignees designated by the central government. I discuss *tahrir* in detail in the section on provincial administration.

The *tahrir-timar* system extended the policy of gradual incorporation. *Tahrir* recorded, rather than altered, existing levies, boundaries, and resources. The *timar* system incorporated many of the existing military elite, both Muslim and Christian, into the Ottoman army. Ottoman records disclose that at least one family of *sipahi*s (Ottoman cavalrymen holding *timar* assignments) remained Christians in Ottoman service for five generations. *Timar*s were not normally heritable—though the status of *sipahi* (cavalryman in imperial service) was—but in various conquered provinces, especially Karaman, many families held heritable *timar*s. In Karaman, the principle families held large assignments in accord with their former status. Allowing families to retain hereditary tenure helped to transform them from Karamanid, Serbian, or Albanian nobles into Ottoman *sipahi*s. It offered some families a considerable incentive to switch allegiance to the Ottomans. In some areas, half the *sipahi*s were Christians. Christians received *timar*s as late as the reign of Bayazid II, but most had become Muslims by the sixteenth century. In some cases, heritable tenure survived until the end of Ottoman rule.

The existing elites did not hold all of the *timar*s in new provinces. Some *sipahi*s who participated in the campaign that conquered the provinces might receive new assignments there, especially if they distinguished themselves. So, too, might their military dependents (discussed below), for whom receiving a *timar* meant a vital confirmation of *askari* status. *Quls* (military slaves) of officers as well as of the sultan also received *timars* in new provinces, again gaining the security of *askari* status for themselves and their families. This political factor—the desire of members of the ruling class to increase their income and standing and the desire of outsiders to become *askari*, a status they could obtain only through receiving a *timar*—created a major substantive incentive for expansion. The *quls* of the sultan and the provincial military notables normally competed for *timars*; both benefited from increases in the supply of *timars*. This common interest explains, for example, the coalescence of both Janissaries and provincial soldiers in favor of the succession of Yavuz Selim. In Halil Inalcık's words,

> The constant demand for *timars* was a vital factor in the internal affairs of the Ottoman Empire during the classical period. Dispossessed *sipâhîs*, *kapıkulu* troops and volunteers in the frontier districts exerted continual pressure for these holdings. The need for land to distribute as *timars* constantly forced the state to undertake new conquests. . . . The need for *timars* was thus a motivating force in Ottoman expansion.[15]

Colonization and population transfers formed an integral part of Ottoman expansion policy. Orkhan forcibly deported a group of Turkmen nomads to populate the new Ottoman possessions in Europe. His son Sulayman deported the Christian military population from the new territories and sent them to Anatolia. These deportations became a pattern for Ottoman policy throughout the entire period of expansion. Such population transfers continued the old pattern of forcing disruptive nomads to the frontier and reduced the threat of revolt in new possessions, both east and west. They also helped to repopulate and restore prosperity to newly conquered areas. The Turkish population of Cyprus began with a massive forced transfer of peasants and craftsmen from Anatolia after the conquest of the island. Fatih Mehmed used forced transfers from newly conquered areas to repopulate the new imperial capital, founding different quarters for new arrivals. Deportations of nomads from Anatolia followed the revolt of Shaykh Badr al-Din and other early disorders in Anatolia. Such population transfers also helped to relieve the population pressure in Anatolia that had been a fundamental factor in Ottoman history from the beginning.

Military Organization

The Ottoman army evolved rapidly over the fourteenth and fifteenth centuries in three phases. In the first few decades of the fourteenth century, the army consisted entirely of the frontier *akinjis*, all of whom were light troops and most of whom were mounted archers. Organization was informal, at least at first, and cohesion limited. In the early decades, the Ottomans lacked the ability to defeat organized forces in open battle and to conduct sieges. They developed both capabilities during the fourteenth century, as the series of battlefield victories beginning in 1363 and the successful sieges of multiple fortresses in the Balkans demonstrate. The two basic components of the Ottoman army, the household troops, or central army, and the provincial *sipahis* (cavalry troopers), began to develop during this period. The household troops were the equivalent of the war band in a tribal confederation. As the principality grew, the Ottomans developed a substantial professional army, paid in cash from the expanding treasury filled by booty and agricultural revenue. By the reign of Murad I, the growth of the empire made the use of land-revenue assignments, known as *timar*, to pay soldiers both necessary and possible. The concept of *timar* resembled the *iqta* but reflected Byzantine practice as well. In the later Byzantine Empire, similar land-revenue assignments were known as *pronoia*, which became the primary form of military organization in the twelfth century. *Pronoia* holders were military officers who supported small contingents of troops. When the Ottomans surveyed new territories after conquest, they frequently assigned what had been *pronoia* as *timar*. The original central army became the new *timar* army. Murad, or perhaps his father, also began the recruitment of a new central army, the *qapiqullar* (slaves of the sultan; literally, "of the sultan's gate"). He thus set the fundamental pattern of the Ottoman army: central army of *qapiqullar*, including the Janissaries, provincial *timar* army, and frontier army of *akinjis*. The leaders of the frontier army, the *uch* (*uç*, frontier) beys, had considerable autonomy in the early centuries and were among the most potent forces within Ottoman politics into the reign of Murad II.

Murad recruited his slave soldiers largely through the famous *devshirme* (*devşirme*). The *devshirme*, literally meaning "collection" and usually translated "levy of boys," was unique in that it involved the enslavement of the sultan's own subjects rather than the capture or purchase of slaves from foreign lands. This practice violated the Shari prohibition on the enslavement of *zimmis*, but the violation never became a major issue. The slaves of the sultans were known as *qapiqullu* (*kapıkulu*, literally, "slaves of the gate"; I use the Turkish plural, *qapiqullar—kapıkullar*—to refer to them as a class). Though the slave system provided administrators and even ulama as well as soldiers, I will offer a brief description of its functioning during its maturity here. It began with the enslavement of a selection of Christian peasant boys. Ottoman officials evaluated the population village by village, selecting the most promising boys at the rate of one in forty. The *devshirme* was undeniably a harsh measure, but it also offered Christian peasant boys the opportunity join the military class and reach the highest offices of state. The boys did not lose contact with their families and frequently used their positions to assist them. After recruitment the boys were divided into two groups. The most promising, called *ichoglani* (*içoğolanı*; the term is singular), were assigned for special training to prepare them for the highest positions in the empire. The most able of them joined the Inner Service (*Andarun, Enderun*) of the administration; the others joined the central army, which included the Janissary infantry, the *sipahis* of the Porte (see below), and the artillery. The boys who did not become *ichoglanis* were sent to Turkish villages in Anatolia for conversion to Islam, then became Janissaries.

The word "Janissary" derives from the Turkish *yeni cheri* (*yeni çeri*, new army). They were originally an infantry bodyguard of a few hundred men using the bow and edged weapons. They adopted firearms during the reign of Murad II and were perhaps the first standing infantry force equipped with firearms in the world. Janissary firepower and discipline turned the tide of numerous Ottoman battles, including Varna, Baskent, Chaldiran, Marj Dabik, and Mohacs. The early adaptation of firearms indicates that there was no cultural or institutional opposition to them. The Janissary corps expanded steadily through the sixteenth century, growing from 18,000 in 1527 to 45,000 in 1597.

The Ottomans began using artillery themselves during the reign of Bayazid I, in the 1399 and 1402 sieges of Constantinople, and a formal corps of artillerymen existed by that time. The Ottomans first used siege guns successfully at Salonica in 1430. They did not make better cannons than their Western foes, but they did make larger ones, like the famous gun Mehmed II used at the final siege of Constantinople. Until the time of Bayazid II, the Ottomans used artillery primarily in sieges; their success depended on their artillery, but their siege guns did not guarantee success or make sieges easy. Bayazid's military reforms included the development of improved field artillery, but firearms had a decisive effect in field engagements during the two previous reigns, beginning with Varna and Kosovo. The artillery corps was quite small, numbering fewer than 3,000 in 1527 and about 8,000 in 1609.

The cavalry component of the central army, known as the *sipahi*s (troopers) of the Porte, resembled the Janissaries in recruitment and the provincial *sipahi*s in training and equipment. As mounted archers, they were the military descendants of the horsemen who created the Saljuq and Mongol empires. The Turkish composite recurved bow was a formidable weapon. John Francis Guilmartin explains that "the Turkish bow of the sixteenth century was capable of delivering a higher volume of accurate and effective fire at longer ranges than any competing weapon."[16] The composite recurved bow used by Ottomans, in the hands of an expert, could hit a man on horseback 280 yards away with one shot in four. A fresh, trained archer could make six aimed shots per minute, far more quickly than any sixteenth-century firearm. The *sipahi*s of the Porte were the most disciplined cavalry component of the Ottoman army and served at the center of the Ottoman battle formation with the sultan and Janissaries. They provided the sultan's escorts and served as pathfinders on campaign. In addition to the *devshirme* boys, the members of these units included the sons of previous members, Janissaries who had distinguished themselves, and some Muslim volunteers from outside the Ottoman Empire. They were paid cash salaries from the central treasury and stationed on the outskirts of Istanbul and other major cities. There were some 5,000 *sipahi*s of the Porte in 1527 and some 14,000 in 1609.[17]

The capability of the Ottoman central army distinguished the Ottomans from their predecessors and contemporaries in the Islamic world. One may describe Islamic polities after the decline of the Abbasid caliphate as points on a continuum between the wholly centralized, bureaucratic state dependent on a slave army and the pure tribal confederation in which the ruler had only a small personal entourage. Although the Ottoman provincial army had far greater numbers, the strength of the Ottoman central army, which alone included all types of land forces—infantry, artillery, and mounted archers—made the central government dominant. Gábor Ágoston observes:

The Janissaries represent the corner-stone of the centralizing political technology of the Ottoman Sultans and provided the ruler with a permanent armed force well before similar standing armies were established in Western Europe. This was an important development, for the Sultans using the Janissaries and the salaried cavalrymen of the Porte could claim a monopoly over organized violence, in sharp contrast to the European counterparts who had to rely upon and negotiate with local power-holders.[18]

Ottoman military organization thus improved upon not only their Muslim predecessors but also their European contemporaries.

The character of the Ottoman provincial army contributed to central power. The *timar* system gave central government effective control over the military potential of the provinces. The parts of the empire not covered by that system were far from the center. The Ottomans had two categories of non-*timar* jurisdictions. The fiscally autonomous *salyanah* (*salyane*) provinces, of which Egypt was by far the most important, supported sizeable units with minimal central oversight. The *hukumet sanjak*s (*hükûmet sancak*; see the section on provincial administration) were mountainous regions dominated by Kurdish tribes. The Ottomans made the tribal chieftains hereditary governors. These areas contributed small tribal components of the Ottoman provincial army. From the development of distinctively Ottoman institutions under Murad I to the Long War, the Ottoman provincial army meant the *timar* army. Though the *timar* system followed Muslim as well as Byzantine precedents, it represented a unique compromise between the requirements of financial decentralization and the need to keep political control of the provincial army.

The Ottomans did not separate the assignment of revenue from administrative responsibility. The provincial army was also the provincial government. But the typical *sipahi* (*timar* holder) was not an officer but a private soldier. The basic *timar*, known as *qilich* (*kılıç*, sword), was sufficient to support a single mounted archer with his horse and personal equipment on campaign. Each increase in the value of the *timar* increased the military obligations of the *sipahi*. He might be required to provide armor for himself or his horse or a tent. When the value of the *timar* was twice the *qilich* level, the *sipahi* had to provide a second mounted archer, called a *jebelu* (*cebelü*). The typical *sipahi* had either one *jebelu* or none. *Beylerbeys* (provincial governors), *sanjakbeys* (*sancakbey*, district governors), and *subashis* (*subaşî*, subdistrict governors) were also compensated through land-revenue assignments and had military obligations proportionate to their incomes. A *qilich timar* normally yielded its holder 3,000 *akche* (*akçe*, the standard Ottoman silver coin). *Sipahi*s could receive *timar*s worth as much as 20,000; the largest assignments required them to furnish six *jebelu*s and other equipment. *Subashi*s received assignments called *zeamet*s, worth between 20,000 and 200,000 *akche*. *Beylerbey*s and *sanjakbey*s held *khass* (*has*) assignments, which provided between 200,000 and 1 million *akche* per year, with provincial governors usually receiving at least 600,000. These officers had to provide one *jebelu*—in other words, they could add someone to their entourage—for every 5,000 *akche*. *Subashi*s thus had personal contingents of between six and forty troopers, between 40 and 120 *sanjakbey*s, and between 120 and 200 *beylerbey*s.

To put these figures in the context of the entire provincial army, one report states that the *sipahi* army numbered 60,000 under Bayazid II. At that time, there were seven provinces and sixty-one *sanjak*s in the empire. The beys would thus have contributed at most 9,000 troops, perhaps far fewer. Though the contribution of the *subashi*s is difficult to estimate, clearly ordinary *sipahi*s comprised the majority of Ottoman provincial forces.

The dual role of the *sipahi*s as the soldiers and provincial policemen and magistrates limited the size of the Ottoman Empire. The *sipahi*s had to be home in their *timar*s in the autumn to collect the agricultural revenue. This requirement, as well as the difficulty of campaigning in winter, constrained the campaign season to March to October—and thus reduced the action radius of the Ottoman army. This limitation determined the maximum size of the empire. Selim I could not continue the occupation of Azerbaijan, and Sulayman could not take Vienna in 1529 because of the limited campaign radius of the Ottoman army. But the *timar* system gave the Ottoman central government direct contact with individual soldiers in the provincial army, a dramatic contrast to the tribal armies of tribal confederations like the Aqquyunlu; the Ottoman Empire had far greater control over its provincial army. This difference made the Ottoman Empire more centralized. *Beylerbey*s and *sanjakbey*s were normally *qapiqullar* (military slaves) of the sultan and thus unlikely to align themselves with the *sipahi*s against the central authority. The beys attempted to strengthen their positions in the provinces by seeking to make their own personal dependents *sipahi*s, thereby asserting control over a larger portion of the armies, and administrators of their provinces. One *daftar* (*defter*), from the *sanjak* of Arvanid in modern Albania in 1431, shows that *qul*s of the sultan or the *beylerbey* and *sanjakbey* held 50 percent of the *timar*s; Turks from Anatolia held 30 percent, and indigenous former Christians, 16 percent. The central government limited the number of *timar*s that the beys could assign to their dependents. *Sipahi* families who wanted as many *timar*s for their dependents as possible frequently complained to the central government about such appointments by beys; their petitions were almost always accepted. The clash of interests between officers and the rank-and-file soldiers of the provincial army strengthened central control. There was no such balance in tribal confederations.

The Ottoman central government took other steps to limit the possibility of successful provincial revolts, meaning revolts by governors and the provincial armies. The Janissary garrisons in provincial fortresses—including urban citadels—were among the most important of these measures. These garrisons were instrumental in the defeat of two significant uprisings, that of Janbardi al-Ghazali, governor of Damascus, in 1520 and that of Ahmed Pasha, governor of Egypt, in 1524. Significantly, these revolts occurred in provinces where there were substantial disaffected pre-Ottoman elites and no fundamental clash of interests between the provincial governors and their troops.

The Ottoman armies also included a wide variety of auxiliary forces, several of which straddled the boundary between *askari* and *raya*. *Akinji*s remained part of the military structure of the empire into the seventeenth century, but as the empire expanded, they inevitably became marginal, literally and figuratively. Expansion moved the frontier further from the capital, inevitably reducing their political and military significance. They became semiautonomous, with hereditary dynasties leading them as Osman had led the original Ottomans. They served as auxiliaries on major campaigns and carried out border raids on their own accounts, receiving tax exemptions rather than salaries. Other auxiliaries included the *azab*s (*azap*), conscript infantry forces recruited primarily to support the professional armies on campaign and in garrison. Other categories of auxiliary forces performed noncombatant duties such as road construction.

The Ottomans made the Janissaries and field artillery the centerpieces of a tactical system that the Ottomans adopted from the Hungarians, who in turn had learned it from the Hussites (the followers of Jan Hus [1372/1373–1415], the Bohemian religious reformer). Known in Turkish as *tabur jangi* (*tabur cengi*)—*tabur* translates the German *wagenburg* (wagon fortress), and *jangi* (literally, fighting) means tactics—this system involved the use of the

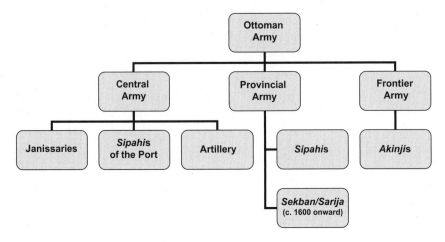

FIGURE 3.1 Ottoman Military Organization

carts and wagons used to transport supplies to construct a field fortification, behind which the sultan and central forces were stationed. The provincial cavalry formed the wings of the formation. At Varna, the Hungarian forces under John Hunyadi survived the rout of the crusader forces because they had a *wagenburg* to which to retreat. At the second Kosovo, four years later, the Ottomans employed one. The combination of infantry with firearms, mounted archers, and *tabur jangi* gave the Ottomans an almost unbroken string of battlefield victories from Varna in 1444 into the seventeenth century. Both the Safavids and Mughals learned *tabur jangi* from the Ottomans. Their combination of firearms and mounted archers enabled them to defeat their opponents consistently. The Ottoman military system fitted that era of warfare perfectly, to judge by the results.

This era of Ottoman superiority coincided with dramatic military developments in western Europe. In sieges and on the battlefield, the Italian wars of the late fifteenth and early sixteenth centuries began a new era. A new generation of siege guns nullified what had previously been formidable fortifications. Eight hours of bombardment smashed forts that had previously withstood siege operations for months. The French victories at Ravenna in 1512 and Marignano in 1515 displayed tactical innovations in the field. For the last fifty years, historians have debated what Michael Roberts named the "Military Revolution" in a 1957 essay. Geoffrey Parker, in the most current exposition on the topic, summarizes the Military Revolution as follows:

First, the improvements in artillery in the fifteenth century, both quali-
tative and quantitative, eventually transformed fortress design. Second,
the increasing reliance on firepower in battle—whether with field artillery
or with musketeers—led not only to the eclipse of cavalry by infantry, but
to new tactical arrangements that maximized the opportunities of giving
fire. Moreover, these new ways of warfare were accompanied by a dramatic increase in army size.[19]

Parker argues that the Ottomans "adopted and mastered Western technology with remarkable speed and thoroughness" and "were clearly equal to
all but the largest forces that the West could throw against them" until the
late seventeenth century.[20] As discussed below, the changing conditions in
the late sixteenth and early seventeenth centuries forced the Ottomans to
make significant changes in military organization, but those changes did
not imply permanent military inferiority. As Gábor Ágoston points out,
the Ottoman approach to firearms indicates "the flexibility of early Ottoman society and the pragmatism of its rulers."[21] There is no evidence that
Islam in any way inhibited the adaptation of new technology. The Ottomans used outside experts, but so did all the European states at this time.
It does not indicate any deficiency on the part of the Ottomans but does
show alertness to, and the willingness to exploit, technical innovations.

Like the Ottoman army, the Ottoman navy had what might be called
provincial and central components. Understanding the Ottoman navy requires a comprehension of what John Francis Guilmartin calls the
Mediterranean system of warfare. His *Gunpowder and Galleys*, one of the
most important pieces of military historiography of recent decades, distinguishes the Mediterranean system from the type of naval warfare depicted by Alfred Thayer Mahan. The war galley dominated warfare on the
Mediterranean Sea, but galley fleets could not stay at sea long enough to
establish and maintain a blockade. Trade and its correlate, piracy, continued unabated whether the Ottomans, the Hapsburgs, or the Venetians
won battles. Because sea control did not exist, none of the combatants attempted to obtain it. Naval warfare existed on two levels. The central activities of major combatants, which produced great battles like Prevesa and
Lepanto and sieges like the Ottoman conquest of Cyprus and the failed
attempt to take Malta in 1565, concerned the conquest of points on land.
Such campaigns punctuated a constant maritime small war, in which raiding, piracy, and commerce overlapped and interacted. Muslim corsairs in

the Mediterranean were thus Ottoman auxiliaries in the wars against Venice and the Hapsburgs, though not paid or maintained from the Ottoman treasury. These forces constituted what might be called the Ottoman provincial navy. The two levels of warfare interacted. The Hapsburgs sought to take Jerba to deny it to *ghazi* pirates; the Ottomans attacked Malta in order to disable the crusader pirates of the Knights of St. John and make the base available to their raiders, or provincial navy.

The Ottomans developed a central fleet of their own as an auxiliary for their wars of expansion in Europe. The Ottoman alliance with Genoa had made the Ottoman expansion into Europe possible, but the lack of a fleet under Ottoman control had severely limited Ottoman operations. The Ottoman navy first appeared in 1416; it grew and developed steadily through the fifteenth century and became capable of countering the Venetians effectively by the Ottoman-Venetian War of 1499 to 1502. When the Ottomans faced the Hapsburgs, served by the formidable Genoese admiral Andrea Doria, later in the sixteenth century, they needed to adapt to face the challenge. The Ottoman fleet, constructed and maintained in major naval yards at Gallipoli and Galata, was physically formidable but lacked effective leadership. That leadership came from the North African corsairs.

The growing prominence of the Ottomans had led to requests for assistance from the Muslims of Granada, the last Muslim state on the Iberian Peninsula, in 1487. Bayazid II responded by equipping an expedition, led by a corsair, Kamal Reis, to investigate the situation in the western Mediterranean. This expedition began the Ottoman connections in North Africa that led to the establishment of Algiers and Tunis as Ottoman provinces and the extension of the struggle between the Hapsburgs and the Ottomans to that arena. Ottoman corsairs used North African bases from 1487 to 1495, when Bayazid recalled them to reinforce the imperial forces. But seamen also immigrated to North Africa from the eastern Mediterranean. These new corsairs became the leaders of the Muslim resistance to Spanish and Portuguese expansion in North Africa. By the reign of Selim I, they could not cope with the forces of Spain, and their leader, the famous Khayr al-Din Barbarossa, who had fled from Ottoman territory after supporting Korkud against Selim, requested assistance from Constantinople. He offered the Ottomans sovereignty over Algiers, which became a *beylerbeylik* (province; see the section on provincial administration) in 1519.

Naval competition between the two empires continued until the middle of the sixteenth century, when Ottomans turned to their continental concerns and the Spanish to their transatlantic ones. This change of focus coincided with the decline of the Mediterranean system of warfare. Both of these changes were extremely complex in their causes and effects. Guilmartin associates these changes with a series of technical developments and tactical responses, as well as financial and demographic factors. In the Ottoman realm, the use of siege artillery at Constantinople and such lesser sieges as the conquests of Coron and Modon in 1500 showed the effectiveness of the new siege guns. The new generation of fortifications made the 1522 siege of Rhodes long and difficult and kept the Ottomans from taking Malta in 1565. Once again, taking a major fortress, whether on land or through an amphibious campaign, had become an expensive, time-consuming proposition. This military stalemate produced territorial stability in the Mediterranean world.

At sea, the same developments led to the decline of the Mediterranean system of warfare. Galleys grew in size, requiring larger crews, which meant a shortage of skilled manpower. A steep rise in the cost of provisions made it too expensive to feed oarsmen the diet they needed to perform at their peak. These developments reduced the strategic mobility of galley fleets. Guilmartin sees Lepanto not as a decisive battle in the normal sense but as the apex of naval warfare in oared ships in the Mediterranean. The increasing size of galleys and the high cost of operating them made galley fleets an evolutionary dead end. The Ottoman defeat at Lepanto cost the empire heavy casualties among its most skilled soldiers, Janissaries, and *sipahis*. The loss of *sipahis*, who fought as marine archers, took a generation to make good, for it took that long to train an expert archer. In order to make naval operations useful, they had to change to a new basis. The decrease in the cost of artillery caused by the development of iron guns disturbed both the strategic equilibrium and the setting of naval tactics. When only a few cannons were available, the bow of a galley was an excellent place for them. Arming a single sailing ship with a broadside of guns meant disarming several galleys. Inexpensive iron artillery and inexpensive, though less effective, iron shot altered this situation fundamentally. Bronze guns with stone cannonballs were more effective but entirely uneconomical. Mass overwhelmed quality and, by the eighteenth century, had reduced the galley to marginal use. The increasing expense of Mediterranean warfare eventually left only the Ottoman Empire capable of mounting offensive expeditions, and the Ottomans, after Lepanto, lacked the man-power to do so. The Ottoman conquest of Genoa's Black Sea colonies removed Genoa from the conquest for Mediterranean superiority. Venice could not compete quantitatively with either the Ottomans or the Haps-burgs, though she could qualitatively. More importantly, after the Ottoman conquest of Egypt, the trade on which Venice depended passed through Ottoman territory. War with the Ottomans thus threatened Venice's jugular, and Venice fought the Ottomans only under severe provocation and in alliance with the Hapsburgs. The most concrete result of the Ottoman victory at Prevesa was the exclusion of the Hapsburgs from the Adriatic theater. In the later sixteenth century, Spain turned from the Mediterranean to the Atlantic.

Both historians and the sources themselves devote little attention to the Ottoman Indian Ocean navy. So far as we know, when the Ottomans sought to project power into the Indian Ocean from the Red Sea and the Persian Gulf, they built Mediterranean-style galley fleets at Suez and Basra. The failure of the Ottoman naval campaigns in the Arabian Sea reflects the unsuitability of the Mediterranean system of naval warfare in the Indian Ocean.

The Ottoman armed forces, in what Inalcık calls the classical period of Ottoman history, represented the essence of the empire. As Guilmartin states, the continuous frontier warfare by which the Ottomans created themselves endowed them with a military machine superior to those of all their neighbors and all their challengers. The combination of infantry, mounted archers, and artillery—employed in *tabur jangi* and buttressed by the discipline of the Janissaries and the *sipahi*s of the Porte—gave the Ottomans their superiority on the battlefield. The classical Ottoman system had one great limitation: its demographics. The *devshirme* produced highly capable, highly trained soldiers and officers; the hereditary military of the provinces likewise produced a limited number of expert soldiers. The demand for *timar*s indicated the existence of a pool of manpower willing to serve the empire in return for the privilege of becoming *askari*. But even the pool of potential *sipahi*s was limited, and few aspiring subjects could actually have been masters of the horse and composite recurved bow. The inability of the classicial system to recruit large numbers of soldiers rapidly meant that the Ottomans had to create new military institutions in order to expand their armies. This change began the military and fiscal transformation of the Ottoman Empire. The casualties at Lepanto and the increasing manpower demands of the galley navy added to the demographic challenge to Ottoman institutions.

CENTRAL ADMINISTRATION

The Ottoman central government developed as the empire expanded. The disruption of the Rum Saljuq state made its officials available to the Ottomans and the other Anatolian *beyliks*. The chief official of Muslim regimes, from Abbasid times onward, was the vizier. Orkhan appointed a minister with considerable authority and the title bey. The title *sadr-i azam* (*sadrazam*), which became the normal title of Ottoman chief ministers and is generally translated grand vizier, appeared about 1360. Different departments, most importantly the imperial treasury (*khazinah-i amirah, hazine-i âmire*), developed in the course of the fourteenth century, but Ottoman central administration did not achieve its mature form until the reign of Fatih Mehmed.

In the early centuries of Ottoman history, members of the provincial military elites, as well as the products of the *devshirme*, served in the central administration. The famous Chandarli family, of Turkmen descent, dominated the administration in the first half of the fifteenth century. Their fall marked the beginning of the total dominance of Ottoman administration by the products of the *devshirme*. Dominance does not mean monopoly. Some freeborn Muslims, most with backgrounds as ulama, held important administrative posts throughout Ottoman history. Members of the ruling classes of conquered principalities played significant roles in Ottoman government well into the sixteenth century.

The Ottoman central government had two components, the palace and the bureaucracy. The palace administration followed the ground plan of the palace, with two main divisions, the Inner (*Andarun, Enderun*) and Outer (*Birun*) services. The *Andarun*, administered by the third-highest official of the empire, the *dar al-saadah aghasi* or *qapi aghasi* (*darüsaade ağası*; literally, "master of the house of felicity"; or *kapı ağasi*, "master of the gate"; also described as the "chief white eunuch"), included the harem and the sultan's actual household. It had six departments. The staff of the privy chamber (*khass oda, has oda*) took precedence, attending the sultan personally. The chief of the privy chamber (*khass oda bashi, has oda başı*) acted as the sultan's personal escort; other members included the sultan's valet, sword bearer, and personal secretary. The second department was the treasury (*Khazinah Odasi, Hazine Odası*), which had two components. The Outer Treasury (*Dish Khazineh, Dış Hazine*) kept the financial records, stored the robes of honor conferred on dignitaries, and dealt with revenues and expenditures outside the palace. The Inner Treasury (*Ich Khazinah, İç Hazine*) provided for all the expenditures of the Inner Service and stored the sultan's personal valuables. The other services were the Imperial Commissary (*Kiler Odasi, Kiler Odası*), the Campaign Chamber (*Seferli Odasi, Seferli Odası*), which had miscellaneous household duties, the Falconry Department (*Doganji Odasi, Doğancı Odası*), and the Large and Small Chambers (*Buyuk* and *Kucuk Odasi, Büyük* and *Küçük Odası*). The last two handled the training of the *devshirme* boys.

The Inner Service included all of the palace women. The harem was an inherent part, symbolic and substantive, of the Ottoman regime, not a private pleasure ground. After the Ottomans abandoned political marriage in the fourteenth century, all of the palace women, except the daughters of the sultan, began their careers as slaves. There was no female *devshirme*. The Ottomans acquired women as prisoners of war and by purchase in slave markets. In 1475, the palace establishment included some six hundred women. The female establishment had a hierarchy similar to that of the male establishment, but the feminine hierarchy was dual. It included the women with personal relationships to the sultan—mothers, concubines, daughters—across several generations and the support staff. The rank-and-file members were known as *jariye* (*cariye*, female slave or concubine). When they first arrived at the palace, the girls received careful training in such skills as sewing, singing, dancing, and puppetry. Their training prepared them to become royal concubines, support staff, or the wives of *qul*s. Most palace women eventually married members of the imperial hierarchy, the equivalent of a man's leaving the central administration for the provinces. The continual passage of women from the palace to the leading families of the empire ensured that those households emulated the norms of palace life.

The chief officials of the Outer Service included the keeper of the standard, chief gatekeeper, master of the horse, chief falconer, and chief taster. There was also the *chavush bashi* (*çavush başi*), who commanded the imperial messengers, *chavush*es. Along with the *agha*s (ağa, lord or master) of the Janissaries and the *sipahi*s of the Porte, these officials were known as *agha*s of the stirrup because they had the privilege of riding with the sultan on campaign. The Ottomans kept the sons of vassal dynasts and important provincial governors at court as hostages; they were known as *muteferrika*s (*müteferrika*) and attached to the Outer Service. The Outer Service also included the ulama who attended the sultan, including his personal religious teacher and the court imam, the superintendent of public buildings in the capital, the commissioner of the imperial kitchen, and the commissioner of grains, who supervised fodder for the imperial stables.

The *ghulam*s (*gulâm*; literally, "young men" or "young male slaves") recruited through the *devshirme* passed through the ranks of the various services. The least promising boys began as outer servants, gardeners, cooks, stablemen, and doorkeepers. They could gain promotion into the Janissaries or *sipahi*s of the Porte. More promising slave recruits either joined the central army after initial training or were prepared for the various components of the Inner Service. The commanders of the Janissaries, *sipahi*s of the Porte, and artillery, as well as the other components of the Outer Service, normally came from the Inner Service. At each level, men could move, either voluntarily or compulsorily, from the palace into the provinces, at appropriate ranks. Gardeners, doorkeepers, or Janissaries could become provincial *sipahi*s; *sipahi*s of the Porte and middle managers like the chief gunner or *muteferrika*s might become *subashi*s; higher officials like the chief falconer or doorkeeper could become *sanjakbey*s; and the most important palace functionaries could become *beylerbey*s. As a rule, the path from the palace went only one way. Palace officials could establish themselves in the provincial administration, but *timar*-holding *sipahi*s and *subashi*s did not move into the central administration.

The importance of the career path from the capital to the provinces offers a key to understanding Ottoman politics. Slave status, whether through the *devshirme* or another means, offered a way to the highest ranks of the empire. It did not, however, offer either security or heritable status. A provincial position, even as a lowly *sipahi*, did. A Janissary who became a *sipahi* knew that his sons would probably become *sipahi*s. This situation created much of the competition between the existing provincial aristocracies and the *qul*s of the sultan. It also offered a means of maintaining the *sipahi* army at strength.

The Imperial Council was the center of Ottoman administration. It consisted of the viziers, the governors of the most important provinces, the *nishanji* (*nişancı*, head of the chancery), the *bash daftardar* (*baş defterdar*, state treasurer), the *agha* of the Janissaries, the *kapudan-i darya* (*kapudan-i darya*, grand admiral), and the chief religious officials of the empire, the *shaykh al-Islam* and *qazi-askar*s (*kadı asker*, see below). Several departments, directed by the *rais al-kuttab* (*reisülküttab*, chief scribe), provided administrative support for the council. In the second half of the seventeenth century, the staff of the grand viziers grew considerably under the name of *pashakapisi* (*paşakapısı*, Pasha's gate) or *bab-i ali* (*babıâli*; high gate; the French translation, "Sublime Porte," became the common term in Europe for the Ottoman government).

Until the reign of Mehmed II, the sultans themselves directly participated in and chaired the meetings of the council. Fatih Mehmed delegated this duty to the grand vizier but observed the council's deliberations through a grilled window. After the meetings, the members of the council attended the sultan to obtain his formal approval of their decisions. The Imperial Council functioned as a court of appeal, an executive, and, in all but name, a legislative body. The concept of just kingship required the king to make himself available to his subjects for the redress of grievances. The sultan heard petitions whenever he appeared in public. These complaints usually concerned heavy or unfair taxation or other forms of oppression by the local authorities; the council also heard appeals against the local authorities. Some rulers, notably Sulayman I, Ahmed II, and Murad IV, made personal inspection tours incognito, following the example of Harun al-Rashid as recorded in *The Arabian Nights*. The rulers also sent slaves from the palace on secret inspection tours to monitor the provincial administration.

For most of the Ottoman period, the grand vizier (*sadr-i azam*) had absolute control of the administration. The *qanunnamah* of Mehmed II describes his position as follows:

> Know that the grand vizier is, above all, the head of the viziers and commanders. He is greater than all men; he is in all matters the sultan's absolute deputy. The *defterdar* is deputy for the Treasury, but under the supervision of the grand vizier. In all meetings and in all ceremonies the grand vizier takes his place before all others.[22]

Unlike most viziers in Islamic history, the Ottoman chief minister was also a military commander. The grand vizier could not make major decisions without consulting the Imperial Council. Though he had the right to supervise the treasurer, he could not make expenditures from the treasury without the treasurer's permission or dismiss him without the sultan's authority. The *agha* of the Janissaries and the *dar al-saadah aghasi* were not under the authority of the grand vizier, and when the sultan did not serve on a campaign, some of the Janissaries remained in the capital. The *agha* of the Janissaries, unlike the *qapi agasi*, did not have direct access to the sultan. The grand vizier could request the dismissal of the *qapi agasi*.

Outside the purview of the grand vizier, the ulama had the greatest power. The two *qazi-askar*s (literally, "judges of the army"; there was one for Anatolia and one for Rumelia) were responsible for the administration of Shari law throughout the empire. They had charge of the appointment and dismissal of the *qazi*s throughout the empire and final power of appeal in Shari cases. The *shaykh al-Islam*, the chief of the empire's ulama, was not actually a government official but had immense influence. He was actually the chief mufti (*müfti*, jurisconsult, authority on the Shariah consulted by other ulama) of Istanbul. The *shaykh al-Islam* decided not cases but points of law. The *shaykh al-Islam* could not direct the disposition of cases and drew no government salary. He and the other muftis—appointed by the *shaykh al-Islam* for the provinces of the empire—were paid consulting fees for their rulings and also frequently received lucrative appointments as the administrators of charitable foundations.

The position of the grand vizier varied significantly. Such energetic rulers as Fatih Mehmed, Yavuz Selim, and Murad IV made their ministers functionaries rather than potentates; the Köprülüs were effective rulers of the empire and made that status the condition of accepting the post. After the murder of Sokollu Mehmed Pasha, who served as grand vizier under Sulayman I, Selim II, and Mehmed III until his assassination in 1579, there were no dominant viziers until the Köprülü period, and there was no dominant sultan except for Murad IV.

Many of the Ottoman bureaucrats began their careers as ulama, gaining the requisite literary skill through their religious training. Others were the sons of bureaucrats or *qul*s. They progressed through various secretarial posts in a form of apprenticeship. Administrative service could lead to financial and even military positions in the provinces. In this way, individuals could make the transition from religious to military careers. Men who entered the provincial regime from the financial service could hope to return to the central government in higher positions.

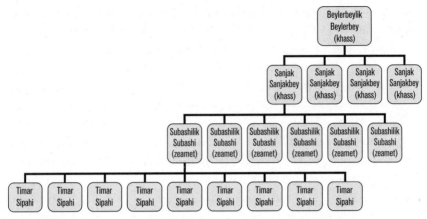

FIGURE 3.2 Ottoman Provincial Government and Military Structure

This chart shows the standard structure of Ottoman provinces and the Ottoman provincial army into the seventeenth century. The first line is the provincial unit; the second line is the governor or administrator, with the type of land revenue assignment he held in parentheses.

PROVINCIAL ADMINISTRATION

In the early years, the basic unit of the Ottoman Empire was the *sanjak* (literally, "banner"). When Osman ruled only a small area, it was referred to as his *sanjak*. In later years, the Ottoman princes ruled *sanjak*s of their own, and eventually beys (governors) were appointed from outside the family. The award of a flag gave the bey his authority. The rapid expansion of the empire in Europe led to the creation of another layer of administration with the appointment of a *beylerbey*—bey of beys—for Rumelia by Murad I. Bayazid I appointed a second *beylerbey* for Anatolia in 1393, with its capital at Kutahya, later moved to Ankara, and a third, called Rum, with its capital at Amasya. The three provinces formed the core of the empire. The Ottomans did not establish another province until 1468, when the difficulty of absorbing the principality of Karaman required a high degree of administrative attention. The conquests of Bayazid II, Selim I, and Sulayman I led to the formation of a series of new provinces, including Damascus, Aleppo, Baghdad, Basra, and Egypt in the Arab lands, Erzurum and Diyar Bakr in eastern Anatolia, and Buda and Temsevar in Europe. There were three basic patterns of Ottoman administration, the *tahrir-timar* system, the *salyanah* provinces, and the *hukumet* *sanjak*s. The *tahrir-timar* system applied to the core of the empire, including all European provinces, Anatolia, and Syria.

Ottoman land theory, generally derived from the traditions of the Islamic world, gave the sultan ultimate control of all lands. There were three main categories of land: *miri* (*mîrî*), *mulk*, and *vaqf* (*vakf*.) In all three categories, the peasants on the land received the right to cultivate it in return for the payment of taxes to a recipient designated, or at least approved, by the sultan. The Imperial Treasury controlled the revenue of *miri* land, receiving it directly, farming it out in return for cash payment, or assigning it as salary. *Mulk* land was granted by the sultan as heritable and alienable freehold. *Vaqf* lands paid their revenues to charitable endowments that served either religious or social welfare purposes. Obviously, much of the income, thus the power, of the empire depended on the amount of land in the *miri* category. Strong and aggressive rulers like Bayazid I, Mehmed II, and Sulayman I sharply curtailed *mulk* and *vaqf* holdings. Such rulers as Bayazid II, Selim II, and Murad III made and allowed more *mulk* and *vaqf* assignments. In 1528, 87 percent of the land was *miri*. Even during periods of central weakness, however, most of the empire's land was *miri*.

To place administration in the context of land theory, Ottoman provincial administration had the responsibility of maintaining order and collecting and, in part, distributing the revenue from *miri* lands. These lands fell into two categories: *timar* and other assignment lands and *khass-i humayun* (*has-i humayun*), which paid its revenue into the central treasury. The *khass-i humayun* consisted of about half of the *miri* lands, usually the most productive areas. The central treasury farmed out most of *khass-i humayun* to wealthy individuals, either from the capital or from the locality involved, in return for advance payment in cash. This division made no difference to the peasants. They paid various fixed duties, including a marriage tax, and a percentage of their produce in cash and the rest in kind. The recipients of the revenue, whether tax farmers, *sipahi*s, or other assignment holders, had the burden of converting what revenue they did not consume themselves into cash.

The *tahrir* (detailed revenue survey) recorded and defined all of these duties, including the proportion of cash. *Tahrir* took place immediately after conquest and every several decades thereafter. The imperial government appointed an *amin* (*emin*) or *il-yazicisi* (*il-yazıcısı*, trustee or district clerk)—different titles for the same position—to survey each *sanjak*. He was assisted by a *katib* (*kâtip*, clerk), who often acted as a local informant and coordinated his efforts with the local *qazi*s. In the initial *tahrir*, the *emin* recorded all existing sources of revenue and customary duties. The Ottomans normally made few changes in existing systems of assessment and collection, happily tapping sources that their standard levies, derived from Byzantine practice, ignored.

Later surveys involved the collection of all revenue records and claims to income pertaining to the *sanjak* and the comparison of them with information collected in each village of the *sanjak*. Each *sipahi* or other holder of an assignment had to produce each of the adult male subjects living in his assignment for the recording of their names and the lands they cultivated. The Ottomans considered the peasant household, called *chift-khanah* (*çift-hane*), the basic unit of taxation. The word *chift*, literally meaning "yoke," refers to the pair of oxen (yoked together) with which peasants plowed. The term *chiftlik* (*çiftlik*), representing the amount of land one pair of oxen could plow, equated to the land a peasant family could cultivate (including fields lying fallow). The *chift-khanah* was, in Halil Inalcık's words, "an indissoluble agrarian and *fiscal* unit" (Inalcık's italics).[23] This system prevented both the formation of large estates and the fragmentation of the *chiftlik*s into smaller units. In addition to the settled peasants, there was a floating, unattached rural population: peasants who had fled their lands, sons who had left their families, and other renegades. They often worked as temporary agricultural laborers and were listed in separate registers, paying a limited amount of tax. Women and children were always exempt from taxation. The right to cultivate *chiftlik*s was heritable in the direct male line. The basic agricultural tax was the *chift-resmi* (*çift-resmi*, known as *ispenje* [*ispence*] if the taxpayers were non-Muslims), which was assessed but not always collected in silver coins. The available land and labor of each household determined the specific amount of tax.

The surveys produced records of the revenue of the district and the assignment of it, including a *qanunnamah* showing the rates and methods of tax collection. Copies of these records were kept in the provincial capitals and in the imperial capital. They defined fiscal propriety in the *sanjak* until the next survey. The *qazi*s of the *sanjak* maintained separate *daftar*s (*defter*, registers) for the *jizya* (*cizye*) tax on non-Muslims and *avariz* (*avarız*, emergency cash levies). The process of *tahrir* extended the knowledge of the central government down to the individual peasant. Aside from the infrequent surveys, however, there was rarely such interaction. The peasants dealt with the assignees and tax farmers or with their agents. Beys and *subashis*, for example, employed agents (*voyvodas*) to collect revenue from their assignments and perform other local duties because their assignments were scattered rather than contiguous.

Three officials controlled the administration of revenue assignments in accord with *tahrir* and were the chief subordinates of the *beylerbeys*: the *timar daftardar* (*defterdar*), the *daftar kadhudasi* (*defter kethüdası*) and the *khazine daftari* (*hazine defterdari*). They had charge of *timar* assignments, *zeamet* and *khass* assignments, and the *khass-i humayun*, respectively. Empowered to communicate directly with the central government, the *khazine daftari* had a more independent status than the other officials. The *beylerbey* could dismiss him, but not without consulting the central government. The chief *qazi* of the province had similar autonomy. The provinces were divided into *qaziliks* (*kadılık*), which did not coincide with the *sanjaks*, for the administration of Shari justice. The *qazis* acted primarily as Shari judges, with police support from the *sipahis* and *subashis*, but they also had administrative responsibilities, even in the fifteenth century, including the collection of the *jizya* and *avariz* taxes. The administrative role of the *qazis* grew significantly in the seventeenth century.

Ultimately, the *timar* system worked because it permitted cavalrymen to maintain their horses in their villages on local fodder. It could not have worked unless the *sipahis* with their small personal establishments had kept order in the villages. They did so. Rural disorders rarely occurred in the Ottoman Empire before the late sixteenth century. Ordinary peasants rarely posed a problem to Ottoman authority, not least because they frequently preferred the Ottomans to previous regimes.

The *sipahis* themselves dealt primarily with the *sanjak* and provincial authorities despite their status as soldiers of the sultan. Once a man held a *timar* in a *sanjak*, he could expect to transmit his position, though not necessarily his actual assignment, to his sons, especially if they served with him on campaign. A son who served with his father could apply for a *timar* before his father's death; a son who did not could only do so afterwards. The size of a son's *timar* depended on that of his father. For example, the three eldest sons of a deceased *sipahi* with a 10,000 *akche timar* could expect to receive *timars* yielding 6,000, 5,000, and 4,000 *akche* in order of their ages. A *sipahi* could lose his *timar* for failing to go on campaign for seven years. *Sipahis* were subject to rotation of assignments within their home *sanjaks*, which meant that they were periodically left without income. This practice must have caused some hardship but apparently provoked little resentment until the end of the sixteenth century.

Until the second half of the sixteenth century, *sanjakbeys* and *beylerbeys* actually made the most of the assignments. In the European provinces of the empire, the provincial authorities could make assignments up to 6,000 *akche*, in Anatolia 5,000, and in Karaman, Zu al-Qadiriyye, and Rum 3,000. The restrictions on assignments in these provinces reflect the role of the pre-Ottoman Turkish elites in the resistance to Ottoman authority in these areas. The discretion allowed to the provincial authorities resulted in two abuses, the appointment of the beys' *quls timar*s and the granting of assignments in return for bribes. In order to prevent these abuses, the central government took control of all appointments and promotions during the reign of Sulayman I, though it did not turn out *sipahi*s who had received their assignments improperly. In addition to *sipahi*s, some court functionaries and religious officials (both Muslim and Christian) received *timar*s.

In the *salyanah* provinces, the central government appointed only a *beylerbey*, *daftardar*, and chief *qazi*. The provinces had complete fiscal autonomy, with the payment of the annual tribute being the only requirement. In Egypt, the Ottomans took over the existing fiscal units of the province, reclassifying Mamluk *iqta*s as *muqataa*s (revenue concessions, a different form of the same Arabic root as *iqta*). Initially, the Ottomans appointed salaried officials to collect the revenue of the assignments. In the later part of the sixteenth century, the local agents employed to make the actual collections, who were compensated with a part of the proceeds, took control of the process of collection. They were normally members of the Egyptian provincial army but did not receive these positions in lieu of salary. Ottoman administration in Egypt had to meet two requirements that did not apply elsewhere. First, rural disorders in Egypt after the Ottoman conquest made a concentrated, rather than dispersed, provincial army a necessity. Second, administrative measures could not interfere with Egypt's position as the granary of the empire. The Ottoman administration in Egypt met these goals and kept effective control of the province for more than a century.

Ottoman provincial administration included specific arrangements for nomads, of whom there were substantial numbers in the Dobruja, Albania, the Balkan Mountains, eastern Anatolia, the Caucasus, and, of course, the Arab lands. The Ottomans recognized them and their subdivisions as peoples (*ulus*), tribes (*boy*), clans (*uymaq, oymak*), and tents (*oba*). It recognized the hereditary chiefs and other leaders, who handled the internal arrangements of the tribes and their interaction with the regime. The Ottomans appointed special *qazi*s and officials with the title *agha* (confirmed chiefs) to collect taxes and transmit orders, usually for support for the Ottoman army, to the chiefs. Most of the tribes did not engage exclusively in animal husbandry but hunted and farmed on their winter pastures. They produced most of the animal products consumed in the empire's cities, served as auxiliaries on military campaigns, and transported supplies for armies in the field.

The policy of the regime favored the city dwellers. They were subject to fewer taxes and had no forced labor requirement like the peasants in the *timar* provinces. This situation created an incentive to immigrate to the cities, contributing to their rapid growth in the late fifteenth and sixteenth centuries. Because the regime depended on the *timar* army, it could not permit mass emigration from the countryside. (The incentives for settlement in Istanbul applied to the residents of other towns, not to peasants.) The regime attempted to force peasants to return to their lands, and they could become legal residents of a city only after remaining there for ten years with a regular occupation. If they met these conditions, they had to pay an annual tax, the *chift bozan resmi* (land-abandonment tax), to the *timar* holder.

The circle of justice helps to explain both the structure and the function of Ottoman administration. The regime had to receive the revenue of the provinces in order to support its army, but oppression of the peasants would ultimately reduce the revenue. The lasting attachment of the provincial *sipahi*s to their *sanjak*s, if not their assignments, made them unlikely to exploit their assignments for immediate gain. The restriction of the provincial elites to the lower ranks and the fundamental division of interest between the *sipahi*s and the *qapiqullar* beys prevented the provincial governors from transforming themselves into autonomous rulers before the eighteenth century. It also permitted them to leave provincial officials on all levels in place for decades, which was vital for the prevention of oppression. The general population also had a voice. *Tahrir*, after all, took place once a generation, not once a year. The annual assessment and collection of those levies dependent on production rather than specified in cash must have involved some element of negotiation. The long-standing relationship and close proximity between *sipahi*s and peasants made Ottoman government in the provinces something other than a distant despotism. Well into the sixteenth century, the Ottoman provincial administration system worked remarkably well.

THE OTTOMAN ECONOMY

In the early decades, the bands that became the Ottomans lived by raiding. By the time the Ottomans took Bursa, however, the principality had gained possession of productive agricultural lands and a major commercial center. As the empire grew, it gained control of agricultural territories in Europe and Anatolia as well as trade networks, first in the Black Sea and Aegean littorals and then throughout the eastern Mediterranean and the Middle East to the Red Sea and Persian Gulf. The empire was as much commercial as agricultural.

Ottoman economic policy reflected the circle of justice. The military power of the empire depended on its wealth, agriculture was the most important source of wealth, and agricultural productivity depended on the welfare of the peasants. The Ottomans sought specifically to increase the specie (money in gold and silver coins) in the central treasury and broadly to ensure adequately supplies of necessities for the general population. They did not regard exports as a source of wealth but as a potential cause of domestic shortages. Ottoman efforts to control and protect trade reflected the desire to increase revenue and avoid domestic shortages, especially in the imperial capital. The regime intervened in the economy primarily to prevent shortages and keep the prices of basic commodities down, not to affect the trade balance as in European mercantilism. The involvement of the Ottoman governing elite in commerce brought governmental attitudes into commerce, not mercantile attitudes into government.

As mentioned earlier, the Ottoman economy was only partially monetarized; many transactions in rural areas, including the payment of taxes, were in kind rather than cash. The use of money in rural areas, among peasants and nomads, became increasingly common during Ottoman times, with a surge in the sixteenth century in particular. Like most of their contemporaries, the Ottomans relied primarily on silver coins. Monetary historian Şevket Pamuk gives periodization of Ottoman monetary history as follows:

> *1300–1477* Silver based and relatively stable currency (*akçe*) of an emerging state on the trade routes of Anatolia and the Balkans.

1477 to 1585 Gold, silver, and copper coinage during a period of economic, fiscal and political strength; the unification of gold coinage, the ultimate symbol of sovereignty; the emergence of different silver currency zones within the Empire; the development of intensive networks of credit in and around urban centers.

1585 to 1690 Monetary instability arising from fiscal, economic and political difficulties compounded by the adverse effects of intercontinental movements of specie; the disappearance of the *akçe* and increasing circulation in the Ottoman markets of foreign coins and their debased versions.[24]

The section below discussing stress and transformation addresses the period of monetary instability and developments after 1690.

The growth of the empire had an immediate effect on the pattern of commerce. Bursa became the most important entrepôt for both regional trade and the long-distance commerce between Asia and Europe. By the end of the fourteenth century, the caravans that carried valuable silk from the Caspian shore of Iran came to Bursa, not the Byzantine port of Trebizond on the Black Sea. The Ottoman capital also attracted European merchants from Constantinople—purchasers of silk, spices, and other eastern commodities and sellers of wool. But Bursa's position as a silk emporium was the key to its importance and a major source of customs receipts for the government. Bursa remained the center of the silk trade after the conquest of Istanbul. Spices, dyes, and drugs also passed frequently through Bursa. The conquests of Syria and Egypt gave the Ottomans control of the traditional routes by which products from South and East Asia reached Europe.

Goods from the Indian Ocean entered Mediterranean trade at the port of Antalya as well as through Bursa and Istanbul. These goods included spices and indigo from the Indies, linen, rice, and sugar from Egypt, and soap from Syria. Antalya was also the major port for Anatolian exports to Syria and Egypt, which included timber, iron, a wide variety of textiles, opium, dried fruit, furs, wax, and pitch. Exports of timber and slaves from Anatolia had formed a vital part of the Ottoman economy from the beginning. White slaves from the north, many of them from the Caucasus, were exported to the Arab lands, and black slaves from Africa went north. The great importance of eastern Mediterranean trade to the empire explains the strenuous Ottoman efforts against Christian corsairs, who would have described themselves as maritime crusaders. In the twelfth and thirteenth centuries, Italian merchants, primarily but not exclusively from Venice and Genoa, dominated the trade of both the eastern Mediterranean and the Black seas. The Black Sea littoral had long been a source of wheat, fish, oil, and salt for the Mediterranean world. Fatih Mehmed excluded the Italian merchants from this trade, placing it entirely in the hands of Ottoman subjects. Though many of the merchants were Christians, including Greeks, the majority were Muslims. Important ports on the Black Sea included Caffa and others in the Crimea, Trebizond on the northeastern coast of Anatolia, Akkerman near the mouth of the Dniester, and Kilia near the mouth of the Danube. A huge variety of goods passed through Caffa. From Anatolia came cotton textiles, mohair, rice, opium, wine, nuts, and timbers. European textiles passed through Caffa to Muscovy and central Asia. From the north came wheat, tallow, butter, cheese, honey, fish, and caviar. Salt mines in the Crimea supplied much of the Ottoman market. Slaves taken by the Tatars on raids into Russian and Polish territory passed through Caffa on the way south. Other exports from Muscovy included furs, flax, and mercury. Goods, especially textiles and spices from Asia and Anatolia, passed through Kilia and Akkerman. The European provinces and the subject principalities of Wallachia and Moldavia exported shoes, woolens, cattle, leather, salt, flax, honey, and beeswax and received spices, cotton and silk textiles, and some foodstuffs from the Indian Ocean and the Mediterranean.

Though the establishment of the Ottoman Empire altered trade patterns in the eastern Mediterranean, it hardly eliminated the role of the Italian cities, especially Venice. Venice and Genoa had traded without restriction in Byzantine territory, enjoying trade relationships with local regimes throughout the Black Sea and the Levant. Venice responded to Ottoman expansion by taking strategic points in Albania, the Morea, and the Ionian and Aegean seas in the fourteenth and fifteenth centuries, finally taking Cyprus in 1489. The Venetians repeatedly attempted to deny the use of the Bosporus and Dardanelles to the Ottomans. Only Mehmed II's construction of new fortresses on the Straits and conquest of Istanbul secured Ottoman control of the passage between Europe and Asia. Genoa chose to cooperate with the Ottomans. Orkhan first granted commercial privileges—later known as capitulations—to the Genoese in 1352. The Genoese colonies of the island of Chios and Foca (modern Foça) on the Anatolian mainland became vital entrepôts for trade between Anatolia and

Europe. In return, the Genoese provided vital naval assistance to the Ottomans, permitting Ottoman forces to cross the Dardanelles.

The Ottomans used economic leverage against Venice. The island city and its hinterland depended on wheat from Anatolia and the Ottoman provinces in Europe. When war with Venice broke in 1463, the Ottomans began economic warfare, imprisoning all Venetian merchants, confiscating their goods, and seeking alternative trade outlets. The Conqueror sought to establish trade with Florence through Ragusa (Dubrovnik, on the coast of modern Croatia) and Ancona, a papal free port on the Adriatic coast of Italy. Ragusa, an Ottoman tributary from the reign of Murad II, became a vital commercial outlet. Wheat, hides, beeswax, and raw and finished silk passed through that city to Italy; woolens were the most important Ottoman import. Ragusa became a major producer of wool products for the Ottoman market, and Ragusan merchant colonies developed throughout the empire. Ragusa's role as intermediary between the Ottomans and Venetians during the series of wars between them led to a massive increase in the city's trade. Ragusans traded with England as well as Italy in the sixteenth century, but the growing importance of direct Ottoman trade with England and France in the seventeenth century caused a decline in Ragusa's importance. Despite the importance of Ragusa and the disruptions caused by war, Venice always dominated the eastern Mediterranean spice trade. Venetian ships carried woolens, silks, paper, and glass products to Egypt and Syria and returned with spices, drugs, dyes, silk, and cotton, along with imports of wheat, hides, wool, cotton, and silk from Anatolia and Rumelia.

These trade patterns changed significantly in the late sixteenth and early seventeenth centuries. Trade between France and the Ottoman Empire began with the Ottoman occupation of Egypt in 1517 when Selim I renewed the capitulations that the Mamluk sultans had previously granted. The French received full trading privileges in 1569, and competition between France and Venice soon began. France exported textiles, paper, and metal goods to the Ottoman Empire and imported wool, cotton, cloth, silk, spices, perfumes, drugs, and mohair. The Ottoman-Venetian War of 1570 to 1573 gave France a great advantage over Venice, and by the end of the seventeenth century, half of French commerce was with the Ottoman Empire. Dutch and English merchants traded under the French flag. Ottoman support for the Protestants in Europe led them to suspend French trading privileges when the principle French port, Marseilles, supported the Catholic League in the French civil wars of the last decades of the sixteenth century. They restored the privileges at the accession of Henry IV in 1589.

English merchants first received trading privileges in 1553 but sought instead to find more direct access to the spices of the Indies. When the Ottoman conquest of the Caucasus in 1578 made overland trade to Iran through Muscovy impossible, the British returned their attention to the Levant. They became vigorous rivals of the French and Venetians, selling woolen goods at lower prices, purveying tin and steel, and engaging in piracy against the competition. The volume of Venetian trade dropped sharply, and France had lost half her markets in the Levant by 1630. The English Levant Company dominated eastern Mediterranean trade. The success of the East India Company in the Indian Ocean reduced, but did not eliminate, the value of the Levant trade to England. Dutch merchants traded under the English flag until they received their own capitulations in 1612.

The tremendous growth of trade with Europe did not harm the Ottoman economy in the sixteenth and seventeenth centuries. It provided considerable customs revenues for the regime and satisfied demand for woolens and other European goods, but the narrow range of imports from Europe did not significantly affect Ottoman industries. The Ottomans sought to foster and protect commerce by constructing a trade infrastructure. These efforts had two aspects: the construction and maintenance of roads and travel facilities and urban development, especially in Istanbul. The Ottomans built roads for strategic as well as commercial purposes. The Ottomans devoted considerable attention to maintaining and improving the Roman road from Istanbul to Belgrade. Other major roads in Europe led from Edirne to the mouth of the Danube and north along the Pruth River into Moldavia, south from Istanbul to Gallipoli, and southwest from the main road through Sofia, Skopje, Pristina, Sarajevo, and Mostar to Ragusa and the Adriatic Sea. In Ottoman times, no less than 232 inns, eighteen caravanserais (large enclosures to shelter caravans at stops between cities), thirty-two hostels, ten *bedestan*s (covered markets for the sale of valuable goods), and forty-two bridges were built in Bosnia and Herzegovina alone. To encourage the construction of such facilities, the Ottomans employed a special form of land grant known as *tamlik* (*temlik*), which gave freehold land to a statesman or notable—including palace women—so that the recipient could then establish a pious endowment, or *vaqf,* to support the construction and maintenance of such establishments, which provided, without charge, for the needs of travelers on the roads from Istanbul to Damascus, Erzurum, and Belgrade. *Zaviye*s were pious foundations established by Sufi *shaykh*s who also received freehold grants from the regime.

The threat of bandits forced the Ottomans to attend to the security of commerce. They constructed caravanserais (between cities) and *bedestan*s (in cities) primarily for security. The Ottomans also employed a variety of provincial paramilitary forces primarily to ensure the safety of commerce. Villagers, especially pastoral nomads, were recruited as *darbandjis* (*derbendçi*, guardians), responsible for keeping order in their localities and maintaining and protecting nearby roads and bridges in return for tax exemptions or even *timar*s.

Roads connected cities, and the Ottomans were city builders. Fatih Mehmed's reconstruction of Istanbul was only the most prominent Ottoman project. The Ottoman regime supported urban development through the *imaret* system. An *imaret* was a complex of institutions, normally a mosque, madrasa, hospital, traveler's hostel, water source, and necessary roads and bridges, with inns, markets, caravanserais, bath houses, mills, dye houses, slaughterhouses, and soup kitchens. The religious and charitable institutions were normally clustered around the mosque, with the commercial institutions located nearby. These complexes, normally supported by *vaqf*s, dominated the structures of Ottoman cites and towns. Mosques and *bedestan*s were the core institutions of Ottoman cities. Fatih Mehmed ordered the construction of a monumental *bedestan* in Istanbul as part of the *vaqf* to support Aya Sofia as the leading mosque of the new capital. The huge stone building functioned as a safe-deposit building for the money and jewelry of the city's wealthy citizens, with doorkeepers and watchmen under government control. The Conqueror's *bedestan* contained no less than 118 shops. The markets arranged around it, roofed over in stone, included 984 shops and remain the commercial center of Istanbul today.

*Bedestan*s played so fundamental a role in Ottoman cities that Evliya Celebi, the famous seventeenth-century traveler, divided Ottoman cities into those with and without *bedestan*s. Orkhan Ghazi constructed the first in Bursa in 1340. *Bedestan*s became the nuclei of the major cities of Ottoman Europe like Salonica, Sofia, and Plovdiv. But the *bedestan* was only the beginning of Fatih Mehmed's efforts in the capital. He required the leading officials of the empire each to endow an imaret in the city. These foundations became the centers of Istanbul's resettlement and gave it its

Ottoman appearance. The Conqueror himself built a monumental mosque of his own, the Fatih Jami (Fatih Cami). The surrounding foundation included eight madrasas, a children's school, a library, a hospital, two hostels, and a dining hall. The market that supported this establishment included 318 shops. The madrasas trained six hundred students at a time, and the hostels sheltered 160 travelers.

At the time of the Ottoman conquest, the population of Constantinople had fallen to 30,000 or 40,000. The Conqueror's efforts had more than doubled that by 1477. In the first half of the sixteenth century, the population reached 400,000, making the Ottoman capital the largest city in Europe. By the end of that century, it may have grown as large as 800,000. Forced resettlement had caused much of the growth in the fifteenth century. To the refugees who had fled Constantinople, the Conqueror had offered the restoration of their property as well as freedom of religion and occupation. He freed prisoners taken in the conquest and settled them in the city, even exempting them temporarily from taxes. But he also ordered the forcible transfer of some 8,000 families, Muslim and Christian, from Rumelia and Anatolia, with at least some of them being wealthy merchants or artisans. Fatih Mehmed and Bayazid II transferred Christians from such newly conquered areas as Trebizond, Karaman, and Caffa, settling different quarters of the city with them. The Ottomans encouraged the immigration of Jews even before their expulsion from Spain in 1492. A 1477 census showed that the Jews made up the third-largest component of the population of the capital. By the middle of the seventeenth century, Istanbul boasted some 152 mosques, 125 madrasas, and one hundred caravanserais. This immense urban agglomeration required huge amounts of provisions; special regulations governed the supply of food to and in Istanbul. By the seventeenth century, more than five ships carrying food arrived daily, bringing wheat, rice, sugar, and spices from Egypt; livestock, cereals, edible fats, honey, fish, and hides from the Black Sea littoral; cereals and hides from Thessaly and Macedonia; and wine and other Mediterranean products from the Morea and the Aegean islands. More wheat came from the Dobruja and Thrace. The demand for wheat from the capital turned the Dobruja into a prosperous agricultural region.

Guilds dominated much of the professional life of Ottoman cities. The history of guilds, in the Islamic world in general and the Ottoman Empire specifically, is extremely controversial. Ottoman guilds were self-help organizations formed by the craftsmen to represent their interests. A guild's members elected the *kadkhuda* (*kethüda*, guild leader) to enforce the guild regulations and petition the administration and courts on behalf of the membership. The existence of the guilds and the elections of their officials were registered in the *qazi's* courts, but the regime accepted the guilds' autonomy. In addition to the *kadkhuda*, each guild had a *yigitbashi* (*yiğitbaşi*), who handled internal guild matters, including purchasing raw materials for the guild and distributing them among the craftsmen, checking products to make sure that they followed guild specifications, and supervising delivery of products to other guilds. Many guilds had other officials who assisted in these duties. Guild regulations were part of *ihtisab* (market standards).

Most Muslim regimes prided themselves on the enforcement of *ihtisab*, the component of the Shariah that dealt with commercial fraud and profiteering. The Ottomans certainly did so. The *muhtasib* (*muhtesib*, market inspector) patrolled the markets ensuring the regulations' enforcement. Some commodities, such as timber and cloth, could not be sold without this official's stamp of approval. The *qazi* and *muhtasib* could set prices for raw materials and finished products, sometimes under the sultan's eyes in Istanbul. Ottoman regulations included which gates and streets of Istanbul various commodities could pass through. Guild masters paid a tax for each shop and for the manufacture of certain materials. There was also a sales tax on each commodity sold in the market. Separate *qanunnamah*s stated the tax rates for the cities and markets of each province.

The government interfered in guild organizations only when a situation threatened tax receipts or the public good, and guild regulations recognized governmental authority. Guild officers relied on the government for support; the guilds formed a means of both economic regulation and tax collection. Guilds limited opportunities for profiteering and thus incentives for popular unrest, and they helped to balance the demand for products, the supply of raw materials, and the number of artisans and shops. This authoritarian structure restricted competition and thus incentives to improve products.

Within guilds, there were significant differences in wealth and status. Often the owners of workshops and their employees both belonged to the same organization. In some guilds, if a master became too wealthy and independent, he was considered a merchant and had to leave the guild, but one member of the velvet weavers' guild of Bursa owned a shop—more accurately, a factory—with fifty looms. In the sixteenth century, guilds that produced export items became subject to considerable friction between the wealthier members and the rank and file.

Guild regulations could not eliminate entrepreneurial innovation. Members found ways to open shops that regulations did not authorize. The owners of new shops frequently broke the guild regulations, producing lower-quality goods at lower prices and changing patterns and styles. The guild masters sought and received the support of the regime against these innovators. Still, the guild structure did not prevent all changes. New guilds evolved from old ones. Their formation required the approval of the *qazi*. Guild masters employed free laborers and slaves as well as apprentices. Some guilds, especially those involved in cotton spinning and silk winding, employed women and children.

Though guilds were primarily organizations of artisans, merchants formed guilds as well. There were two categories of merchants: the *isnaf* (*esnaf*) and the *tujjar* (*tüccar*). The *esnaf* handled local trade in guild products, and the *tujjar* handled long-distance commerce. The *tujjar*, free from guild regulations, participated in a wide variety of enterprises and were the truest capitalists in the Ottoman Empire. Wealthy members of the *askari* class frequently invested funds in their ventures. The wealthiest private citizens of the empire were money lenders, who were frequently also goldsmiths; merchants, usually those involved in the silk trade; and silk weavers, who were the wealthiest of the guild members. The *tujjar* frequently employed slaves as agents.

The Ottoman economic system thus reflected the Ottoman economic mind set, which in turn reflected the circle of justice. The function of the economy is the function of the peasantry in the classic formulation of the circle—to provide tax revenue for the treasury. The prevention of shortages, profiteering, and deceptive practices, as well as efforts to keep prices low, are the equivalent of providing justice for the peasants. Although the Ottoman policy sought to gain control of trade routes and the Ottoman elite participated in trading ventures, their outlook was not truly capitalist. Like their Spanish and Portuguese contemporaries, the Ottomans saw commerce as a source of tax revenue rather than of general wealth.

OTTOMAN SOCIETY AND POPULAR RELIGION

This section seeks only to open a window onto the vast assortment of information and insight that the study of Ottoman social history—based largely, but not exclusively, on records of legal proceedings—has produced in the past four decades. Social historians have explored Ottoman society from many angles. There is a significant literature on the roles of coffee, which spread to Europe from the Ottoman Empire, wine, opiates, and tobacco in Ottoman social interaction. There are explorations of sex and sexuality through the medium of lyric poetry. There are studies of popular festivals, literature, entertainment, and, of course, piety. Naturally, given the increasingly prominent role of female historians, there is a growing literature on Ottoman women. Various aspects of slavery and the role of slaves in Ottoman households have drawn attention. The wealth of sources has permitted significant exploration of the experience of the groups ignored by the narrative of power, which is the primary concern of this text. This section presents Ottoman society through examination of the various groups within it. The most important point, however, is that Ottoman society was just that, Ottoman. No other adjective—certainly not Turkish or Islamic—fits it.

Although Ottoman Turkish was never the native language of a majority of Ottoman subjects, it was the dominant language not only in politics and government but in commerce and popular culture. Social and cultural patterns spread downward from the Ottoman court and outward from Istanbul. As the next section explains, Ottoman high culture was Persianate, but it also embodied numerous other influences, the most important being Byzantine. The result was a distinctly Ottoman synthesis, not a random or syncretic mixture, in social as well as cultural patterns.

Inevitably, given the size and complexity of the empire, Ottoman society consisted of numerous groups divided across numerous lines. The divisions between male and female, *askari* and *raya*, and Muslim and non-Muslim were only the most fundamental. There were numerous ethnic divisions, as well as the divisions between urban and rural, nomad and settled, free and slave. Each of these major divisions had subdivisions. The general category of *askari* encompassed two different cultural orientations, one courtly and secular, rooted primarily in the Iranian tradition of statecraft, and one religious and legal, rooted in Shari learning. As already noted, the *askari* consisted of two main components, the provincial military gentry and the *qapiqullar*. Each of these groups was diverse in itself. The common Ottoman identity, though powerful, did not submerge prior ties. Grand Vizier Sokollu Mehmed Pasha, for example, was an ethnic Serb and used his position to revive the Orthodox patriarchate at Pec in Serbia and to have a relative appointed to the position. The tensions between the two orientations and between the two components of the *askari* influenced Ottoman politics significantly.

The diversity among the *raya*, however, far exceeded that among the *askari*. Historians have traditionally emphasized the religious divisions among Muslims, Christians, and Jews. These fractures mattered, but so did numerous lines of difference within these groups. The religious divisions did not align neatly with ethnic and linguistic ones. Many Orthodox ethnic Greeks and religious and ethnic Armenians used Turkish in day-to-day language. One Orthodox group, the Karamanlis, used the Greek liturgy transcribed in Turkish (Arabic) script. They were otherwise entirely Turkic and probably descended from a Turkic tribe or clan that became Christian rather than Muslim. In eastern Anatolia, Armenians called Armenian converts to Islam Kurds. The general autonomy of the non-Muslim religious communities did not mean a lack of interaction between Muslims and non-Muslims. Even though Christian and Jews had their own courts, they frequently resorted to the Shari courts, even in routine matters within their own communities, such as the registration of marriages. Since non-Muslim Ottoman subjects had at least three different mechanisms available for the resolution of grievances (their own courts, the Shari courts, and appeal to executive jurisdiction), the pattern of resort to Shari courts had to reflect the belief that they offered the best chance of a favorable resolution. There is no question that confessional divisions were the most important in the empire after the *askari/raya* division and that non-Muslim groups suffered significant legal disabilities and social restrictions. But non-Muslims faced discrimination rather than active oppression and were far from voiceless. The common characterization of the Christian peoples of the Ottoman Empire as captive both exaggerates and distorts the situation.

The situation in Constantinople was unique but not unrepresentative of the situation in the empire as a whole. The fundamental split between Muslims and non-Muslims did not coincide with categories of wealth, occupation, and status. Merchants and craftsmen of different faiths worked together, and Jewish, Greek, and Armenian merchants imitated Muslim clothing and behavior. Periodic efforts by the regime and by professional guilds to enforce differences in dress between faiths and to prevent non-Muslims from riding horses and owning slaves did not succeed. The different communities worked and traded together but lived apart, in different quarters of the city and under the administration of officials from their own *millet*, priests and rabbis for Christians and Jews and imams (prayer leaders) and *kadkhuda*s (*kethüda*, local headmen) for Muslims. Relations between the communities were generally amicable, with marriages between Muslim men and non-Muslim women not uncommon.

There were several divisions within the Ottoman Muslim community, the Sunni-Shii split being the most important. Ottoman Shiis had a less favorable position than any other religious group. After the advent of the Safavids, the Ottomans had good reason to regard Shiis, especially among the Turkmen of eastern Anatolia, as traitors. Ottoman troops killed tens of thousands of them during Selim and Sulayman's eastern campaigns. But Shiis were a small fraction of the Muslim population of the empire, concentrated in Lebanon and southern Iraq. Within the Sunni population, there were definite, but not serious, divisions.

Ottoman Sunnis adhered to all four Sunni schools of law; most were Hanafis, but the differences among the schools did not matter much. Many, perhaps most, Ottoman Sunnis respected, even if they did not participate in, Sufism. There was no fundamental antipathy between Shari Islam and Sufism. The most inflexibly Shari Muslims condemned Sufism in general; the more extreme Sufi groups ignored some provisions of the Shariah. The Bektashis, for example, believed that such Shari restrictions as the prohibition of alcohol applied only to believers without spiritual insight. Women participated in Bektashi rituals. Many, probably most, Muslims accepted Sufi beliefs to some degree, participating in such customs as pilgrimage to the shrines of various Sufi saints. These ranged from the tombs of saints with reputations throughout the Islamic world, like Jalal al-Din Rumi, the founder of the Mavlavi (Mevlevi) order in Konya, to local shrines that had been Christian before they became Muslim and pagan before they became Christian. The most influential orders, including the Halvatis, Mavlavis, and Bekatshis, had enough influence that the Ottoman administration certified the selection of their leaders.

Within the Greek Orthodox Church, there was a significant break between the popular faith of the countryside, where priests and monks often had no formal training, and the orthodoxy of Constantinople, which had a far more rigorous intellectual tradition, including connections to the University of Padua in Venetian territory. Members of the Orthodox elite thus had access to Western secular learning.

Like their Eastern Roman predecessors, the Ottomans regarded Catholicism as a hostile faith and ideology. After the alliance with France, however, the French ambassadors in Constantinople acted as advocates for Ottoman Catholics, providing them with a modicum of official protection. The Ottomans were ambivalent about Protestantism. They welcomed the Protestants of western and central Europe as allies against their Catholic and papal allies, but on their own territory they considered Protestants a threat to orthodoxy.

Ottoman Muslims, like their Christian neighbors, participated in networks that extended beyond the imperial borders. The major Sufi orders and educational hierarchies of the ulama reached beyond the Ottoman borders. And mercantile networks extended outward from Istanbul and Cairo in all directions. The boundaries between the Ottomans and the Christian powers in the Mediterranean world and between the Sunni Ottomans and Shii Safavids rarely interfered with commerce and even more rarely with the passage of individuals and ideas. People even crossed the line between Islam and Christianity in both directions and back with some frequency, mostly, but not always, as the result of capture in war followed by escape or release. When captured, Muslim and Christians often entered the service of their erstwhile enemies rather than becoming prisoners, at least until they had the opportunity to return to their own side.

From some perspectives, Muslim Ottoman women had greater freedom than their Christian counterparts before the nineteenth century, since they had the right to own property and some access to the courts, although they were not the legal equals of males. Although polygamy was legal for Muslims, the court records suggest it was quite rare, even among the wealthy. The men who married Ottoman princesses could take no other wife or concubine; this practice set a pattern among the Ottoman elite. Except for the poor, women generally wore a full veil in public. Armenian and Orthodox women often covered most of their faces, following the dominant pattern. Women had little opportunity for independent economic activity, though some inherited businesses from their husbands or fathers and operated them on their own. Women participated in the transmission of traditional Muslim learning, in Sufi spirituality, and in the arts and literature to a limited degree.

All of the categorical divisions within Ottoman society were fuzzy to a greater or lesser extent. Nomad groups engaged in agriculture as well as animal husbandry. Artisans and small merchants supplemented their incomes with produce from small garden plots. Such groups as the *darbandji*s, mentioned above, even straddled the *askari/raya* boundary.

OTTOMAN CULTURAL AND INTELLECTUAL HISTORY

It is no more possible to describe Ottoman cultural and intellectual history in a few paragraphs than it is to describe the culture and intellectual history of Renaissance and Reformation Europe in the same space. There were great Ottoman achievements in prose and poetry, the Islamic sciences, architecture and painting, and music. This section deals only with some aspects of Ottoman prose. It does not touch on the majesty of Ottoman architecture or the sheer beauty of Ottoman miniature painting. The size of the only major Western study of Ottoman poetry, E. J. W. Gibb's massive six-volume *History of Ottoman Poetry*, gives some idea of what is missing.

Ottoman cultural and intellectual history has received far less attention from historians than Ottoman social history. As Suraiya Faroqhi points out, Ottoman historiography offers no consensus vocabulary comparable to such standard Western concepts as Renaissance, Reformation, Enlightenment, baroque, and rococo, except for the Tulip Period. She identifies two turning points in literature and architecture: the middle of the fourteenth century, with the conquest of Constantinople and the establishment of mature political, military, and administrative institutions, and the late sixteenth and early seventeenth centuries, in which Ottoman high culture reached its culmination and began to suffer from the political, social, and economic stresses of the empire.

The Ottomans built their great mosque complexes—most importantly, the Fatih Jami, the Sulaymaniyyah, and the Blue Mosque in Istanbul and the Selimiyyah in Edirne—between these two turning points. These great mosque complexes articulate the majesty and grandeur of the Ottoman Empire. If the Hagia Sophia symbolized the Byzantine political and cultural order, Fatih Jami, Sulaymaniyyah, and the Blue Mosque did the same for the Ottoman world. Fatih Mehmed replicated the work of Justinian (r. 527–583), the great Byzantine emperor responsible for the Hagia Sophia, in promulgating a code of law, rebuilding a capital, and expounding his sovereignty through a monumental religious structure.

Ottoman literature existed on two levels: classical and popular. Classical literature consisted primarily of poetry, which followed Persian models, but also included prose historiography, mirrors for princes, and religious, legal, and scientific works. Ottoman historical writing developed, again following Persian originals, in the reigns of Murad II and Fatih Mehmed. Chroniclers in

IMAGE 3.6 *Fatih Jami, Sultan Mehmet II Mosque Complex (1463–1471), Istanbul.*
Mehmet II ordered the construction of this mosque complex as the visual symbol
of the Ottoman conquest of Constantinople. It replaced the fifth-century
Byzantine Church of the Holy Apostles which was razed for the new complex.

IMAGE 3.7
*Selimiye Jami, Sultan Selim II
Mosque Complex (1568–1574),
Edirne.* The Selimiye Jami is
considered the penultimate
masterpiece of Koca Sinan. Sinan
was conscripted via the devshirme
and entered the Janissary corps
where he became an accomplished
military engineer. However,
Sinan's enduring legacy was his
nearly fifty-year career as Mimar
Bashi (Chief Architect)
successively under the Ottoman
sultans Sulayman, Selim II,
and Murad III.

IMAGE 3.8 *Interior view of the Sultan Ahmet Jami, Ahmet I Mosque Complex (1609–1617), Istanbul.* Foreign travelers called this beautiful building the Blue Mosque because of the predominance of blue-hued ceramic tiles adorning its interior surfaces. This photograph shows the muezzin seated in the raised platform (*mahfil*) and, in the background, two of the four enormous piers that support the central dome.

this period provide the earliest Turkish sources on the development of the Ottoman polity. Bayazid II continued official patronage of Ottoman chronicles. Ottoman historians wrote in Persian and Greek as well. Some high officials also wrote history. Ahmed Shams al-Din Ibn-i Kemal (d. 1536), known as Kemalpashazade, offers an interesting example of Ottoman career paths.

He began his career as a *sipahi*, following the example of his ancestors, before obtaining religious and legal training. He gained some of the highest ulama posts, including *qazi* of Edirne, *qazi-askar* of Anatolia, and *shaykh al-Islam*. Though best known as the author of the *Tarikh-i Al-i Osman*, the best narrative source for his time, he also produced works in the religious sciences and poetry. Two later Ottoman historians, Mustafa Ali (d. 1599) and Mustafa Naima (d. 1716), have generated sufficient interest to inspire English monographs. Both men served as bureaucrats; Naima was the first official historian of the regime. The son of a Janissary in Aleppo, he began his career as a palace secretary and remained in the administrative bureaucracy all his life. Ali, the son of a Muslim merchant, began his career with education as an *alim* (singular of ulama); then, as was not uncommon, he took advantage of his literary training and ability to begin a career in the bureaucracy. He remained in that career throughout his life, though it led him to serve for seven years in the provinces as the secretary of a *sanjakbey* in Bosnia and as a *sipahi* in his own right. Both men wrote works other than their chronicles; Ali's included one of the most famous of the Ottoman mirrors for princes, the *Nasihat al-Salatin* (Counsel for Sultans).

These summaries of the careers of Ottoman scholars give some idea of the milieu in which Ottoman writers operated. Though few worked to official commissions, as Naima did, most wrote in the hope of obtaining rewards and earning appointments from the sultan or high officials. Cornell Fleischer's account of Ali's long and only partially successful search for patronage describes that environment cogently.

Into the seventeenth century, in addition to history, Ottoman writers produced works not inferior to Western works on mathematics, medicine (which received considerable official patronage), astronomy, and geography. The most famous geographic works were those of two Ottoman admirals who had journeyed to the Indian Ocean, Piri Reis and Sidi Ali Reis. Ottoman geographers were well aware of the European discoveries in the Americas.

Fleischer explains the tension between Muslim and Ottoman identities: As a *Rumi*, one born and raised in the Ottoman domains, Ali identified with the distinctive regional culture that had developed in Anatolia and Rumeli. As a graduate of the religious educational system, he also identified with the universal religious tradition of the madrasa and the cosmopolitan Arabo-Persianate high culture to which the Ottoman Empire was heir. This dual orientation reflected the polarity between the Shariah and the *qanun* of the Ottoman Empire. For Ali and many other Ottomans, *qanun*, "promulgated by the sultans on the basis of dynastic prestige and the conditions peculiar to Rum, was the very embodiment of regional Ottomanism."[25] Ali's Islam often conflicted with his Ottomanism, and he was hardly the only intellectual discomfited by the clash between the Shariah and *qanun*, though *qanun* was indispensable to the order of the state. The incorporation of the Shariah into Ottoman *qanun*, as well as massive state patronage for the ulama, made for the best possible resolution of the conflict. But conflict or no, the servants of the Ottoman state—the lettered classes of the empire—took pride in defining themselves as Ottomans, even if that pride could trouble their Muslim consciences.

STRESS AND ADAPTATION

During the past hundred years, the interpretation of Ottoman history from the reign of Qanuni Sulayman through the Tulip Period has changed from decline as a result of moral degeneracy at the top to decline as a result of military, financial, and socioeconomic stresses to successful transformation in response to those same stresses. Comparison with the Safavids and Mughals makes Ottoman success clear. In 1730, the Safavid regime had disappeared; a Safavid prince survived as puppet for Nadir Khan Afshar. The Mughal emperor Muhammad Shah was an emperor in name only, without the power, revenue, or territory to match his unquestioned imperial status. But the Ottoman Empire survived, despite some loss of territory and control of commercial networks.

The current interpretation of this era does not deny that the power and wealth of the Ottoman Empire declined relative to the rising powers of western Europe. It does, however, assert that the Ottoman Empire adapted to the global military and commercial environment with considerable, though hardly complete, success. Deviation from the "classical" Ottoman patterns and practices of the late fifteenth and early sixteenth centuries did not imply degeneration. The decline of specific institutions like the *timar* army did not imply systemic failure. The empire faced the inherent challenge of the position of incumbent power. Because Ottoman policies and institutions fitted the conditions of the late fifteenth and early sixteenth centuries so superbly, change was inevitably disruptive, not only to the empire's geopolitical position but also to its internal power structure. Internal politics, not religious or attitudinal reluctance to change, hindered the Ottoman "military and fiscal transformation," to use Halil Inalcık's expression.[26]

The *qapiqullar*, who had dominated the Ottoman regime since the reign of Fatih Mehmed, had become a coherent political class pursuing its own interests, not merely acting as servants to the sultan. They saw no distinction between their group interests and the interests of the empire as a whole. During the empire's time of troubles, the *qapiqullar* redefined themselves as a hereditary class and assumed control of the provincial as well as the central government. The new provincial *qapiqullar* became the feedstock of the *ayan*, the provincial notable class that came to dominate the empire in the eighteenth century. The *qapiqullar* secured their dominance of the Ottoman system during the reign of Selim II. As the Janissaries had secured his succession to the throne, he had no choice but to reward them, and then the other *qapiqullar* units, with generous bonuses and with one other vital concession: He granted the Janissaries the privilege of enrolling their sons in the corps, thus effectively making Janissary, and *qapiqullu*, status hereditary. The Janissaries had leverage not only because of their pivotal political significance but because of the growing military requirement for them as a result of the Military Revolution.

Of Geoffrey Parker's three dimensions of the Military Revolution, the growth in the size of European armies challenged the Ottomans far more than the increase in firepower and improvement in fortification. Charles VIII of France invaded Italy with 18,000 men in 1494; Francis I led 32,000 there in 1525. His son, Henry II, led 40,000 to take Metz from the Hapsburgs in 1552. The army that Charles V led in Hungary six years after Mohacs consisted of 100,000 troops. Between 1630 and 1700, the French army increased in size from 150,000 to roughly 400,000. The military challenge grew steadily through the seventeenth century as European armies adopted drill. In the 1590s Maurice and William Louis of Nassau originated the complex maneuvers by which a unit of musketeers could maintain a steady fire, one rank firing while the others—nine at first—reloaded their weapons. Other European powers, notably Sweden and Austria during the Thirty Years War (1618–1648), improved this Dutch innovation. The Ottomans, however, did not adopt drill until the eighteenth century. This situation prompted the remark of the great French commander Marechal de Saxe (1696–1750) that "it is not valor, numbers, or wealth they lack; it is order, discipline and military technique."[27]

The classical Ottoman military system could not match the growth in European armies. The provincial *sipahi* army could grow only with conquest of new provinces. Because it took a lifetime to train a mounted archer, the Ottomans could not rapidly expand the *sipahi* force or recoup the heavy losses Ottoman armies sustained in the late sixteenth century, notably in the campaign to take Astrakhan in 1569, Lepanto in 1571 (*sipahis* served as marines), and the Caucasus in the 1570s. With the supply of provincial *sipahis* limited and a continuing need for more troops, the Ottomans inevitably responded by expanding their central forces. The number of Janissaries and *sipahis* of the Porte increased from 16,000 in 1527 to 67,000 in

1609. But expanding the central forces could not meet the need. Military slavery created highly reliable, expert armies, not mass forces. In order to compete against the Europeans, the Ottomans had to use a different mechanism of recruitment and create a different kind of soldier.

For this reason, Ottomans began to recruit peasants for infantry units, known as *sekban* or *sarija* (*sarıca*), outside the existing military structure. These groups were organized into companies, called *boluk*, organized and led by *boluk-bashi*s (*bölük başi*), who were hired by the central government or provincial governors. The Ottomans developed large infantry forces with firearms in order to match the growth of European armed forces in size, not because of the superiority of infantry over mounted archers in battle. Mounted archers retained huge tactical advantages in the seventeenth century. François Bernier, the French traveler who visited all three empires in the seventeenth century, wrote that a mounted archer could shoot six arrows before a musketeer could fire twice. Even in the seventeenth century, the longbow had significant advantages over the flintlock musket. The advantage of the musket was not tactical but in training and procurement. In John F. Guilmartin's words, "Where a few days and a good drill sergeant might suffice to train a reasonably good arquebusier, many years and a whole way of life were needed to produce a competent archer."[28] Likewise, guns and ammunition could be produced quickly and cheaply. Making bows and arrows involved highly skilled labor, and some of the glues took more than a year to cure. Infantry were superior to *sipahi*s only in sieges, where the cavaliers could not use their horses and were unwilling to undertake other tasks like construction. The Ottomans recruited mass infantry armies not because they preferred infantry to cavalry or wanted to exploit the military potential of peasant manpower but because they had no alternative.

The dominance of the *qapiqullar* prevented the Ottomans from developing a standing professional infantry force large enough to match developments in Europe. Military service had defined status in the Ottoman Empire. Neither the regime nor the provincial governors assumed that *sekban* became *askari* when they were hired as salaried troops. As far as the regime was concerned, the soldiers of each *boluk* reverted to *raya* status as soon as their contract to fight expired. The armed peasants were rarely content to return to the role of taxpaying cultivators. Like unemployed soldiers in other historical contexts, they became insurgents, known as the *jalali*s. The term referred to the uprising of Shaykh Jalal, a Safavid sympathizer, in

Anatolia in 1519. But the *jalali*s had no connection, social or political, to the earlier rebels. They were not rebels in the normal sense. They sought not to overthrow the Ottoman regime but to gain secure status within it. In William Griswold's words, "Neither religious traitors, nor founders of a new breakaway state, these rebels mixed a cunning, self-centered leadership and the desire for unlimited power with a demand for security, income from lands, and rank within the Ottoman system for themselves and their followers."[29] They sought *askari* status; the individual rebels wanted to be *sipahi*s or Janissaries, their leaders, *sanjakbey*s or *beylerbey*s. After the victory at Mezo-Keresztes in 1596, the central government created a second pool of manpower for the *jalali*s. Chagalzade Sinan Pasha, appointed grand vizier after the victory, ordered a muster of the army and deprived all *sipahi*s who did not report of their *timar*s. Most of the alienated *sipahi*s fled to Anatolia and became *jalali*s. The mass confiscation of *timar*s was the final act of the political struggle between the *sipahi*s and the *qapiqullar*, excluding a substantial fraction of the *sipahi* class from *askari* status.

Karen Barkey describes the *jalali* problem as the product of deliberate state policy. The regime "created disenfranchised groups with access to weaponry, whom it directed toward actions consistent with the state's goal of increased coercion and control at the central and regional levels."[30] The state at this time meant the *qapiqullar*. Writers associated with the *qul* regime described the efforts of the *raya* to infiltrate the Janissary corps as a central problem in the empire; it was in fact a direct challenge to the *qapiqullar*. Osman II sought to restore vigor to the empire by substituting the insurgent *sekban* for the incumbent *qapiqullar*. His assassination led to a major *jalali* uprising headed by Abaza Mehmed Pasha, the governor of Erzurum. The rebels justified their uprising by the need to avenge the slain sultan. The rebel pasha dominated eastern Anatolia from 1623 to 1628; his forces hunted down and massacred Janissaries in their territory.[31] Murad IV eventually pardoned Abaza Mehmed Pasha and incorporated his forces into the official army, a significant victory for the *jalali*s. Similar uprisings by governors continued into the Köprülü era.

When the *jalali*s were not engaged in organized rebellion, they acted as organized bandits. Dispersed *sipahi*s, who had been responsible for rural order, could not cope with these armed bands. The *jalali*s extorted funds from defenseless towns and villages, pillaging those that did not submit. Even this activity, however, fits into the pattern of struggle between the *sek-*

ban and the *qapiqullar*, for the revenue the *jalalis* extorted would, in all probability, have gone to the *qapiqullar* as taxes. The rebels did not represent the *raya* but fought against the *quls* of the sultan for revenue and status.

The failure of the *timar* system also meant a breakdown of the restraints on provincial governors, since there was no longer a class of rooted military notables to restrain their power. Governors hired and used their own mercenary bands to establish independent power bases and collect illegal taxes, in part because their legal income, for reasons discussed below, no longer sufficed to support their positions. These depredations led to a massive flight of Anatolian peasants to cities and to Europe. To protect the general population from the ravages of bandits and officials alike, the central government used general mobilization (*nefer-i am*) to form local emergency militias. The *qazis* organized these forces, which were led by local *ayan* (notables), who in turn recruited subordinate officers and troops from each of the local villages. The inadequacy of the *timar* army to meet the needs of the later sixteenth century thus caused severe disruption of the provincial political and financial structure. But the Ottoman regime endured this prolonged turmoil.

The Ottomans experienced a similar challenge in naval warfare, though its political consequences were less far reaching. The rising cost of Mediterranean warfare (the result of the increasing size and rising costs of galleys and their crews) and the proliferation of inexpensive cast iron artillery and cannon balls (and thus of broadside sailing warships) made the Ottoman galley fleet an expensive anachronism.

The struggle between the *qapiqullar* and the insurgents took place during a period of monetary and economic turmoil, Pamuk's period of "monetary instability arising from fiscal, economic and political difficulties compounded by the adverse effects of intercontinental movements of specie."[32] A generation ago, the interpretation of the Ottoman economic difficulties of the late sixteenth century emphasized the effect of "intercontinental movements of specie," specifically, the effects of the influx of American silver, the so-called Price Revolution. Even in Europe, the precise relationship between the increase in the silver supply, silver inflation, and other factors, such as population growth, appears less clear than before, although the extent and impact of the inflation does not. European prices, in sliver, at least doubled, and in some areas tripled, between 1500 and 1650. Further east, in the Ottoman Empire and beyond, the picture becomes murkier.

Inflation certainly took place in the Ottoman Empire. Pamuk's analysis indicates that Istanbul prices in *akche* increased roughly 500 percent between 1500 and 1700. But debasement—reduction in the silver content—of the *akche*, rather than silver inflation, explains much of that change. Prices in weight of silver, rather than number of coins, increased much less. From a base year of 1489, prices had risen some 80 to 100 percent by the first quarter of the seventeenth century, but then actually declined to 140 percent of the base level by 1680 and 120 percent by 1700. Pamuk concludes that the demographic and economic growth of the sixteenth century, which led to increased monetarization of trade in small towns and rural areas (an increase in the velocity of the circulation of money), in addition to the increased supply of specie, caused the inflation in the sixteenth century.

In 1585–1586, the Ottoman regime debased the *akche* by 44 percent for reasons that are not yet clear. This action coincided with rising demands on the treasury and began the long era of monetary instability in the empire. The Ottoman treasury operated in substantial surplus for most of the first three quarters of the sixteenth century; the debasement began, or coincided, with the beginning of a century of substantial deficits. The changes in the military system were expensive. Unlike earlier wars in Europe, the Long War produced no profit. The *jalali* disorders disrupted the economy of much of Anatolia. The *timar* army cost the central treasury almost nothing in cash; the central army and the *sekban* required cash payment, but the dwindling number of *sipahis* and the need for the larger armies that only the *sekban* could provide forced the Ottomans to alter the provincial financial, administrative, and military structure. They transferred much of the provincial revenue from *timar* holders to tax farmers and used the revenue to support *sekban* infantry rather than *sipahi* cavalry. This policy reflected not the military obsolescence of the *sipahis* but their dwindling numbers, the need for larger armies, and the interests of the *qapiqullar*.

The Ottoman term for tax farming was *iltizam*; a tax farmer was a *multezim (mültezim)*. *Iltizam* involved the sale of a given revenue source (*muqataa, mukataa*), usually for three years. The *multezim* made a down payment and regular payments for the term of the contract in return for the right to collect the statutory revenue from that source. The provincial authorities had to assist the *multezim* in the collection of the revenue, with military force if necessary, and the government appointed an accountant to monitor the *multezim's* collections and payments. *Multezim*s could in turn divide their *muqataa*s and farm the parts out to subordinate tax farmers. The regime transformed a significant part of what had been *timar* land, including *khass* and *zeamet* assignments, into *muqataa*s. In theory, *iltizam* did not imply less central administrative control than the *timar* system. Government officials supervised assessment and collection of revenues to prevent exploitation and oppression. As the stress on the revenue system increased through the seventeenth century, however, the oversight system often failed, especially because of personal relationships between *multezim*s and other officials. In 1699, the Ottomans began allowing tax farmers to purchase *iltizam*s for life and pass them on to their children.

The new tax system started with two existing levies, the *avariz-i divaniye* (*avarız-i divaniye*) and the *tekalif* (*tekâlif*). These levies had been emergency cash taxes, assessed and collected by the local *qazi*s; they became standard levies during the Long War. The *avariz* was a capitation tax, imposed on all adult males, Muslim and non-Muslim, at a variable rate. The *qazi*s conducted revenue surveys, although we know less about these than about those for the *timar* system. They focused, apparently, on the population, rather than actual productive assets, as the locus of assessment. Especially later in the seventeenth century, the assessment became subject to negotiation between the *qazi*s and the local notables; the notables (*ayan*) frequently actually paid the taxes themselves and then collected the balance from the general population. These taxes became extremely onerous, causing many peasants to flee to avoid paying them.

Just as the *avariz* had been an emergency tax collected by the regime, the *tekalif* had been a legitimate emergency levy imposed by provincial governors. It became routine because of the need for governors to support their *sekban* retinues; the central regime allowed them to collect such levies routinely in order to prevent the governors from becoming rebels and collecting them anyway. Governors frequently collected *tekalif* levies even though they had no authorization to do so. In the later seventeenth century, the *ayan* became the primary conduit for the collection of *tekalif*. The regime extracted forced loans from them as well, requiring them to collect the repayment from the general population, a form of forced tax farming. The role of the *ayan* in the new revenue system became the springboard to *ayan* dominance in the provinces in the eighteenth century.

In this political, military, and financial turmoil, official corruption became rampant. Inflation made it impossible for *sipahi*s to perform their duties with the funds they received legitimately; even beys and *qazi*s demanded bribes and extorted funds to meet the requirements of their stations. It was difficult to distinguish the activities of legitimate officeholders from brigandage. The sale of offices became prevalent as well. The expense of gaining appointments forced *voyvoda*s to oppress subjects in order to make their short tenures in office profitable, leading to depopulation and revolt in these areas. This depopulation countributed to a fundamental change in the social and political structure of the Ottoman countryside. Large landholdings, confusingly also known as *chiftlik*s, produced cash crops. The tax farmers frequently became the propietors of these large farms. The change in the meaning of *chiftlik* demonstrated the extent of transformation of rural society and economy.

The change in provincial finance and administration meant, of course, a change in administrators. Many of the tax farmers and their agents were members of the central armed forces, especially the central cavalry. The new provincial administration, then, meant the transfer of the provincial revenue that had supported the old provincial elite to the central elite. It thus completed the dominance of the *qapiqullar*, even as it provided the cash revenue the empire needed to fund the new infantry armies and respond to monetary stresses. In the course of the seventeenth century, however, this system also helped to empower a new provincial elite, which became known as the *ayan*. The eighteenth century became the era of the *ayan*.

According to Halil Inalcık, the principle interpreter of the *ayan* era, the central government turned to the *ayan* as a means of protecting the general population from the depredations of both rebels and legitimate officials collecting illegal taxes, and then as tax collectors themselves. From this limited military and financial role, the *ayan* became autonomous potentates in the provinces. The frequent transfer of provincial officials, especially *sanjakbeys* and *beylerbeys*, forced them to rely on local deputies (*mutesellims*, *mütesellim*). The frequent absences of, and changes in, governors made the *mutesellims*, who held their positions for long periods, more important than the actual governors. They were normally tax farmers with large *muqataas*. They used this income to maintain large retinues of *sekban*. In Inalcık's words,

> While steadily making themselves indispensable to the government, especially in times of war, by providing revenues, men, provisions, and animals, the *ayan* deputies at the same time used (and often abused) their state-delegated authority to reinforce their influence in the provinces.[33]

Ayan families competed for the office of *mutesellim*, but it generally became hereditary. Later in the eighteenth century, what amounted to a series of local *ayan* dynasties ruled much of the empire through what amounted to local *ayan* councils.

Less prominent *ayan* acted as *voyvodas*, leading *multezims* in areas within a given *sanjak*. The *mutesellims* attempted to secure their control of the situation by making their own dependents the *voyvodas* in their territories. The *mutesellims* and *voyvodas* became indispensable intermediaries between the regime and the *raya*.

Several categories of people constituted the *ayan*: ulama, *qapiqullar* who had provincial assignments, wealthy merchants who frequently served as *multezims*, and leading members of guilds. Ulama, especially descendants of the Prophet, had extremely prominent roles in the life of Ottoman cities and considerable wealth. But the provincial role of the *qapiqullar* requires further discussion. Even in the classical period of Ottoman history, the regime had sent *quls* to the provinces, especially Janissary garrisons. In the eighteenth century, however, people of provincial origin who had never served in the palace began to claim this status for themselves and actually acquired the title of Janissary and bey. They did so at first by bribery, but the transfer of the unique status of *qapiqullar* to provincial elements followed the transfer of governmental responsibility to them. The process was no more even or neat than the admission of *sekban* to *askari* status, but was analogous to it. In the seventeenth century, officials of *raya* origin contented themselves with the titles of *mutesellim* or *voyvoda*; in the eighteenth century they became beys and pashas. The *qapiqullar* had succeeded in defining themselves as the governing elite of the empire; the transfer of financial and military power to the *ayan* made the transfer of the outer trappings of *qapiqullar* status to them inevitable. Conversely, the wealth and security of the *ayan* offered much to the *qapiqullar*. Wealth was apparently the most important criterion for receiving these titles; it was what made individuals from the constituent categories *ayan*. Within provincial cities and towns, the *ayan* were the leading citizens, acting as representatives of the general population with the central government and maintaining public works. Beginning in the 1680s, the central regime began to designate one *ayan*, chosen by his peers, to act as its local representative and as the guarantor for the collection of the *avariz*.

The Ottoman Empire in the *ayan* era differed dramatically from the classical empire of the late fifteenth and early sixteenth centuries. But the *ayan* system offered both the regime and the general population a number of benefits. Because of their lasting local connections, the *ayan* had incentives to protect the interests of the general population and to invest in the economic development of the area, rather than to exploit their positions for short-term gains. But they also offered the central government an effective way of drawing on the resources of the provinces, not only in routine taxation but in support of military campaigns; for example, *ayan* families often acted as contractors to provision armies on campaign.

The turmoil of the early decades of the seventeenth century produced a religious reform movement, the Kadizelis. Their leaders came from the class of popular preachers. They criticized the elite, both political and religious, for luxury and laxity, contrasting Ottoman practices with an austere image of Prophetic ideals. The Kadizelis attacked Sufism as well. Like later reform movements, the Kadizelis sought to address contemporary problems by calling for a return to true Islam. They were unable to win power in the empire but formed a part of its seventeenth-century difficulties.

The Ottoman Empire of 1730—shorn of much of its European possessions, beset by internal disorders at the center, without central control of much of its hinterlands, and with its rulers cowering in the palace seeking to survive by manipulating political factions—appeared a pitiful remnant of its era of grandeur. But it was no mean achievement to survive as a remnant when its contemporaries had become ghosts.

Though debilitating, these changes did not make the Ottoman Empire impotent. In all probability, the Ottoman victories over Peter the Great on the Pruth in 1711 and the reconquest of the Morea in 1715 made the survival of the empire into the twentieth century possible. Commenting on the early *jalali* revolts, William Griswold argues that the loyalty of the civilian bureaucrats and the general population carried the empire through the first *jalali* crisis. The commitment of the empire's subjects, Muslim and Orthodox, to the regime and the expectation of continuing success lasted through the troubles of the seventeenth century and into the eighteenth.

THE OTTOMAN SYSTEM

The Ottoman Empire appeared as the result of the transplant of the Irano-Islamic tradition of bureaucratic empire to the fertile lands of western Anatolia and the Balkans. Since the decline of the Abbasid caliphate, no polity in the central Islamic lands had followed the patterns of bureaucratic empire, but the bureaucrats who could not execute its provisions nonetheless continued to carry and transmit that pattern. The presence of this tradition, as well as the Byzantine example from the more recent past, produced the transformation of the frontier principality into an empire. The pushing of the *ghazi*s to the frontier, to a political as well as a geographical margin, was the inevitable consequence of the development of bureaucratic institutions. Along with the *ghazi*s, the original Ottoman elite consisted of survivors of the ruling classes of conquered principalities, the ulama—a certain proportion of whom always made careers in government service—and a growing number of military slaves. In the course of the fifteenth century, the balance of political power moved steadily away from the provincial elites to the slaves of the sultan's household. The *qapiqullar* never had a monopoly on power or on high office, and the group's composition changed, from actual slaves captured, purchased, or taken through the *devshirme* to children and personal dependents of other *qapiqullar*. But the group retained a firm grip on the high offices of the central government into the nineteenth century at the cost of the increasing impotence of the central government in the eighteenth century.

Ottoman military dominance in the fifteenth and sixteenth centuries stemmed from a fortunate happenstance. The comparatively humble situation of the Janissary corps in the fifteenth century made it possible for them to accept firearms when most professional military forces in the Islamic world were unwilling to do so. The Ottoman mating of firearms—artillery for sieges, muskets in the field—with traditional Islamic means of recruitment and training, as well as the adoption of *tabur jangi*, made them dominant militarily for more than a century. The Ottomans lost this dominance as a result of the Military Revolution, but this loss did not imply degeneration or somnolence.

Notes

1. Heath W. Lowry, *The Nature of the Early Ottoman State* (Albany: State University of New York Press, 2003), 54.

2. Donald Quataert, *The Ottoman Empire, 1700–1922*, 2nd ed. New Approaches to European History, ed. William Beik and T. C. W. Blanding (Cambridge: Cambridge University Press, 2005), 44.

3. M. Guboğlu, *Paleografia ği diplomatica turco-osmanâ* (Bucharest, Romania: n.p., 1958), 133, quoted and translated in Halil İnalcık, "State, Sovereignty and Law During the Reign of

Sülaymân," in *Sülaymân the Second and His Time*, ed. Halil İnalcık and Cemal Kafadar (Istanbul: Isis Press, 1993), 77–78.

4. Colin Imber, "Ottoman Dynastic Myth," *Turcica* 19 (1987): 16–20.

5. Halil Inalcık, "Emergence of the Ottomans," in *The Cambridge History of Islam*, ed. Bernard Holt, Ann K. S. Lambton, and Bernard Lewis, 2 vols. (Cambridge: Cambridge University Press, 1970), 1:287; reprinted as "The Rise of the Ottoman Empire," in *A History of the Ottoman Empire to 1730*, ed. M. A. Cook (Cambridge: Cambridge University Press, 1976), 35.

6. Cornell H. Fleischer, "The Lawgiver As Messiah: The Making of the Imperial Image in the Reign of Sülaymân," in *Sülaymân the Magnificent and His Time*, ed. Gilles Veinstein (Paris: La Documentation Français, 1992), 167.

7. Gülrû Necipoğlu, "Sülaymân the Magnificent and the Representation of Power in the Context of Ottoman-Hapsburg-Papal Rivalry," in *Sülaymân the Second and His Time*, ed. Halil Inalcık and Cemal Kafadar (Istanbul: Isis Press, 1993), 209.

8. Necipoğlu, "Sülaymân the Magnificent," 219.

9. Leslie P. Peirce, *The Imperial Harem: Women and Sovereignty in the Ottoman Empire*. Studies in Middle Eastern History, ed. Bernard Lewis, Itamar Rabinovich, and Roger Savory (New York: Oxford University Press, 1993), 185.

10. Peirce, *Imperial Harem*, 283.

11. Colin Imber, *Ebu's-Su`ud: The Islamic Legal Tradition*. Jurists: Profiles in Legal Theory, ed. William Twining and Neil MacCormick (Stanford, CA: Stanford University Press, 1997), 106.

12. Peirce, *Imperial Harem*, 41.

13. Carl Brockelmann, *History of the Islamic Peoples*, trans. Joel Carmichael and Moshe Perlmann (New York: Capricorn Books, 1960), 331. The German original was published in 1939.

14. Palmira Brummett, *Ottoman Seapower and Levantine Diplomacy in the Age of Discovery*. Studies in the Social and Economic History of the Middle East, ed. Donald Quataert (Albany: State University of New York Press, 1994), 175.

15. Halil Inalcık, *The Ottoman Empire: The Classical Age, 1300–1660*, trans. Norman Itzkowitz and Colin Imber (London: Weidenfeld and Nicholson, 1973), 115–116.

16. John Francis Guilmartin Jr., *Gunpowder and Galleys: Changing Technology and Mediterranean Warfare at Sea in the Sixteenth Century*, 2nd ed. (London: Conway Maritime Press, 2003), 161.

17. All the figures for the size of the central army are from Rhoads Murphey, *Ottoman Warfare, 1500–1700* (New Brunswick, NJ: Rutgers University Press, 1999), 45.

18. Gábor Ágoston, *Guns for the Sultan: Military Power and the Weapons Industry in the Ottoman Empire*. Cambridge Studies in Islamic Civilization, ed. David Morgan (Cambridge: Cambridge University Press, 2005), 23.

19. Geoffrey Parker, *The Military Revolution: Military Innovation and the Rise of the West, 1500–1800*, 2nd ed. (Cambridge: Cambridge University Press, 1996), 24.

20. Parker, *The Military Revolution*, 126.

21. Ágoston, *Guns for the Sultan*, 21.

22. Halil Inalcık, *Fâthi Devri Üzerinde Tetkikler ve Vesikalar* (Ankara: Türk Tarih Kurumu, 1954), cited in Inalcık, *The Ottoman Empire*, 94.

23. Halil Inalcık, "The Ottoman State: Economy and Society, 1300–1600," in *An Economic and Social History of the Ottoman Empire*, ed. Halil Inalcık with Donald Quataert (Cambridge: Cambridge University Press, 1994), 146. This book appears in one-and two-volume editions with the same pagination.

24. Şevket Pamuk, *A Monetary History of the Ottoman Empire*. Cambridge Studies in Islamic Civilization, ed. David Morgan (Cambridge: Cambridge University Press, 2000), 20.

25. Cornell H. Fleischer, *Bureaucrat and Intellectual in the Ottoman Empire: The Historian Mustafa Ali* (Princeton, NJ: Princeton University Press, 1986), 261.

26. Halil Inalcık, "Military and Fiscal Transformation in the Ottoman Empire," *Archivum Ottomanicum* 6 (1980). Reprinted in *Studies in the Social and Economic History of the Ottoman Empire* (London: Variorum, 1985).

27. Marechal de Saxe, *Mes Reveries*, ed. l'Abbe Perau (Amsterdam and Leipzig: n.p., 1757), 1:86–87, quoted in V. J. Parry, "La manière du combattre," in *War, Technology and Society*, ed. V. J. Parry and Malcolm Yapp (London: Oxford University Press, 1968), 256.

28. Guilmartin, *Gunpowder and Galleys*, 162.

29. William J. Griswold, *The Great Anatolian Rebellion, 1000–1020/1591–1611*. Islamkundliche Untersuchungen 83 (Berlin: Klaus Schwarz Verlag, 1983), 23.

30. Karen Barkey, *Bandits and Bureaucrats: The Ottoman Route to State Centralization* (Ithaca, NY: Cornell University Press, 1994), 141.

31. Inalcık, "Military and Fiscal Transformation," 297–299.

32. Pamuk, *A Monetary History*, 20.

33. Halil Inalcık, "Centralization and Decentralization in Ottoman Administration," in *Studies in Eighteenth Century Islamic History*, ed. Thomas Naff and Roger Owen. Papers on Islamic History 4 (Carbondale: Southern Illinois University Press, 1977), 31.

Chapter 4

THE SAFAVID EMPIRE

The Safavid Empire never equaled the size, power, or wealth of the Ottoman or Mughal empires. Its history had a different pattern. It did not grow steadily over many decades but reached its maximum size within a few years of its foundation and maintained those boundaries only briefly. Safavid rule transformed the religious life of the empire but had a much less significant effect on its ethnic composition and social structure. Some historians have questioned whether it qualifies as an empire at all, though the Ottomans and Mughals had no difficulty identifying the Safavids as peers. The Safavid polity began as a confederation of Turkmen tribes, led not by the leader of one tribe but by a Sufi *shaykh*, Ismail Safavi (I use the anglicized Safavid for the order and dynasty but Safavi in personal names). The Safavid ideology—a blend of *ghuluww*, Turko-Mongol conceptions of kingship, and the folk Sufism of the Turkmen—energized the tribes. This ideology and Ismail's consistent military success from 1501 to 1512 suspended the normal political operation of the tribal confederation. After the first Safavid defeats, at Ghujduvan in 1512 and Chaldiran in 1514, Ismail's loss of prestige altered the balance of power within the confederation, giving the tribal leaders decisive authority and making their struggle for dominance the central issue in Safavid politics. After 1530, Ismail's son, Shah Tahmasp, gradually strengthened his position enough to manipulate, rather than be manipulated by, the tribes. After his death, however, the tribal

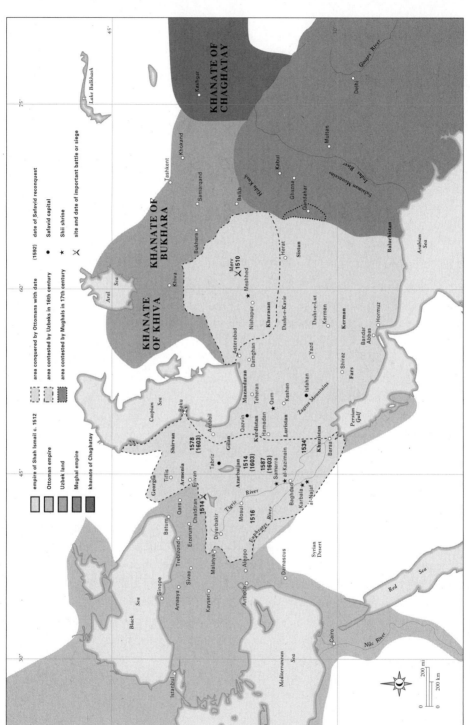

MAP 4.1 Safavid Empire

chiefs again dominated the empire until the time of Abbas I (1588–1629). Abbas transformed the Safavid polity from a tribal confederation into a bureaucratic empire. The primacy of the bureaucracy, with the tribes present but peripheral, survived until the rapid collapse of the empire in 1722.

The Ottoman and Mughal empires clearly deserve the title agrarian. They represented transplants of the agrarian bureaucratic traditions of the Middle East to rich agrarian regions elsewhere. The Safavids had no such advantage; the tribal resurgence in the eighteenth century showed that the ecology of the Iranian plateau continued to favor pastoral nomadism. The Safavid regime relied not on broad agricultural prosperity or control of major trade networks but on the export of a single commodity: Abbas I's central army and central bureaucracy depended on income from the export of silk. The Safavid polity thus became a gunpowder empire because of the increase in global trade in the sixteenth century. Otherwise, the Safavid Empire, in all probability, would have remained a tribal confederation, held only the central and western parts of the Iranian plateau, and had a shorter lifespan. The income from this commerce did not, however, permit a return to the previous agrarian pattern of Abbasid times, based on massive irrigation works. The empire thus became a peculiar hybrid. Under Abbas I, the center became strong enough to reduce the Qizilbash tribes to political insignificance but could not eliminate them. There was no open frontier to divert them to. When the central regime failed, the tribal forces became dominant by default.

The Safavid Empire was neither a revival of the ancient empires of the Achaemenians (the Persians who fought the Greeks) and Sasanians nor the beginning of the modern state of Iran. Although the Safavids united most of what had been the Persian-speaking areas of the earlier empires, they did not claim to be their heirs or legitimate successors. They were no more or less Iranian than their Timurid and Turkmen predecessors. Although the Safavid unification of the eastern and western halves of the Iranian plateau and imposition of Twelver Shii Islam on the region created a recognizable precursor of modern Iran, the Safavid polity itself was neither distinctively Iranian nor national. In the words of Rudi Matthee, "Though not a nation-state, Safavid Iran contained the elements that would later spawn one by generating many enduring bureaucratic features and by initiating a polity of overlapping religious and territorial boundaries."[1]

The establishment of Twelver Shiism dominated the social, religious, and cultural history of the Safavid period. Earlier dynasties frequently had

---

BOX 4.1 Twelver Shiism

The Twelver (Ithna-Ashari; also known as Imami) branch of Shii Islam asserts that the line of imams, the legitimate leaders of the Muslim community after the death of the Prophet, ended when the Twelfth Imam disappeared in 873 in Samarra. Known as Muhammad al-Muntazar (the Expected), he will eventually return as the messiah, the Mahdi. The absence of the true imam creates a problem of political leadership. Some Twelvers have adopted an entirely quietist position, arguing that legitimate political activity in the absence of the imam is impossible. As noted below, the Safavid rulers, and their Zand, Qajar, and Pahlavi successors, considered themselves legitimate rulers in the absence of the imam. From the late seventeenth century onward, the Shii ulama have presented themselves as the representatives of the imam, with the most senior of them, the grand ayatollahs, having the status of *marja al-taqlid* (pattern for imitation), providing guidance for the believers. The leading ulama had a significant political voice, but none before the Ayatollah Ruhullah Khomeini claimed actual political authority.

Twelver Shiism did not become the largest and most influential variety of Shiism until the Safavids imposed it on their empire.

Shii tendencies or preferences; none in the post-Mongol era had made Shiism a political platform or sought to impose it. The Safavid imposition of Shiism broke precedent and began the pattern of confessionalization. But Safavid *ghuluww* had little in common with the Twelver Shiism that eventually became the faith of the general population. There is no consensus on why the Safavids made this innovation in religious policy.

By the time of Abbas I, the religion the Safavids had imposed had become their principle source of legitimacy. Abbas I posed as the protector and chief patron of Shari Shii Islam the basis of the regime. He began the establishment of Shii madrasas especially at Isfahan and made great display of his personal piety. The Shii ulama responded by justifying Safavid sovereignty in Shari Shii terms. The personalities of the next rulers made the ulama supreme in the regime. The survival of Safavid prestige into the nineteenth century suggests that the ulama domination of the Safavid regime won considerable legitimacy for it among the general population. But that new legitimacy did not translate to military power, as the regime's rapid downfall showed.

This apparent dichotomy reflects the division between the general, settled population and the military classes typical of the Islamic world since Abbasid times. The settled population, urban and rural, had little military potential, except when trained and equipped as infantry with firearms. The Safavid relationship with the Turkmen tribes gave them control of most of the military manpower of the country, except in such marginal areas as Baluchistan and the Afghan mountains. The diffusion of firearms had little political or social effect in the Safavid domain. The Safavids recruited few peasants for military service, and they never became a political force, unlike in the Ottoman case. Safavid politics and military recruitment followed the patterns common in the Islamic world before the gunpowder period. Muslim nomads and mainly Christian outsiders recruited primarily through the mechanism of military slavery dominated the armed forces.

Historians of the Safavid period have emphasized the division between Turks and Tajiks. In the words of Vladimir Minorsky, "Like oil and water, the Turcomans and Persians did not mix freely and the dual character of the population profoundly affected the military and civil administration of Persia."[2] This duality was not a simple struggle for power. The Tajik bureaucrats, administrators, and ulama did not wish to become the chiefs of Turkmen tribes; the Turkmen chiefs could not function without Tajik administrative expertise. The relationship was always symbiotic; within the symbiosis, there was a struggle for dominance. In that struggle, however, the Tajiks were the allies of the ruler, for their perceived interests—the political theory they believed and transmitted—lay in the concentration of power at the center. The inherent military power of the Turkmen chiefs made aspirations to autonomy natural. The Tajik administrators had no such ambitions; the power that they sought could come to them only as extensions of the ruler. Andrew Newman insightfully describes the Safavid polity as a "project":

> The Safavid story is the story of the growth of its composite constituencies: where from well prior to the capture of Tabriz throughout most of the sixteenth century allied Turk political-military and Tajik administrative interests dominated the project's political center, [the last Safavid ruler] Sultan Husayn commanded the recognition of an array of foreign commercial, political and religious interests, as well as Turk and non-Turk tribal, Tajik, and *ghulam* military, political and administrative court

elements, and indigenous Muslim, Christian and foreign artisanal and commercial-political classes.[3]

When Shah Ismail appointed the Tajik Amir Yar Muhammad Isfahani, known as Najm-i Sani, to command the army he sent to Khurasan in 1512, he did so to establish his own authority—to make himself the orderer of the Safavid polity. The insubordination on the part of the Qizilbash amirs, which led to the defeat at Ghujduvan (see below), showed that he could not do so. The Qizilbash resented Tajik authority—not necessarily Tajiks as a group—because it implied the loss of their autonomy to the central government. The Turk-Tajik dispute was not, ultimately, ethnic, though ethnic rivalry was certainly present. It was a clash over the nature of the polity. The reforms of Shah Abbas indicated a victory for the Tajik agenda, but the Tajiks did not enjoy many of the rewards. And the victory for centralization proved temporary.

CHRONOLOGY

I divide Safavid history into five phases: (1) Sufi order, from the establishment of the Safavid Sufi order by Shaykh Safi to the accession of Shah Ismail; (2) the establishment of empire, from 1501 to 1514; (3) tribal confederation, from 1514 to 1588; (4) the Abbasi transformation, from 1588 to 1629; and (5) inertia and devolution, from 1629 to 1722.

Sufi Order

Shaykh Safi, the founder and namesake of the Safavid Sufi order, lived from 1252 or 1253 to 1334. He established a typical order of mystics, without a political agenda or a sectarian Shii allegiance. The Safavid order's transformation into an organization of religious extremists with a political agenda was not unique in its context. In the thirteenth, fourteenth, and fifteenth centuries, a variety of extremist religio-political movements developed in greater Iran and Anatolia. The Babai movement, mentioned earlier, was perhaps the first of them. They espoused *ghuluww* ideology, denied the legitimacy of existing political arrangements, and generally focused on a messianic figure who would bring true justice. One such group, the Sarbadars, combined peasants, urban dwellers, and rural notables in an uprising against Mongol rule in Khurasan in 1337 and established a state that survived for fifty years, the only state in greater Iran in that era not to claim some form of Mongol legitimacy. Another group, the Mushasha, began as an uprising against Timurid rule in Khuzistan. Its leader, Sayyid Muhammad ibn Falah, claimed to be the Mahdi but succeeded only in establishing a durable provincial dynasty. Clearly, the political and religious atmosphere of this period fostered revolutionary and messianic expectations. The mixture of political disorder, the breakdown of the structure of Sunni authority after the destruction of the Abbasid caliphate, responses to the presence and rule of the non-Muslim Mongols, and the interaction of popular or folk Islam with Sufi theory all contributed to the mixture.

The melding of *ghuluww* and Turkmen clan confederation began with the association of Shaykh Junayd Safavi with Uzun Hasan Aqquyunlu. Before Junayd's time, the Safavid order had no political power, though it was prominent and influential. Shaykh Safi al-Din had established the headquarters of his order in Ardabil, near the shore of the Caspian Sea in Azerbaijan. In his lifetime and that of his son, Shaykh Sadr al-Din (1304/1305–1391), the Safavid order spread throughout greater Iran and as far as Egypt and Sri Lanka. It gained many adherents among the Turkmen of eastern Anatolia and Syria. Historians have sought to establish exactly when the Safavids became a Shii order and whether they were actually descendants of Muhammad and Ali. Zeki Velidi Togan and Ahmad Kasravi have shown that the Safavids were not actually descended from the Prophet. Kasravi contends that the family was Tajik but spoke Azeri Turkish; Togan contends that they were Kurds. There can be no firm answer to the question of when the Safavids became Shii. There was no sharp line between Sunni and Shii Islam in the middle periods of Islamic history. The transition from Sufi order to empire had two components: the beginning of political and military activity and the activation of messianic claims.

Junayd, Safi al-Din's great-grandson, became *shaykh* after the death of his father, Ibrahim, in 1447. His paternal uncle Jafar challenged his succession and won the support of Jahanshah Qaraquyunlu, the ruler of the Turkmen confederation that dominated the western Iranian plateau at the time. Junayd was exiled from Ardabil. At this time, he first gathered a military retinue. In 1456, he took refuge with the major opponent of Jahanshah, Uzun Hasan Aqquyunlu. Uzun Hasan sheltered Junayd for three years and allowed him to marry his own sister. Presumably, Uzun Hasan, who had secured his paramountcy among the Aqquyunlu only in 1457, sought to gain the support of Junayd's followers among the Turkmen. Junayd later led a series of raids into the Christian areas of the Caucasus but could not reestablish himself in Ardabil. In 1460, Junayd and his forces were attacked by the Muslim ruler of Shirvan, Khalilullah, during their return from a raid on Georgia, and the Safavid leader was killed. Junayd's participation in *ghaza* fits the association of *ghaza* non-Shari religiosity and pastoral nomadism familiar from the early phase of Ottoman history. Junayd's son, Haydar, spent his childhood at the court of Uzun Hasan and married the ruler's daughter (and thus his own first cousin). Uzun Hasan installed Haydar as the *shaykh* of the Safavid order in Ardabil in the early 1470s, after his victories over Shaykh Jafar's protectors, Jahanshah Qaraquyunlu and Abu Said Timuri. Haydar introduced the distinctive red turban that gave the followers of the Safavids their name, Qizilbash (redheads). Though most of the tribes that had formed the Qaraquyunlu confederation until Uzun Hasan defeated Jahanshah in 1467 joined the Aqquyunlu confederation, many of their members became adherents of the young *shaykh* of Ardabil instead. Haydar's growing power, militant stance, and theological extremism led to a dispute with Uzun Hasan's son and successor, Yaqub.

Yaqub, who had become effective leader of the Aqquyunlu in 1481, and his chief minister, Qazi Isa, sought to alter the Aqquyunlu regime fundamentally. His program "aimed at the complete reorganization of the empire along the lines of traditional Irano-Islamic statecraft."[4] This agenda alienated many of the Turkmen and probably increased the influence of the Safavids. Haydar first led the Qizilbash into the field against the Circassians in 1484 with Yaqub's grudging permission and obtained transit rights through Shirvan from its ruler, the *Shirvanshah*, Farrukhyasar, the son of Junayd's killer. Haydar led a second raid in 1486, but Yaqub then forced him to swear an oath to end his military activity and devote himself to the spiritual guidance of his followers.

Haydar did not keep his vow for long; Yaqub actually asked his cousin for military assistance two years later. Haydar mobilized his troops but then obtained Yaqub's permission to raid Circassia and passage rights from the *Shirvanshah*. Instead of passing through Shirvan, however, Haydar attacked Farrukhyasar. The *Shirvanshah* appealed for help to Yaqub, who sent a large Aqquyunlu force. The combined Aqquyunlu-Shirvani army crushed the Safavids on July 9, 1488. Haydar was killed, and his three sons, Sultan Ali, Sayyid Ibrahim, and Ismail were imprisoned far from Ardabil. This apparent victory weakened the Aqquyunlu regime, for many of the disaffected Turkmen were sympathetic to the Safavids.

After Yaqub's death in 1490, the Aqquyunlu Empire collapsed into a series of conflicts among the descendants of Uzun Hasan. One of his grandsons, Rustam bin Maqsud, established a modicum of order in 1493. He permitted the three sons of Haydar to return to Ardabil, and the Safavids supported Rustam against other Aqquyunlu princes. The Aqquyunlu administration could not, however, control the Safavid forces once they were in being. Several Aqquyunlu princes decided to arrest the three sons of Haydar in the summer of 1494. The brothers attempted to flee to Ardabil, but Aqquyunlu forces overtook them outside the city. In the ensuing battle, Sultan Ali was killed. Ibrahim renounced extremism, and the Aqquyunlu authorities installed him in Ardabil. His seven-year-old brother, Ismail, became the bearer of the Safavids' militant tradition. He escaped the Aqquyunlu and found refuge at the court of Ali Mirza Kiyai, the Shii ruler of Gilan, in the city of Lahijan. Ismail remained in hiding there for five years.

The Establishment of Empire, 1499–1514

Ismail emerged from his exile in Gilan in the summer of 1499, at the age of twelve. The disorders within the Aqquyunlu realm had continued during this period and prevented an immediate response to Ismail's reappearance. He rapidly attracted a huge following, including seven major tribes: the Ustajlu, Shamlu, Takkelu, Varsaq, Rumlu, Zul Qadr, Afshar, and Qajar. These tribes formed the Qizilbash confederation. He led these forces against the old enemy of his family, the *Shirvanshah*, and by the end of 1500 had killed Farrukhyasar and subjugated the rich province he had ruled. The Safavid order had become a principality.

In 1501, Ismail's forces occupied Tabriz, the Aqquyunlu capital and the most important commercial center of western Iran. Ismail then defeated a series of Aqquyunlu princes, most importantly Sultan Murad, near Hamadan on June 20, 1503. The urban centers of southern and western Iran—Isfahan, Shiraz, Yazd, and Kirman—accepted Safavid rule. The Aqquyunlu held Baghdad until 1508 but ceased to be a major political factor.

Following the victory at Hamadan, the Safavids conquered the Caspian littoral (Mazandaran and Gurgan) in 1504, occupied the Aqquyunlu

IMAGE 4.1
The battle between Shah Ismail I and Muhammad Shaybani Khan in 1510: folio from the *Kebir Musavver Silsilename*. Murals in Shah Abbas II's Chihil Sutun palace (1642) also depict this battle. According to Safavid accounts, after killing Shaybani Khan, Ismail had the skin removed from the skull and gilded it to use as a wine goblet.

heartland of Diyar Bakr between 1505 and 1507, took Baghdad in 1508, and finally, in 1510, occupied Khurasan. There, Shah Ismail encountered two rivals, the incumbent Timurids and the insurgent Uzbeks. The consequences of collective sovereignty and the appanage system had shrunk Timurid control to Khurasan and Mawaralnahr (Mawara al-Nahr, meaning "the land between the two rivers," the Amu-Darya and Syr-Darya), with major centers at Herat and Samarqand. The Timurids faced increasing pressure from the Uzbeks in the north. The Uzbeks, Turkic nomads ruled by descendants of Chingiz Khan through his son Jochi and grandson Shayban, had migrated southwest from their homeland between the Ural Mountains and the Irtysh River in the second quarter of the fifteenth century and controlled the north bank of the Syr-Darya by 1450. In 1490, one of the Uzbek princes, Muhammad Shaybani Khan, began the conquests that made the dynasty a significant power. Between that year and 1507, Shaybani Khan took Tashkent, Khwarazam, Balkh, and Herat, effectively ending Timuri rule in central Asia. His last Timuri opponent was the intrepid Zahir al-Din Muhammad Babur, who later carried Timuri sovereignty to the Indian subcontinent.

In 1509, Uzbek forces raided Kirman, which was Safavid territory. Shah Ismail sent two embassies to Shaybani Khan to dissuade him from expansion westward; Shaybani Khan responded by demanding that Ismail accept Uzbek (Chingiz Khanid) suzerainty and return to the spiritual vocation of a Sufi. Ismail then led Safavid forces into Khurasan, met Shaybani Khan's forces at Marv, and defeated them decisively on December 2, 1510. In 1511, Safavid forces assisted Babur in retaking Samarqand and Bukhara from the Uzbeks. When the Safavids then withdrew, the Uzbeks drove Babur off. Ismail sent another army to Babur's assistance, but dissension among the Safavid commanders led to a rout when the allies met the Uzbek forces at Ghujduvan. Though Ismail later drove the Uzbeks out of Khurasan, which they occupied after the battle, Ghujduvan ended expansion of the Safavid Empire.

The strength of the Safavid following among the Turkmen of Anatolia made a clash with the Ottomans inevitable. The Ottomans had begun efforts to suppress Qizilbash sympathizers from their Anatolian provinces in 1501, but the cautious Bayazid II avoided open hostilities with Ismail. This passive policy was the immediate cause of Selim I's revolt against his father. There were widespread disorders among the Anatolian Turkmen during the succession war, and many fled to Safavid territory. As soon as Selim I took the throne, he began the thorough suppression of the Qizilbash in Ottoman Anatolia. He then invaded Safavid Azerbaijan. Ismail offered battle at Chaldiran, northeast of Lake Van, on August 23, 1514. The Ottoman tactic of *tabur jangi* defeated the Safavid cavalry. The Safavids suffered extremely heavy casualties. The Ottomans occupied Tabriz, but the limited campaign radius of the Ottoman army prevented them from holding it.

The defeat at Chaldiran ended the first phase of Safavid history. Geographically, the Safavids lost only the province of Diyar Bakr, but the momentum of expansion was gone. Ismail, who had been a charismatic, aggressive leader, became passive. He never led his troops in battle again. Of the last ten years of his reign, there is little to report.

The establishment phase of the Safavid Empire ended with a Qizilbash confederation ruling Azerbaijan, Iraq, western Iran, and Khurasan. It confronted the Ottomans in the west and Uzbeks in the east and was committed to Shii Islam as the religion of the general population. With the exception of the loss of Iraq to the Ottomans in 1534, this description remained accurate until 1588.

Qizilbash Confederation, 1514–1580

Ismail's passivity transferred real authority to the leaders of the Qizilbash tribes and the leading civilian officials. For most of the remainder of Ismail's reign, a Tajik vizier, Mirza Shah Husayn Isfahani, dominated the administration. His supremacy eventually led to his assassination in 1523. Most of the Qizilbash chiefs were also provincial governors and resided in the provincial capitals rather than at the court, reflecting the comparative unimportance of the center. The governors of the most important provinces acted as the guardians of Ismail's five sons. Tahmasp Mirza, the eldest, was titular governor of Khurasan, under the tutelage of Amir Khan Mowsillu at Herat; the Mowsillu *uymaq* (*uymaq* was the standard term for tribe) thus dominated the province of Khurasan. Ismail died of natural causes on May 23, 1524, aged only thirty-seven despite his twenty-three years of rule.

Tahmasp, aged ten, ascended the throne, apparently without dispute. Historians have described the first decade of Tahmasp's reign as a Qizilbash interregnum, since the Qizilbash chiefs clearly controlled the empire. Internal stresses always took priority over external dangers, and the Ottoman threat always came before the Uzbek threat. The leaders of two Qizilbash tribes, Div Sultan Rumlu and Kopek Sultan Ustajlu, established themselves as coregents at the shah's enthronement. Shah Ismail's last *vakil* (chief officer) had been an Ustajlu, so the new arrangement meant a loss in influence for that tribe. Div Sultan's efforts to eliminate the Ustajlu from power entirely dominated the first two years of Tahmasp's reign. By 1526, the Ustajlu had fled to Gilan, and Juheh Sultan Takkalu had joined Div Sultan Rumlu as regent. The instability at court interfered with the defense of Khurasan against the Uzbeks.

Between 1524 and 1540, Ubayd Khan Uzbek invaded Khurasan five times. Shah Tahmasp "led" four campaigns to drive the Uzbeks from the province, the Ottomans conquered Iraq and temporarily occupied Azerbaijan, and the dominant *uymaq* changed four times in that period. Considering the combination of internal weakness and external dangers, it is remarkable that the Safavid polity survived at all. When Tahmasp faced the Ottoman invasion of Iraq, he had only 7,000 troops, not all of them reliable, to face the victor of Mohacs. Only the limited campaign radius of the Ottoman army prevented them from holding Tabriz. The Uzbeks had a comparable limitation.

The Uzbek principalities—there were separate kingdoms in Mawaralnahr and Khwarazam—were appanage states in the extreme. Separate dynasties, both descended from Shayban, the son of Jochi, ruled the two kingdoms. Within the principality of Mawaralnahr, four different lines ruled the main appanages of Bukhara, Samarqand, Balkh, Miyankal, and Tashkent. The senior male member of the family had only limited authority as grand khan. The principal opponent of Shah Tahmasp, Ubayd Khan, did not become grand khan until 1533 and, even in that position, had only limited success in swaying the other Uzbek leaders to his agenda. Only his own appanage family, the Shah Budaqids of Bukhara, showed a consistent interest in the acquisition of Khurasan. He was able to persuade the rest of the Uzbek princes to join him in a united effort against the Safavids only in 1524 and 1528.

Tahmasp defeated the Uzbeks decisively at Jam on September 24, 1528. The defeat made the other Uzbek clans unwilling to support him against the Safavids. It was thus responsible for the hardening of the frontier between Safavid Khurasan and Uzbek Mawaralnahr. The Safavids had won at Jam using firearms. Though far more obscure than the major battles of the early gunpowder era, like Chaldiran, Mohacs, and Padua, Jam ranks among them. The gunpowder forces that won the battle, however, did not alter the internal political balance of the Safavid Empire, and the victory over the Uzbeks did not give the Safavids the confidence to challenge the Ottomans in the field.

The Ottomans invaded three times in Tahmasp's reign, in 1534, 1548–1549, and 1553–1554. Each time, Tahmasp refused battle, ceded territory, and survived. Tabriz fell in all three invasions; Ottoman forces advanced as far east as the old Mongol capital of Sultaniyyah, two hundred miles southeast of Tabriz, but could not hold the territory or subdue the Safavids. Sulayman sought to put Tahmasp's brothers Sam Mirza, in 1533, and Alqas Mirza, in 1548, on the Safavid throne. The Ottomans might then have governed the Safavid Empire indirectly, as they did the Crimean khanate, another nomad-dominated principality, but neither effort succeeded.

The Ottoman invasion of Iraq in 1533–1534 caused the greatest crisis of Tahmasp's time. Its events are difficult to reconstruct. Sometime on the march westward, a Shamlu agent attempted to poison the shah. Apparently, the Shamlu and Takkalu *uymaq*s had aligned against the Ustajlu and the shah; Sam Mirza, who was governor of Herat with Husayn Khan Shamlu as his guardian, was the rebels' candidate for the throne. The Takkalu-Shamlu party sought Ottoman support. Sam Mirza sent his submission to Sulayman during the Ottoman ruler's march west, and Sulayman recognized him as the ruler of Iran west of Azerbaijan. This situation caused panic at Tahmasp's court, but Sam Mirza did not leave Herat until after the Ottomans had withdrawn, at which point he submitted to his brother immediately. After weathering this storm, Tahmasp was able to manipulate the *uymaq*s rather than being manipulated by them.

The city of Herat had been the central objective of the struggle between the Safavids and the Uzbeks; the city changed hands several times. Tahmasp regained it from the Uzbeks in 1537 and briefly conquered the city and province of Qandahar from the Timurids the same year. Qandahar controlled an important overland trade route between the Iranian plateau and the Indo-Gangetic plain; it became a point of contention between the Safavids and the Mughals (Timurids), as Herat was between the Safavids and the Uzbeks. In 1543, Timurid prince Humayun came to Tahmasp's court, a refugee from the Suri Afghans and his brother Mirza Kamran. Tahmasp made Humayun's conversion to Shiism a prerequisite for his assistance; the Timurid prince acquiesced reluctantly. In 1545, Tahmasp provided Humayun with a small army to regain his empire from Mirza Kamran, requiring in return that Humayun relinquish Qandahar to him. Humayun conquered Qandahar and began the reestablishment of what became the Mughal Empire. He duly transferred Qandahar to Safavid sovereignty but took it back when the Safavid governor died. Tahmasp led an expedition to Qandahar in 1558 and reconquered it.

Even during the second half of his reign, Tahmasp had little political leverage compared to his Ottoman contemporaries. Despite his limited freedom of action, however, he laid the foundation for Abbas I's transformation of the Safavid polity. In a series of raids into the Caucasus, Tahmasp took large numbers of Georgian, Armenian, and Circassian prisoners, who became military slaves. Though the first unit consisting of military slaves did not exist until the reign of Abbas I, most of its members actually entered Safavid service in Tahmasp's time. Tahmasp thus created the nucleus of the force that changed the political balance of the empire in his grandson's time. Tahmasp also moved the capital of the empire from Tabriz, the principal city of western Iran since Mongol times but impossible to defend from the Ottomans, southwest to Qazvin.

For a monarch who reigned more than fifty years, Tahmasp leaves a remarkably vague impression. He must be judged by his most positive accomplishment, the establishment of his dynasty. He may not have been a great monarch, but had he been a lesser one, the Safavid Empire might well have split into two separate principalities (not uncommon in tribal confederations with weak rulers and strong tribal chiefs) or been destroyed entirely. Circumstances made Tahmasp a passive figure; Chaldiran had taught the dangers of activity.

Although Tahmasp had nine sons, only two, Ismail and Haydar, became candidates for the throne when he died. Neither played an active role in the contest; Ismail had been a prisoner since 1556, and Haydar was young and inexperienced. Each had the backing of a coalition of Qizilbash tribes and other elements at court. Ismail's supporters triumphed without much difficulty.

Ismail reigned for fourteen months before his death, either by poison or from an overdose of opium. His reign was as violent as it was brief. He ordered the execution of all of his brothers (Muhammad Khudabandah, his older brother, who had not been a contender for the throne because he was nearly blind, survived only because of Ismail's own death) and all but three of his nephews and male cousins, as well as numerous Qizilbash chieftains. Often taken as an indication of insanity, these executions may well have been part of an effort to make the empire more stable by eliminating the elements that had restricted Tahmasp's power. Though seen as a mad tyrant, had he lived, Ismail might have become the empire builder his nephew Abbas later became. His death began a decade of disorder.

Muhammad Khudabandah and his three sons, Hamza Mirza, Abbas Mirza, and Abu Talib Mirza, were the only Safavid princes to survive Ismail's reign. The Qizilbash chiefs chose Muhammad Khudabandah as shah. His reign had four phases: the dominance of his chief wife, Mahd-i Ulya, from his enthronement to her murder in 1579; the dominance of the vizier Mirza Salman and Hamza Mirza until the vizier's assassination in 1583; the supremacy of Hamza Mirza alone until his assassination in 1586; and the final denouement until the accession of Shah Abbas in 1588. At his enthronement, no one expected Khudabandah to govern and he did not disappoint. At first, his sister, Pari Khan Khanum, who had considerable support among the Qizilbash and had orchestrated the enthronement of Ismail, and a Circassian uncle in an important court office held the strongest positions at court. Mirza Salman, who had been Ismail II's vizier and feared his master's sister, collaborated with Mahd-i Ulya to eliminate Pari Khan Khanum, but Mahd-i Ulya took effective power, issuing royal commands and appointing officers. She apparently sought to establish a centralized regime and ensure the accession of her son Hamza Mirza. The Ottomans exploited the new Safavid weakness by invading Azerbaijan and Georgia in 1578. Hamza Mirza and Mirza Salman took the field the next year and regained much of the lost territory. The Qizilbash chiefs found Mahd-i Ulya's hostile dominance intolerable and had her strangled.

Mahd-i Ulya's son Hamza Mirza and protégé Mirza Salman inherited her position and agenda. The Ottoman threat, together with an Uzbek invasion of Khurasan, did not alter the behavior of the Qizilbash. The empire was effectively partitioned. The Turkmen and Takkalu controlled Qazvin; an Ustajlu-Shamlu coalition governed Khurasan with the young Abbas Mirza as titular governor. The Khurasani coalition revolted in 1581, seeking to substitute Abbas for his father. Mirza Salman and Hamza Mirza led the royal army to Khurasan the next year. The Ustajlu leader, Murshid Quli Khan, surrendered to Hamza Mirza, and the royal forces besieged the Shamlus in Herat. The Qizilbash chiefs resented the authority of the Tajik vizier, and Mirza Salman accused them of dereliction of duty in prosecuting the siege. The Qizilbash demanded the dismissal of the vizier and the shah, and Hamza Mirza saw no choice but to surrender Mirza Salman to them. He was executed shortly afterwards. The young Hamza Mirza was eventually murdered while campaigning against the Ottomans in December 1586. The empire now had no effective leadership.

After Hamza Mirza's death, the Qizilbash broke into eastern and western factions. Abbas became the tool of Murshid Quli Khan Ustajlu in Khurasan; the Iraqi faction supported his brother Abu Talib Mirza, expecting to partition the Safavid realm between them. But Abd Allah Khan Uzbek, the greatest of the Shaybani rulers, invaded Khurasan and drove Murshid Quli Khan west with Abbas. Once back at Qazvin, Murshid Quli Khan created a consensus of the leading Qizilbash officers for the enthronement of his protégé. Abbas took the throne on October 1, 1588.

Imperial Transformation:
The Reign of Shah Abbas I, 1588–1629

When he placed his young ward on the throne, Murshid Quli Khan Ustajlu expected to govern the empire as *vakil*. Abbas I, at sixteen, hardly

IMAGE 4.2
Portrait of Shah Abbas I.
Bishn Das, one Jahangir's
finest court artists,
accompanied a Mughal
embassy to the court of
Shah Abbas I. Upon
returning home, Jahangir
awarded him an elephant by
appreciation for the
naturalistic portraits of
Abbas that no doubt aided
Jahangir in taking the
measure of his rival.

seemed likely to succeed in taking control of the empire from the Qizil-bash chieftains. Murshid Quli Khan rearranged the offices of the court and provincial governorships, without making major changes. The strength of his position inevitably provoked a challenge from the other Qizilbash chiefs. Abbas sought to rally support for himself as shah, not as the tool of the Ustajlu or any other tribe. He employed the concept of *shahisivani* (literally, "love for the shah"). Intended to recall the loyalties of individual Qizilbash to the shah rather than to their individual *uymaqs*, *shahisivani* became one of Abbas's mechanisms for strengthening his position.

Abbas had Murshid Quli Khan executed on July 23, 1589, less than nine months after taking the throne. This action marked the beginning of Abbas's actual authority. In order to undertake a fundamental transformation of the empire, he had to secure his frontiers and could do so only by making concessions. He opened negotiations with the Ottomans, and on March 21, 1590, the Safavid representatives signed a peace treaty surrendering all of Azerbaijan and Iraq, as well as parts of Shirvan, Daghistan, and Kurdistan. There was no treaty with the Uzbeks, but after an abortive expedition in 1591, Abbas made no effort to retake Mashhad and Herat until 1598. In 1594, the Safavid governor of Qandahar transferred both his loyalty and the city to the Mughals. Abbas did not respond. He thus obtained the breathing space necessary to transform the Safavid polity.

Abbas's program had three elements: two fiscal and administrative and one military. In order to obtain the income necessary, he established direct Safavid rule over the silk-producing regions of Gilan and Mazandaran, south of the Caspian and Qarabagh and Shirvan, further west. These operations lasted from 1593 to 1607. Abbas thus ensured that most of the profits from the empire's most valuable export went into the central treasury. He also began a significant change in provincial administration, the transfer of provinces from *mamalik* (provincial) to *khass* (central government) administration. I discuss these concepts in depth in the sections on military organization and provincial administration. Briefly, Qizilbash chiefs governed *mamalik* provinces and distributed their revenues to their *uymaq*s, with little or none going to the central government. *Khass* provinces paid their taxes into the central treasury. The *mamalik* structure reflected the practice in tribal confederations. The transfer of provinces from *mamalik* to *khass* shifted the balance of power from the Qizilbash to the ruler. In some cases, the transfer amounted to the conquest of provinces from the Qizilbash.

With this new revenue, Abbas paid for the construction of a new imperial capital at Isfahan, which began in 1597–1598, and for his military reforms. He expanded the infantry, cavalry, and artillery units that his grandfather had created, with soldiers primarily of slave origin, which could defeat any tribal force just as the Safavid army had defeated the Uzbeks at Jam. Abbas also transferred the capital to Isfahan, far from the Ottoman frontier. His military reforms coincided with periods of weakness in the Ottoman Empire and the Uzbek principalities. The Jalali uprisings and the Long War distracted the Ottomans. The death of Abdullah Khan in 1598 ended Uzbek unity, opening the way for the Safavids. Abbas led his army from Isfahan in the spring, took Mashhad on July 29, and defeated the Uzbeks outside Herat on August 5.

In 1603, the Ottoman garrison abandoned the fortress of Nihavand in Iraq, and a Kurdish chieftain revolted against the Ottomans. These events and the Jalali disorders further west left the eastern Ottoman Empire in a shambles. Exploiting this weakness, Abbas occupied Tabriz in 1603 and

Erivan, in eastern Anatolia, in 1604. In 1605, the Safavid army crushed an Ottoman army sent to Sufiyan near Tabriz. This victory marked the transformation of the Safavid Empire into a bureaucratic polity with a gunpowder army. In 1622, Abbas conquered Qandahar from the Mughals and, with the help of the British East India Company, took Hormuz from the Portuguese. He later established a new port, Bandar Abbas, on the mainland opposite Hormuz. It became the major outlet for exports, especially silk. After a pause, Abbas initiated hostilities against the Ottomans again in 1623, retaking Iraq and a considerable part of Kurdistan. The Safavids repulsed an Ottoman siege of Baghdad the next year. Abbas's military achievements matched the magnificence that his new imperial capital at Isfahan symbolized and articulated.

Abbas took drastic measures against his own family to secure his position. His eldest son, Muhammad Baqir Mirza, known as Safi, may or may not have been guilty of the plot for which his father executed him in 1615. Two other sons were blinded in 1621 and 1626 because he interpreted their efforts to secure succession as disloyalty to him. These steps brought stability to the dynasty. Abbas imitated the Ottoman practice of confining princes to the palace, making all future succession disputes a matter of court politics. Before his death on January 19, 1629, Abbas had nominated his grandson Sam Mirza, the eldest surviving Safavid prince who had not been blinded, to succeed him. The young man took the throne on February 17, using the name of his father, Safi.

Inertia and Devolution, 1629–1722

The French jeweler Jean Chardin, who spent eight years in Iran during the reigns of Abbas II and Sulayman, wrote that the prosperity of Iran had ended when Abbas I died. Western historians have generally accepted Chardin's view. Andrew Newman interprets the reigns of Safi (1629–1642), Abbas II (1642–1666), Sulayman (1666–1694), and Sultan Husayn (1694–1722) differently. He argues that the Safavid project, as he calls it, remained successful throughout this period and that the sudden fall of the empire to the Ghalzay Afghans indicated not the complete degeneration of the regime but a narrow military failure. The character of the rulers certainly changed. With the exception of Abbas II in the earlier part of his reign, the later Safavid rulers generally remained in the palace and divided their time between pleasure and piety. But, as mentioned above, the character of the monarch does not necessarily indicate the strength of the regime. As in the Ottoman Empire, strong grand viziers emerged to fill the gap left by the withdrawal of the monarchs. The Qizilbash grew less and less influential in politics; competition between palace officials, bureaucrats, and the ulama became a central feature. No healthy government, however, would sink into the military impotence that led to the fall of the Safavids.

From a military perspective, the revived conflict with the Ottomans dominated Safi's reign. Murad IV renewed hostilities against the Safavids in 1629; the Ottoman army defeated the Safavids in the field near Hamadan in November 1630 but then withdrew. After four years without a major expedition on either side, the Ottomans took Erivan and plundered Tabriz in 1635. Safi recaptured Erivan, but in 1638 the Ottomans took Baghdad. The next year Safi relinquished the Safavid claim to Iraq in the treaty of Qasr-i Shirin, signed on May 17, 1639. The treaty ended hostilities between the Safavids and the Ottomans. In the east Safi lost Qandahar in 1638, though not to a Mughal siege. There was also a series of minor Uzbek incursions, none of which had any major effect, and the Portuguese raided the town of Qishm on the island of that name in the Persian Gulf.

Politically, Shah Safi had some significant successes. He gradually replaced the close associates of Abbas who had overseen his accession with his own loyalists. He and his supporters overcame succession challenges from an uncle and a nephew after his enthronement. The changes in court offices took three years. In 1633–1634, Safi eliminated the most powerful man in the kingdom after himself, Imam Quli Khan. Imam Quli, the son of Abbas's leading officer, Allahverdi Khan, was the effective ruler of southern Iran as the governor of Fars. Safi had him and his entire family executed. The principal officers of Safi's time illustrate the change in Safavid politics wrought by his grandfather. Only one was a Qizilbash tribal leader, two were Georgians (one of whom commanded the imperial slave forces and the imperial musketeers), and one was a Turkmen not affiliated with a major tribe. He prevented further challenges to his position from within the dynasty by ordering the execution of all Safavids other than his own children. They also faced, and suppressed, a series of *ghuluww* uprisings early in the reign. Safi continued Abbas's alliance with the Shii legal specialists against the continual rumblings of *ghuluww*.

Safi's reign did show evidence of significant fiscal strain. His vizier, Saru Taqi, sought to enforce fiscal discipline. His rigor cost the empire

Qandahar. Summoned to court over a fiscal dispute, the governor, Ali Mardan Khan, shifted his allegiance to the Mughals. Safi and Saru Taqi's program also included further transfers of provincial revenue from the Qizilbash tribes to the central treasury and imposition of an array of new taxes. Safi ended Abbas's monopoly on silk exports at the beginning of his reign, and the treasury apparently received significantly less revenue from silk as a result, but the picture is far from clear.

Safi died unexpectedly on May 12, 1642, leaving a sound if diminished empire. His nine-year-old son, Sultan Muhammad Mirza, took the throne on May 15 as Abbas II, with Saru Taqi still in control. The vizier's dominance continued until 1645, when Qizilbash officers successfully conspired to have him assassinated, with Abbas's consent. The Qizilbash success in eliminating Saru Taqi was their last; the Qizilbash leadership was no longer at the center of power. No single officer dominated the administration, and the young shah took a major role in government. Abbas II maintained the strength of the Safavid armed forces and continued the transfer of provinces from *mamalik* to *khass* jurisdiction. Previously, only the interior provinces of the empire had been shifted, but Khurasan and Azerbaijan came under crown control in Abbas II's reign. During his rule the Safavids achieved their last significant military success, the reconquest of Qandahar from the Mughals in 1649. Perhaps the enormous expense of this expedition and the lack of any comparable objective, rather than a lack of military energy, prevented any further expansion in this period. The fundamental economic weakness of the Safavid regime, demonstrated by its inability to halt the steady outflow of specie, remained. Newman considers this problem one of the two major challenges Abbas II faced; the other was continuing *ghuluww*-inspired unrest, or rather unrest among the urban lower classes suffering from "the combined effects of specie outflow, currency devaluations and price inflation"[5] and inspired by *ghuluww*. Despite these challenges, there is little ground for asserting that the Safavid enterprise had become substantially weaker under Safi and Abbas II. Abbas showed signs of a debilitating illness in 1662 but remained active until his death in October 1666.

The reigns of the last two Safavids continued the trends that existed under Safi and Abbas II. Abbas's eldest son, also named Safi, took the throne as Safi II and was then reenthroned as Shah Sulayman on November 1, 1666. The young prince panicked when he was taken out of the harem, fearing that he was to be killed or blinded. He showed few positive characteristics after that incident. He rarely attended meetings of the council of state, communicating with state officials through his eunuchs. The nexus of power moved entirely inside the palace. The Western writers who describe him depict an alcoholic and libertine who alternated between parsimony and profligacy. Without royal supervision, the Safavid army and civil administration degenerated. There was no check on official corruption. The lack of significant external threats and prior elimination of internal factionalism allowed the reign to pass without serious disruption, and the borders remained peaceful. Fiscal weakness, however, continued, exacerbated by the forces of nature. The empire suffered a series of poor harvests in the 1660s and 1670s, which led to repeated regional famines. Several parts of the empire also suffered serious outbreaks of plague from 1680 onward. The tax shortfalls that these events inevitably caused put severe stress on the Safavid treasury. The empire also suffered external pressure from the Uzbeks, Kalmyks, and Cossacks on its northern borders.

In response, Sulayman and his chief minister, Shaykh Ali Khan (a Sunni Kurd), used various means to increase income and reduce expenditures, including reduction of military expenditures, a tax on silver exports, aggressive collection of taxes and fines in arrears, and attempts to increase income from the sale of silk to the Dutch East India Company, which purchased the material from the government instead of private suppliers. None of these measures made a significant difference. The model of the sericultural empire could not last. Too much of the wealth that flowed into Iran from Europe in return for silk continued eastward to India and the Dutch East Indies in return for spices, drugs, cotton textiles, and other goods to sustain wealth. The English East India Company (EIC) and the Dutch East India Company (VOC) had alternative sources of silk in Bengal and China. Sulayman's most significant action was the appointment of Muhammad Baqir Majlisi as the empire's chief religious official. Majlisi sought to transform Safavid society into an entirely Shii environment and called for the forced conversion of all non-Shiis. There is little information about the enforcement of this policy on the ground. But in Sulayman's time, the military and financial weakness did not undercut the legitimacy or resilience of the regime. Sulayman died on July 29, 1694.

Sulayman's courtiers chose his older son, Sultan Husayn, as his successor. He took the throne using that name on August 6, 1694. Enormously pious, he was nicknamed Mulla Husayn. His piety distracted him from government, though it did not prevent him from drinking. Majlisi remained in office and continued his policy. The shah went on massive pilgrimages, in 1706 traveling to Qum and Mashhad with a retinue of 60,000. The appearance of new military threats in the east did not cause any significant reaction. When Baluchi tribesmen revolted in 1698–1699, raiding Yazd and Kirman and almost reaching Bandar Abbas, the Safavid court had no army to send against them. Sultan Husayn called upon Gurgin Khan, also known as Giorgi XI, a Georgian prince, to assemble an army. Since Abbas I had established Safavid sovereignty in Georgia, the Safavids had ruled the region through a prince, chosen from one of the two royal houses. Gurgin Khan had recently been dismissed as governor because he had become too powerful; apparently his power was excessive because the Safavids had so little of their own. Appointed governor of Kirman, Gurgin Khan defeated the Baluchis and retained that office. In 1704, when the Baluchi menace reappeared in Qandahar province, Sultan Husayn appointed Gurgin Khan there, and he had similar success. The Georgian's policies in Qandahar, possibly oppression of the Sunni Afghans, provoked resistance among the Ghalzay Afghans, the dominant tribal group in the area, under their leader Mir Uvays. Gurgin Khan defeated the uprising without difficulty and sent Mir Uvays to Isfahan as a prisoner. But the Afghan leader proved a more dangerous foe in the capital than in the field, for he won the favor of Shah Sultan Husayn and was allowed to return to Qandahar.

In 1709, Mir Uvays staged a coup in Qandahar and killed Gurgin Khan. An anti-Georgian faction at court delayed a punitive expedition for eighteen months; then two separate expeditions failed to dislodge the Ghalzays. Mir Uvays ruled Qandahar until his death in 1715. His brother Mir Abd al-Aziz succeeded him and wanted to come to terms with the Safavids, but he was overthrown by his nephew Mahmud, who had greater ambitions. The Abdali Afghans, a rival group located primarily in Khurasan, gave Mahmud his chance. Like the Ghalzays, they expelled the Safavid authorities and defeated a series of punitive expeditions. Sultan Husayn's advisers, concerned about events in the east, had him move his court from Isfahan to Qazvin in 1717. But the shah remained in Qazvin for three years without mounting a single expedition against either the Abdalis or Ghalzays. Finally, Mahmud led the Ghalzays into the field, not against the impotent Safavids but against his Abdali rivals as putative servants of the shah. When Mahmud defeated the Abdalis, Sultan Husayn rewarded him with the title Husayn Quli Khan and recognized him as governor of Qandahar.

A year later, Mahmud attacked Kirman. Local Zoroastrians, disaffected by persecution, opened the gates of the city for Ghalzays. Mahmud remained in Kirman for nine months, appropriating food and supplies from the population, before returning to Qandahar. In 1721, he again led his army westward and took Kirman, but the city's citadel had been strengthened, and the Ghalzays had no siege equipment. Mahmud eventually accepted a bribe from the garrison to abandon the siege, but he led his army westwards toward Isfahan. Mahmud's approach caused panic. Shah Sultan Husayn chose to offer battle outside the city rather than prepare for a siege. The two armies met at Gulnabad, outside Isfahan, on March 7, 1722. Although Safavid forces greatly outnumbered the ragtag Afghan army, their lack of discipline and coordination led to an overwhelming Afghan victory. The Safavids could not drive the Afghans away; the Afghans could not breach the city walls. Thus began the siege of Isfahan.

The ordeal lasted for seven months. Starvation and cannibalism became commonplace; 80,000 people died. Mahmud crushed several relief expeditions. Shah Sultan Husayn sent his son Tahmasp out of the city to organize another effort, without result. Thousands perished trying to escape the city. On October 20, Shah Sultan Husayn Safavi surrendered his throne and royal insignia to Mahmud. He had to borrow a horse from Mahmud to ride out to surrender; the imperial stables had been emptied for food. The Safavid regime had ended. Power in Iran had reverted to the tribes.

Safavid prestige did not end, of course. Safavid pretenders did not disappear from the scene for fifty years. But it swiftly became clear that they would never be more than pretenders. The former shah was executed in 1726; Tahmasp became a puppet for Qizilbash chiefs, first Fath Ali Khan Qajar and then Nadir Khan Afshar. Nadir Khan drove the Ghalzays from Isfahan and enthroned Tahmasp there, but three years later he deposed him in favor of his infant son, Abbas. In 1736, Nadir Khan deposed the young boy and took the throne himself as Nadir Shah. He had the two deposed rulers and another Safavid prince executed in 1740.

SOVEREIGNTY, RELIGION, AND LAW

Safavid conceptions of sovereignty evolved over time and addressed multiple audiences, though the evolution was less complex and the number of audiences smaller than in the Ottoman Empire. Andrew Newman's conception of the Safavid polity as a project which used different narratives to appeal to different constituencies has considerable merit, though it does not of course apply exclusively to the Safavids. Turks and Tajiks were, of course, the most important of the constituencies, but, as explained above, these terms did not simply refer to ethnic groups. The Safavids also confronted religious diversity along several different axes. In addition to the divisions between Muslim and non-Muslim and between Sunni and Shii, the Safavids' environment included an assortment of mystical and esoteric Muslim beliefs, some with messianic overtones and some without. The Safavids also sought to articulate their sovereignty to outsiders, not only their Ottoman, Uzbek, and Mughal neighbors but also Europeans. The Safavid efforts to address all of these audiences succeeded for more than two centuries, but not easily or evenly.

In the most recent significant work on Safavid political ideas, Kathryn Babayan discusses the ideology of the Safavid movement within the general category of *ghuluww*. In Babayan's conception, *ghuluww* denotes a world view of opposition, political and religious, drawing upon an intellectual and spiritual legacy far older than Islam. *Ghuluww* was the continuation of such dissents against dominant faiths and the establishments which supported them as Manicheanism and Gnosticism. These traditions emphasized a cyclic conception of time, not in the sense of endless repetition but of successive cycles of prophecy and the incarnation of God or pure spirit in humanity. They denied a strict separation between creator and created. In Babayan's words, *ghuluww* "was a repository of different traditions that with the cultural project of Islam came to be marginalized and cast as heretical."[6] Shah Ismail's poetry, written in Turkish under the pseudonym Khatai, places him in the *ghuluww* tradition: "I am Very God, Very God, Very God! / Come now, O blind man who has lost the path, behold the Truth!"[7] The tradition of *ghuluww* provided the background for the widespread messianic speculation toward the end of the first *hijri* millenium; it also interlocked with the religious traditions of central Asian origin. Although the Turkmen had been Muslims for centuries and lived far from the central Asian steppes, many of the traditions of the steppe remained alive. Ismail presented his authority in the idiom of the Turkmen. Sufism among the Turkmen had mimicked the shamanism of their central Asian past, in which charismatic individuals claimed direct personal connections with the divine. Ismail was a charismatic young man of striking physical appearance; his poetry articulated that connection.

Safavid *ghuluww* encompassed and expressed the lasting tradition of nomad dissent against settled rule. From a social and political perspective, and perhaps from ideological one as well, the young Ismail Safavi had much the same agenda as had Baba Ishaq in Anatolia in the thirteenth century: the establishment of a social and religious order in which Turkmen could migrate, maraud, and pursue their own religious practices without concern for a settled administration, formal taxation, or Shari strictures. Ismail's messianism expressed and channeled the resentment of the Turkmen of eastern Anatolia and western Iran against the agrarian/bureaucratic/Shari policies of the Ottomans and of the Aqquyunlu under Qazi Isa. offered his leadership to the Turkmen as an alternative to Aqquyunlu, and Ottoman, oppression. Ismail's was a revolutionary messianism, as opposed to the imperial messianism of the contemporary Ottomans.

Ismail promised to address two sets of grievances, those of the Turkmen against the Aqquyunlu ruling house and those of the house of Ali— by extension all true Muslims—against the established order. At least some Safavid adherents considered Ismail the harbinger of the coming of the Hidden Twelfth Imam, a connection to Twelver Shiism, or, alternatively, as the return of Abu Muslim, the military leader of the Abbasid movement which overthrew the Umayyad dynasty in the eighth century. Abu Muslim had become a central figure in *ghuluww* lore. Ismail's poetry also emphasized his descent from Ali and Fatimah, as well as from Safi, Junayd, and Haydar. His alleged ancestry lent credence to his claims and contributed to his charisma. Some of his followers believed that Ismail projected a charismatic authority that nullified the Shariah. His Aqquyunlu descent also influenced them. His enmity toward the other members of the Aqquyunlu ruling family knew no bounds. Taking revenge for his father and brother, he personally executed at least one Aqquyunlu prince and ordered the execution of all pregnant Aqquyunlu princesses. But by doing so, he made himself the only heir to the Aqquyunlu legacy. Shaybani Khan Uzbek mocked Ismail's descent from Aqquyunlu women; if it had been meaningless he would not have done so.

Ismail triumphed as the carrier of messianic expectations, but, according to all available evidence, he was neither God nor the messiah. To make his triumph the basis of an enduring polity required the transformation and elaboration of Safavid political doctrine. Ismail's appeal to the Turkmen brought him to Tabriz in 1501. Probably, success plunged Ismail and his advisors into wild uncertainty. They could not expect their new Tajik subjects to become Qizilbash. They could, however, expect them to accept Safavid rule, for the Shari ethos emphasized acceptance of authority in order to prevent anarchy. The decision to impose Twelver Shiism as the sovereign faith of what had become the Safavid principality did not facilitate gaining popular support, since Shiis were a distinct minority in Azerbaijan and the rest of the areas the Safavids conquered. It was, not, apparently, planned in advance, but it must have had an ideological purpose. The Safavids went beyond the positive promulgation of Shiism; they instituted the cursing of Abu Bakr, Umar, and Uthman, the three men who became caliph before Ali, and other early Muslims who had opposed Ali. Merely asserting the precedence of Ali over the three caliphs was not inherently sectarian. Anathematizing was and created a decisive difference between the Safavids and their neighbors. In the negotiations that produced the treaty of Amasya, for example, the Ottomans insisted on an end to the practice. Similarly, when the Uzbeks occupied Herat in 1507, they demanded an end to the cursing of the caliphs.

The sources do not disclose the rationale for the imposition of Twelver Shiism decision and historians do not agree on an explanation. The standard argument, that the Safavids imposed Twelver Shiism in order to create a sharp distinction between themselves and the Sunni Ottomans and Uzbeks and to establish a national identity is both teleological and anachronistic. Other historians have speculated that the Safavids had become sectarian Shiis in the course of their evolution from a quietist Sufi order to an extremist political movement, and that Ismail and his immediate advisors did not in fact accept the *ghuluww* of their order and were actually Twelver Shiis themselves. The proclamation of Shiism continued the revolutionary agenda of the Safavid movement, redressing the grievances of the family of the Prophet. Acceptance of the status quo might have meant a compromise offensive to the Qizilbash

The proclamation of Twelver Shii Islam created a dual religious policy: messianic extremist Sufism for the Turkmen, Shari Twelver Shiism for the settled population. This pattern did not persist. In the course of the sixteenth century, the Safavids discarded *ghuluww*.

Eventually, Shari authority, along with its correlate, settled bureaucratic government, triumphed. But in the beginning, it was the secondary component of a dual doctrine of kingship and a dual religious policy. Court practices followed the pattern of the Safavid order. Ismail required that his subjects and servants prostrate themselves before him. Many Muslims considered this practice contrary to the Shariah, but it was a fundamental part of Safavid Sufi practice, and not only in the Safavid order.

The defeats at Ghujduvan and Chaldiran ended the myth of Ismail as the messiah, but left the Safavids in control of most of the Iranian plateau. The Qizilbash disappointment must have been bitter, but not complete. They had hoped to escape the irksome strictures of settled administration and Shari religious leadership; they had done so. They had every hope of maintaining their dominance in a Safavid system despite the disappointing persistence of mundane reality. In this context, the Safavid leader still served as a source of spiritual guidance and confirmation of divine support, without necessarily interfering with the Qizilbash-dominated political and social order. This state of affairs persisted into the reign of Tahmasp.

The imposition of Shii Islam did not interfere significantly with the incorporation of the Persian notables, including the hitherto Sunni ulama, into the Safavid regime. The Safavids were not gentle; many Sunni ulama fled or were executed, but most of the prominent ulama of greater Iran accepted both Twelver Shiism and Safavid rule. The imposition of Shiism did not prevent the Safavids from taking over the machinery of the administration of Shari justice more or less intact. The old ulama elite came from families with both large landholdings and significant religious prestige, most often as *sayyids* (descendants of Muhammad, though not everyone who claimed the status was actually a descendant). They dominated most important posts in the religious hierarchy before the Safavid conquest and continued to do so. Most importantly, they controlled the posts of *sadr* (chief religious administrator, responsible for overseeing charitable endowments) and *qazi* (Shari judge). These offices belonged to a hereditary class. The change from Sunni to Shii altered their intellectual background and behavior remarkably little.

The need for experts in Shii theology and jurisprudence led to the establishment of a second class of ulama, with narrow expertise in Shii learning. Most came from outside Safavid territory, primarily from the Jabal Amil in contemporary south Lebanon or from Bahrain, and all, at first, had neither landed wealth nor hereditary association with official positions. They rarely became *qazis* or *sadrs*, but often held the post of *shaykh al-Islam*, in greater Iran the chief religious authority in a city or province, and *pish namaz* (prayer leader). Their status depended on their knowledge of Shii law and theology and the patronage of the regime, not on their descent or charisma. In the words of Jean Calmard, "their main function was to re-elaborate, teach and propagate the Imami doctrine to fit the new situation created by the existence of an officially Shii state."[8] They also played the major role in the propagation of Shii Islam among the general population. Rula Jurdi Abisaab's major study analyzes the role of the scholars from the Jabal Amil through the Safavid period. She contends that the Amili jurists, unlike other Shii ulama, "were prepared to transform Shiism from a religion of the community to that of the state, proposing significant modifications in political theory and becoming highly equipped to circumvent Ottoman and Uzbek propaganda and ideological expansion."[9] The Amilis became the opponents of, and eventually the victors over, *ghuluww* and the voice of the Safavids in the ideological struggle against the Ottomans and Uzbeks.

The official imposition of Shiism was neither uniform nor immediate. Sunnis did not disappear; there were some substantial communities even when the dynasty fell. The Sunni community of Qazvin remained influential until after Tahmasp made the city his capital. The Safavid authorities used several methods of enforcing Shiism, including substituting ritual cursing for conventional prayer, employing groups of public cursers (*tabarrayyan*; literally, "disavowers"; sing. *tabarray*), to anathematize the enemies of Ali and his family in public places, and, "extortion, intimidation and harassment."[10] These measures never provoked widespread popular opposition. They resemble the methods used in the process of confessionalization in Europe at the same time.

From the beginning, the Safavids demanded that other Sufi orders accept the ruling ideology and regarded alternate claimants of sovereignty in the *ghuluww* tradition as dangerous enemies. Two major orders with definite Sunni identities, the Qadiris and Naqshbandis, abandoned Safavid territory entirely. Other major orders, including the Zahabis, Nurbakhshis, and Nimatullahis, conformed outwardly to the Safavid requirements. The leaders of the Nimatullahis formed close family connections to the Safavids, including marriage alliances with the royal family; one served as a high official. They remained influential through the sixteenth centuries. The Nurbakhshis had a messianic ethos of their own, survived in Safavid territory only into the late 1540s. Other groups with *ghuluww* mindsets, including Nizari Ismailis (Sevener Shiis) faced persecution.

Tahmasp altered the Safavid ruling ideology fundamentally. Babayan uses two different versions of the life of Ismail by court historians to explain the change, one by Khwandamir completed just after Ismail's death in 1524, and one by Amini, completed some five years later. Both writers refer to a dream of Shaykh Safi's as a prophecy of the family's sovereignty, similar to Osman's dream in Ottoman ideology and other portents in the biographical myths of other conquerors. Khwandamir's version, in Babayan's words, "[locates] Isma'il's mandate of sovereignty . . . within the Irano-Islamic idiom of the messiah king" and employs Shii rhetoric associated with the return of the awaited imam."[11] Amini's version emphasizes Ismail's role as a *ghazi*, fighting both Sunnis and Christians, and the founder of Shii government. Amini uses the term *panah* (refuge) which the Ottoman sources apply to Sulayman in the later part of his reign, after the Ottoman ruler had abandoned his messianic pretensions. Tahmasp himself and his brother Sam Mirza both wrote about their father themselves, portraying him more as a world conqueror guided by the Imams than as a messianic figure. Shii divines depicted the Safavids as necessary prerequisites for the return of the Hidden Imam, establishers of the just world order necessary for his return. Tahmasp presents himself as a "pious Shii mystic king."[12] He looked to the Twelver Shiism imposed by his father for a new doctrine of kingship; he substituted conventional piety for *ghuluww* and charisma. He deferred to the ulama in religious and legal matters and attempted to suppress extremism. In 1533, he designated Shaykh Ali al-Karaki, the first of the prominent Amilis, as the deputy of the Hidden Imam and most authoritative interpreter of the Shariah. This action clearly aligned the regime with ulama and against *ghuluww*. The appointment also began the rise to prominence of the Shii religious specialists.

Following this lead, Abbas I substituted *shahisivani* (loving the king) for *sufigari* (Sufi conduct, meaning loyalty to the Safavid order and its leader) as the defining characteristic of his loyal followers. He ended prostration, eliminated the rituals associated with his function as the spiritual guide of the Qizilbash, and became the major patron of the Shari religious establishment. More importantly, Abbas began to emphasize, and patronize, specifically Shii rituals and popular celebrations. The observance of the martyrdoms of Husayn (during the first ten days of the month of Muharram) and Ali (the twenty-first of Ramadan) became enormous public festivals. Violent clashes between urban factions became a standard feature; Abbas apparently enjoyed watching them. The rituals included the symbolic recreation of the circumstances of Husayn's death at Karbala and Ali's at Najaf, ritual flagellation (punishment for collective guilt for permitting the deaths to occur), and other mass expressions of grief. The rituals became increasingly more dramatic in the later Safavid period. They became the principle nexus of popular piety. The Shii specialists apparently did not approve of this extravagantly emotional religiosity, but accepted it as a means of spreading and reinforcing Shii Islam. Abbas articulated his doctrine of sovereignty through construction and pilgrimage. In addition to the monumental capital at Isfahan, described below, he sponsored the elaborate reconstruction of the tomb of the Imam Riza at Mashhad, the only major Shii shrine safely in Safavid control. (The shrine of Riza's sister at Qum was also in undisputed territory, but did not become a major focus of patronage until after Abbas's reign.) He made pilgrimages to both Ardabil, the ancestral home of the Safavids, and to Mashhad. In 1601, he made his most famous pilgrimage, walking from Isfahan to Mashhad. This immense symbolic undertaking was an integral part of Abbas's imperial restoration of the dynasty. Abbas's demonstration of his devoted subordination to the Imam showed the new basis of Safavid sovereignty.

The Nuqtavis Sufi order became sufficiently popular as carriers of *ghuluww* expectations that Abbas suppressed them with extreme brutality. The Shii specialists, and ultimately the Safavid regime, sought to make Shari, Twelver Shii Islam the only form of Muslim religiosity in the Safavid Empire. In the early years, Ismail I ordered the repression of popular Sufi orders except, of course, for the Safavids themselves. The Shii specialists saw extremist Sufism, including that of the Qizilbash, as unacceptable. They could do little as long as the Qizilbash dominated the empire. As Qizilbash power declined, the Shii ulama began to redefine the spiritual landscape. Essentially, they defined popular Sufism, as well as Sunni Islam, as heretical. In the later decades of Safavid rule, they extended the ban to intellectual Sufism as well, though a school of Sufi philosophy flourished during the seventeenth century. The term Sufi, which had been a standard description of the Qizilbash and their leader, became a term of opprobrium. The Safavids thus became the upholders of Shii, Shari Islam just as the Ottomans were the champions of Shari Sunni Islam.

The Safavid commitment to Shii rigor as the basis of legitimacy had unpleasant consequences for non-Muslim populations, but not serious ones. The later shahs, notably Abbas II, sought to demonstrate their commitment to Islam by pressuring Jews, Christians, and Zoroastrians to convert.

They did so frequently at the beginning of their reigns, as proof of their piety. The prominent participation of Jews and Armenians in commerce made them targets of popular resentment. The most important instance of persecution of Jews, in 1657, reflected economic pressures. These episodes of persecution never lasted long, even though the ulama supported such efforts at conversion.

Muhammad Baqir Majlisi (1628–1699 or 1700) had enormous influence on both religious policy and popular religion in later Safavid times. He was Shah Sultan Husayn's tutor, became *shaykh al-Islam* of the empire in 1686 and remained in that office until he died. Majlisi sought to restore vigor to the Safavid regime through theological rigor. According to Ruli Jurdi Abisaab, his program had four main components: the promotion of Shii practices, patronage of Shii rituals such as the celebration of Ali's birthday, attacks on immoral behavior such as fornication, and forced conversion to Shiism, especially of non-Muslims. Majlisi "revived the power of the ulama and promulgated a 'missionary' Shi'ism of a public devotional character."[13] Majlisi apparently did not seek to suppress Sufism entirely, but to confine speculation and Sufi practices within acceptable limits, prohibiting music and dancing. It is unclear to what extent his policies actually led to forced conversion; it is possible that Majlisi's anti-Sunni policies provoked the Afghan uprising which led to the collapse of the regime.

The Shii specialists had won enormous prestige as the closest available link to the Hidden Imam, and became a focus of popular devotion. Shii jurists argued that pious Muslims had to follow the example of a living authority on the Shariah in ritual and legal issues. This view ensured the continuing importance of each generation of scholars. The leading *mujtahid*, not the shah, represented the Hidden Imam in the daily life of the believers. By the end of the seventeenth century, partially because of the support of Shah Sulayman and Shah Sultan-Husayn, the Shii specialists had secured dominance over the religious life of the country and a significant voice in the political life as well. They engaged in an unceasing rhetorical battle against Sufism.

The Safavid rulers after Abbas I depicted themselves as pious servants of Ali and the Imams. They claimed to fill the gap caused by the absence of the Twelfth Imam on the basis of their competence and Alid descent. This stance dovetailed with the traditional Irano-Islamic depiction of the ruler as the Shadow of God. The Shii doctors supported this position be-

cause they needed the support of the rulers against the clerical notables. Sulayman and Shah Sultan Husayn gave the Shii doctors their way, permitting them to complete the suppression of Sunnis and Sufis. Said
Arjomand describes the clash between the Safavid doctrine of kingship
and the views of the Shii doctors. The role of the Alid descent in the justification of sovereignty and the lack of emphasis on the enforcement of
the Shariah reveals the conflict. Despite the dominant influence of the
ulama in the late Safavid period, they remained dissatisfied with the
regime. This tension permeated Iranian politics from the late Safavid period through the Iranian Revolution.

Safavid dynastic theory has attracted little attention from historians.
Like the Ottomans, the Safavids clearly began with collective sovereignty.
In the early decades, brothers, sons, and nephews of the rulers served as
provincial governors. Even more than the Ottomans, they avoided its worst
consequences. Ismail and Tahmasp both faced challenges from, or in the
name of, brothers. After the defeat at Ghujduvan, Ismail's half-brother Sulayman mounted a short-lived challenge to his rule. In 1533, the Takkalu
and Shamlu rebels used Tahmap's brother Sam Mirza against him. In 1536,
another brother, Alqas Mirza, governor of Shirvan, rebelled against Tahmasp. He eventually took shelter with the Ottomans and participated in
their 1546–1548 campaign in Azerbaijan but gained no support. In 1556,
Tahmasp imprisoned the future Ismail II, presumably because he feared the
popularity Ismail had won as the successful governor of Shirvan.

Nine sons survived Tahmasp, but only two of them were serious candidates for the succession, Ismail and Haydar. Haydar, born in 1556 to a
Georgian wife of Tahmasp, had become a favorite of his father's. He received the support of a complex coalition including several Qizilbash tribes,
Georgian elements at court, and others. Ismail, born about 1533, had
been imprisoned for twenty years. He had distinguished himself as a
soldier while serving as governor of Shirvan in 1547. Neither prince
played an active role in the contest. At Ismail II's death, there was only
one adult male prince who could be enthroned, his half-blind older brother,
Muhammad Khudabandah. He held the throne until Murshid Quli Khan
Ustajlu found it expedient to dethrone him in favor of his own protégé,
Abbas. Abbas's early experience caused him to see his own sons as a threat.
He began confining them to the harem and sought to prevent the development of alliances between his sons and his officers. The execution or
blinding of all of his sons and brothers prevented any succession dispute

at his death. Abbas's policies made pawns of Safavid princes in future successions. Though Abbas II ruled actively, he took the throne as the nine-year-old tool of his father's vizier Mirza Taqi. At Abbas II's death, the leading officers of the empire chose his elder son Safi, who ruled as Sulayman, over his younger son Hamza. A similar decision brought Shah Sultan Husayn to the throne.

This brief review of succession reveals how rarely the Safavid rulers had the political initiative. The Qizilbash leadership determined the successions of Tahmasp, Ismail II, Muhammad Khudabandah, and Abbas I. The palace elite, and the lack of other candidates, determined the later successions. The Safavid period produced no succession clashes between mature capable princes or succession wars between parties. During the period when princes held provincial governorships, there were no adult princes capable of taking power on their own.

Although there is no study of Safavid royal women comparable to Leslie Peirce's landmark work on their Ottoman sisters, they evidently played similar roles. Two women, Tahmasp's daughter Pari Khan Khanum and Muhammad Khudabandah's wife Mahd-i Ulya, played major roles in the disordered period between Tahmasp's death and Abbas I's accession. One must assume that royal mothers had significant influence in the seventeenth century, when dynastic politics moved inside the palace, but the topic has not yet received close attention.

Although the Safavids must have relied on administrative regulations to address the practical problems of government as much their predecessors and contemporaries did, there was no tradition of Safavid *qanun*. Given the influence of the ulama from the earliest decades of the empire, the absence of an explicit *qanun* tradition is no surprise. The Safavids also did not face the task of asserting administrative control over what had been Christian areas, and thus did not need to undertake anything equivalent to Ottoman *tahrir*, one of the basic components of *qanun*.

EXPANSION AND MILITARY ORGANIZATION

The Safavid Empire was not a conquest state: Safavid conquest did not imply a change in the form of administration. During the expansion of the empire, the Safavid regime closely resembled the Aqquyunlu and Timurid regimes that it supplanted. It also came to terms with the Tajik aristocracy, which included the established ulama. Their religious prestige,

status as landholders, and role in the transmission of land revenue to recipients designated by the regime made them indispensable. In many areas,
the notables made the regime real by connecting it to the peasants. Safavid
conquest meant continuity, not change, except for the establishment of
Shiism. The mode of expansion did not define the regime, as it did for the
Ottomans and Mughals. Substantial parts of the Aqquyunlu confederation,
including some components of the paramount Bayandur clan and of the
Timurid confederation, joined the Qizilbash confederation.

Safavid military organization inevitably resembled that of the Aqquyunlu
and Timurids. The Safavid army had two main components before the
time of Shah Abbas, the confederate *uymaq*s and the *qurchi*s. The *qurchi*s
were the Safavid war band but differed from the pattern of earlier tribal
confederations. They were recruited as individuals and paid from the central treasury but came from the Qizilbash tribes and retained tribal affiliations. Some 1,500 in number under Ismail I, they served as the retinue
of the shah in battle, as palace guards, and as royal couriers and occasionally went on independent expeditions. Positions in the corps were frequently hereditary, and officers were promoted from within. Before the
reign of Abbas I, the chief of the *qurchi*s, or *qurchibashi*, normally came
from the dominant *uymaq* and had little political power. The *qurchi*s were
part of the tribal power rather than a means of counterbalancing it. They
did, apparently, begin to use firearms during the reign of Shah Tahmasp,
who increased their number to 5,000.

Under Abbas, the political and military significance of the *qurchi*s
changed. He expanded the corps to 10,000. The *qurchibashi* became one
of the most prominent officials of the state. Abbas appointed *qurchi*s to
provincial governorships in place of Qizilbash chiefs. The expansion of the
size and role of the *qurchi*s was a central aspect of Abbas's military reforms.
The *qurchi*s were a different mechanism for drawing upon the same pool
of manpower that provided the Qizilbash tribal forces. Though becoming
a *qurchi* did not extinguish tribal loyalty, it diluted tribal ties and reinforced fidelity to the ruler.

The early Safavid rulers drew on other sources of soldiers and military
technology to strengthen their positions. Ismail sought artillery and technicians from Venice in 1502 and 1509. The defeat at Chaldiran gave further impetus to the acquisition of firearms. A small corps of artillerymen
(*tupchi*s) and infantry (*tufangchi*s) had firearms by 1516. Descriptions of
the Safavid order of battle at Jam in 1528 and of a military review in 1530

show that the Safavid forces then included both battlefield artillery—several hundred light guns at Jam—and several thousand infantrymen armed with guns. At Jam, the forces with firearms served in the center of the formation, as the Janissaries and *sipahi*s of the Porte did in the Ottoman army. In the first phase of the battle, the Uzbek tribal cavalry engaged and defeated the Qizilbash tribal cavalry on both wings of the Safavid formation. The Uzbeks did not, however, engage the Safavid center, which was deployed in the Ottoman *tabur jangi* formation. The Uzbek forces reached the rear of the Safavid army, but this success did not affect the outcome of the battle. When the Uzbek forces were disorganized by victory, the Safavid center, under Tahmasp's personal command, charged the Uzbek center. The Uzbek forces scattered. At Jam, the Safavids fielded a typical gunpowder-empire army and won a typical gunpowder-empire victory, even though the Qizilbash continued to dominate internal politics.

Under Abbas and afterwards, the *tupchi*s and *tufangchi*s remained important components of the Safavid army. One historian asserts that each corps had 12,000 men. The Safavids apparently recruited new cavalry units from tribal groups, Iranian and Turkic, outside the Qizilbash, in addition to expanding the *tupchi*s and the *tufangchi*s. Infantry units became a substantial part of the army by the time of Abbas's wars with the Ottomans in Iraq. According to Willem Floor, the *tufangchi*s were local peasant levies, organized for local defense but also liable for service on imperial campaigns far from home. *Tufangchi*s from Khurasan fought in Anatolia. At least some, probably most, *tufangchi*s were Tajiks; some must have been peasants. But they never became a potent force in Safavid politics. Since the Safavid Empire had a far weaker agrarian base than the Ottoman Empire, it is not surprising that the peasants carried less political weight.

Military slaves (*qullar*) frequently commanded the *tupchi*s and *tufangchi*s. Tahmasp apparently began development of a military slave corps. The prisoners from his Caucasian campaigns, converted to Islam and made military slaves, probably became the nucleus of the corps of *ghulaman-i khassay-i sharifa* (slaves of the royal household; also called the *qullar*), which is first mentioned under Abbas. The ethnic origin of the *ghulam*s did not matter; the extraordinary loyalty and reliability of military slaves in general, coupled, apparently, with same high level of military training as the Janissaries, did. Because all of the new corps apparently served in the center of the battle formation, the precise tactical role of the *ghulam*s is unclear. They were mounted but used firearms; presumably they fought as dragoons (mounted infantry). There may have been separate cavalry and infantry components, on the Ottoman model. Contemporary historiography on the Safavids pays little attention to military history; Martin Dickson's description of Jam is the only battle history. For this reason, assessment of the precise military roles and effectiveness of the new army units is difficult. As the next two sections explain, *ghulam*s frequently served in high positions in the central and provincial administrations during and after the reign of Abbas I. Abbas created the office of *sipahsalar* (commander-in-chief) for the commander of the central army, supplanting the Qizilbash *amir al-umara*, mentioned below.

Abbas's reforms created an army capable of meeting the Ottoman army in the field. The Safavids no longer needed the Fabian strategy of Tahmasp's time. Though they were recruited directly, these forces were not always paid directly from the central treasury. They actually constituted a new provincial army because many of them, especially the *qullar*, held land-revenue assignments (*tiyul*, a Turkic word comparable to the Arabic *iqta*) in the provinces. In fact, these corps constituted a new provincial army, drawing revenue from the *khassa* provinces rather than the *mamalik* provinces. (I discuss these terms in the section on provincial administration.) Because they held, apparently, individual *tiyul*s assigned by the central government, these corps, or some components of them, resembled the Ottoman *sipahi* army. Abbas's reforms thus created a new provincial army, supported by a new form of provincial administration.

The original provincial army, of course, was the Qizilbash confederation. It first materialized as an army when Ismail summoned his followers to Erzincan in 1500, uniting his distant tribal followers with the men who had been his entourage in hiding in Lahijan. At that time, rivalry between Ismail's personal followers and the chiefs of the Qizilbash tribes began. Within a decade, the original Sufis of Lahijan, to use Masashi Haneda's phrase, had lost most of their influence. Turkmen chieftains occupied most high offices. Like other tribal confederations of the period, the traditional battle formation of the Qizilbash reflected the hierarchy of tribes within a confederation. The battle formations reflected the dominance of the Shamlu and Ustajlu tribes.

At the time of the 1530 military review, the Qizilbash tribes provided 84,900 of 105,800 troops. The tribal proportion of actual fighters was probably greater. The chief of the most powerful Qizilbash *uymaq* normally held the posts of *vakil* (royal deputy and chief minister) and *amir al-umara* (commander in chief) as long as the Qizilbash dominance lasted. The Qizilbash tribes were not, however, taut hierarchies with a single leader. Each normally had two major leaders, one at court and one in the provinces. Tahmasp increased his leverage against the Qizilbash by cultivating lesser chieftains within the tribes.

In the Qizilbash army, the individual soldiers had no direct ties to the ruler at all. Their loyalties were to their relatives and, ultimately, to their tribal leaders. Aside from occasional reviews like that of 1530, the central administration had little or no control over the size, equipment, or composition of the Qizilbash forces. Before the Abbasi transformation, Qizilbash chiefs were provincial governors and the commanders of the troops supported by their provinces. The central regime had minimal control over the provincial forces and governments. From the perspective of military administration, the weakness of the Safavid regime between 1514 and 1594 consisted of the lack of central control over the provincial army or of loyalty on the part of the provincial army to the ruler. One aspect of Abbas's reforms addressed this issue.

Abbas used the principle of *shahisivani* to rally Qizilbash to his cause, beginning early in his reign, to gain support against the dominance of Murshid Quli Khan Ustajlu. Abbas organized the Qizilbash who responded to such calls for action into new military units. Like the expansion of the *qurchi*s, the creation of the *shahsivin* units drew on Qizilbash manpower but bypassed the tribal leadership. The new pattern of provincial administration, with Tajiks, *qurchi*s, and *ghulam*s supplanting Qizilbash chiefs, did not end the role of the Qizilbash tribesmen in the provincial army. They continued to serve under the new governors and were paid either by land-revenue assignments or in cash from provincial treasuries.

The institutional structure of the Safavid army changed little after the time of Abbas I, but its fighting power degenerated considerably. External threats did not disappear entirely, but the Uzbeks remained weak and divided; the Treaty of Qasr-i Shirin marked the end of the Ottoman threat, and the Mughal threat to Qandahar ended in 1653. The Safavids did not attempt expansion, perhaps because of the enormous cost of their Qandahar expedition. Financial pressure led to significant reductions in military expenditure, including the abolition of the posts of *sipahsalar* in 1653–1654 and *tupchibashi* in 1658.

CENTRAL ADMINISTRATION

Compared to the majestic edifice of the Ottoman regime, Safavid central administration appears both fluid and crude. In the early decades of Safavid history, the governing elite came from three sources, the leaders of the Safavid order, the Aqquyunlu bureaucracy, and the chiefs of the Qizilbash tribes. When Ismail emerged from Gilan as the *pir* of the Safavid order, the functionaries of that order inevitably dominated his regime. The inclusion of the other two elements marked the transition from Sufi order to polity. Once Ismail emerged from Gilan, Safavid administration followed Aqquyunlu precedents.

Ismail's entourage became the central administration of the empire. There were at first four leading officials, the *amir al-umara*, *qurchibashi*, vizier, and *sadr* (chief religious official). Three of these four posts went to companions of Ismail in exile. The exception, the post of vizier, went to a veteran Aqquyunlu vizier, Amir Muhammad Zakariyya Tabrizi. This arrangement reflected the nature of the Safavid conquests; the Turkmen elite changed while the Tajik leadership remained, for the most part, intact. The *amir al-umara*, Husayn Beg Lala Shamlu, who had been Ismail's guardian during his exile, dominated the regime and had the additional title of *vakil*, which probably referred to Husayn Beg's status as regent. It might well be accurate to describe Husayn Beg as the actual founder of the Safavid empire. He was Ismail's deputy in the capacities of *shaykh* and shah. His position as *amir al-umara* meant that he had control of the tribal military forces, but he was not a tribal chief. His status derived from his relationship to Ismail. This arrangement differed from Aqquyunlu precedents in two ways. First, the vizier had far less influence than in previous regimes; he was merely chief of the fiscal bureaucracy rather than head of government. Second, the *sadr*, whose office normally dealt primarily with the administration of charitable land grants to religious figures, had the task of establishing Twelver Shiism.

This arrangement lasted until 1508, when Ismail appointed another of his followers from Gilan, Amir Najm al-Din Masud Gilani, to the office of *vakil*. This appointment did not end the dominance of Ismail's entourage, since Najm al-Din had attached himself to the young exile in Gilan though he had not accompanied him when he left that province. A Tajik who had no ties with Aqquyunlu officialdom, Najm al-Din quickly came to dominate the administration. In 1509, Ismail deprived Husayn

Beg of the office of *amir al-umara* and replaced him with Muhammad Beg Sufrachi Ustajlu, who took the title Chayan Sultan. Though associated with one of the most powerful tribes, he had no particular status within it; his appointment indicated that Ismail controlled the status of his officers. Husayn Beg retained high rank and, after the Safavid conquest of Khurasan, received the governorship of Herat, effectively becoming viceroy of Khurasan. This appointment removed Husayn Beg from the center of politics and reduced his influence without demoting him.

When Najm al-Din died in 1509 or 1510, Ismail appointed another Tajik, Amir Yar Muhammad Ahmad Khuzani, to replace him. Known as Najm-i Sani (second Najm), he became the dominant figure in Safavid administration and, in 1512, provoked the first crisis of Ismail's reign. Ismail appointed him to command the army sent to Khurasan to oppose the Uzbek invasion under Jani Beg Sultan. The Qizilbash officers assigned to the province served under him. Supported by Babur and his followers, the Safavid army besieged Ghujduvan in the autumn of 1512. When the siege became prolonged, and supplies ran short, Najm-i Sani refused the advice of his subordinates to withdraw. When the Uzbeks attacked, the Qizilbash chiefs abandoned him, and he was captured and executed. The sources make clear that the Qizilbash resented Najm-i Sani's power, influence, wealth, and arrogance. They begrudged their subordination to him on the grounds of his appointment to high office by the shah, perceiving themselves as independent chiefs rather than extensions of the ruler. This issue, not ethnic rivalry in and of itself, caused the recurrent clashes between Qizilbash chiefs and Tajik officials in Safavid history before the reign of Shah Tahmasp. Though the Tajik *vakil*s did not have the title of vizier, they functioned as viziers normally did, with the individuals who held the title vizier having a subordinate position.

After Najm-i Sani's death, Ismail appointed Amir Najm al-Din Abd al-Baqi, one of Najm-i Sani's assistants who also held the office of *sadr* as *vakil*; he was killed at Chaldiran. The next *vakil*, Mirza Shah Husayn Isfahani, held that office for nine years. Ismail's withdrawal after his great defeat left the *vakil* in control of the administration, but his position was really that of vizier. His authority naturally led to Qizilbash resentment. In 1523, he was assassinated by a Qizilbash officer from whom he had been attempting to collect a large debt owed to the treasury. The event reinforces the impression that the clash between Qizilbash and Tajik concerned the terms of the relationship between the shah and his officers.

Were they servants of the ruler, subject to punishment as well as reward, holding office and status at his pleasure, or independent chiefs ritually subordinate to the ruler but serving him at their own pleasure? Mirza Shah Husayn's successor as *vakil* had previously served as vizier and continued to hold that office as well.

During the period of Qizilbash dominance in the first years of Tahmasp's reign, the chief of the paramount tribe held the title of *vakil*. This designation reflected the status of the dominant chief as the effective ruler of the empire. The chief of the administration, though also holding the title *vakil*, had little power. The administrative consequence of Tahmasp's emergence was the resurgence of the civilian bureaucracy. Masum Beg Safavi played a pivotal role. Descended from a brother of Shaykh Haydar, he served as *vakil* from 1550 or 1551 to 1569. He steered a middle course between the Tajik and Qizilbash agendas, one that characterized most of Tahmasp's reign. The office of *qurchibashi* also became more prominent. Sevinduk Beg Afshar held this office from 1538 or 1539 until his death in 1561 or 1562, despite the fluidity of tribal politics in this era. With the disappearance of a religious challenge within the empire, the office of *sadr* reverted to its prior status of administering land and funds assigned to the religious establishment.

The disordered period of Tahmasp's final illness, Ismail II's brief reign, and Muhammad Khudabandah's ineffective rule meant a return to Qizilbash dominance and chaos in administration. Ismail II gave considerable authority to his vizier, Mirza Salman. Mirza Salman led the forces of centralization, at first in association with Mahd-i Ulya, then with Hamza Mirza, until the Qizilbash *amir*s demanded his dismissal in 1583. Mirza Salman had consistently sought to increase the power of his benefactor, Hamza Mirza, and frequently accused Qizilbash officers of disloyalty. They, in turn, accused him of exceeding his authority and position, for instance, by participating in military affairs rather than confining himself to the Tajik pursuits of administration, and of having an inappropriate military retinue. Hamza Mirza surrendered him to the Qizilbash leadership, who had Mirza Salman executed. He was accusing the Qizilbash not of treason in the sense of aiding the Ottomans or the Uzbeks but of being more loyal to themselves than to the shah and heir apparent. The Qizilbash condemnation of Mirza Salman's usurpation of military status has more than ethnic content; it resists the transfer of military assets that ought to be the exclusive preserve of the Qizilbash to an outsider. Had Mirza

Salman happened to be a native speaker of Turkish without connection to the Qizilbash confederation, he would probably have met the same fate with a different rhetorical justification.

The accession of Shah Abbas in 1588 appeared to mark a return to the situation at the beginning of Tahmasp's reign, with the dominant Qizilbash officer holding the office of *vakil* and *amir al-umara*. The execution of the young ruler's former patron, Murshid Quli Khan Ustajlu, two years later ended forever the Qizilbash pretension to political domination. Under Abbas, no single office dominated the others; the shah reserved domination for himself. Four officers—the *qurchibashi, qullaraqasi, tufangchibashi*, and grand vizier, now given the title *sadr-i azam* (following Ottoman practice) or *itimad al-dawlah* (pillar of state)—controlled the administration. The *qurchibashi* ceased to be associated with a dominant tribe, for there was none. For much of Abbas's reign, Isa Khan Safavi, the grandson of Tahmasp's *vakil*, held the office, removing it from Qizilbash control entirely. The office of *amir al-umara* effectively ceased; the term was used primarily for important provincial governors. Abbas made all officers, Qizilbash chiefs included, into his own functionaries. The issues and conflicts that had dominated Safavid politics and administration receded into insignificance.

The transfer of much of the empire from *mamalik* to *khass* jurisdiction primarily concerned provincial administration. But just as this change had military consequences, for the reclassified land supported *qurchi*s, *ghulam*s, and musketeers instead of Qizilbash soldiers, it affected the central administration as well. *Mamalik* provinces ruled by Qizilbash governors paid little or no revenue to the central government and were thus mostly outside its purview and its civilian bureaucracy. *Khassa* provinces, however, were the exclusive realm of the central administration. Abbas thus greatly increased the importance of the civilian bureaucracy and its head.

After the death of Abbas, the system of administration he created remained in force, though not unaltered, until the fall of the dynasty. There were three major changes: the withdrawal of the rulers (except for Abbas II) from day-to-day administration, the growing influence of palace officials, and the growing importance of the ulama, inside and outside official positions. The power of the vizier and the size of the civilian bureaucracy increased. Tension between the civil bureaucracy and the palace bureaucracy became a major feature of Safavid politics. The palace bureaucracy had always been both sizable and influential; it also had much better access to, and often closer relationships with, the rulers themselves. The chief court official, the *ishiq-aqasi-bashi*, reported to the grand vizier and controlled the entire court establishment, including eunuchs, doorkeepers, and other court functionaries. His duties had two main components, palace administration and court protocol. The chief eunuch of the harem, who had the title *ishiq-aqasi-bashi* of the harem, or *qapuchi-bashi*, was subordinate to the *ishiq-aqasi-bashi*. The eunuchs played a particularly pivotal role during the long reign of Shah Sulayman, who had spent his entire life in the harem before his enthronement and rarely left it afterwards. The harem officials became the intermediaries between the actual government and the ruler.

The Safavid royal establishment had another important component, controlled by the *nazir-i buyutat* (superintendent of the royal workshop). The *nazir-i buyutat* represented the ruler in the capacities of artistic patron and industrialist. Ismail and Tahmasp supported huge artistic establishments. The imperial workshops produced the most famous Iranian illuminated manuscript, the stunning Tahmasp *Shah-namah*, in the early years of Tahmasp's reign. Safavid patronage of the arts declined in the second half of Tahmasp's reign, though royal patronage did not stop entirely and members of the *ghulam* elite became important cultural patrons in the provinces. The royal workshop continued, however, to produce a wide variety of products until the end of Safavid rule. There were thirty-three different workshops during the reign of Shah Sultan Husayn. They produced clothing, shoes, carpets, metalwork, and other commodities for court consumption, as well as provided foodstuffs.

The growth of the religious establishment and its political influence has often been treated as a part of Safavid decline; there is some justification for this. For Shah Sultan Husayn, religious matters were as much of a distraction as the affairs of the harem were for his father, Sulayman. But the institutional developments deserve treatment on their own. In addition to and above the standard religious offices of *qazi* (judge) and *sadr* (administrator of religious grants), two new offices were created, that of *mullabashi* and that of *divan begi*. Shah Sultan Husayn apparently created the office of *mullabashi* for Mulla Muhammad Baqir Majlisi to recognize to his status as the leading Shii divine. The office of *divan begi*, which appeared considerably earlier, might effectively be translated as "lord chief justice." As chief magistrate and appeals judge of the empire, the *divan begi* had jurisdiction over capital crimes in the capital of the empire, as well as appeal and administrative control of provincial courts, and also heard civil cases. His jurisdiction involved both the Shariah and administrative or customary law; the *sadr* advised him in Shari matters.

The Safavid imperial bureaucracy, the *divan-i ala* (literally, "high court") had two main components, the *daftar-khanah* (literally, "notebook house"), which handled financial administration, and the *dar al-insha*, which handled correspondence. The *mustawfi* or *munshi al-mamalik* ran the *daftar-khanah* as chief accountant; he had some five chief subordinates, of whom one was the *mustawfi-yi khassa*, who had specific responsibility for *khass* revenues. As more provinces moved from *mamalik* to *khass* jurisdiction, this office became steadily more important. The *majlis-nivis* (literally, "recorder of audiences") acted as both the recording and the corresponding secretary of the ruler. The *majlis-nivis* also became more important in the second half of the seventeenth century. Other officials included the chief falconer and two officials in charge of stables.

One unique office, the *khalifat al-khulafa*, remains. The shah was still the head of the Safavid order. The *khalifat al-khulafa* was the shah's chief subordinate in that capacity. The representatives of the Safavid *shaykh*s who spread the order among the Turkmen of Anatolia and western Iran had the title *khalifa*; they played a considerable role in rallying the Turkmen to the Safavid cause, before and after the advent of Ismail, and remained active among the Turkmen of Ottoman Anatolia. As the Sufi aspect of the Safavid polity became less important, the importance of the *khalifat al-khulafa* dwindled until he became nothing more than the chief of the Sufis at court in their capacities as jailers and executioners.

The Safavid palace establishment and bureaucracy have not received the decades of close atttention that their Ottoman equivalents have. The existing studies do show that the both entities were ethnically diverse. The bureaucrats included Kurds, Armenians, Georgians (Armenian and Georgian converts to Islam retained their ethnic identities), and Tajiks.

The Ottoman and Safavid empires shared the basic distinction between the palace and the bureaucracy, but the differentiation between inner and outer components of the palace, though present, was much less pronounced. Perhaps as much because of the large amount of literature on the Ottoman court and regime as because of the common antecedents of the two empires and actual Ottoman influence on the Safavids, Safavid institutions seem like pale and imperfect copies of Ottoman originals. Just as Safavid Isfahan, despite its remarkable beauty and grandeur, could hardly compete with Ottoman Istanbul, the Safavid government could not compare, in scope or capability, with the Ottoman regime.

PROVINCIAL ADMINISTRATION

The Safavid Empire began as a tribal confederation; Safavid rule thus meant tribal control of the provinces. The Safavids generally assumed the relationships with Tajik provincial notables that their Aqquyunlu and Timurid predecessors had had. Since many of the components of the Qizilbash confederation had been part of the Aqquyunlu or Timurid confederations, the continuity was sometimes complete. In a tribal confederation, provincial rule meant the assignment of provinces to tribes, with their chiefs serving as provincial governors. Until Abbas's reforms, the Safavids did not actually govern the provinces; the Qizilbash tribes did. It was natural in this circumstance for the most common title for a governor to be *beylerbey*, for as a tribal chief he was indeed a bey of beys. This situation also reduced the division between military and fiscal responsibility, common in Aqquyunlu as well as Ottoman practice, to a mockery. Essentially, the provinces were the land-revenue assignments (for which the Safavids normally employed the Turkish term *tiyul*) of the governors; the regime thus transferred the land revenue from the agricultural producers to the tribal followers of the Qizilbash chieftains. The central regime had virtually no control over the administrative practices of the Qizilbash governors and received very little revenue from them. This situation both reflected and perpetuated the Qizilbash dominance of the regime before Abbas I.

Safavid provinces generally followed the previous boundaries of Aqquyunlu and Timurid jurisdictions. The following list of provinces includes areas that were not always under Safavid jurisdiction; indeed some were rarely under Safavid control: Shirvan, Qarabagh (as in Nagorno-Karabagh), Erivan, Azerbaijan (Tabriz), Diyar Bakr, Erzincan, Hamadan, Iranian Iraq, Kirmanshah, Arab Iraq (Baghdad), Fars (Shiraz), Kuh-Giluya, Kirman, Qandahar, Balkh, Marv, Mashhad, Herat, and Astarabad. In addition to these provinces, the Safavids had several vassals whose leaders, whether chiefs or kings, bore the title *vali*. The vassals included Kurd and Lur tribes and local dynasties in Gilan, Mazandaran, Arabistan (Khuzistan), and Georgia. The Georgian vassals contributed important military

forces to the Safavids in campaigns against the Ottomans and became increasingly influential in the later stages of Safavid history. The Kurdish
and Lur vassals served as buffers between the Safavids and the Ottomans.
Unlike the Ottomans, the Safavids never obtained the supremacy over a
major rival necessary to treat its subjects as a vassal, except when Babur
acted as a subordinate ally of Ismail and his son Humayun then took
refuge with Tahmasp.

Before Abbas's time, individual Qizilbash tribes dominated individual
provinces. Governors changed, but the tribes they led did not. In Fars, for
example, the Zul Qadr tribe dominated the province from its conquest by
Ismail in 1503 until Abbas I took it from its last Zul Qadr governor in
1590. In this period, then, Fars was actually an autonomous Zul Qadr
principality, ritually subordinate to the Safavid monarchs and sometimes
providing military support but neither subject to central administrative
control nor paying a meaningful amount of revenue to the center. The
Safavids did appoint royal viziers to the provinces, but until about 1630
they were distinctly subordinate to the governors. The economy of the
province supported the Zul Qadr tribe, which also formed the military
forces of the "principality." The Tajik administrators served the Zul Qadr,
not the Safavids. This description of provincial administration explains
the weakness of Tahmasp in the face of the Ottoman threat and the fragmentation of authority during his minority and the ineffective reign of
Muhammad Khudabandah. Once the defeats at Ghujduvan and Chaldiran
shattered Ismail's charismatic authority, there were few institutional arrangements to control the Qizilbash chiefs cum military commanders cum
provincial governors. Conflicts between provincial governors were not uncommon; clashes within the *uymaqs* were routine.

Abbas thus had to establish central authority in the provinces, but he
received almost no revenue from the provinces to support this effort.
Using administrative language, there was little *khass* or *khalisa*, land that
paid its revenue to the central treasury. Other categories of land included
tiyul (land-revenue concessions in return for service), *soyurghal* (heritable
land-revenue grants normally for charitable purposes), and *vaqf* (charitable endowments by individuals). During and after Abbas's reign, the term
khass came to refer to provinces assigned to the central treasury. Neither the
Ottomans nor the Mughals had a comparable practice, but because a substantial part of the land of *khass* provinces was frequently assigned to individuals, the difference was more apparent than real.

In a sense, Abbas's reforms in the provinces began with the annexation of the vassal states of Mazandaran, Lahijan, and Rasht in Gilan and of Lar between 1592 and 1602. Gilan and Mazandaran produced much of Iran's silk, by far the most valuable export commodity. The silk-producing regions became *khass* provinces, and silk became a royal monopoly. Exports of silk and silk products provided the critical mass of revenue necessary for Abbas's reforms. Qazvin, Kashan, and Isfahan, parts of which had been *khass* territory under Tahmasp, became *khass* territories at the beginning of Abbas's reign; part of Kirman, Yazd, Qum, Mazandaran, and Astarabad were incorporated into *khass* between 1590 and 1606. All of these areas were far from the disputed frontiers, so they did not require standing armies. The administrative structure of these provinces is not entirely clear. In some cases at least, no governor was appointed, only a provincial vizier. Substantial parts of the *khass* provinces paid their taxes directly to representatives of the central government, but much of the *khass* territory was also given in land-revenue assignments. Unlike the *mamalik* provinces, these assignments went to individuals, like Ottoman revenue assignments, not to tribal chieftains. These individuals included servants in every component of the court and royal administration, including the provincial officials themselves. The end result resembled the Ottoman *timar* provinces quite closely, though apparently without detailed revenue surveys. There were no provincial military elites comparable to the Ottoman *sipahi* families, so all of the assignments went to imperial functionaries, military or civilian.

Abbas's reforms also involved the transformation of the Qizilbash tribal organization itself. Because the Qizilbash tribes were substantial population groups, they could not be eliminated, and Abbas did not require this in any case. Qizilbash troops were useful; Qizilbash challenges to royal authority were intolerable. Because such challenges could only come from the leaders of strong tribal groupings; Abbas set out to eliminate them. He broke the power of the Qizilbash by breaking the Qizilbash into smaller pieces and by transferring land to other tribal groups, including Lurs, Arabs, and Baluchis. The holdings of Qizilbash tribes did not always shrink, but those of their leading families, which had provided the Qizilbash contenders for power, did. Because the most powerful Qizilbash chiefs had entourages that included military slaves of their own and could thus have competed with Abbas's new army, this step was essential for the centralization of power. Under their lesser chieftains, the Qizilbash clans served under royal governors in *mamalik* provinces.

Abbas's success shows that these reforms served the purpose he intended. They moved the Safavid regime closer to the Ottoman model. In addition to the central army, which included gun-armed infantry, artillery, and cavalry, there was a new provincial army in which the individual soldiers had direct ties to the regime. After Abbas's death, the extension of the *khass* administration continued. Under Safi I and Abbas II, the provinces of Fars, Lar, Hamadan, and Ardabil, as well as all of Kirman, were transferred to *khass* jurisdiction. Power moved from the provinces to the court, and income followed. The *khass* territories now provided revenue for the court elite rather than supporting the army. *Khass* revenue administration was consistently more lax than *mamalik* administration. As time went on, the *khass* provinces produced less and less military power.

THE SAFAVID ECONOMY

The Safavid Empire was far less prosperous and economically complex than its Ottoman and Mughal contemporaries. Its predominantly arid territories were less productive and encompassed a less elaborate commercial network. The Safavid economy resembled that of the Uzbek principalities, which never developed the centralized, bureaucratic institutions of the three empires, more than it did the prosperous agrarian economies of the Ottoman and Mughal realms. Lucrative silk exports did not mean broad agricultural prosperity.

The lack of information on the Safavid economy and society reflects the lack of development. Population data is hard to come by. The population of the core territories was perhaps 5 or 6 million and reached 7 or 8 million when the Safavids held Iraq. Most of that population lived from hand to mouth. Only about 15 percent lived in cities; the remainder subsisted by agriculture or pastoral nomadism in the countryside. There was no hard-and-fast distinction between nomads and peasants. Political, fiscal, and social conditions restricted incentives for the investment and innovation necessary for economic development. The conditions of land tenure and management and peasant status limited economic opportunity. The different categories of land paid their revenue to different classes of recipients, but the collection of revenue and the conditions of peasant life varied little. Outside the areas controlled by Qizilbash tribes, whose society and economy we know little about, land revenue was assigned, or conceded, not in discrete, compact units but in shares. The revenue of a single village could be parceled out to as many as forty-eight different recipients, not as specific plots of land but as shares of what the village produced. The produce the individual peasants received was likewise shared out from the total. The various assignment holders did not normally collect their shares directly but hired a manager or agent, who collected all the revenue and divided it among the recipients. In general, the Safavids used the term *tiyul* for revenue assigned as salaries and *soyurghal* and *vazifah* for revenue grants to individuals.

Peasants were effectively tied to the soil and could not migrate freely. Within the villages, they formed cultivation units. These groups were most frequently called *joft* (pair, referring to the area that could be cultivated with a single team of oxen). These units negotiated the level of rent, or tax (there was no meaningful distinction), with the landlords or their agents. The peasants had little leverage; commands from the shah to treat peasants fairly did not protect them. Peasants were effectively subsistence farmers, seeking to grow as much of their own food as possible and meet their other requirements without recourse to the market. Even in areas that produced cash commodities such as silk, peasants cultivated food to live on and other commodities to pay taxes or rents with. The peasants thus did not participate in the markets for the commodities they grew. The landholders' agents constituted one of several layers of middlemen between the peasants and the merchants, who were the ultimate purchasers within the empire.

This system discouraged landlords and peasants from innovation and investments. A landlord who could raise revenues simply by raising rents had little incentive to increase the productivity of his holdings; what cash he had was normally used to purchase goods, especially luxuries, that his holdings could not supply. Peasants had little incentive to expand a surplus they could not keep. Landholders with funds available for investment could often make greater profits in trade than in agricultural investment. The revenue demand was essentially the entire surplus, meaning that the peasants had to surrender everything they grew beyond their own needs and seed for the next year's crop. European travelers gave descriptions of the conditions of peasant life in the various parts of Safavid Iran. Some felt that the peasants lived well by outwitting the tax collectors; others emphasized how much the actual revenue demand exceeded the amount set by administrative regulations. In general, peasants on *mulk* (hereditary freehold) or *vaqf* (charitable endowment) land did the best; peasants did better on *khass* land than *tiyul*. Almost all the items the peasants used—clothing, utensils, furniture, tools—were made in their villages. Few goods intended for consumption outside the individual village were produced in rural areas, though some luxury goods were.

Guilds dominated the economic life of Safavid cities. In the major cities like Isfahan, Kashan, and Tabriz, guilds produced consumer goods as well as luxuries. They functioned as much as administrative units for the authorities as trade associations. Guild leaders bore the title *rais* and were elected by the members, then approved by the town headman (*kalantar*), a royal appointee. The *kalantar*s and the guild leaders negotiated tax assessments for the guild members, and the guilds acted as conduits for revenue collection. Like peasants, guilds members often paid taxes in kind (the goods they produced) rather than cash. A *muhtasib al-mamalik* (royal market inspector), with a deputy in each city, enforced fair-trade regulations in association with the guild leadership. In the larger cities, guilds produced a broad range of commodities. The largest single industrialist was, of course, the shah. Royal workshops produced some goods for market, including carpets, which competed directly with privately produced goods.

Guild members did their business in bazaars. Like the urban foundations of the Ottoman Empire, bazaars in Safavid Iran were often constructed and supported by charitable endowments; tradesmen rented their shops from the foundations. Major cities had covered markets (*qaisariyyah*, equivalent to the Ottoman *bedestan*) in which expensive luxury items were sold. Many of the guilds, bazaars, and charitable endowments predated the Safavid period.

Turning from production to commerce, most merchants were closely associated with recipients of land revenue. Iranian commerce was comparatively unsophisticated at this time, with almost all transactions in cash. Trade was nonetheless highly profitable; it was not unusual for a merchant to make a 40 percent profit in a single year. Small merchants supplied urban goods to the hinterlands of their cities; they lacked the capital necessary for long-distance trade, especially because of high tolls charged for long-distance travel. Long-distance trade, however, formed the basis of the transformation of the Safavid confederation into an empire.

Before Safavid times, two major trade routes passed through what became Safavid territory. The east-west route led across northern Iran from central Asia to Anatolia, with the port of Trebizond and later Ottoman Bursa as its major western terminus. The north-south route went from the Persian Gulf north to Azerbaijan where it met the east-west route. The route from Khurasan to Azerbaijan was the western part of the Silk Road and carried both Chinese and Iranian silk to the Ottoman and European markets. Tabriz, Sultaniyyah, and Herat were the major cities on this route; Tabriz served as the commercial as well as the political center of western Iran. The overland trade to India, mostly in horses and textiles, passed from eastern Iran through Afghanistan to the Indus Valley. The southern route passed through the great marketplace of Hormuz. Merchants exchanged spices and precious stones from India and Indonesia, Iranian carpets and horses, pearls from Bahrain, and a wide variety of textiles. One merchant wrote of pepper, cloves, ginger, cardamom, tamarind, rare woods, saffron, indigo, wax, iron, sugar, rice, coconuts, porcelain, precious stones, silk and cotton textiles, copper, mercury, vermilion, musk, rhubarb (a medicinal root, not the vegetable), pearls, horses, raisins, dates, salt, and sulfur passing through the great island port. It formed one of two routes, the other passing through the Red Sea, that brought the spices of the Indian Ocean to the Mediterranean world. Iran thus formed a vital part of the caravan trade of Asia which had existed, with variations, for millennia.

Compared to the other great events of the late fifteenth and early sixteenth centuries, the establishment of the Safavid polity had neither a profound nor a prolonged effect on global trade. In the east, the Safavid wars with the Uzbeks interfered with the east-west trade route. Herat, the focal point of the struggle, lost much of its commercial importance. In the south, the Portuguese, led by the redoubtable Don Afonso d'Albuquerque, occupied Hormuz in 1507, forcing the local Muslim ruler to pay tribute to Portugal as well as to Shah Ismail. The diplomatic interaction between Albuquerque and Ismail included the question of cooperation against their mutual enemies, the Ottomans and Mamluks, as well as discussion of Hormuz and trade in the Gulf. Ismail's interest in Persian Gulf trade primarily concerned keeping it from passing through Ottoman territory. Hormuz remained a great emporium; the range of goods did not change significantly. The one item in which the Portuguese tried to establish a monopoly, pepper, continued to pass through the island beneath the blind eyes of corrupt officials. As Niels Steensgaard has demonstrated, the Portuguese did not seek to divert the trade of the Indian Ocean from the Red Sea and Persian Gulf to the Cape Route, except in pepper, merely to tax it. Portuguese dominance in the Indian Ocean thus did not significantly alter the overall trade pattern, except in pepper.

Just as the Portuguese conquest of Hormuz did not block the Persian Gulf route to the Mediterranean, the Ottoman-Safavid conflict did not end trade between western Iran and the Ottoman commercial centers. Selim I attempted a commercial blockade. This effort, as well as Selim's deportation of artisans from Tabriz, did not terminate the passage of silk and other goods from western Iran to the Mediterranean. Until the destruction of the Mamluk kingdom, trade could flow from Iraq, which Ismail controlled, to Syria rather than Anatolia. The Ottoman conquest ended that outlet. Selim sought to deprive the Safavids of military equipment as well as to cut off their exports. The embargo was ineffective. The effort at blockade ended with Selim's death. This temporary and incomplete interruption of the trade from western Iran and the Persian Gulf had little permanent effect.

Shah Abbas's trade policy did not deviate from the overall Safavid pattern. All of the Safavid rulers pursued a bullionist policy, seeking to increase the inflow and decrease the outflow of specie, meaning to increase exports and reduce imports. This principle applied to the economy in general and to the central treasury in particular. What made Abbas different was his success; in this area as in most others, he completed projects that his grandfather and great-grandfather had begun. His projects went far beyond silk. In modern terms, he promoted import substitution. He sought to expand domestic production of cotton, indigo, and rice, to replace imports from South Asia, and, in the case of cotton, to increase the amount of silk available for export. He aimed to make Isfahan a center of commerce, most famously by forcing Armenian merchants to migrate from Julfa to New Julfa, outside Isfahan, and settling a community of Chinese potters there to establish a domestic ceramic industry. Abbas also supported trade with the construction of numerous caravanserais. These grand but utilitarian structures provided secure shelter for merchants and pilgrims on the road. Abbas also built a series of bridges and other road improvements. The security of the roads in Abbas's time became proverbial. But silk was the centerpiece of his program.

Abbas's silk policy began with, and depended entirely upon, gaining control of its supply. The incorporation of Gilan, Mazandaran, Shirvan, and Qarabagh into the empire between 1595 and 1607 gave him that control. The designation of these areas, except Shirvan, as *khass* provinces passed that control to the central treasury. Abbas succeeded in ensuring that however the silk reached the European market, by land or sea, he gained most of the profits. He did seek to use the growth of global trade to increase his income, but the presence of the European traders in the Indian Ocean did not contribute significantly to his success. Abbas's diplomatic initiatives mixed trade with attempts to gain political and military support against the Ottomans and, less prominently, the Portuguese. Abbas sent no less than seven missions to Europe between 1598 and 1600 without result. He did explore the possibility of working with the Portuguese to block Ottoman access to the products of the Indian Ocean by blockading the Red Sea and diverting the flow of silk from the Mediterranean to the Cape Route, but nothing came of the idea. Rudi Matthee describes the concept as more a "diplomatic gambit . . . rather than reflective of realistic options."[14]

Since no diversion of silk took place, Abbas's success did not depend on the arrival of the EIC and VOC in Indian Ocean trade, which happened at the same time. The companies sought to open new routes between Atlantic Europe and the Indian Ocean and to take over the trade of the Indian Ocean, not merely to tax it. They were not interested in Iran at first; the notion of diverting the silk trade failed to gain the immediate interest of the EIC. But an English evaluation of the Persian market in 1614 led to negotiations with Abbas. The EIC obtained trading privileges in the Safavid Empire in 1615, and trade began in 1616. In 1617, Abbas granted extraordinary concessions to the English, including a customs exemption. English commerce in Iran, however, had anything but a smooth beginning, for Abbas declared his monopoly on silk exports in the same year and the English were unwilling to pay the price he demanded. The negotiations between the East India Company and Abbas proceeded simultaneously with the maritime rivalry between Portugal and England. When an English flotilla defeated a larger Portuguese force in the Gulf of Oman off Jask in 1620, the benefits of military cooperation became obvious. Abbas and the East India Company agreed to swap commercial privileges for naval support in 1621. The combined forces conquered Hormuz on May 3, 1622. This event marked the downfall of the caravan trade and the beginning of company dominance. It also marked the end of the commercial significance of Hormuz; Abbas developed the port of Jarun on the mainland, renamed Bandar Abbas, as the new center of Gulf commerce.

Because it was a waterless, barren island whose sole virtue was its separation from the mainland, the abandonment of Hormuz made sense. Bandar Abbas grew rapidly; the EIC and VOC traded there. They carried goods consigned by the former peddler merchants as freight in addition to their own merchandise. The variety of goods equaled that which had passed through Hormuz. Though the overland peddler trade did not disappear, the companies came to dominate the trade in Indian Ocean spices and to carry a substantial amount of silk. In the later decades, goat wool from Kirman became another major export to Europe.

Although the European merchants have received far more attention, a prosperous network of Indian merchants extended through the Safavid Empire into the Uzbek principalities and Muscovy. These merchants, not the European companies, handled most of the commerce between India and Iran. Aside from silk and horses, Safavid exports to India consisted of limited specialty items, such as asafetida and assorted fruits. Iranian merchants imported cotton textiles, indigo, and sugar from India. The trade balance was unfavorable to Iran.

The roads that Abbas made safe and passable led to Isfahan, his capital. Tabriz, the first capital, had been too vulnerable. Tahmasp moved the capital to Qazvin in 1548. His efforts to develop the city as a symbolic capital prefigured the work of his grandson. Abbas developed Isfahan as an imperial capital to rival Ottoman Istanbul and Mughal Agra and as the venue for the commerce on which his treasury depended. In addition to the monumental *Maydan* (square) of Isfahan, which was the physical symbol of Safavid sovereignty, Abbas financed the construction of a new covered bazaar; the great square was lined with markets as well. Safavid courtiers also devoted some attention to urban development, though their activity did not approach that of their Ottoman counterparts. Ganj Ali Khan, one of Abbas's governors of Kirman, constructed a complex there that included a mosque, madrasa, caravanserai, and bazaars.

All of Mazandaran and most of Gilan were *khassa* provinces; Abbas used forced migration of Georgians and Armenians to increase silk production in these areas. Most of the silk grown was collected as taxes by the royal treasury; purchasers of silk could sometimes buy it outside official channels but not for less than the official price. The viziers of the silk-producing provinces collected the silk and were responsible for storing it and having it transported to Isfahan. There, royal merchants arranged for sale and delivery to the purchasers. The merchants, whether or not they were representatives of the companies, had to pay the cost of transportation to Bandar Abbas, tolls, and any applicable customs dues. The direction of the silk trade mattered less to the Safavid regime than the royal monopoly. The outlet for silk mattered less than who received the profits.

Abbas's "state-capitalist" manipulation of the Safavid economy to permit his military and political reforms differed significantly from the policies of his contemporaries.[15] In general, the Ottoman and Mughal rulers

IMAGE 4.3 *Caravanserai at the Ganj ʿAli Khan Complex (1598–1619), Kerman.* Ganj Ali Khan served as Shah Abbas I's governor of Kerman, Qandahar, and Sistan. A great patron of public works, Ali Khan's most important commission was the complex in Kerman which included this magnificent double-storied caravanserai, a small mosque, public bathhouse, and three bazaars.

pursued a more laissez-faire economic approach, benefiting from the prosperity of their realms as a whole. Abbas could compete only through mercantilist manipulation.

Like his politics, the commercial pattern created under Abbas continued after his death but gradually degenerated. Safi ended the silk monopoly, and the Armenians secured their dominance among the domestic merchants of the country. More silk was exported, via both the Gulf and the Levant; the EIC and the English Levant companies both benefited from the expansion. Holland, France, and Venice also purchased large amounts of Iranian silk. The East India companies continued to dominate the seaborne trade, and the EIC sought to establish a silk monopoly. This effort failed, but both the English and Dutch companies became extremely prominent in Iranian commerce. Their silk purchases were a vital source of income for the Safavid regime. The Dutch were more successful for most of the seventeenth century, owing to their victory in the First Anglo-Dutch War and use of military power to gain improved commercial terms. The French Compagnie des Indes was also active.

The peace on the Safavid frontiers for most of the seventeenth century stimulated trade in all directions. Trade with and through Russia grew considerably during the Safavid period. On the northeastern frontier, Mashhad became the major commercial center in the Safavid period; Qandahar likewise was the major entrepôt on the land route to India. Both routes remained active until the degeneration of public order in the early eighteenth century made trade difficult.

Abbas's economic policy obviously strengthened his regime and made his political and military successes possible. From the perspective of the Iranian economy, however, his reforms' effect was not entirely beneficial. In Amin Banani's words, they were "structural manipulations to increase his immediate power and wealth. Compared with contemporary economic changes in Western Europe, Abbas's reforms of the Persian economic structure lacked altogether the dynamic element of capital investment necessary for greater production."[16] By emphasizing the export of raw silk (not finished silk products), Abbas helped to move Iran into the passive role of exporter of raw materials and importer of finished products, mostly textiles. The obstacles to capitalist development were not of Abbas's making or even limited to the Safavid period. The Safavids made few major alterations in the system of landholding that discouraged innovation and increases in production.

SAFAVID SOCIETY AND POPULAR RELIGION

A generation ago, the historiography of Safavid society had barely begun and did not extend beyond the study of land tenure and agrarian social conditions. Even today, it lacks the breadth and depth of the work on Ottoman social history, in part because of the comparative paucity of documentary sources and difficulty of doing research in postrevolutionary Iran. In particular, the court records that underlie so much recent Ottoman historiography either did not survive or have not been available to historians. Nonetheless, Safavid historians have begun exploring the same themes that have drawn attention in the Ottoman historiography and elsewhere: changing patterns of social interaction associated with the consumption of coffee, wine, and narcotics and the roles of women in the various levels of society. As in the Ottoman Empire, the diffusion of coffee created new patterns of social interaction, with the coffeehouse rivaling the mosque as a venue for social interaction.

Although Safavid society was less diverse than Ottoman or Mughal society, it was hardly homogenous. The Turks and Tajiks were only the most prominent ethnic groups. There were also Chaghatay Turks in Khurasan, non-Turkic nomad groups such as the Lar and Bakhtiyari, and of course the Kurds. The Christian population included both Georgians, who were Orthodox Christians, and Armenians, who generally adhered to the Armenian Apostolic Church. There was considerable tension between these two groups. Armenians and Jews had leading roles in commerce throughout the empire.

Social life in the Safavid Empire probably changed less than in the Ottoman or Mughal empires because the Safavid economy changed less, and the empire participated less in the nascent world economy. But the Safavid regime did transform the religioius life of the country. The imposition of Twelver Shiism in the lands of the Safavid Empire created a national identity that overlay the distinction between Turk and Tajik. Before the Safavid era, the majority of Persian speakers were not Shii, and the majority of Shiis did not speak Persian. The Safavid effort to impose uniformity bore durable fruit.

SAFAVID CULTURAL AND INTELLECTUAL HISTORY

Safavid Iran produced some of the greatest achievements of Irano-Islamic civilization. Critics disagree about the poetry of the time, but Safavid achievements in art, architecture, and philosophy are beyond dispute. This cultural flowering took place even though there was clearly a flow of talent out of Safavid Iran. Intellectuals, especially ulama, fled Safavid territory because of the establishment of Shiism; poets, artists, and other intellectuals fled to the greater rewards of Mughal India.

The two great schools of Persian painting, the Turkmen school of western Iran and the Timurid school of Herat, came together when Shah Ismail united the two halves of the Iranian plateau. This coalescence of talent and artistic traditions produced a marvelous series of illuminated manuscripts during the reign of Shah Tahmasp, the greatest Safavid patron. He supported a royal painting workshop housing a hierarchy of artists organized as masters, journeymen, and apprentices with access to such exotic materials as ground gold and lapis lazuli. Tahmasp's interest in painting decreased in the second half of his reign as he focused more on personal piety. The patronage of Tahmasp's nephew Ibrahim Mirza, governor of Mashhad, and then of Ismail II during his brief reign produced a second creative burst later in the sixteenth century. But Shah Abbas's monuments were public buildings, not paintings.

IMAGE 4.4

Feast of Sada: folio from the Shah Tahmasp *Shahnama*. Containing the finest paintings in the history of Persian art, this *Shahnama* manuscript was among the gifts from Shah Tahmasp to the Ottoman Sultan Selim II in 1568. Hushang (the earth's second king in Iranian mythology) is shown celebrating his fortuitous discovery of fire.

IMAGE 4.5

Firdawsi's Parable of the Ship of Shiism: folio from the Shah Tahmasp *Shahnama*. In the prologue of the *Shahnama*, Firdawsi describes the world as a turbulent sea and exhorts the reader to take refuge with the Prophet, Ali, and Imam Ali in their ship. Emphasizing the Safavid claim to descent from Ali, the artist has portrayed the Prophet and his family wearing Safavid headgear.

IMAGE 4.6
Aerial view of the Maydan-i Shah (1590–1595), Isfahan. The centerpiece of Shah Abbas I's new urban center was the Maydan-i Shah. The Maydan was the forecourt of the Shah Mosque (foreground), the Ali Qapu (left), and the Shaykh Lutfullah Mosque (right) and a venue for state ceremonies and public entertainments.

References to Safavid architecture point primarily to Shah Abbas's Isfahan. His lesser projects at Ardabil, the original home of the dynasty, and at the pilgrimage center of Mashhad rival any attempted by his ancestors or descendents. There is no question that Abbas considered his new capital a symbol of his sovereignty and intended for it to outshine Istanbul and his older contemporary Akbar's works at Agra and Fatehpur Sikri. If Isfahan never matched its Ottoman rivals in wealth or population, it certainly did in magnificence, giving rise to the saying *Isfahan nisf-i jahan* (Isfahan is half the world). Abbas's works at Isfahan had two foci, the Chahar Bagh garden and the great square, the Maydan-i Naqsh Jahan (Image of the World Square). The Chahar Bagh, a broad, tree-lined avenue, stretched four kilometers from the center of the city across the Zayandarud (Isfahan's river) to a royal country estate. A parkway rather than an avenue of commerce, the Chahar Bagh is flanked alternately by gardens and palaces. The Maydan, at the northern end of the Chahar Bagh, was the ceremonial center of the empire. A rectangle half a kilometer long, the Maydan served alternately as a market, polo ground (the marble goal posts survive), and setting for public ceremonies.

Attached to the Maydan are two mosques, the Masjid-i Shah and Masjid-i Shaykh Lutf-Allah. The magnificent structures are the greatest triumphs of Safavid architecture. The Masjid-i Shah is not the congregational mosque of

IMAGE 4.7 *View of the Shah Mosque (1611–ca. 1638) and Ali Qapu (early 17th century), Isfahan.* Shah Abbas's largest architectural commission was the Masjid-i Shah which featured monumental marble and tile-mosaic portals and elegant, tall minarets. The Ali Qapu, initially a gate, was expanded and became the main royal residence with a loggia where Shah Abbas and members of the court could observe activities on the Maydan.

the city—Abbas's foundation was adjacent to the existing town and thus did not require a new mosque for the citizens—but the ceremonial place of worship for the ruler. It articulated the Safavid commitment to Shii Islam.

The smaller Masjid-i Shaykh Lutf-Allah, named for a father-in-law of Abbas, is a grand and beautiful setting for the ruler's private contemplation. Across the Maydan from the Shaykh Lutf-Allah is the Ali Qapu (Sublime Gate), a gateway, hall of audience, and reviewing stand leading to the Maydan and the imperial gardens. The Ali Qapu was elaborately decorated with wall paintings. Later Safavid rulers and other officials financed the construction of mosques, religious colleges, and other structures in Isfahan but none on a monumental scale.

Three major intellectual developments occurred in the Safavid period: the growth of Shii law and theology, including the beginning of the Akhbari-Usuli controversy; major developments in philosophy; and the appearance of the *sabk-i Hindi* (Indian style) in poetry. The advent of the Safavids gave Shii ulama and theologians greater official patronage than they had received in earlier centuries. Ismail and Tahmasp encouraged Shii scholars

IMAGE 4.8
*Masjid-i Shaykh Lutfullah (1617),
Isfahan.* The exquisite, colorful
glazed-tile decoration that adorns
the Shaykh Lutfallah mosque
contrasts with the Maydan's
comparatively austere brickwork.
Named for Shah Abbas' father-
in-law who was a prominent
religious scholar, the mosque was
used by the Shah's family and as
a women's sanctuary.

to settle in their empire; Abbas continued this pattern of recruitment and established religious colleges in Isfahan. They became the precursors of the religious colleges of Qum, Mashhad, and Najaf, which have dominated Shii religious life since the eighteenth century.

Shii thought changed considerably in Safavid times. The doctrine that Shii ulama capable of independent legal reasoning (*ijtihad*; the ulama were *mujtahids*) should exercise the religious and judicial authority of the Hidden Imam gained acceptance during the sixteenth century, though it was developed in Lebanon rather than Iran. This principle came to underlie Twelver Shii thought and practice up to the present, but not without controversy. The advocates of this position came to be known as Usulis (adherents of legal reasoning). In the seventeenth century, opposition to this position appeared; the opponents became known as Akhbaris. The Akhbaris rejected independent legal reasoning and the dominance of the *mujtahids*; instead, they emphasized the Quran and *akhbar* (reports) of the sayings and actions of the Prophet and imams as the authoritative pattern for human action. As noted above, the Shii doctors, the specialists in Shii theology and law who immigrated from Lebanon and Bahrain to

Iran, and their physical and intellectual descendents generally took the Usuli position; the provincial clerical notables frequently became Akhbaris. The dispute between the two schools continued through the Safavid period until the Usuli triumph in the eighteenth century. But the establishment of the Shii doctors as the major recipients of royal patronage in Safavid times determined the pattern of religious practice in Iran.

The flowering of Islamic philosophy in the Safavid era demands attention even though it took place within an intellectual tradition alien not only to contemporary Westerners but to contemporary Muslims. Seyyed Hossein Nasr, a profound and sympathetic student of this tradition, asserts that the "Safavid renaissance," as he calls it, developed as a product of the synthesis of four separate intellectual currents: "peripatetic (*mashshāī*) philosophy, illuminationist (*ishrāqī*) theosophy, gnosis (`*irfān*) and theology (*kalām*)," which had been gradually converging before Safavid times.[17] There was no hard separation between these esoteric disciplines and Shari learning. The major figures included Shaykh Baha al-Din Amili, known as Shaykh-i Bahai (1546–1621); Mir Muhammad Baqir Damad Husaini, known as Mir Damad (c. 1561–1630); and Sadr al-Din Shirazi, known as Mulla Sadra (c. 1571–1648). Shaykh-i Bahai's works encompassed every field of traditional Islamic learning, including commentary on the Quran, hadith study, jurisprudence, religious rituals, and Sufi doctrine and practice, as well as rhetoric, mathematics, and astronomy. He wrote the most famous work in Persian on Shii jurisprudence but was also a prominent Sufi poet.

Mir Damad also worked in the traditional religious disciplines but achieved his fame in philosophy, or rather in the combination of philosophy and Sufi mysticism known as theosophy. He became known as the third teacher in Islamic philosophy, after Aristotle and al-Farabi, and founded what came to be known as the School of Isfahan. His student Mulla Sadra, in Nasr's view, completed the integration of the philosophical and mystical traditions. Modern scholars, such as Fazlur Rahman and S. H. Nasr, consider Mulla Sadra's School of Shiraz one of the last truly creative intellectual enterprises of the Islamic world before the encounter with the modern West began.

The development of the Indian style of poetry has been a matter of controversy. Since the eighteenth century, critics, both Iranian and Western, have denigrated the Persian poetry of this period in comparison with the works of earlier years. The Safavid court could never rival Timurid Herat as a literary center. But literary production does not observe political boundaries. Safavid patronage fell short; poets from Safavid territory frequently sought patronage in the Mughal Empire and the other Muslim principalities of the Indian subcontinent. To distinguish Safavid from Mughal poetry is artificial and useless. The poetry produced in this environment differed in style and content from the great works of earlier Persian masters like Hafiz and Jami; some observers liken it to the symbolist poetry of England in the sixteenth and seventeenth centuries, such as the work of John Donne. Indian-style poetry is subtle and intricate, difficult to appreciate. But to regard it as a symptom of decline involves an aesthetic judgment, a matter of preference. There was no consciousness at the time of literary decline. There were also significant developments in prose, notably historiography, which have received significant attention from later scholars.

SAFAVID DECLINE

Andrew Newman, in his effort to provide an "alternative synthesis" of Safavid history, argues that Safavid historiography has given undue attention to the fall of the empire. Historians have considered the fall of Isfahan an inevitable consequence of the steady weakening of the empire after the death of Abbas I, of "the darkness of the fanatical religious orthodoxy amid military, political and economic chaos and 'weak' leadership at the center."[18] These studies, Newman argues, rely uncritically on Persian sources written long after the period in question and on Western sources; they are also teleological, judging the empire by its end. No historian has devoted a detailed study to later Safavid study after Abbas since Laurence Lockhart's 1958 work. The absence of contemporary Safavid sources on the reigns of the later shahs and the need to explain the fall of the empire remain, whatever agenda brings a historian to the problem. There is no way to deny that the Safavid project collapsed in 1722 because it lacked the military capability to defeat an enemy far less capable than many adversaries the empire had faced before. The empire that had retaken and held Qandahar more than half a century earlier could not muster a force capable of defending its own capital. The Ghalzay threat was not new; the earlier Baluch incursions had shown the military weakness of the empire decades earlier. It is impossible to escape the conclusion that the higher leadership of the empire did not seriously concern itself with military matters and that this inattention made it possible for Afghan tribal forces without siege weapons to defeat what had been a great power. The unmilitary nature of the leadership reflected the change in the character of Safavid rulers, which may well have reflected a change in the conception of monarchy, with piety replacing military prowess, as Leslie Peirce suggests for the Ottomans.

In the Ottoman case, the transfer of the focus of government inside the palace did not cause the military capability of the empire to atrophy entirely, but the Ottomans faced continuous external challenges. Senior officials of the regime led campaigns on a regular basis and had a stake in military success. The ruling elite of the Safavid Empire apparently had no such motivation. Without active supervision from the top, the military system atrophied. The tribal armies that established the empire had inherent military capability; the new central army required active maintenance. The continued transfer of land from *mamalik* to *khass* jurisdiction thus steadily weakened the empire militarily in the long run. By 1700, the provinces of Fars, Lar, Hamadan, and Kirman had been transferred to *khassa*. Crown provinces had the same military potential as treasury provinces, but they did not have it automatically. Tribal levies existed as long the tribes did; professional armies actually had to be recruited and paid. This system required vigorous oversight, which did not exist under Safi, Sulayman, and Shah Sultan Husayn. For this reason, the expansion of crown administration debilitated the Safavid military. Shah Sultan Husayn's royal pilgrimages cost as much as military campaigns; his construction program must also have been expensive. Government expenditures clearly did not fall when revenues did. This apparently led to increasing revenue demands and oppression of the population because the bureaucrats in charge of tax collection were frequently transferred and thus had no interest in the welfare or development of their temporary jurisdictions. Vigilance from the center could have minimized both of these trends. As it was, the oppression of crown administration caused significant population declines in some areas.

The ulama, the other group that gained power in the late Safavid period, pursued their own agenda without reference to the political interests of the regime. Whether or not they led to the Afghan uprising, Muhammad Baqir Majlisi's efforts to convert non-Shiis, Muslim or not, to Shii Islam clearly did not strengthen the regime. Though the courtiers persuaded the shah not to live by Majlisi's ban on alcohol, he determined Safavid religious policy. His aim was simple: the elimination of all other religions in Iran, including Sunni Islam. But however brutal it may have been, the application of this policy to the Christian, Jewish, and Zoroastrian communities of the country had little political effect.

From another perspective, Safavid decline needs less explanation than the existence of the empire at all. The Safavid project might easily have followed the common pattern of tribal confederations and collapsed into fragments rather than developed bureaucratic institutions and patterns after the death of Shah Tahmasp.

THE SAFAVID SYSTEM

Hans Robert Roemer, in one of the last publications of his long career, calls the Qizilbash the "founders and victims" of the Safavid Empire.[19] His description is apt. The Qizilbash flocked to the Safavid standards in response to the Shari Sunni bureaucratic rule of the Ottomans under Fatih Mehmet and Bayazid II and of the Aqquyunlu under Yaqub. Ismail's messianic claims promised the justice they sought. For nearly a century, the Qizilbash got what they wanted. Under Abbas, they lost out to the same bureaucratic authority and the same form of military organization that the Ottomans had created and Yaqub Aqquyunlu sought to emulate. Once the defeats at Ghujduvan and Chaldiran had dissipated the messianic impulse, the same political forces that had alienated the Turkmen from the Ottomans and Aqquyunlu became active in the Safavid realm.

With the exception of the substitution of Sunni for Shii Islam, political alignments in the Safavid realm resembled those in the Ottoman Empire before military and fiscal transformation. The *ghuluww*/nomad forces faced the Shari/bureaucratic/agrarian/*ghulam* (*qul*) coalition, which had the support of the crown. Abbas's fiscal and military reforms gave the victory to the forces of centralization. The Qizilbash tribes did not disappear but became fragmented and lost pasture grounds to other nomad groups like the Lur and the Bakhtiaris. The social power of the agrarian, bureaucratic regime with gunpowder weapons kept the nomads on the political periphery despite the lack of inspired leadership and effective oversight for most of the century between the death of Abbas I and the fall of Isfahan. Once the regime fell, however, the nomads regained the upper hand in Iranian politics and held it into the nineteenth century.

Though centralized bureaucratic rule did not survive, the Safavids clearly left an enormous impact on the area they ruled. Sunni Islam had virtually disappeared, the importance of Sufism in popular religion had declined enormously, and the Shii ulama had come to dominate the religious life of the country. Safavid achievements in architecture and painting are notable by any standard. The Safavids won and held the allegiance of diverse and divergent political constituencies. Legitimacy and loyalty, however, did not produce military power. The Safavid project did not fail, perhaps, but the Safavid regime certainly did.

Notes

1. Rudolph P. Matthee, *The Politics of Trade in Safavid Iran: Silk for Silver, 1600–1730.* Cambridge Studies in Islamic Civilization, ed. David O. Morgan (Cambridge: Cambridge University Press, 1999), 231.

2. Vladimir Minorsky, introduction and appendices to *The Tadhkirat al-Muluk: A Manual of Safavid Administration*, ed. and trans. Vladimir Minorsky. Gibb Memorial Series n.s. 14 (1943; rpt. London: E. J. W. Gibb Memorial Trust, 1980), 188.

3. Andrew J. Newman, *Safavid Iran: Rebirth of a Persian Empire* (London: I. B. Tauris, 2006), 8.

4. John E. Woods, *The Aqquyunlu: Clan, Confederation, Empire*, rev. ed. (Salt Lake City: University of Utah Press, 1999), 144.

5. Newman, *Safavid Iran*, 83.

6. Kathryn Babayan, *Mystics, Monarchs, and Messiahs: Cultural Landscapes of Modern Iran.* Harvard Middle Eastern Monographs 35 (Cambridge: Harvard University Press for the Center for Middle East Studies, 2002), xxiii.

7. Quoted in Vladimir Minorsky, "The Poetry of Shah Isma`il," *Bulletin of the School of Oriental and African Studies* 10 (1942): 1047.

8. Jean Calmard, "Shii Rituals and Power II: The Consolidation of Safavid Shiism: Folklore and Popular Religion," in *Safavid Persia*, ed. Charles Melville (London: I. B. Tauris, 1996), 80.

9. Ruli Jurdi Abisaab, *Converting Persia: Religion and Power in the Safavid Empire* (London: I. B. Tauris, 2004), 4.

10. Rosemary Stanfield Johnson, "Sunni Survival in Safavid Iran: Anti-Sunni Activities During the Reign of Tahmasp I," *Iranian Studies* 27 (1994): 131.

11. Babayan, *Mystics, Monarchs, and Messiahs*, 299.

12. Babayan, *Mystics, Monarchs, and Messiahs*, 313.

13. Abisaab, *Converting Persia*, 127.

14. Newman, *Safavid Iran*, 82.

15. Stephen Frederick Dale, *Indian Merchants and Eurasian Trade, 1600–1750.* Cambridge Studies in Islamic Civilization, ed. David Morgan (Cambridge: Cambridge University Press, 1994), 32.

16. Amin Banani, "Reflections on the Economic and Social Structure of Safavid Persia at Its Zenith, *Iranian Studies* 9 (1978): 93.

17. S. H. Nasr, "Spiritual Movements, Philosophy, and Theology in the Safavid Period," in *The Timurid and Safavid Periods*, ed. Peter J. Jackson and Laurence Lockhart, vol. 6 of *The Cambridge History of Iran*, ed. Harold Bailey et al. (Cambridge: Cambridge University Press, 1986), 658.

18. Newman, *Safavid Iran*, 6–7.

19. H. R. Roemer, "The Qizilbash Turcomans: Founders and Victims of the Safavi Theocracy," in *Intellectual Studies on Islam: Essays Written in Honor of Martin B. Dickson*, ed. Michel M. Mazzaoui and and Vera B. Moreen (Salt Lake City: University of Utah Press, 1990), 27–34.

Chapter 5

THE MUGHAL
EMPIRE

Like the Ottomans, the Mughals carried the dilemma of post-Abbasid politics outside the Arid Zone and resolved it. Unlike the Ottomans, the Mughals did not expand the frontiers of Muslim political power, except on some fringes. They established a new polity ruled by an established dynasty in territory that Muslims already ruled. The dynastic setting and the environment—physical, social, and cultural—requires careful explanation in order to make the Mughal success comprehensible. This section describes the multiple contexts in which the Mughal Empire developed and then summarizes the most important characteristics of the Mughal polity.

Historians have traditionally identified Babur as the founder of the Mughal Empire and considered his invasion of northern India in 1526 as the beginning of Mughal history. Both the identification and date are misleading. Babur's grandson, Akbar, established the patterns and institutions that defined the Mughal Empire; the prehistory of the empire dates back to Babur's great-great-grandfather Timur's invasion of north India in 1398. Because Timur remained in Hindustan (literally, "the land of Hindus"; the Persian word for northern India) only a short time and his troops sacked Delhi thoroughly, historians have traditionally treated his incursion as a raid rather than an attempt at conquest. Timur, however, did not attempt to establish direct Timurid rule in most of the areas he conquered;

he generally left established dynasties in place or established surrogates of
his own. His policy in Hindustan was the same; he apparently left one
Khizr Khan as his governor in Delhi. Khizr Khan and his successors remained formally subordinate to the Timurids for more than forty years,
probably until after the death of Timur's youngest son and effective successor, Shah Rukh, in 1447. Peter Jackson, the leading historian of the
Delhi sultanate, asserts that "Shah Rukh's influence in the subcontinent
seems to have been extensive."[1] Timurid prestige existed in the Deccan
(roughly the middle third of the Indian subcontinent) as well. Babur was
well aware of his ancestor's exploits and probably of the lasting connection
between the Timurids and Indian rulers. He did not describe his invasion
of Hindustan as a reassertion of Timurid governance there, but he certainly entered a region in which the image of Timurids as imperial sovereigns already existed.

   This emphasis on the Timurid identity of the Mughal dynasty raises
the question of nomenclature. Mughal is the Persian word for Mongol,
but the Timurids considered themselves Turks. They were known as
Mughals in the Indian subcontinent because there the term had come to
designate the Turkish-speaking military elite of central Asia. But neither the
dynasty that ruled the Mughal Empire nor the followers who helped establish the empire considered themselves Mughals. The dynasty was
Timurid; its Turkic followers were Chaghatays, taking their name from
the second son of Chingiz Khan. Chaghatay and his descendants had
ruled northeastern Iran and much of central Asia; the Turkic nomads of
that region took their identity from them. For the purposes of this chapter, the term *Mughal* refers to the distinctive set of political and military
institutions, political symbols and rituals, and cultural forms developed
during the reign of Akbar: Mughal could be glossed as Akbari. Akbar's
grandfather, Babur, who brought Timurid sovereignty to the subcontinent, and father, Humayun, were Timurids in the subcontinent, not
Mughals. The transition was not instant, especially since Akbar took the
throne as an adolescent and Humayun's chief officer became his regent.
Babur, not Akbar, won the great battles with the gunpowder techniques
that made the Timurids the greatest power in the subcontinent. But Akbar
established the durable political patterns and institutions of the empire.

   At its greatest extent the Mughal Empire extended from Kabul, Ghazni,
and Qandahar in contemporary Afghanistan east beyond Bengal into
Assam and south to the Cauvery River. The proclamation of sovereignty

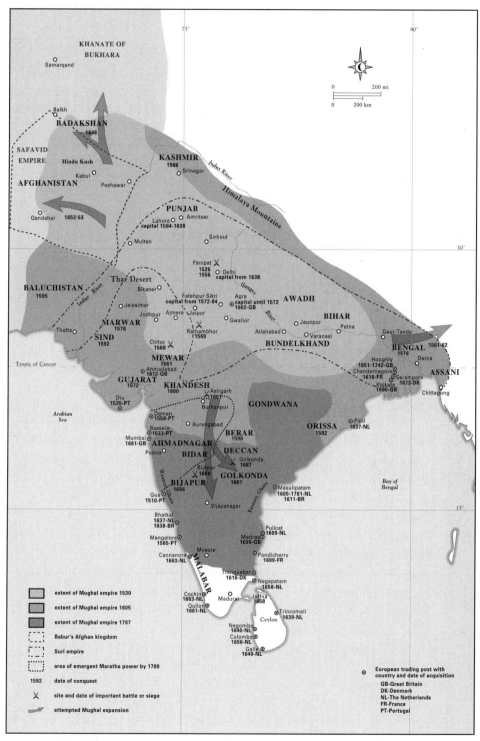

KHANATE OF
BUKHARA
Samarqand

Balkh
BADAKSHAN
1646

SAFAVID
EMPIRE   Hindu Kush
              Kabul
AFGHANISTAN   Peshawar

Qandahar 1652-53

KASHMIR
1586
Srinagar   Indus River

PUNJAB   Himalaya Mountains
Amritsar
Lahore
capital 1584-1638
              Sirhind
Multan

BALUCHISTAN   Panipat
1595   1526   Delhi
          Thar Desert 1556   capital from 1638
          Bikaner   Ganges
                  Fatehpur Sikri Agra   AWADH
          Jaisaimer capital from 1572-84 capital until 1572
          Jodhpur Ajmere Jaipur 1602-GB
MARWAR   Gwalior   Jaunpur BIHAR
1576   Rathambhor   Allahabad Patna
Thatta SIND I 1569   Varanasi Gaur-Tanda
1592   Chitor   BUNDELKHAND   BENGAL 1561-62
       1568   1576
MEWAR   Hooghly Dacca
1561   1651-1742-GB
Ahmadabad GUJARAT   Chandernagore
1612-GB 1572   KHANDESH   1616-FR   Serampore
          1600   Asirgarh   Kolkata 1673-DK ASSAM
Diu   1601   1690-GB
1535-PT   Burhanpur GONDWANA   Chittagong
Daman
1558-PT   Aurangabad
Bassein
1533-PT   BERAR   ORISSA
Mumbai   1596   1592   Pipli
1661-GB AHMADNAGAR   1637-NL
Poona   BIDAR DECCAN
        BIJAPUR Golkonda
        1686   1687
Goa BIJAPUR GOLKONDA   Bay of
1510-PT 1686   1687   Bengal
        Vijayanagar   Masulipatam
Bhatkal   1605-1781-NL
1637-NL   1611-BR
1638-BR
Mangalore Mysore Pulicat
1565-PT   1609-NL
Cannanore Madras
1663-NL MALABAR 1639-GB
          Tranquebar Pondicherry
          1616-DK   1699-FR
Cochin   Negapatam
1663-NL Madurai 1658-NL
Quilon   Jaffna
1661-NL   1658
          Trincomali
Negombo   Ceylon 1639-NL
1640-NL
Colombo
1656-NL
Galle
1640-NL

Arabian
Sea
Tropic of Cancer

extent of Mughal empire 1530
extent of Mughal empire 1605
extent of Mughal empire 1707
Babur's Afghan kingdom
Suri empire
area of emergent Maratha power by 1700

1592   date of conquest
✗   site and date of important battle or siege
         attempted Mughal expansion

European trading post with
country and date of acquisition

GB-Great Britain
DK-Denmark
NL-The Netherlands
FR-France
PT-Portugal

MAP 5.1 Mughal Empire

over that huge region did not, however, imply effective governmental control of all of it. In most of it, the Mughal regime did not interact directly with the general population but collected revenue through local intermediaries (zamindars); in some mountainous or remote areas, they exerted no authority at all.

Jos Gommans explains Mughal political and military geography superbly in his *Mughal Warfare*. The region that became the Mughal Empire included three general types of land: well-watered, intensely cultivated agricultural areas that commonly produced two crops of rice per year; more arid areas that produced wheat and millet with irrigation and were excellent pasture lands for horses and camels; and dense, humid forests that produced elephants but little else the Mughals, or any other regime, could use. Political power came from control of the revenue from the densely cultivated areas and from the animals and soldiers of the arid areas. The Arid Zone, which covers much of North Africa and Southwest Asia, extends south and east into the Indian subcontinent, from the Indus Valley to the head of the Ganges delta and south through the central part of the peninsula. In Gommans's words, "Mughal expansion was most successful in Arid India and in those parts of Monsoon India that were accessible by riverboats."[2] The swamps and forests of eastern Bengal, Assam, and Gondwana formed natural frontiers. Where arid territories formed the boundaries, they did so because the Mughals could not obtain any benefit by crossing them. The Mughal unification of the subcontinent consists, in Gommans's view, of a series of "nuclear zones of power" that had the desired combination of agricultural surpluses, extensive grazing lands, and access to major trade routes.

Most accounts of the cultural geography of the subcontinent before, during, and after the Mughal period emphasize the divide between Hindu and Muslim far more than any other factor, if not to the exclusion of all other factors. The religious divide separates polities and cultures and generates constant conflict, in which the Hindus steadily lose. The South Indian kingdom of Vijaynagar appears "a Hindu bulwark against Muhammadan conquests"; its fall to a coalition of Muslim regional kingdoms at the Battle of Talikota in 1565 is the final collapse of Hindu power at the hands of the aggressive and expansionist Muslims.[3] The current generation of historians, notably Richard Eaton and Phillip Waggoner, has exploded this image. By the time the Mughals came upon the scene, an Indo-Iranian political culture already dominated the subcontinent, encompassing the principalities of both Hindu and Muslim rulers. Hindu officers shifted allegiances between Muslim and Hindu rulers; it was possible to build a mosque in honor of a Hindu ruler. The ruler of Vijaynagar called himself "sultan among Hindu kings." Sufism and popular Hinduism intertwined, with some Sufi teachers accepting Hindu students and some Muslim adepts studying under Hindu gurus. Mystic literature also united Muslim and Hindu elements, and, as elsewhere in the Islamic world, folk Sufi practices incorporated indigenous elements. Not all Muslims accepted this tolerance and syncretism, but their objections did not prevent or terminate it. The tension between the two approaches to the Hindu environment was a lasting feature of Islamic culture in South Asia.

The conquests of Muhammad ibn Tughluq (r. 1324–1351) created the space in which the Indo-Iranian culture flourished. Muslim rulers had dominated the Indo-Gangetic plain since the end of the twelfth century. Expansion into the Deccan had begun under Ala al-Din Khalji (1296–1316). Muhammad ibn Tughluq extended his rule over virtually the entire subcontinent, but extremely briefly. His effort to solidify his control of the Deccan and South India by creating a second capital city at Daulatabad failed. By the end of his reign, the Bahmani sultanate and the kingdom of Vijaynagar had taken control of the Deccan and most of the south. The ability of the Mughals to conquer most of the subcontinent did not distinguish them from their predecessors. The ability to establish a lasting polity encompassing most of South Asia did.

Historians have categorized the Mughal polity in three ways. Most historians of the colonial era and the most influential group of postcolonial historians, the quasi-Marxist Aligarh School, have described the empire as a highly centralized bureaucratic despotism with an unquenchable drive to increase revenue. Tapan Raychaudhuri describes the Mughal state as "an insatiable Leviathan . . . [with an] unlimited appetite for resources."[4] In perhaps the most definitive statement of that position in an article addressing its critics, M. Athar Ali states, "The picture of the Mughal Empire in its classic phase, as a centralized polity, geared to systematization and the creation of an all imperial bureaucracy . . . still remain[s] unshaken."[5] Steven Blake developed the concept of the Mughal Empire as a "patrimonial-bureaucratic state," occupying a middle ground between traditional patrimonial monarchies, ruled essentially as family possessions and modern bureaucracies.[6] J. F. Richards supports this position in the most important book on the Mughals, his volume of the *New Cambridge*

History of India. All of these conceptions focus on the central government and, to a lesser degree, the imperial ideology of the Mughals. Farhat Hasan, I, and others, looking to the provinces as well as the center, come to different conclusions. The rhetoric of the central government, in words and rituals, articulated the image and intent of centralization and bureaucratization in accord with the Irano-Islamic tradition of statecraft. Conditions in the provinces, however, sharply restricted the ability of the central government to impose its will in the provinces. The Mughals had in theory, and sought in practice, the same direct relationship with individual peasants and soldiers that the *tahrir-timar* system gave the Ottomans. In practice, the Mughals rarely approached that standard. Most of their soldiers served an officer, who frequently had a power base (military and fiscal) that did not depend primarily on his position in Mughal service. Intermediaries, sometimes in multiple layers, separated the central government from the cultivators, who were the ultimate source of tax revenue.

Bernard S. Cohn's conception of multiple levels of politics, developed in a study of the Varanasi region in the eighteenth century, clarifies the situation. Cohn describes four levels of political activity: the imperial, secondary, regional, and local. The Mughals occupied the imperial level; only they participated in politics throughout South Asia. All participants in politics on the other levels conceded sovereignty to the Mughals, even though the Mughals had little effective authority in the period Cohn analyzes. The secondary actors, dynasties like the Nizams of Hyderabad, which had developed out of Mughal provinces, sought to dominate, in Cohn's words, "major historical, cultural, and linguistic" zones.[7] Regional actors sought to establish control of smaller areas within the secondary zones, generally receiving, or at least seeking, certification for their positions from imperial or secondary actors. Local actors, who generally had roots in established local lineages, received certification from secondary and regional actors and exerted control over the cultivators, merchants, and artisans who actually paid taxes. All of these actors sought freedom of action and security on their own levels and often to participate on a higher level.

All of these levels of politics operated throughout Mughal times. Imperial power consisted of the ability to manipulate and control actors on the other levels. Mughal officers (*mansabdars*; literally, "officeholders") occupied what would become Cohn's secondary and regional levels of politics. They controlled most of the empire's military manpower and collected and disbursed most of its revenue. Mughal power in the provinces was thus indirect, as in a tribal confederation or the indirectly ruled, as opposed to core, provinces of the Ottoman Empire. The Mughals governed indirectly because they ruled an armed population. The image of India as a peaceful society inhabited by seekers after spiritual enlightenment, now epitomized by the figure of Mohandas Karamchand Gandhi, has never fit the reality of the subcontinent. D. H. A. Kolff has demonstrated that Indian peasant men were normally skilled with weapons and frequently accepted military service far from their home villages. Some of them spent much of their lives as professional soldiers. The Mughals had to co-opt much of this massive indigenous manpower pool. To do so, they had to incorporate its leaders into their ruling class. The process of expansion was the process of incorporation. It brought such local potentates as the rajahs of Amber and Jodhpur into the Mughal system with military followers whose loyalty was to their own masters rather than the empire. The terms of incorporation defined the relationship of the emperor to his officers.

The empire could never have existed, of course, if the Mughals had not had sufficient military superiority to defeat their opponents. The same combination of artillery and mounted archers that enabled the Ottomans to defeat the Safavids, Mamluks, and Hungarians and the Safavids to defeat the Uzbeks gave the Mughals a definite but limited military superiority in the subcontinent. The Mughals, as well as their opponents, expected Mughal victories in battle. There were few major battles in Mughal history for that reason. Sieges were far more difficult, although the Mughals could normally force their opponents to surrender for terms. But this military superiority went only so far. It could not guarantee the modicum of order in the countryside necessary for the collection of revenue. The imperial army provided the ultimate sanction on which the regime depended, but the empire could not have survived on the basis of that sanction alone. The Mughals could not continuously fight to collect their taxes. They had to absorb, or at least neutralize, the peasant soldiers. They did so by giving status to the group known as zamindars (literally, "land-holders"), who held power on the local level.

The zamindars served as intermediaries between the actual cultivators and the imperial regime. They were an extraordinarily diverse group, ranging from peasants who collected revenue from their neighbors to regional potentates like the rajahs of Amber who became influential *mansabdar*s. A typical zamindar, if he ever existed, collected agricultural revenue, primarily in kind, from a village or group of villages, with the support of a small private army of peasants, and had his headquarters in a small wooden fort. He kept about 10 percent of the revenue and paid the balance to the designated imperial recipient, either a tax collector or assignee. The zamindar and imperial recipient normally negotiated the actual amount of tax paid each year. The imperial regime confirmed zamindars in their positions but rarely actually interfered with them. The zamindars stayed in place; the imperial recipients changed frequently. Most peasants had dealings only with a zamindar, not with the imperial regime. In some areas, several layers of zamindars separated the cultivators from the imperial administration. From one perspective, then, the empire was actually a series of small zamindar principalities that paid tribute to the imperial center.

The imperial *mansabdar*s, except for those who were also zamindars, ruled what might be conceived of as mobile principalities. Their private armies made up most of the imperial army but owed loyalty primarily to individual officers, not the emperor. Most of the empire's land revenue was assigned to the *mansabdar*s; the assignments were called *jagir*s (literally, "place taking"). The holders of assignments were *jagirdar*s (*jagir* holders). The same individuals were simultaneously *mansabdar*s and *jagirdar*s in different capacities. Since they collected taxes and maintained armies, the *mansabdar*s were de facto rulers. They were, however, subject to frequent changes in their assignments and official posts, which prevented them from transforming themselves into local potentates. The Mughal combination of imperial prestige, material incentives, and mechanisms of control persuaded the *mansabdar*s to act more like bureaucrats than like independent chiefs. This fact differentiates the Mughal Empire from the early Safavid Empire and other tribal confederations. There were remarkably few *mansabdar* rebellions in Mughal history. The complete absence of any reflection of *mansabdar* independence in Mughal political theory makes this situation appear even odder. Mughal political texts, notably the *Ay'in-i Akbari* (the official description of Akbar's empire and the most important single source on the Mughals), and court rituals depicted *mansabdar*s as extensions of the ruler. Their status and authority came from the emperor and was a product of their subordination to him. In fact, and in the provinces, a *mansabdar*'s rank often recognized his military following and prestige; in theory, and at the capital, his appointment created his status and power. This description may seem more appropriate for a degenerating empire, but it fits the Mughals at their zenith.

None of the earlier Muslim rulers or dynasties of South Asia had achieved the prestige or legitimacy that the Timurids had in central Asia. Timur's brief conquest of Delhi had extended his prestige to northern India. Babur's great military victories reinforced the status of his family. Akbar's charisma and record of success confirmed it. His alteration of the theoretical basis of his sovereignty both broadened and deepened his appeal. By ending the collection of the *jizya* in 1579, Akbar recast the theory that justified his position. Timur had presented himself simultaneously as the prop of the Shariah and the restorer of the Mongol Empire to what it should have been. His descendants discarded the Chingiz Khanid linkage and claimed a divine mandate through him. Akbar asserted that the divine mandate of sovereignty that had manifested itself in both Chingiz Khan and Timur reached complete fruition in him. But he abandoned the Islamic side of Timurid political theory and, with it, the definition of Muslims as the ruling class of the empire. Rather than upholding Sunni Islam, Akbar espoused *sulh-i kull* (peace with all, universal toleration) as the sovereign cult of the empire. He removed himself from the category of Muslim—though he never formally abandoned Islam—by claiming independent spiritual insight. He also incorporated both Muslim and Hindu officers and chiefs into a single ruling class. At court, clan leaders from central Asia, Iranian bureaucrats, Indian Muslim local leaders with prestige as Sufis, and Hindu Rajput chiefs and clerks were all *mansabdars*. Though Mughal officers learned Persian, the court language, they did not shed their ethnic and local identities in the way that Ottoman officials recruited through the *devshirme* and trained in the palace school generally did. Whoever their fathers had been, most Ottoman officers were Turkish-speaking Muslims. In the Mughal case, there was no linguistic or religious uniformity and no formal distinction between the rulers of subordinate principalities and purely imperial servants.

Also, the distinction between imperial servants and subjects, so crucial in the Ottoman system, was blurred under the Mughals. There were too many overlapping layers. Personal employees of ranking *mansabdars* could have greater income and influence than obscure imperial servants. Zamindars theoretically held office by imperial decree; they paid taxes as well as collected them. They did not normally contribute to the imperial army but did have to support imperial operations close to their territories. The division of the subjects of the Ottoman Empire into *millets* also had no Mughal parallel. There were no hierarchical organizations of Mughal subjects, Muslim or Hindu, and there was no official distinction between Muslims and Hindus.

This emphasis on the Mughal political theory and the empire's governing elite should not distract attention from the material basis of the Mughal regime, its wealth. The modern association of India with searing poverty had no place in the Mughal period. The Indo-Gangetic plain is an extraordinarily wealthy agricultural region by premodern standards. It routinely produces two harvests a year. The agrarian wealth of Hindustan (the northern third of the subcontinent, in the usage of the time) made the Mughal Empire far more prosperous than arid Safavid Iran. The subcontinent offered substantial mineral wealth as well and was a major center of commerce. Only a prosperous region could have supported the multiple and competing levels of politics that existed in the Mughal realm.

Mughal wealth provided cultural patronage. Indeed, the Mughal Empire became the center of Iranian culture during Akbar's reign. Mughal architecture and visual arts reflect fusion between Persianate and Indian traditions; such monuments as the Taj Mahal are the fruit of that merger. The Persian poetry of this period is called the Indian style (*sabk-i Hindi*) as a result of the primacy of Mughal patronage. But the Mughals also stimulated indigenous traditions as well, notably prose in Hindi, the north Indian vernacular descended from Sanskrit; their patronage helped to create literary Hindi.

CHRONOLOGY

Prehistory

When Babur invaded Hindustan in 1526, nothing remained of the Timurid connection to that region save the memory. Afghan tribesmen who had migrated into Hindustan had become the dominant military group. An Afghan leader, Bahlul Lodi, established a dynasty at Delhi in 1451. The Lodi rulers became important patrons, with close ties to the Muslim cultural elite of the region. Sultan Bahlul Khan ruled until 1488. His son and successor, Sultan Sikandar, founded Agra as a new capital. After his death, his sons Ibrahim and Jalal divided the kingdom between them, and it fell into disorder. This situation created the opportunity for the Timurids to return to the subcontinent.

BOX 5.1 The Delhi Sultanate

Although the Umayyad general Muhammad ibn Qasim conquered Sind (the lower Indus Valley) in 692 and Mahmud of Ghazna launched a series of raids into the Indo-Gangetic plain in the late tenth century, permanent Muslim rule in northern India did not begin until the early thirteenth century, under the Ghurid dynasty. Qutb al-Din Aybak (r. 1206–1211), a military slave commander under the Ghurid ruler Muizz al-Din Muhammad, became the ruler of an independent principality dominating north India when his master died in 1206. Aybak's slave Iltutmish (r. 1211–1236) succeeded him and received the title sultan of Hindustan from the Abbasid caliph. His capital was at Delhi, which became the political, cultural, and spiritual center of Muslim life in the subcontinent, and he and his successors were known as the Delhi sultans. A monarchy of military slaves similar to the contemporary Mamluk kingdom of Egypt and Syria ruled the sultanate until 1290. Two subsequent dynasties, the Khaljis (1290–1320) and Tughluqs (1320–1412), expanded the Delhi sultanate steadily south and east until Muhammad ibn Tughluq (1325–1351) briefly united the subcontinent under his rule, but his empire had begun fragmenting into regional kingdoms even before his death. After Timur's invasion of Hindustan in 1398, the sultanate was only one of several regional kingdoms. Khizr Khan, appointed governor of Delhi by Timur, founded the Sayyid dynasty, which ruled Delhi as a tributary of the Timurids. The Sayyid principality was the least of the Muslim regional sultanates, the others being Gujarat, Malwa, Jaunpur, Bengal, and the Bahmani sultanate in the Deccan.

The Sayyid dynasty survived in Delhi until 1448. Its army had come to consist primarily of Afghan tribesmen. One of their leaders, Bahlul Lodi, supplanted the last Sayyid ruler in Delhi and established the Lodi dynasty as well as the era of Afghan dominance in Hindustan. Under the Lodis, the Delhi sultanate regained a significant amount of territory in the east and south, including Jaunpur. Bahlul Lodi's son Sikandar established the new city of Agra in 1505. The Lodi rulers became major patrons of Islamic culture and learning and developed close ties to the leading ulama and Sufi families. Babur invaded Hindustan in response to the invitation of Daulat Khan Lodi, the Lodi governor of the Punjab, who resented Sikandar's efforts to establish a more centralized government.

Zahir al-Din Muhammad Babur Padishah Ghazi (1483–1530) undertook that enterprise, not by choice but for lack of an alternative. He was a fifth-generation Timurid; Timur's son Miran Shah was his great-grandfather. Babur's grandfather, Abu Said, had been the preeminent Timurid until his death in 1469; his father, Umar Shaykh, ruled the Farghana Valley from Andijan. When Umar Shaykh died in 1494, he left Babur (the name means "the Tiger") his small principality and, apparently, great aspirations. Babur's mother was a Chingiz Khanid Mongol princess; he thus combined both Timurid and Chingiz Khanid descent, but he considered himself a Turk and Timuri. The consequences of collective sovereignty had caused the Timurid realm to degenerate into a patchwork of warring principalities. From 1494 until 1514, Babur strove to unite the Timurid principalities under his leadership and above all to defend the Timurid lands against the Uzbek onslaught. He cooperated with the Safavids in the victory over Shaybani Khan at Marv in 1510 and the defeat at Ghujduvan in 1512. Three times he occupied Timur's old capital of Samarqand, which symbolized his ambitions; three times he had to abandon it. In search of a secure base, he had taken the city of Kabul in 1504. He led a brief raid into Hindustan, his first journey there, in 1505 but did not direct his ambitions south until after 1514. Though the precise narrative of Babur's invasions of Hindustan is uncertain, the one that mattered began in the late autumn of 1525. He had received an invitation from Daulat Khan Lodi, the governor of Lahore, to assist him in a rebellion against his master, Sultan Ibrahim Lodi. At Panipat, the Timurid army met Ibrahim Khan's much larger force on April 21, 1526. Babur used a wagon fortress, and the tactic worked as well for him as it did for the Ottomans later that year at Mohacs. He entered Delhi six days later. On March 16, 1527, Babur won another great victory at Khanua near Agra over Rana Sanga of Mewar, the leading Hindu ruler in Hindustan. With these two victories, Babur disposed of the two leading claimants to primacy in the northern subcontinent. The Afghans assembled a coalition against him in 1529. Babur won a third major battle on the Gogra River on May 6. He died in 1530, without an opportunity to transform his military superiority into durable political arrangements. Babur wrote one of the greatest autobiographies of world literature, the *Babur-Namah*, and was an extremely attractive character—but not the founder of the Mughal Empire.

Babur left four sons—Humayun, Mirza Kamran, Mirza Askari, and Mirza Hindal—each of whom received an appanage. Humayun received the throne of Hindustan and Kamran Kabul, Qandahar, and the Punjab. His experiences from 1530 to 1556 resembled Babur's from 1494 to 1526: He was beset both by powerful external enemies and threatened by fellow Timurids. He faced two great opponents, the new Afghan leader Shir Khan (later Shir Shah) Sur, and Mirza Kamran. Shir Khan was an Afghan officer in Lodi service but sought to gain power for himself and to expel the Mughals from Hindustan. He obtained both objectives. Humayun spent the first several years of his reign attempting to secure control of Hindustan and absorb the regional kingdoms of Gujarat and Malwa. This distraction provided Shir Khan with the opportunity to secure control of Bihar and Bengal. When Humayun finally engaged Shir Khan, the Afghans defeated the Mughals twice, at Chausa on June 26, 1539, and at Kanauj on May 17, 1540. Humayun fled to Lahore, where the four brothers met. Rather than allying against the Afghan danger, they split up. Mirza Kamran cooperated with Shir Shah, who claimed the throne of Hindustan, against Humayun. Eventually, Humayun fled through Sind and Qandahar and took refuge with Shah Tahmasp at Qazvin in 1544. Mirza Kamran ruled the remnants of Babur's realm from Kabul, and Shir Shah dominated Hindustan.

Shir Shah died in 1545. Shah Tahmasp provided Humayun with a small army. He had apparently demanded and received Humayun's acceptance of Shii Islam in return and also expected Humayun to cede the vital fortress and trade center of Qandahar to him. Humayun took Qandahar in 1545 and Kabul in 1547, regaining unmistakable primacy among the surviving Timurids and in Afghanistan. By 1552, he had finally eliminated the threat from his brothers. In Hindustan, Shir Shah's son Islam Shah had taken the throne after his father's death but was not an effective ruler. At his death in 1554, three contenders struggled for the throne. This disunity created an unmistakable opportunity for Humayun, who advanced from Kabul in December, defeated three Afghan forces, and on July 23, 1555, took Delhi. Six months later, on January 26, 1556, he died of injuries sustained in a fall.

Akbar

Jalal al-Din Muhammad Akbar was enthroned as ruler of Hindustan at Kalanaur in the Punjab on February 14, 1556. He was less than fourteen solar years old, his followers had only a tenuous hold on the Punjab and the Delhi-Agra area, and his father's inability to hold the empire his grandfather had conquered could hardly have engendered confidence. When Akbar died nearly fifty years later, he was one of the most powerful and wealthy monarchs in the world. The Mughal Empire was his achievement. In the beginning, however, he and his guardian, Bayram Khan Khan-i Khanan (khan of khans; the title implied primacy among Mughal officers), had to think of survival. At least there was no succession contest; Akbar had only two close living male relatives, his infant brother, Mirza Muhammad Hakim, in Kabul and a cousin who was a nonentity. But Akbar faced a host of other enemies. The greatest threat came from the Sur Afghan forces, now led by the Hindu commander Himu. Himu defeated the Mughal governor of Delhi and Agra, but the main Mughal army met his force at Panipat, the same field where Babur had defeated Ibrahim Lodi thirty years earlier, on November 5, 1556. Both sides fought hard, but the Mughals triumphed. Within two years, the Mughals had disposed of the Suri claimants and had extended their authority south to Gwalior and east to Jaunpur.

Bayram Khan governed the empire as Akbar's regent for four years. He consolidated Mughal power in western and central Hindustan and began expansion southward and eastward. But his position as regent could not last; his power annoyed his colleagues—and eventually Akbar. The young ruler dismissed Bayram Khan in 1560. Maham Anagah, his foster mother, dominated the regime for the next year, working with various officers. The officers who had held high rank under Humayun were especially disaffected and incited Maham Anagah's son Adham Khan to kill Shams al-Din Muhammad Khan Atgah, the husband of Akbar's wet nurse and Maham Anagah's final choice as chief officer. After Adham Khan had Shams al-Din Muhammad Khan murdered, Akbar ordered Adham Khan's immediate execution; Maham Anagah died forty days later. From this time on, Akbar governed for himself.

The expansion of the empire had begun during Maham Anagah's dominance. Malwa, the regional kingdom to the south of the Delhi-Agra region, had fallen into chaos under the misrule of Baz Bahadur, famous as an innovative musician but not as a political leader. A Mughal expedition conquered the province in the spring of 1561. Later the same year, Mughal forces commanded by Ali Quli Khan Khan-i Zaman, the governor of Jaunpur, defeated an Afghan attack on that city, which formed the eastern frontier of the empire. In 1562, Akbar made his first pilgrimage to the shrine of Khwaja Muin al-Din Chishti at Ajmer in Rajasthan, a standard practice among Muslim rulers seeking to establish their legitimacy. At this time, he entered into his first alliance with a Rajput prince, Rajah Bihara Mal of the principality of Amber (near modern Jaipur). To show that he accepted Akbar's sovereignty, Bihara Mal offered his daughter to Akbar in marriage. The Mughals also took a number of minor fortresses and obtained the submission of several small principalities between 1561 and 1563. When the governor of Malwa attempted to conquer Khandesh, the smallest of the principalities of the Deccan, he was defeated by Baz Bahadur, who then reoccupied Malwa. Baz Bahadur surrendered to a Mughal punitive expedition.

When Akbar took control of the government himself, his chief political and military subordinate was Munim Khan, a Chaghatay who had been one of Humayun's chief officers. He received the title *khan-i khanan*. Akbar's first financial minister was Itimad Khan, who had held a similar post under the Surs. Expansion continued. In 1563, two principalities, Bhath, or Panna, near the famous temples of Khajuraho, and the Gakkar country in the Punjab, surrendered to Mughal expeditions. The Mughals also conquered part of the great Rajput principality of Marwar, including its capital, Jodhpur. In the Gakkar and Marwar cases, a member of the ruling family of the principality entered Mughal service and obtained assistance in expelling a relative from the throne.

From 1564 to 1567, Akbar faced a serious challenge, the Uzbek rebellion. The Uzbeks in question were a family of Shaybani Uzbeks, relatives of the rulers of the Uzbek principalities. Their leader, Khan-i Zaman, was governor of Jaunpur and thus guardian of the eastern frontier of the empire against the Afghan threat from Bihar and Bengal. One of the most important Chaghatay officers, Khan-i Zaman did not seek to overthrow Akbar; his grievances concerned the terms of service of Akbar's officers. Many other Chaghatay officers, including Munim Khan-i Khanan, sympathized with the Uzbeks. Akbar sought repeatedly to reach a compromise with them, but the revolt did not end until Khan-i Zaman was killed in battle on July 9, 1567, more than two years after Akbar first marched against him. Akbar appointed Munim Khan governor of Jaunpur in Khan-i Zaman's place. This step removed the leader of the Chaghatays, and of the officers who had served Humayun, from the center of political activity.

During the same three years, Akbar faced two threats from other Timurids. Mirza Muhammad Hakim invaded the Punjab in 1566, perhaps because his advisors believed he would receive the support of the Uzbeks.

Akbar hastened northwest from Agra, and his approach was enough to drive his brother back Kabul. The next year, during the last phase of the Uzbek disorders, the sons of Muhammad Sultan Mirza revolted in the Punjab. Muhammad Sultan Mirza, a descendant of Timur's son Umar Shaykh and thus a distant cousin of Akbar, had served under Babur and Akbar; his sons had followed his allegiance. In the spring of 1567, they revolted in the Punjab, then joined Khan-i Zaman, and eventually fled to Malwa and then to the independent principality of Gujarat. The rebel Mirzas troubled Akbar again in 1568, during the conquest of Gujarat in 1572–1573 and again in 1577. Eventually, Akbar pardoned the last rebel.

Akbar next moved against the Sisodias of Mewar. Even after Babur's victory over Rana Sanga at Khanwa, the Sisodias had remained the most prestigious Hindu dynasty and the standard bearers for Hindu sovereignty. Their fortress capital of Chitor was among the strongest in the subcontinent. If Akbar could humble the rana, Udai Singh, other Rajput rulers might submit. Hoping to lure Udai Singh into battle, he approached Chitor with a small army. But Udai Singh fled, leaving Chitor prepared for a siege. Akbar sent a field force after the rana; the Mughals defeated Sisodia forces repeatedly but failed to capture Udai Singh. Though the rana did not submit to Akbar, there could no longer be any doubt of Mughal supremacy. The main force besieged the fortress for four months and finally took it by storm. The Mughal triumph at Chitor facilitated the conquests of two other major fortresses, Ranthambor, between Agra and modern Jaipur, and Kalinjar near Allahabad, in 1569.

Between the conquests of Chitor and Ranthambor, Akbar took another significant step. He dispersed the assignments of his foster family, known as Atgah Khayl. Akbar had given high positions to the son and brothers of Shams al-Din Muhammad Khan Atgah, his foster father, who had been murdered by Adham Khan. They held virtually the entire province of the Punjab. In 1568, Akbar summoned his foster uncles to court and assigned them new *jagirs* (land-revenue assignments, in Mughal parlance) in different areas of the empire. This peaceful dispersion of a powerful faction indicated Akbar's growing personal power.

In 1569 and 1570, Akbar's sons Salim, the future Jahangir, and Murad were born. Akbar attributed their births to the spiritual intervention of Shaykh Salim Chishti, a descendant and spiritual follower of the saint buried at Ajmer. Shaykh Salim's hermitage was located at Sikri, a village west of Agra. Akbar's wives both gave birth there. In response to this in-

IMAGE 5.1 *Buland Darwaza (1521–1522 to 1574) at Fatehpur Sikri, Uttar Pradesh.*
Literally the "Great Gate," this monumental portal leads to Fatehpur Sikri's
congregational mosque and the tomb of Shaikh Salim Chishti. This entire palatial
complex articulates Akbar's conception of sovereignty in red sandstone, combining
Central Asian with indigenous Indic architectural forms and decoration.

dication of Sikri's auspicious location, Akbar ordered construction of a
new capital complex there, to be called Fatehpur Sikri, in 1570. He also
continued regular pilgrimages to Ajmer.

In 1572, Akbar confronted the two remaining regional kingdoms in the
northern subcontinent, the sultanates of Gujarat and Bengal. Both kingdoms
were important centers of trade; Bengal, ruled by the Afghan Kararani dynasty, embodied the Afghan claim to supremacy in Hindustan. Akbar led an
expedition to Gujarat in the summer of 1572, obtained the surrender of the
leading Gujarati officers, and took possession of the capital of Ahmadabad.
The citadel of the port city of Surat, held by one of the rebel Mirzas, required
siege operations. The garrison surrendered in February 1573, apparently securing Mughal control of Gujarat. As soon as Akbar departed, however, the
Gujarati officers attacked the Mughal governor. In one of the most famous
episodes of his career, Akbar raced to the rescue, covering the 450 miles from
Agra to Ahmadabad in nine days with a small force and defeating a much
larger Gujarati army. This victory secured Mughal control of Gujarat.

Akbar sent Munim Khan against Daud Khan Kararani in Bengal. The Mughals took the frontier fortress of Patna after a long siege. Akbar sent Munim Khan to pursue Daud Khan and conquer Bengal and Bihar. The Mughal forces occupied the provincial capital, Tanda, with little resistance in September 1573. Munim Khan spent the next two years defeating the dispersed Afghan forces in detail. On March 3, 1575, Munim Khan defeated Daud and the main Afghan army in a hard-fought battle at Tukaroi; Daud surrendered. Seven months later, Munim Khan died, the Mughal army and administration in Bengal fell apart, and Daud regained control. Akbar sent a second army eastward under Khan-i Jahan Husayn Quli Khan, a nephew of Bayram Khan. He defeated Daud Khan in another battle at Raj Mahal on July 12, 1576. In the wake of this victory, the Mughals occupied several fortresses that had held out in Bihar and Bengal. In this way, the struggle for dominance in Hindustan between the Mughals and the Afghans, which began at the first Panipat, came to an end.

Akbar also continued operations against Mewar. Negotiations with Rana Pratap, who had succeeded his father, Udai Singh, in 1572, failed. Akbar then sent Man Singh, the grandson of Rajah Bihara Mal of Amber, against Rana Pratap. The two Rajputs met in battle at Haldighati on June 18, 1576; the Sisodia forces were overwhelmed. Rana Pratap escaped and evaded a series of expeditions between 1576 and 1585. The rana could not challenge the Mughal forces in the field or prevent them from sweeping through his principality, but he alone of the Rajput dynasts refused to submit to Akbar.

Administrative changes continued in parallel with expansion. In 1574, Akbar, assisted by a cadre of expert bureaucrats, established the defining institution of the Mughal regime, the *mansabdari* system. It placed all the officers of the empire in a single hierarchy with numerical ranks that represented the number of troops they were required to support. These measures, together with simultaneous alterations in provincial administration, decreased the political and fiscal autonomy of Mughal officers. Naturally, many of the officers resented these changes, especially Chaghatays like Munim Khan. Akbar dealt with their resentment by assigning them to the eastern frontier and softening enforcement of the new regulations. The dissidents conquered Bihar and Bengal. The concentration of Chaghatays in the east gave rise to the greatest crisis in Akbar's reign after the second Panipat.

In 1580, Akbar ended the exemption of the officers stationed in Bihar and Bengal from the new administrative regulations. The officers in both provinces, still predominantly Chaghatays, revolted, directing their operations against the officers Akbar had sent to enforce the new regulations. Historians have most commonly interpreted these revolts as responses to Akbar's religious innovations, discussed below. This interpretation does not fit the historical record. The Bihar rebels had no single leader, and Akbar defeated them without difficulty. The Mughal forces, under Tudar Mal, one of the architects of Akbar's program, then defended the fort of Monghyr on the Ganges against the rebels. The Bengal rebels attacked the imperial forces there.

Muzaffar Khan provoked the Bengal uprising by instituting severe salary reductions that Shirazi had ordered for the officers there and attempting to collect their debts to the treasury. Chaghatay officers of the Qaqshal clan led the uprising. The rebels stormed the provincial capital, Tanda, and executed Muzaffar Khan. They established a Timurid government, with the distant Mirza Muhammad Hakim as emperor; Masum Khan Kabuli, a leader of the Bihar rebels with personal ties to the Mirza, as regent; and Baba Khan Qaqshal, the actual leader of the rebels, as governor of Bengal and chief officer. Faced with this crisis, Akbar sent a second army east, this time commanded by Khan-i Azam Mirza Aziz Kukah, his foster brother, and Shahbaz Khan Kambu, one of the administrative reformers. Despite their personal connection, Akbar had dismissed Khan-i Azam from service because of his opposition to the new regulations. His reappointment indicated Akbar's willingness to compromise with the opponents of his policy. Khan-i Azam reached Monghyr in September 1580. The rebel forces dispersed, ending the threat, but operations against them continued until 1583.

The rebels had called upon Mirza Muhammad Hakim to invade Hindustan in order to force Akbar to fight on two fronts and to give additional legitimacy to their efforts. But Akbar had remained in Agra rather than going to the front because he expected his brother to march. When the Mirza invaded Hindustan in 1581, Akbar marched from Agra to meet him, and the invaders dispersed. Akbar pressed on to Kabul, was well received there, and left his chastened brother in place. Minimal though it was, the threat from Mirza Muhammad Hakim led to the execution of Khwajah Shah Mansur Shirazi as the result of false accusations that he had supported the Mirza. In this way, the leading officers eliminated their enemy.

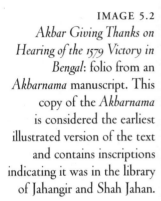

IMAGE 5.2
*Akbar Giving Thanks on
Hearing of the 1579 Victory in
Bengal*: folio from an
Akbarnama manuscript. This
copy of the *Akbarnama*
is considered the earliest
illustrated version of the text
and contains inscriptions
indicating it was in the library
of Jahangir and Shah Jahan.

In the wake of the revolts, Akbar adjusted many of the administrative regulations that had provoked them. The revolts, as well as the compromise that they brought about, completed the maturation of the Mughal Empire. For a century afterward, the institutions and practices that Akbar and his advisors had evolved functioned effectively and without major changes. The Mughals had also established unquestioned dominance in northern India and looked elsewhere for lands to conquer. There were only four possible choices: north, south, east, and west. Though the Mughals eventually absorbed Kashmir and part of Tibet in the north, these countries offered little wealth or prestige. The eastern border in Bengal, and beyond that Assam, received a significant amount of attention from the Mughals over the years but lacked large cities and major principalities. The governors of Bengal continued expansion in the east, but it was never a major focus of

Mughal policy. Due west lay the barren desert of Baluchistan. The major opportunities lay on the northwest frontier, beyond Kabul and in the Indus Valley, and on the southern frontier, in the Deccan. Events outside the empire forced Akbar's attention first to the northwest. The great Uzbek ruler Abdullah Khan forced Akbar's attention northwestward first.

Abdullah Khan had established his dominance over all the Uzbek principalities in 1582 and, like Akbar, was looking farther afield. In 1584, he invaded and conquered Badakhshan, the only surviving Timurid territory north of the Hindu Kush. But Abdullah Khan was too preoccupied with Khurasan to cross the mountains. No Timurid could ever discount the Uzbeks, however, and Abdullah Khan's success led Akbar to focus on the northwest for nearly a decade. Akbar moved to the Punjab to parry the Uzbek threat. Lahore became the center of his activities for most of the next decade. In 1585, Mirza Muhammad Hakim died. Akbar took direct control of Kabul.

Akbar sent expeditions to Baluchistan, to Kashmir, and to the Afghan tribal regions of Swat and Bajaur against the powerful Yusufzai tribe. The ruler of Kashmir had submitted to Akbar previously but refused to attend him personally. The remoteness of Kashmir made it difficult to subdue. The first expedition sent there in 1586 left the Kashmiri ruler in place as a tributary. Akbar did not approve of this arrangement, and a second invasion in 1588 led to the incorporation of Kashmir into the empire; its ruler became a Mughal officer stationed elsewhere. The leading Baluchi chiefs submitted to the Mughal expedition and attended Akbar at court in 1586. But the Afghan tribes proved a more serious challenge, as they remain today. The Mughals faced two centers of resistance, the politico-religious movement known as the Raushaniyyah (Illuminati) and the Yusufzai tribe. The Raushaniyyah were another *ghulat* movement, similar to the Safavids under Junayd and Haydar. The Yusufzai were a powerful tribal grouping that dominated the triangle formed by the Indus and Kabul rivers. The first Mughal expedition against the Yusufzai in 1586 ended in a disastrous ambush. A second expedition brought temporary order to the Yusufzai. The Mughals inflicted a crushing defeat on the Raushaniyyah in 1587, capturing their leader, Jalala, but he later escaped.

Although Akbar's attention was focused on the northwest, he missed no opportunity for expansion in the Deccan. The Bahmani sultanate, which dominated the Deccan for more than a century after the short-lived Tughluq control of the Deccan, had splintered at the end of the fifteenth century.

What had been Bahmani provinces became the Deccan principalities that the Mughals encountered: Khandesh, Ahmadnagar, Bijapur, and Golconda.

Expansion in the Deccan began slowly. The principality of Khandesh, just south of Malwa, was a natural refuge for enemies of, and rebels against, the Mughals. This circumstance led to Mughal expeditions into Khandesh in 1562 and 1576. The latter expedition forced the ruler of Khandesh to accept subordination to Akbar. In 1585 and 1589, Akbar sent Mughal forces to support a candidate for the throne of Ahmadnagar without positive result. In 1590, Akbar's candidate won the kingdom on his own, then renounced his allegiance to Akbar. This rebellion, as it was seen in Mughal eyes, led Akbar to send embassies to demand the submission of all the Deccan potentates and to prepare a major expedition south, to be commanded by his second son, Murad. The embassies failed. Before the Mughal army reached Ahmadnagar, however, war broke out between Bijapur and Ahmadnagar. The Nizam-Shah (ruler of Ahmadnagar) was killed in battle, leading to a scramble for the throne. This disorder prevented effective resistance to the Mughal expedition, which began siege operations against Ahmadnagar city in 1595. Murad was not an effective commander, and Chand Bibi, a Nizam-Shahi princess who had become regent of the kingdom, defended the city effectively. Relief expeditions from Bijapur and Golconda forced the Mughals to abandon the siege after nearly six months.

Akbar's forces had greater success elsewhere. A Mughal expedition conquered the principality of Sind in 1590. In 1594, Akbar gained control of Qandahar when the Safavid governor, fearing arrest and execution at the hands of Shah Abbas, surrendered the province to Akbar. He and his followers became loyal Mughal officers. In the east, Rajah Man Singh, the governor of Bengal, conquered the province of Orissa and extended the Bengal frontier eastward.

After Abdullah Khan died in 1598, Akbar returned to Agra to prepare his own Deccan expedition. He sent his chief minister and propagandist, Abu al-Fazl, to take charge of events until he arrived. Murad had died of natural causes, leaving the Mughal forces in complete disarray. Abu al-Fazl restored order and led another invasion of Ahmadnagar. Akbar's third son, Danyal, took titular command. The Mughals took Ahmadnagar and several other fortresses in 1600–1601. These conquests ended the first phase of Mughal expansion in the Deccan. The Mughals had absorbed Khandesh and most of Ahmadnagar. Bijapur, Golconda, and a rump of Ahmadnagar remained autonomous.

IMAGE 5.3
Jahangir and Shah Abbas (Jahangir's Dream): folio from the St. Petersburg Album. Contemporary European allegorical compositions probably inspired the wish-fulfilling compositions painted for Jahangir. This portrayal of amicable dominance depicts Jahangir towering over a diminutive Abbas with the Mughal lion pushing the Safavid lamb into Ottoman territory.

At this time, the succession to Akbar became an issue. Salim had revolted against Akbar in 1599 but won little support. In early 1605, Danyal died of natural causes, and Akbar's physical condition began to deteriorate. It appeared that Salim would succeed without a contest. A rival appeared in the form of Salim's own eldest son, Khusraw. He had the support of Rajah Man Singh of Amber and Khan-i Azam Mirza Aziz Kukah, both of whom were close to Akbar and feared exclusion from power. The majority of officers, however, supported Salim. Akbar died on October 15, 1605. He had ascended a shaky throne as a boy; he left an empire dominating the subcontinent.

Jahangir

Salim took the throne under the name Jahangir and appointed his own followers to high offices. The next year, Khusraw fled from the court, which constituted revolt. He apparently feared exclusion from the succession and imprisonment, but his earlier backers did not support him. Jahangir pursued his son with overwhelming force, defeated and captured him, and executed many of his supporters. The victims included Guru Arjun Singh, the fifth leader of the Sikh faith, who had not actually supported Khusraw but had offered the desperate young man his blessing. Jahangir's purely political vengeance for an act of kindness to a renegade began the poisoning of relations between Sikhs and Muslims that led to centuries of violence.

Though neither energetic nor gifted, Jahangir reigned effectively from 1605 to 1622. The Mughal garrison of Qandahar fought off a Safavid siege in 1606. Further south, the Mughals finally won the submission of Mewar. Campaigns in 1606, 1608, and 1609 to 1611 failed to put an end to Sisodia resistance, despite numerous battlefield victories. In 1614, Jahangir's second son, Khurram, took the field. His forces devastated the country and starved the rana, Amar Singh, into submission. In return for his acceptance of Mughal authority, Amar Singh was allowed to keep all his territory and pay no tribute. There was only one symbolic condition: Chitor, the capital that represented the Sisodia claim, could not be refortified or repaired. This submission by Rana Amar Singh was the greatest triumph of Jahangir's reign, but it was Khurram's achievement, not Jahangir's. For this victory, Khurram received the title by which he is known to history, Shah Jahan.

Jahangir's weakness gave greater influence to his ministers and confidants than people in those positions had under the other Mughal rulers. The most famous of them, of course, was Nur Jahan, whom Jahangir married in 1611. The romantic story of Jahangir's attachment to her dominates popular accounts of the reign. Nur Jahan was clearly the most influential woman in Mughal history; she set an enduring pattern for feminine apparel. But her actions were responsible for years of turmoil in the empire, and her political influence depended in great part on the political and administrative abilities of her father and brother, not her hold over her husband. The sordid reality of Nur Jahan's efforts to perpetuate her power at the cost of imperial unity and family harmony outweighs the romance. Nur Jahan's father, who had the title Itimad al-Dalwah, was one of the leading figures of the regime until his death in 1622. Her brother Asaf Khan remained prominent after Nur Jahan's marriage to Jahangir until his own death in Shah Jahan's reign. He benefited from both his sister's marriage to Jahangir and that of his daughter, Arjomand Banu Begum (later known as Mumtaz Mahal) to Shah Jahan. The third dominant figure of the time was Mahabat Khan, a remarkable and determined military commander. Nur Jahan, Asaf Khan, Shah Jahan, and Mahabat Khan were the four dominant figures of Jahangir's court. But before discussing that struggle, we must turn our attention to the Deccan and the fifth great figure of the period, Malik Ambar.

Malik Ambar was among the greatest African statesmen and warriors of history. Brought from the Horn of Africa as a military slave, he made himself the effective ruler of the rump of Ahmadnagar. His strategy of avoiding battle with Mughals while harassing their forces and threatening their supply lines became the pattern of resistance to Mughal power in the Deccan. He defeated a series of Mughal expeditions between 1608 and 1616. Jahangir sent Shah Jahan to the Deccan in 1617. His strength and prestige persuaded Malik Ambar and his allies in Bijapur and Golconda to accept Mughal sovereignty, repay tribute, and restore territory conquered by Malik Ambar to Mughal control. Shah Jahan's success in the Deccan complemented his triumph in Mewar.

In 1620, when he was forty-eight, Jahangir's health, weakened by prolonged abuse of alcohol and opium, deteriorated visibly. The specter of his death began the struggle for succession, though he lived for another seven years. He had four sons, Shah Jahan, triumphant and well connected; Khusraw, capable but long imprisoned; Parviz, an ambitious drunk supported by Mahabat Khan; and Shahryar, a weak adolescent whom Nur Jahan supported in order to remain in control. Jahangir and Nur Jahan had no children together; Nur Jahan arranged the marriage of Shahryar to her own daughter by a previous marriage. Asaf Khan played a double game, supporting his sister and Shahryar openly but actually working for his son-in-law Shah Jahan.

In 1620, Malik Ambar broke his agreement with the Mughals. Jahangir deputed Shah Jahan to deal with this threat. The prince, fearing that his father would die in his absence, demanded custody of Khusraw, his most dangerous rival. In August 1621, hearing that Jahangir was dangerously ill, Shah Jahan had Khusraw executed. The struggle for succession had begun.

In 1622, Shah Abbas besieged Qandahar. Jahangir ordered Shah Jahan to march north from the Deccan. He refused, demanding various conditions to safeguard his interests. Nur Jahan turned to the only man capable of defending Jahangir from his son, her enemy Mahabat Khan, to command an army against the prince. The two armies met at Bilochpur on

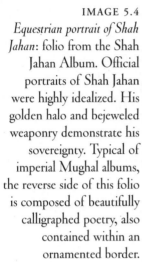

IMAGE 5.4
Equestrian portrait of Shah Jahan: folio from the Shah Jahan Album. Official portraits of Shah Jahan were highly idealized. His golden halo and bejeweled weaponry demonstrate his sovereignty. Typical of imperial Mughal albums, the reverse side of this folio is composed of beautifully calligraphed poetry, also contained within an ornamented border.

March 29, 1623. Mahabat Khan triumphed and continued southward. For four years, the struggle between Mahabat Khan, fighting for himself and Parviz and for Nur Jahan and Shahryar, and Shah Jahan, fighting to succeed to a throne he could not claim, convulsed the empire.

In the end, Shah Jahan took refuge in Ahmadnagar. Malik Ambar welcomed him. With the defeat of Shah Jahan, Nur Jahan's enmity toward Mahabat Khan outweighed her need for him. When Mahabat Khan returned to court, he took desperate action to protect his interests, launching a coup d'état and removing Jahangir from Nur Jahan's control by kidnapping him. Eventually, Nur Jahan submitted, and Asaf Khan fled. It appeared that Mahabat Khan had secured control of the empire and the succession of his protégé, Parviz. But he had little support from other officers and none from Jahangir. Nur Jahan arranged a countercoup. Shortly afterwards, Parviz died, leaving Mahabat Khan without a candidate for the throne. He joined Shah Jahan in Ahmadnagar. Nur Jahan remained in control until Jahangir's death.

Shah Jahan

When Jahangir died on October 29, 1627, Shah Jahan was in exile in the Deccan, and Shahryar was at court. Asaf Khan swung the balance of power to Shah Jahan. He enthroned a tool of his own, Dawar Bakhsh, a son of the late Khusraw, so as not to appear a rebel in challenging Shahryar in Shah Jahan's absence. Nur Jahan was unprepared for this move, and Asaf Khan's forces defeated the army she had assembled on behalf of Shahryar. Virtually all the leading officers of the empire supported Asaf Khan. Shah Jahan, accompanied by Mahabat Khan, had marched north. Before Shah Jahan arrived, Asaf Khan dethroned Dawar Bakhsh. Shah Jahan was enthroned in Agra on January 28, 1628, and ordered the execution of all his male relatives except his own sons. Asaf Khan and Mahabat Khan, formerly opponents in the struggle for power, became his chief officers.

Shah Jahan's reign had three phases: from his accession through 1635, from 1635 through 1653, and from 1653 through his deposition in 1658. During the first phase, he resolved a series of problems resulting from his accession and on the empire's eastern and Deccan frontiers. Two of Jahangir's high officers, Khan-i Jahan Lodi, the governor of the Deccan, and Jujhar Singh Bundilah, the ruler of the principality of Bundelkhand in central India, had influential positions because of their personal connections to Jahangir. Khan-i Jahan fled from court, implying rebellion, to Ahmadnagar in 1629. His flight led to the renewal of hostilities between the Mughals and Ahmadnagar, in the course of which he was caught and killed. Jujhar Singh eventually rejected Shah Jahan's repeated efforts to reconcile and eventually was killed as a rebel in 1635.

In the east, Shah Jahan had a grievance against the colony of Portuguese renegades at Hooghly in Bengal (across the Hooghly River from modern Kolkata) because they had not supported him during his rebellion and because they enslaved Muslims and forced them to convert to Christianity. The Mughals eliminated the colony in 1632 after a long siege.

Mughal forces were also active on the northern, northeastern, and northwestern frontiers of the empire and in central India, forcing submission from various local rulers and subduing disorderly tribes. They parried an attack by Nazr Muhammad Khan, the Uzbek ruler of Balkh, on Kabul. In the Deccan, Shah Jahan sought to eliminate Ahmadnagar once and for all. Operations began during the pursuit of Khan-i Jahan. There was little doubt that the

Mughals would succeed, and many Deccani chiefs defected to the Mughals. They included the first Marathas to enter Mughal service. The heart of the Nizam-Shahi kingdom was now the great fortress and city of Daulatabad. When the Mughals began siege operations against Daulatabad after conquering several lesser forts, the Nizam-Shahis, led by Fath Khan, Malik Ambar's son, accepted Mughal sovereignty. During this campaign, Mumtaz Mahal, who as usual had accompanied Shah Jahan, died at Burhanpur on June 7, 1631, after delivering their fourteenth child. Shah Jahan's devastating grief contributed to his decision to accept the Nizam-Shahi submission and to return to Hindustan in 1632. Construction of her magnificent tomb, the Taj Mahal, began shortly thereafter and continued until 1659.

After Shah Jahan withdrew, the Adil-Shahis of Bijapur sought to gain control of Ahmadnagar as a buffer against the Mughals. Fath Khan switched sides. Mahabat Khan, commanding the Mughal force, besieged Daulatabad and forced Fath Khan to surrender, thus ending the history of Ahmadnagar as an independent principality. A number of Nizam-Shahi officers, including a Maratha chieftain named Shahji Bhonsle, continued to resist. In 1634, Mahabat Khan besieged the Adil-Shahi fortress of Parenda but failed and died shortly afterwards. Shahji and the Adil-Shahis kept the Mughal forces under pressure. In 1635, however, the Mughal emperor returned to the Deccan in person. He coordinated operations against Shahji and the Adil-Shahis. To avert disaster, the Adil-Shahis agreed on a settlement, offering recognition of Mughal sovereignty, tribute, and military cooperation against Shahji. Shah Jahan then turned against Golconda, which accepted a similar settlement. Its Shii Qutb-Shahs were required to name Shah Jahan, rather than the Safavid shah, in the *khutba*. The Mughals promised to protect Golconda from Bijapur. The treaties with Golconda and Bijapur symbolically incorporated the two surviving Deccan principalities into the Mughal Empire and produced almost two decades of stability in the Deccan.

The resolution of the extended Deccan crisis freed Shah Jahan to look elsewhere. Elsewhere meant northwest and especially toward Qandahar, which had remained in Safavid hands since 1622. In 1636, Shah Jahan proposed an alliance with the Ottomans and Uzbeks against the Safavids and offered the Safavid governor of Qandahar a bribe to surrender the city. Nothing came of this effort at first, but two years later, it bore unexpected fruit. The governor, Ali Mardan Khan, surrendered the city to the Mughals rather than face probable execution at the hands of the Safavid government. Hoping to keep this fortuitous acquisition without going to war with the Safavids, Shah Jahan offered Shah Safi financial compensation and an alliance against the Uzbeks. Safi would accept no deal, but the Ottoman threat prevented him from acting. The acquisition of Qandahar permitted Shah Jahan to undertake the conquest of central Asia, his family's dream since Babur's time.

Conditions in the Uzbek principalities favored the Mughal chances. Nazr (or Nadir) Muhammad Khan, the Uzbek prince who had attacked Kabul in 1628, became the paramount khan of the Uzbek principalities in 1641. His policies provoked widespread opposition, and in 1646 he requested Shah Jahan's assistance against his rivals. Shah Jahan assembled a major army, commanded by his youngest son, Murad Bakhsh, to conquer Balkh and Badakhshan and extend Mughal power north of the Amu-Darya. The Mughal forces occupied Badakhshan and Balkh with little difficulty, but Nazr Muhammad Khan grew wary of his powerful ally. He fled to Safavid territory. Rather than press on across the Amu-Darya, Murad Bakhsh returned to Hindustan without orders. He left the Mughal forces in remote and difficult country, without an effective leader, facing a dispersed and mobile opponent. Shah Jahan dispatched Aurangzeb, his third son and a capable soldier, to replace Murad. He arrived in Balkh just in time to face a counterstroke from Abd al-Aziz Khan, the new ruler of Bukhara. The Mughals defeated the Uzbeks in a battle on May 31, 1647. This struggle, so obscure it lacks a name, was perhaps the last major battle between a gunpowder empire and a tribal confederation; it resembled closely Fatih Mehmed's triumph over Uzun Hasan Aqquyunlu in 1473. Despite this victory, the Mughals had no choice but to withdraw to Kabul, leaving Balkh and Badakhshan to the Uzbeks. A folk etymology explains the name of the Hindu Kush (Hindu killer) mountains as a reference to the many Hindu troops killed in this campaign.

The next year, Abbas II reconquered Qandahar. Shah Jahan sent expeditions to recover the city in 1649 and 1652 under Aurangzeb and in 1653 under his eldest and favorite son, Dara Shukuh. All three expeditions failed; despite victories against Safavid field forces, the Mughals could not take the fortress. Qandahar remained in Safavid hands until the Ghalzay uprising. The Mughals thus failed to hold either of the northwestern conquests of Shah Jahan's reign.

During this preoccupation with the northwest frontier, Shah Jahan began construction of a new imperial capital adjacent to the existing urban center at Delhi. Called Shah Jahanabad and now referred to as Old Delhi, it replaced Akbar's buildings at Agra as the symbolic center of the empire, though the actual capital was always wherever the ruler happened to be. Both Agra and Lahore were cramped and dominated by earlier Mughal structures; Delhi retained prestige as the traditional Muslim capital and was a major pilgrimage center. Construction began in 1639; the major projects were the citadel now called the Red Fort and the Jama Mosque adjacent to it. Shah Jahan made a symbolic entrance to the completed complex in 1648. His construction program also included the Taj Mahal, marble buildings inside the Agra Fort, and improvements to the imperial complex at Lahore.

The era of stability in the Deccan ended in 1653. Aurangzeb, now governor of the Deccan, found pretexts for invading both Golconda and Bijapur. In 1656, Aurangzeb invaded Golconda and besieged the capital, but failing to obtain his father's permission to conquer it, he withdrew. That same year, Bijapur fell into disorder, and Aurangzeb sought and received authorization to annex it. In the midst of successful operations, however, Shah Jahan changed his mind, and again Aurangzeb withdrew, having extracted an indemnity and several frontier districts. In 1652, Rana Jagat Singh of Mewar began repairs on the fortress of Chitor in contravention of the agreement Shah Jahan had imposed on his grandfather three decades earlier. A massive Mughal expedition demolished the repairs, and Rana Raj Singh, Jagat Singh's successor, submitted without resistance.

In September 1657, Shah Jahan, now sixty-five, fell seriously ill. His affliction precipitated the greatest of the successor wars in any of the gunpowder empires. The contending princes were the leading officers of the empire. The eldest, Dara Shukuh, whom Shah Jahan had designated his heir apparent, effectively acted as his father's chief officer at court and governed the provinces of Lahore, Multan, and the Punjab through deputies. The second son, Muhammad Shuja, governed the wealthy province of Bengal; the third, Aurangzeb, governed the Deccan; and the fourth, Murad Bakhsh, governed Gujarat. The three younger brothers were jealous and suspicious of Dara. When Shah Jahan's illness prevented him from appearing in public, they believed their father dead or incapacitated and Dara to be securing his own succession, as indeed he was.

Shah Jahan wanted his eldest and favorite son to succeed; Dara desired to secure the throne. But the father was ill, and the eldest son incompetent. Late in 1657, Murad and Shuja both claimed sovereignty for themselves. Shah Jahan had recovered by this time, but none of the absent princes believed it. Dara sent armies east against Shuja and south to face Murad and Aurangzeb, who had joined his brother but not claimed the throne for himself, under Maharajah Jaswant Singh Rathor, the hereditary ruler of Jodhpur. These expeditions produced the first two battles of the succession war, at Bahadurpur near Benares on February 15, 1658, and at Dharmat near Ujjain on April 15, 1658. Dara's army scattered Shuja's force at Bahadurpur but withdrew after the news of Aurangzeb's triumph at Dharmat.

Aurangzeb, the only brother with a military reputation, had agreed with Murad to partition the empire. They broke Jaswant Singh's force in the field. Aurangzeb gathered the booty and swiftly marched north toward Agra. The victory confirmed his military reputation and added to his prestige. Dara set about assembling another army at Agra while his older sister Jahan Ara and Shah Jahan himself sought to avert another battle in letters to Aurangzeb. But Aurangzeb now considered his father only a tool of Dara Shukuh and made clear that he would seize power to deny the throne to his eldest brother. Aurangzeb forced his brother to accept battle at Samugarh, outside Agra, on May 29, 1658, before the eastern army had returned. Though outnumbered, Aurangzeb had every other advantage; Dara's own troops fought hard, but not all his officers did, and he himself made serious tactical errors. Dara's army was routed with heavy casualties. Dara fled toward Delhi, his reputation and confidence shattered. Aurangzeb camped outside Agra, the officials of his father's government submitted to him, and Shah Jahan surrendered Agra Fort a few days later. Aurangzeb thus gained possession of the imperial treasury and arsenal and reduced his imperial father to a prisoner. Shah Jahan now proposed that his sons partition the empire and offered to make Aurangzeb his heir, but the prince rejected any compromise that included Dara. He refused to visit his father, fearing assassination, and placed him in close confinement. When Murad grew jealous of his dominance, Aurangzeb imprisoned and later executed him.

Shah Jahan's submission made the elimination of Dara Shukuh Aurangzeb's first priority. Dara had fled from Delhi to Lahore. Aurangzeb pursued, pausing at Delhi long enough to be enthroned on July 21. When Aurangzeb and his formidable army approached Lahore in August, Dara retreated to Multan and down the Indus. Defections weakened Dara's forces. In November, he fled from Sind to Gujarat. The news of Aurangzeb's westward pursuit of Dara encouraged Shuja to make another bid for the throne. He set forth from Patna at the end of October 1658. Aurangzeb abandoned his pursuit of Dara and hastened east. The two brothers met in battle on

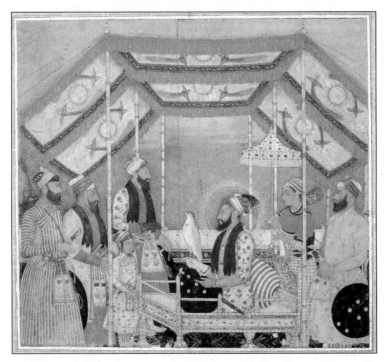

IMAGE 5.5 *Darbar of Aurangzeb*. Seated amid the trappings of imperial
opulence, Aurangzeb is shown receiving his young son and noblemen.
His shield, sword, and the trained falcon reflect the ruler's martial
prowess. Later images of Aurangzeb emphasize his piety.

January 5, 1659, at Khajwa. Aurangzeb's forces' superior numbers and discipline won the day; Shuja fled and eventually disappeared.

Encouraged by false reports that Shuja had defeated Aurangzeb, Dara
challenged his brother once more. The two armies met near Ajmer and
waited for the final denouement to the succession war on March 14, 1659;
the battle is called Deorai or Ajmer. Aurangzeb again triumphed, and Dara
fled. He was finally captured in Sind, paraded through Delhi in chains, and
executed as an apostate from Islam. So ended the struggle for succession. On
June 5, 1659, Aurangzeb was enthroned for a second time in Delhi.

Aurangzeb

Aurangzeb's reign had two phases, from 1659 to 1679 and from 1679 to
his death, at the age of eighty-nine, in 1707. The first phase was relatively

uneventful, with no major political changes or conquests. The second began with a major change in religious policy, thus in the constitution of the empire, and continued with the final conquest of Bijapur and Golconda and perpetual warfare against the Marathas in the Deccan. The second phase of Aurangzeb's reign coincided with the beginning of the loss of Mughal control of many of the provinces of the empire. The two phases also differ geographically; Aurangzeb spent the first in northern India and the second entirely in the Deccan.

With Dara dead, Shah Jahan feeble and imprisoned, Murad Bakhsh likewise confined, and Shuja defeated and fleeing, Aurangzeb had little to fear. His repeated victories in battle had demonstrated his legitimacy, and there was no widespread opposition among his officers. In 1659 his eldest son, Muhammad Sultan, titular commander of the army pursuing Shuja, defected to his uncle, and Aurangzeb prepared an expedition east to restore the situation. The actual commander of the expedition, Mir Jumlah, resolved the difficulty before Aurangzeb could join him, and Muhammad Sultan returned and was imprisoned.

In the Deccan, the struggle that was to dominate Aurangzeb's time had begun to take shape. The Marathas were a highland people who originated in the region of Nasik, Poona, and Satara in the western Deccan, upland from the modern city of Mumbai. Their local chieftains were a peripheral concern for the Deccan rulers, but Maratha peasants had a long tradition of military service, including under the Mughals. The first great Maratha leader, Shivaji Bhonsle, was the son of Shahji, who had alternately served the Nizam-Shahis, Adil-Shahis, and Mughals. Shahji was still in Bijapuri service when Shivaji, without his consent, began attempting to construct a principality of his own by taking control of small forts and districts assigned to his father. The Adil-Shah imprisoned Shahji in 1648, and Shivaji surrendered his conquests to gain his father's release. In 1656, he established control of the area around Pune and Satara. This led to confrontation with the Mughals, for it coincided with Prince Aurangzeb's effort to conquer Bijapur. After flirting with the possibility of alliance with the Mughals, Shivaji joined the Adil-Shahis. When the Adil-Shah made peace with the Mughals, he also offered submission. He and Aurangzeb could not, however, reach an agreement before the prince marched north to contend for the throne. During the succession war, Shivaji conquered the coastal district of Konkan and defeated the Adil-Shahi forces sent against him. Aurangzeb thus faced a growing Maratha power in the west Deccan.

In 1660, the Mughals and the Adil-Shahis began a series of expeditions against Shivaji. They had considerable success until 1663 when Shivaji made a daring night raid on the Mughal camp. The next year, he raided Surat, the commercial center of Western India. Aurangzeb assigned his best general, Rajah Jai Singh of Amber, against Shivaji. Conducting a masterful campaign, Jai Singh forced Shivaji to surrender, but on generous terms. In return for payment of tribute, surrendering two-thirds of his forts, and maintaining a substantial force to serve with the Mughal army, Shivaji was allowed to keep the remainder of his dominion and excused from entering Mughal service personally. His son Shambhuji was to become a Mughal officer. Shivaji agreed, however, to accompany Jai Singh, apparently hoping to receive a high rank and an important office in the Deccan.

His welcome, however, did not meet his expectations. The rank he received placed him behind several other officers, including some whom he had humiliated in battle. Considering this a grave degradation, he complained that Aurangzeb had broken his word and petitioned for a higher rank and position. Because of his terrifying reputation, Aurangzeb ordered him imprisoned. Shivaji escaped and fled back to the Deccan. The inability of Aurangzeb to grant the intrepid Maratha leader the status he desired set the stage for the Maratha war that lasted for the rest of his reign. After defeating Shivaji, Jai Singh had pressed onward against Bijapur. He faced no opposition in the field and reached the city of Bijapur but could not sustain a siege. This failure left Shivaji secure even though his flight from the Mughal court constituted rebellion. He negotiated a three year peace with the Mughals.

Shortly after Shivaji's flight, Aurangzeb faced a crisis in the northwest. The Yusufzais rebelled, threatening communication between Hindustan and Kashmir and raiding imperial territory. A Mughal punitive expedition defeated them. Five years later another Afghan tribe, the Afridis, challenged Mughal authority in the Jalalabad region, cutting the road to Kabul. They inflicted crushing defeat on the Mughal force sent against them. Khushhal Khan of the Khatak tribe, the greatest Pashtun poet and the founder of Pashtun nationalism, joined resistance to Mughal authority. Several Mughal governors attempted and failed to reestablish Mughal authority and order in eastern Afghanistan and open the Khyber Pass route without success. In the summer of 1674, Aurangzeb himself went to Hasan Abdal, close to Peshawar, to direct operations. The Afghan problem absorbed his attention for four years before order was restored; even then Khushhal Khan continued resistance. The Mughals reopened the road between Kabul and Peshawar but achieved little else.

Shivaji renewed hostilities in 1670. The Marathas again looted Surat and defeated a Mughal detachment in a pitched battle. Before his death in 1680, Shivaji established his control over the western coast of the subcontinent from just south of Surat all the way south to Gokarn, with the exception of the Portuguese enclaves of Daman and Goa. He had also extended his power eastward into the Karnatik, as far as the fortresses of Vellore and Jinji, near the French colony of Pondicherry (now Puducherry) and the British colony of Fort St. David (later Madras, now Chennai). He had achieved these gains through continuous raiding, shifting alliances and hostilities with Bijapur and Golconda, conquering fortresses, and avoiding battle against superior Mughal forces. In 1674, Shivaji had himself crowned as *chatrpati* (lord of the universe), signifying his claim to independent and absolute sovereignty. Between Shivaji's enthronement and his death in 1680, he expanded his realm south and east at the expense of Bijapur and Golconda.

Aurangzeb's other initiatives between 1659 and 1679 reflect his puritanical nature and devotion to Shari Sunni Islam. They included deemphasizing the solar Ilahi calendar, banning the performance of music at court and ending the imperial patronage of musicians, making changes in court rituals, attempting to suppress alcohol consumption and prostitution, and, in some cases, destroying Hindu temples. As Muslim rulers in India had for centuries, he treated the Hindus as *zimmi*s rather than idolaters, but he broke Akbar's pattern of not imposing the Shari regulations on *zimmi*s. The Shariah permits the destruction of temples in conquest and forbids the construction and improvement of them in areas under Muslim rule, but it allows existing temples to continue to function. Aurangzeb sought to apply this regulation, which meant the destruction of new temples in Varanasi and elsewhere, as well as the deliberate destruction of temples in military campaigns within imperial territory. He did not, however, order the general destruction of temples throughout the empire.

Har Rai, the seventh Sikh guru, had continued his ancestors' unfortunate habit of backing the wrong contender for the Mughal throne, being a friend of Dara Shukuh. Although Aurangzeb took no direct action against him, he held his son Ram Rai as a hostage, hoping to use him as a tool to control the Sikhs. Har Rai, however, designated another son, Hari Krishen, as his successor. Hari Krishen died in 1664, after eight years on the throne and designated his great-uncle Tegh Bahadur, to succeed him. Tegh Bahadur won the devotion of the Sikhs of the Punjab and inspired them to resist Mughal authority. Aurangzeb summoned him to court and, when he did not respond, had him arrested and then executed on November 11, 1675. Tegh Bahadur's son Gobind Singh, the last of the Sikh gurus, succeeded him. Unsurprisingly, he became a bitter enemy of the Mughals.

In 1679, Aurangzeb reimposed the *jizya*. This step indicated his intention to govern in accord with the Shariah and again to define Muslims as the ruling class of the Mughal Empire. Neither an effort to induce Hindus to covert to Islam nor simply a revenue-raising measure, this decision apparently provoked widespread discontent in Delhi, where Aurangzeb was when it was imposed, but its political effects, direct and indirect, are uncertain. There was initial protest, at least in Delhi, and passive resistance to payment, at least at first. The sequence of events known as the Rajput Rebellion was not, however, a response to Aurangzeb's religious policies.

The death in 1678 of Jaswant Singh Rathor, the ruler of Marwar and one of the most prominent Rajput *mansabdar*s of the time, without an obvious heir began the crisis. The Mughal rulers had traditionally overseen, and frequently intervened in, the process of succession in the Rajput principalities; it was thus not unexpected that Aurangzeb did so. Mughal troops occupied Marwar, a normal and temporary step in supervising the transfer of the principality to a new rajah, but in this case the occupation provoked widespread resentment. Eventually, Aurangzeb appointed a nephew of Jaswant Singh's to the throne, although two of Jaswant Singh's wives had born him posthumous sons. This action provoked widespread opposition in Marwar that took the form of the enthronement of Jaswant Singh's infant son Ajit Singh. The Rathor rebels sought assistance from Rana Raj Singh Sisodia of Mewar, the most prestigious of the Rajput potentates though far less prominent in Mughal service than Jaswant Singh had been. Though he had no personal grievance against Aurangzeb, Raj Singh feared the concentration of Mughal power in Rajasthan and supported the Rathor rebels. Aurangzeb responded with a massive expedition against the Sisodias and Rathors. The Mughals had no difficulty defeating the Sisodia and Rathor forces in the field, with Aurangzeb's son Sultan Akbar in field command. Events took an unexpected turn, however, when the prince declared himself emperor on January 3, 1681, with the support of the rebels.

Aurangzeb dealt with the threat efficiently. Through the adroit use of disinformation, he alienated most of Sultan Akbar's Rajput supporters from him, leaving the prince too weak to fight. Rana Jai Singh, who had succeeded his father, Raj Singh, surrendered to Aurangzeb on generous terms. Sultan Akbar and a small cadre of rebel Rathors eventually sought refuge with Shivaji's son and successor, Shambhuji, in the Deccan. The situation in Marwar remained unsettled until 1699, when Ajit Singh entered imperial service, but had only local significance.

After the resolution of the Rajasthan crisis, Aurangzeb departed Ajmer for the Deccan, where he arrived early in 1682. He stayed for the remaining twenty-five years of his reign and life, attempting to establish order and Mughal authority and to subdue the Marathas. Shambhuji had taken advantage of Aurangzeb's distraction in Rajasthan and raided the outskirts of the two chief Mughal centers in the Deccan, Burhanpur and Aurangabad. Sultan Akbar's alliance with Shambhuji raised the possibility of a Maratha-Bijapur-Golconda alliance, with the prince providing Mughal legitimacy. Some historians believe that Sultan Akbar might have attracted a broad base of support from Mughal officers who disapproved of Aurangzeb's religious policy, treatment of the Rajputs, and expansionist policy in the Deccan. But there is little evidence of significant support for the prince among the Mughal ruling class.

Aurangzeb began energetic operations as soon as he reached the Deccan but faced the same problems that had bedeviled Mughal armies in the Deccan before. The Marathas still could not face the Mughals in the field, but their attacks on Mughal supply lines made sustained campaigns, especially sieges, difficult. Mughal armies won a steady stream of small victories from 1682 to 1684 and took control of a considerable amount of Maratha territory without altering the strategic situation. At this time, Aurangzeb shifted his attention from the Marathas to Bijapur.

Aurangzeb expected the Adil-Shahis, who were theoretically subordinate rulers, to support him against the Shambhuji, but the Adil-Shahis feared the Mughals more than the Marathas. When they did not respond to his orders, Aurangzeb began operations against Bijapur, hoping also to increase the pressure on Shambhuji. The Adil-Shahis surrendered their capital, the city of Bijapur, on September 12, 1686, after a twenty-two-month siege. Supply problems, not the difficulties of the siege itself, prolonged it. The besieging forces came close to starvation. Golconda, the last remaining autonomous Muslim principality in the Deccan, fell on

September 21, 1687. As at Bijapur, starvation and disease took a heavy toll on the besiegers.

The conquests of the city of Bijapur and Golconda Fort did not automatically give the Mughals effective control of all of Bijapur and Golconda. The Adil-Shahi and Qutb-Shahi provincial administrations had fragmented; the Mughals had to reestablish order and administration in much of what had become two new provinces. They never did in some parts of Bijapur and Golconda, especially along the coast of Hyderabad. The struggle to assert Mughal authority over the new conquests overlapped with the continuing war against the Marathas.

Although Aurangzeb stayed in the Deccan from 1687 to 1707, conflicts elsewhere in the empire required attention. In addition to the continuing minor disorders in Marwar, there were several other problems. The Jat peasantry of the Agra and Mathura region, led by local landholders, had challenged Mughal authority even in Shah Jahan's time. A long series of expeditions against them between 1680 and 1705 failed to end the disorder. There were minor uprisings in Malwa and Bihar. More importantly, Guru Gobind Singh had begun assembling an army and transforming Sikh resentment of the Mughals into a militant faith. In 1686, his growing power alarmed the local chieftains who had hitherto sheltered him. He defeated them in battle and became the leader of a regional uprising against Mughal authority. They defeated the first punitive expedition sent against them but then submitted to avoid a second imperial invasion. The Mughals took no punitive action against Gobind Singh at this time. He devoted the next twelve years to securing his authority in the hill country between the Jumna and the Sutlej, building a series of fortresses, and giving to the Sikh faith the form it has retained to this day. The growth of Sikh power again led the local zamindars to call for Mughal assistance, and hostilities between the Mughals and the Sikhs began again. Fighting continued until Aurangzeb's death.

The Maratha wars, however, dominated Aurangzeb's last twenty years. The long, painful struggle, replete with fruitless Mughal victories, makes effective narration extremely difficult. The struggle began well enough, but even success did not help the Mughals. The capture of Shambhuji in 1689 did not end the Maratha will to resist.

After his capture, the remainder of the Maratha leadership, including his younger brother and successor, Rajaram, was besieged in the fortress of Raigarh, southeast of modern Mumbai. Rajaram escaped from there and established a new headquarters at Jinji, across the peninsula northeast of Fort St. David and the French colony at Pondicherry. Raigarh and numerous other Maratha forts in modern Maharastra fell to the Mughals in 1690, but Rajaram's escape kept these victories from being decisive. A Mughal force initiated a siege of Jinji but made little progress. In 1692, another Mughal army began operations against the fortress of Panhala. The Marathas could not retake fortresses from the Mughals or defeat Mughal armies in the field. But the enormous length and expense of sieges and the inability of the Mughals to win political advantage from their continuing victories made the struggle impossible for either side to win.

Rajaram's flight to Jinji forced the Mughals to accelerate their efforts to subdue the surrounding region, the eastern Karnatik. This region had been divided between Bijapur and Golconda, so Mughal forces were already active there. Rajaram's presence made the eastern Karnatik (now southern Andhra Pradesh and northern Tamil Nadu) the focus of operations. The Mughals reached Jinji in 1691, suspended siege operations in 1693, renewed them in late 1694, and finally took the fortress in that year. From 1699 to 1705, the Mughals captured eight major Maratha fortresses, sometimes with massive siege operations, sometimes by bribery. But these victories did not end Maratha resistance. Although the death of Shambhuji had deprived the Marathas of an effective and united leadership, it also deprived them of a leader who could make a peace. Though Aurangzeb's advancing age did not affect his vigor until his last few years, the prospect of his death and a succession struggle distracted his sons and officers from current operations; the Marathas were as much potential allies in future conflicts as enemies in present ones.

In 1705, Aurangzeb apparently gave up hope of defeating the Marathas. He suffered a serious illness and withdrew from operations. He sought primarily to prevent a succession war among his sons and especially to protect the youngest and least capable, Kam Bakhsh, from the wrath of his brothers. He hoped for a peaceful partition of the empire. He died, in despair, on February 21, 1707. The struggle that he had hoped to prevent began almost immediately.

Bahadur Shah

Aurangzeb had left three sons: Sultan Muazzam, the governor of Kabul; Muhammad Azam Shah, who had supported his father in the Maratha wars; and Kam Bakhsh, who was governor of Bijapur. Each had a considerable personal following, but two major factions of officers were tied to neither. Asad Khan, Aurangzeb's vizier, and his son Zul Fiqar Khan led the first faction; Ghazi al-Din Khan Firuz-i Jang, Aurangzeb's most successful general, and his son Chin Qulich Khan, who later founded the principality of Hyderabad, led the second. The nature of the factions, as well as the dissimilarity between them and earlier factions among Mughal officers, receives detailed attention in the section of this chapter on decline. Unlike during previous succession wars, the two factions retained their own agendas rather than simply aligning with the princes. The Firuz-i Jang faction took no part in the struggle whatsoever, waiting instead for the winner to come to them. Muhammad Azam Shah was only a short distance from the court when his father died and swiftly returned there. He receive Asad Khan's support immediately and offered the Firuz-i Jang faction great incentives to join him but without success. Azam marched north to face his brother, leaving his artillery behind. Sultan Muazzam gained possession of the imperial treasuries and artillery parks at Lahore and Agra. The two brothers met in combat at Jaju, near Samugarh, on June 18, 1707. Azam Shah was beaten and killed; Zul Fiqar Khan withdrew his forces before the end. Both factions accepted Bahadur Shah's rule.

Sultan Muazzam had received the title Shah Alam as a prince and ruled as Bahadur Shah. In his brief reign, he resolved the conflicts with the Marathas and Sikhs that had tortured his father for so long. He was clearly an effective ruler, but his success was temporary and superficial. He dealt with Rajasthan and the Punjab first. In Rajasthan, Ajit Singh had taken advantage of the succession war to expel Mughal forces from Jodhpur and won the support of the other two most important Rajput rulers, Jai Singh of Amber (grandson of the Jai Singh of Aurangzeb's time) and Amar Singh of Mewar. Within Jodhpur, Ajit Singh ordered the destruction of mosques and prohibited Muslim prayer. After two years of Mughal expeditions and intricate political maneuvering, all three Rajput princes won the right to hold their principalities as Mughal appointees. Bahadur Shah apparently considered a renewed Sikh uprising, closer to the Lahore/Delhi/Agra core of the empire, a greater threat than the Rajputs.

The Sikh leader, Guru Gobind Singh, had been involved in a struggle against the Mughal governor of Sirhind, Wazir Khan, through the later years of Aurangzeb's reign. He attended Bahadur Shah shortly after Jaju, hoping to win his support against Wazir Khan. Before Gobind Singh could reach an agreement with Bahadur Shah, assassins, probably agents of Wazir Khan, killed him. His death ended the line of ten Sikh gurus and began a new era of Sikh resistance to Mughal authority under his agent, Banda, who mobilized the Jat peasants of the Punjab. The Sikh forces began major operations in November 1709 and defeated Wazir Khan in May 1710. Within a few months, they dominated the Punjab except for Delhi, Lahore, and a few other towns. Banda adopted the title of *padishah* (emperor) and minted coins, thus claiming sovereignty for himself. Bahadur Shah moved north to address this threat but died at Lahore on February 27, 1712, before he had the opportunity to engage the Sikhs.

The Maratha situation was out of Bahadur Shah's control from the beginning. In the immediate aftermath of Aurangzeb's death, Azam Shah permitted Shahuji, the son of Shambhuji, who had been raised as a hostage at the Mughal court, to depart and contend for leadership of the Marathas against his aunt Tara Bai, the widow of Rajaram, acting in the name of her son Shivaji. When Bahadur Shah came south to confront Kam Bakhsh, he awarded Shahuji high rank in return for his cooperation. When Bahadur Shah returned to the north, he appointed Zul Fiqar Khan governor of the Deccan. Zul Fiqar Khan, whose faction had consistently supported a compromise peace with the Marathas, proposed a settlement with Shahuji in which the latter would become governor of the Deccan, with a 35 percent share of the revenue of the province. Tara Bai made a counteroffer, demanding only 10 percent of the revenue. Bahadur Shah refused to choose, and for the remainder of his reign, Maratha armies, affiliated at least formally with Shahuji or Tara Bai, desolated much of the southern and central provinces of the empire. Shortly before Bahadur Shah died, Daud Khan Panni, acting governor of the Deccan, granted Shahuji the terms he wanted, but this agreement had little actual impact. The Mughals had lost effective authority in the Deccan.

The Final Phase

The death of Bahadur Shah left a gap that no Timurid ever filled. Only one of his four sons, Muhammad Azim al-Shan, had demonstrated the ability to govern. He had assisted his father ably in 1707 and gathered considerable wealth and power as governor of Bengal. Zul Fiqar Khan, however, had during the later stages sought to concentrate power in his own hands and did not want a capable emperor. Zul Fiqar Khan united the three weak brothers against Azim al-Shan, planning to partition the empire among them with himself as common vizier. The coalition defeated Azim al-Shan, and Zul Fiqar Khan enthroned Bahadur Shah's eldest son, Jahandar Shah, on March 12, 1712. But Jahandar Shah remained on the throne only for ten months. The change in emperor, however, meant less than changes in the empire. The Mughals had lost control not only of the Deccan but of much of the northern heartland as well. The revenue system had broken down; the central government no longer received much revenue from the provinces.

The challenge to Jahandar Shah and Zul Fiqar Khan came from Farrukhsiyar, a son of Azim al-Shan, who had become governor of Bengal in his father's place. His military support came from Sayyid Husayn Ali Khan Barahah and Sayyid Abdullah Khan Barahah, known as the Sayyid brothers. They had become the governors of Bihar and Allahabad as clients of Azim al-Shan and had significant military following in those areas from their own kinsman. Farrukhsiyar promised them the leading offices of the empire in return for their support in seizing the throne and avenging his father. After defeating Jahandar Shah and Zul Fiqar Khan without difficulty, they ordered their execution, along with that of many of the other leading officers, and the blinding of the three most capable Mughal princes, including one of Farrukhsiyar's sons. Only Farrukhsiyar and the Sayyid brothers remained to contend for power.

Farrukhsiyar reigned for six eventful years. He sought, ultimately unsuccessfully, to wrest effective control of the government from the Sayyid brothers; they sought to retain power. This struggle dominated politics and hindered government, becoming intertwined with the contests against the Marathas, Sikhs, and Rajput rebels. Mughal forces did finally defeat the Sikhs, in great part because many of Banda's supporters deserted him. Farrukhsiyar had Banda and some seven hundred of his followers executed publicly in Delhi in March 1716. At the end of February 1719, the Sayyid brothers finally deposed Farrukhsiyar and replaced him with the young Rafi al-Darajat, son of Rafi ush-Shan, another son of Bahadur Shah. Their opponents enthroned Niku-Siyar, a grandson of Aurangzeb through the rebel Akbar. The Sayyids defeated and killed Niku-Siyar, but Rafi al-Darajat died of natural causes shortly afterwards. The kingmakers enthroned his brother, Rafi al-Daulah. He also died within a few months.

The enthronement of Muhammad Shah, son of Bahadur Shah's fourth son, Jahan Shah, on September 28, 1719, ended the series of short reigns;

Muhammad Shah reigned until 1748 but not over an intact empire. During the six years of political confusion, Mughal authority had ceased to exist in much of the empire. The Sayyid brothers and their opponents controlled different provinces. The kingmakers had effectively ceded the Deccan to the Marathas in return for tribute and recognition; the Marathas rarely paid the tribute. In 1720, a coalition of almost all of the other leading officers of the empire defeated the Marathas and Sayyids in battle at Shakarkhedla in the Deccan, ending the period of Sayyid dominance. But the effective authority of the emperor had already ended. Secondary, regional, and local potentates had become the effective rulers. The idea of Mughal sovereignty remained intact and unquestioned; Mughal government had disappeared.

SOVEREIGNTY, RELIGION, AND LAW

The unchallenged position of the Mughals as imperial sovereigns, even when they became impotent figureheads, demonstrates their enormous success in establishing their legitimacy throughout South Asia—and not only among Muslims. Since the eighteenth century, historians have regarded the Mughal concept of kingship and political theory as the critical element in Mughal success and later failure. Most historians, including those of the British era and Indian nationalists, have attributed Mughal success to Akbar's policy of religious tolerance and inclusion, which won the loyalty of Hindus and Shiis, and Mughal decline to Aurangzeb's bigoted folly in abandoning this policy. Some Muslim, mostly Pakistani, historians invert this interpretation. They condemn Akbar's religious liberalism and experimentation and argue that the inclusion of Shiis and Hindus made the empire inherently weak because of the questionable loyalty and reliability of these groups. They laud Aurangzeb for piety and absolve him and his policies from causing the collapse of the empire. These present-minded interpretations both fall short. Akbar's ideology facilitated the incorporation of Hindus and Shiis into the ruling class, but his measures did not represent as significant a deviation from past practice in the subcontinent as most historians have asserted. There is no indication that either Shiis or Hindus in general were less loyal to the Mughals than Sunnis. Aurangzeb's change in the governing ideology did not, in and of itself, lead to the collapse of the regime. Although the time frame differs, the evolution of Mughal ideology paralleled developments in the Ottoman and Safavid empires.

Babur claimed sovereignty as a descendant of Timur and upheld the Timurid dispensation of sovereignty against the Uzbeks and his own primacy among Timurids. His invasion of Hindustan was a reassertion of Timurid primacy over what had been part of the Timurid Empire, though never under direct Timurid rule. Although his Sunni allegiance did not prevent him from allying with Shah Ismail against the Uzbeks and perhaps formally becoming a Shii for that purpose, he supported Sunni Islam for most of his career, patronizing Sufis as well as ulama. The Timurid concept of collective sovereignty still operated, as the division of the empire among Babur's sons and the struggle among them demonstrates. There is no evidence that Babur intended to make any significant change in the Timurid doctrine of kingship or that he claimed to represent a new dispensation of sovereignty. Humayun, however, had such intentions.

Before his early death Humayun promulgated a new doctrine of political organization that implied a change in the doctrine of kingship. He divided his subordinates into three groups. The men of *daulat* (fortune) were his brothers and other relatives, his military and bureaucratic officers, and his soldiers. The men of *saadat* (happiness) were the ulama, religious administrators, Sufis, and poets. The men of *murad* (hope) were artists, singers, and musicians. The classification of Humayun's brothers and other relatives with his officers and soldiers contradicts the idea of collective sovereignty—no surprise, given Humayun's bitter experiences with the consequences of collective sovereignty. He did not live long enough for this change to have any effect.

Akbar's early efforts to define his ruling position show no sign of innovation beyond the combination of Timurid and Indo-Muslim conceptions. In 1562, shortly after he began to rule independently, Akbar took up the standard practice of Indo-Muslim rulers by venerating the saints of the Chishti Sufi order. The Chishtis had been instrumental in the spread of Islam through South Asia; their shrines were major pilgrimage centers for Muslims and Hindus. Muslim rulers had venerated Chishti tombs and patronized living Chishtis for two centuries. Akbar visited the most important Chishti shrine, the tomb of Muin al-Din Chishti in Ajmer, ten times between 1562 and 1579. In 1569, he visited Muin al-Din Chishti's living successor, Shaykh Salim Chishti, at the village of Sikri, seeking the saint's intercession for the birth of a son. Salim, the future Jahangir, was born at Sikri later that year. Akbar began construction of a new capital at Sikri in 1571. The veneration of the Chishtis did not imply that previous rulers emulated their policy of tolerance and inclusion toward non-Muslims, so Akbar's continuation of the pattern did not imply anything about his views.

Also in 1562, Akbar married the daughter of Rajah Bharmal of Amber, his first marriage connection with the ruler of a Rajput principality. Earlier Muslim rulers had married the daughters of Hindu potentates, and, as already discussed, it was not unusual for non-Muslim officers to serve in prominent positions under Muslim rulers. Akbar's policy differed because the marriage connections and appointments came with a close personal connection between the ruler and his relations by marriage. Bharmal's descendents were legal officers in the empire for generations.

Abu al-Fazl, who became Akbar's confidant, political theorist, and biographer but was not associated with him at this time, reports several early decrees consistent with his later program, including a ban on the enslavement of the families of enemy soldiers in 1562 and the abolition of the *jizya* in 1564. Historians differ on the validity of these reports; they may represent a projection backwards. Even if Abu al-Fazl did not fabricate them, these measures did not form part of a coherent and consistent program. There is no indication that Akbar's religious views had deviated from conventional Muslim piety at this time. He was also cultivating connections with the established Indo-Muslim cultural and intellectual elite, which opposed such connections. These efforts, however, failed. The leading Muslim families of Delhi, who had developed close ties to the Afghan dynasties, refused to lend their prestige to Akbar's project or to marry their daughters to him. In 1564, he was wounded in an assassination attempt in Delhi. Akbar then turned away, literally and figuratively, from Delhi, the traditional capital and center of Muslim life in South Asia.

The construction of Akbar's great fort at Agra, begun in 1565, and then the new capital complex at Fatehpur Sikri in 1571 started the articulation of what became the mature Akbari constitution. Although the prominence of mosques makes explicit the Muslim nature of the spaces created, the style of the structures themselves combines Timurid and Indian architectural elements in a uniquely Akbari style. The combination of Timurid and Indian components in a new order inspired by the sovereign replicated the creation of the Mughal ruling class in the *mansabdari* system.

The *mansabdari* system, which defined the status and income of officers by ranking them in a numerical hierarchy, began in 1572 or 1573. It was primarily a mechanism of military organization and is discussed in the next section for that reason. It formed, however, a fundamental aspect of Akbar's political program as well. By treating Muslims and Hindus as imperial servants without reference to their confessional or ethnic status, it stated unambiguously that the unifying principle of the empire was Timuri, or rather Akbari, rather than Muslim. Following the precedent of Humayun's tripartite division of society, Akbar in 1577 assigned numerical ranks to his sons, classifying them as officers, extensions of himself, rather than fellow sovereigns. Although Mirza Muhammad Hakim continued to rule in Kabul until his death in 1585, the classification of the princes as *mansabdar*s ended collective sovereignty. Mughal princes served as provincial governors and commanded military expeditions, sometimes using those positions as the basis for rebellion, but these assignments were not appanages.

The articulation of the mature Mughal constitution began in 1579 with the promulgation of the Mahzar, an imperial order often inaccurately called the Infallibility Decree, and the abolition of the *jizya*. In 1575, Akbar had begun to sponsor discussions among leading representatives of all the major religions in the Ibadat-Khanah (literally, "house of worship") at Fatehpur Sikri. The performance in these debates and elsewhere of the leading ulama, both Sunni and Shii but especially of the two leading Sunnis, Shaykh Abd al-Nabi and Makhdum al-Mulk Sultanpuri, apparently led Akbar to come to regard them as intellectually inadequate, biased, and small-minded. The promulgation of the *mahzar* responded to that perception. According to Abu al-Fazl, Akbar acted on the suggestion of Shaykh Mubarak Nagawri, Abu al-Fazl's father. The Mahzar designated Akbar as a *mujtahid* (capable of independent legal reasoning), *amir al-muminin* (commander of the faithful, the title normally used by the early, Umayyad, and Abbasid caliphs but rarely by other Muslim rulers), and just sultan. At the same time as the promulgation of the *mahzar*, Akbar recited the *khutba* at a Friday prayer in Fatehpur Sikri, a part of the traditional duties of the caliph but not part of the normal behavior of other Muslim rulers. The *mahzar* and recitation of the *khutba* defined Akbar's position as supreme Muslim ruler capable of making independent legal judgments and thus of going beyond the established principles and patterns and ignoring the strictures of the ulama. In a sense, it gave Akbar the same position as that held by the early caliphs, who, before the emergence of the ulama, were the chief religious authorities as well as sovereigns. Akbar's support for hajj caravans and for charitable causes in Mecca in the late 1570s was consistent with this program. The negative Ottoman reaction to these measures, mentioned in the Ottoman chapter, shows that the Ottomans considered Akbar a rival for prestige among Sunni Muslim rulers.

The abolition of the *jizya* has a logical connection to the *mahzar* because it reflects Akbar's superseding of the normal practices of Muslim rulers. Collection of the *jizya*, the capitation tax on non-Muslims, was a fundamental component of government in accord with the Shariah. It defined Muslims as the ruling class and others as subjects. Akbar's abolition of the *jizya* rendered Hindus and Muslims equally subject to his authority, making it far easier to give Rajputs and other Hindus a lasting place within the Mughal regime. Abu al-Fazl describes the abolition as the foundation of social order and says that its collection was unnecessary because adherents of all religions joined Akbar's service as if they were adherents of the same faith. Abolition of the *jizya* thus altered the nature of the regime fundamentally.

Abu al-Fazl's comment describes the new religious base of the Mughal rule: *sulh-i kull* (peace with all, universal toleration). Loyalty to Akbar superseded sectarian allegiance; Muslims and Hindus were equal in subjection to his authority. As a corollary, Akbar himself did not appear as either a Muslim or a Hindu. He abandoned public observance of Muslim rituals and substituted a personal ritual of sun worship, for which Abu al-Fazl advances a justification from the Quran. He explains Akbar's abandonment of conventional rituals by asserting that kings worship through justice and good government. Because Islam emphasizes public conformity rather than uniform belief, Akbar's avoidance of Muslim rituals constituted a sort of apostasy, but he never publicly abjured Islam. He defined his sovereignty in a manner that both Muslims and Hindus could understand and accept. *Sulh-i kull* was not merely a declaratory policy. As Richard Eaton points out, Akbar's policies had a concrete effect on the administration of justice in the provinces.

Akbar claimed independent religious insight. He made no overt or explicit claim to be a prophet—though some of his contemporary critics believed he wished to—and did not attempt to found a new religion with a mass following. Instead, he made careful use of ambiguity, giving sufficient justification for those who wished to see him as prophet without making categorical claims that would provoke opposition. He emphasized, for example, the phrase "Allahu Akbar," a part of the traditional Muslim call to prayer that literally means "God is great." No Muslim could object to it, but it could also be construed to mean "God is Akbar." In addition to these ambiguous claims, Akbar founded a court religious cult, similar to a Sufi order and most often called the Din-Illahi (divine faith), with himself as master, thus providing basis for the mistaken belief that Akbar intended to start a new religion. He did not; only a few of Akbar's intimates joined, swearing an oath in which they abjured "insincere and imitative Islam" and offered their property, life, honor, and faith to Akbar. They also went through an initiation ceremony in which they did obeisance and received a special token of their devotion. Akbar encouraged, but did not require, his officers to become devotees. Accepting Akbar's spiritual guidance demonstrated the absoluted loyalty that he wanted. His role as spiritual guide was thus a component of his kingship.

Akbar developed a set of court rituals that expressed his conception of sovereignty. These rituals remained extremely important throughout Mughal history. Sir Thomas Roe, who arrived at the Mughal court in 1615 as the second English ambassador there, described Jahangir as a virtual prisoner of court ritual: "As all his subjects are slaves, so he is in a kind of reciprocal bondage, for he is tied to observe these howres and customes so precisely that if he were unseene one day and noe sufficient reason rendred, the people would mutinie."[8] Several aspects of the court rituals require attention. Two specific practices, *jharuka darshan* and the weighing ceremonies, connected Mughal practices to Hindu patterns. *Darshan* (literally, "seeing") is an important feature of the interaction of Hindu spiritual teachers and their students. Akbar showed himself to the general public from the *jharuka*, a small balcony, as the first public act of his day. The crowd acknowledged the privilege of *darshan* by giving a form of salute. This custom presented Akbar as a spiritual guide without Muslim affiliation. The weighing ceremonies took place on the sovereign's solar and lunar birthdays and consisted of distributing the sovereign's weight in various commodities. On the solar birthday, they included gold, silk, perfumes, coppers, grains, and salt; on the lunar, they included silver, tin, cloth, fruits, and vegetables. This ceremony has some resemblance to the royal ceremonial bath (*rayjabhisheka*), one of the central rituals of Hindu monarchy, symbolizing the status of the king as the cosmic man, the embodiment of all elements of the earth. The weighing ceremony did not make Akbar and his successors into Hindu kings, but it stated their sovereignty in Hindu terms. The Mughals made themselves available daily to the general public for redress of grievances, in accord with the Iranian tradition of kingship.

The physical arrangement in which the *mansabdars* stood in the court reflected their status in the imperial hierarchy. The princes had a unique status but were clearly officers, not subordinate sovereigns. Individuals of different ranks saluted the emperor differently. Above the simple salute came a bow; beyond that came complete prostration, which only the highest officers performed in the hall of private audience. The lower an officer prostrated himself before the emperor, the higher his status. This ritual requirement made it unmistakable that all status came from the ruler, even though the political reality did not coincide with this image. The symbolic paraphernalia of royalty included the royal throne, a parasol, a polished ball suspended from a long pole, two types of yak tail standards (or whisks), and several flags. Akbar's thrones were stone platforms set with precious stones. Later thrones became more elaborate, culminating in Shah Jahan's famous Peacock Throne. Jahangir made the importance of these practices clear by prohibiting imperial officials, including princes, from imitating them. *Mansabdars* could not build a *jharuka*, hold court in the imperial style, compel men to prostrate themselves, or use any of the symbols of imperial authority. The exchange of gifts between sovereign and officers comprised much of the business of the Mughal court. Gifts from the emperor to the *mansabdars* transformed them into extensions of the ruler. Gifts to the ruler from the *mansabdars* signified their subordinate status. Mughal court chroniclers devote considerable space to the exchange of gifts, revealing its importance in maintaining the relationships that made the empire function.

Abu al-Fazl propounds the theory of sovereignty that the court rituals symbolized. In his view, Akbar represented the complete maturation of the divine light of sovereignty, which had previously manifested itself in Chingiz Khan and Timur himself. Abu al-Fazl connected this notion of divine light to Sufi doctrine of illuminationism, the belief that God created the universe by emanating light. Akbar possessed a purer light than other men, indicating his sovereignty. To this view, Abu al-Fazl connects a second Sufi doctrine, that of the Perfect Man. The Perfect Man is a microcosm of the universe, an expression of the essences from which the universe is produced. Abu al-Fazl connects Sufi illuminationism to the Timurid claim for sovereignty. Timurid mythology claimed that Timur and Chingiz Khan had a common ancestress, Alan-Qua, who had been impregnated by a beam of light. Akbar represented the full maturation of the light of sovereignty carried by her descendants. As the perfect manifestation of the light of sovereignty, Akbar's advent signaled the beginning of a new era in human history. In accord with this claim and with the end of the first millennium of the *hijri* calendar in 1591, Akbar ordered the calculation of a new solar calendar, called the Illahi calendar, intended not just for administrative use but to supplant the *hijri* calendar. The new Illahi calendar did not win broad acceptance but remained in use at court into Aurangzeb's time. Although there is no evidence of a direct connection, Abu al-Fazl's conception of kingship has some common features with the Hindu doctrine expressed in the *rayjabhisheka*. It may have facilitated the acceptance of Akbar's rule by Hindus.

The establishment of the Illahi calendar reveals the similarity between Akbar's political theory and the esoteric, messianic concepts of the Ottomans and Safavids half a century earlier. But Akbar, unlike Sulayman the Lawgiver and Shah Tahmasp, never confronted circumstances that forced abandonment of his extreme claims. No other ruler in the subcontinent articulated imperial sovereignty. The Mughals had no great rival capable of fighting them to a standstill or exhausting their resources.

Muslim reaction to Akbar's policies is a matter of controversy. Some historians claim that they produced widespread opposition among Muslims and led to the rebellions in Bihar and Bengal from 1580 to 1582. The evidence indicates, however, that resentment of Akbar's military and fiscal policies, far more than his abandonment of Islam as a justification for sovereignty, motivated the rebels. Akbar's critics also contend that he actively persecuted orthodox Islam during the last twenty-five years of his reign. Persecution, however, is too strong a term, especially given what it has come to mean in the last hundred years. Akbar did persecute some individual political opponents who opposed him on religious grounds and certainly withdrew much patronage from ulama and Sufis who had previously received it. The image of Shaykh Ahmad Sirhindi, the influential Sufi teacher, as a vociferous and influential critic of Akbar's religious views and policy, is an anachronism.

The historiographic controversy extends to the succession of Jahangir. Akbar's critics claim that the pious Muslim reaction against Akbar's program led Muslim officers to rally behind the accession of Jahangir on the condition that he would restore traditional Muslim governance, and supporters of Akbar's program backed Khusraw. This interpretation does not fit the facts. The vast majority of officers backed Jahangir and made their decision on the basis of the customs of the Timurid dynasty. The two officers who supported Khusraw did so because they had close personal relationships with the young prince, thus expected to receive high office from him, but were not close to Jahangir. Jahangir also made no significant changes in the Mughal constitution. He refers positively to *sulh-i kull* in his memoirs and continued to act as spiritual guide to some of his officers, though he did not follow Akbar's personal religious usages. He did, however, excuse religious officials from prostration, and the court atmosphere changed in favor of Shari, Sunni Islam.

Shah Jahan, however, altered his grandfather's formula substantially. He did not act as a spiritual guide to officers. Within a year of taking the throne, he ended the practice of prostration before the ruler, reserving it for God in accord with Muslim custom. More significantly, he returned temporarily to enforcement of the Shari ban on the construction of new non-Muslim houses of worship. He took this action in 1633 in response to a petition from the Muslims of Varanasi, who complained that a large number of temples were under construction, but he enforced it through much of the empire. Mughal armies returned to the practice of destroying temples and idols in newly conquered territory. Shah Jahan also returned to Muslim rulers' traditional policy of trying to prevent marriages between Muslim women and Hindus, and he temporarily reimposed taxes on Hindu pilgrims. In 1637, he abruptly reversed all of these changes, except in court rituals, and returned to previous Mughal customs. Unlike his father and grandfather, however, he presented himself as an observant Muslim. Shah Jahan apparently decided to return to Muslim monarchy and then changed his mind. For most of his reign, he did not alter Akbar's constitutional arrangements. He ruled in accord with *sulh-i kull*, acting as a Muslim personally but not ruling as one.

Aurangzeb, however, altered the Mughal regime fundamentally. Historians have often presented him and Dara Shukuh as polar opposites, representing the two basic Muslim responses to the South Asian environment. Aurangzeb stands for particularism or communalism, which emphasizes the need to preserve and purify Islam and to establish a society in which Islam will flourish. Dara exemplifies universalism, accepting and seeking to understand Hinduism and finding much in common between Islam and Hindu ideas. In their personal philosophies, Aurangzeb and his brother did represent these two positions. Aurangzeb presented himself as the guardian of Islam, condemned Dara as an unbeliever, and had him executed as an apostate. He contended that his Sunni Islam made him more fit to rule than the Shii Shah Shuja or the syncretist Dara. But the struggle for succession did not take the form of a war between universalist and particularist parties. Aurangzeb's supporters included Shiis, Rajputs, and Maratha officers. There is no indication that he won support with promises or expectations of a change in the Mughal constitution after he took power; the documentary evidence is all to the contrary.

Although Aurangzeb's recasting of the Mughal regime culminated in the reimposition of the *jizya* in 1679, he began changes immediately. He restricted the use of the Illahi calendar and terminated celebration of the traditional Iranian New Year, Nawruz. In 1668, he banned the performance of music at court and ended the institution of the *jharuka*. In 1669, he ended the weighing ceremonies and ordered a return to the Shari policy of banning construction of new temples and the destruction of temples built contrary to the ban. Aurangzeb did not order the wholesale destruction of temples, only the enforcement of Shari restrictions. The 1679 reimposition of the *jizya* marked the completion of Aurangzeb's ideological program. Several of his measures went far beyond a return to the Timurid status quo before Akbar. Muslim rulers had celebrated Nawruz since Abbasi times and sponsored musicians since Umayyad times. Aurangzeb's monarchy thus responded to Shariah-minded criticisms of previous Muslim regimes. His program was also consistent with the pattern of confessionalization, though more than a century later than similar trends began in the Ottoman and Safavid realms and in Europe. Aurangzeb's program was far less forceful and comprehensive than that of his contemporary Majlisi. It did not involve forced conversion or an effort to enforce a specific Muslim creed. But Aurangzeb's patronage of Shari Sunni Islam, along the lines preached by Shaykh Ahmad Sirhindi half a century earlier, altered Muslim identity and practice in the subcontinent significantly.

Although there is no doubt about the nature and scope of Aurangzeb's constitutional changes, there is considerable debate about their political effects. Some historians argue that Aurangzeb's religious policy led to the collapse of Mughal power on the grounds that it caused, or at least prevented the resolution of, the three conflicts that consumed the second half of his reign. Plausible as this argument appears, it fails on several grounds. The struggles against the Marathas, Rajput rebels, and Sikhs were three separate wars with unique and unrelated causes. They clearly did not reflect a general Hindu resistance to Aurangzeb's policies or reluctance on his part to include non-Muslims in the Mughal ruling class. As M. Athar

Ali demonstrated four decades ago, the ethnic composition of the Mughal ruling class did not change substantially during Aurangzeb's reign. Without the specific trigger of Jaswant Singh's death without a living heir, the Rajput rebellion might not have occurred at all. As the discussion in the section on Mughal decline below indicates, Aurangzeb sought not to extirpate either the Maratha or Rajput leaders but to incorporate them into the empire. Both cases ultimately became irresolvable disputes over the terms of incorporation.

Although the Mughals disposed of the concept of collective sovereignty, they did not evolve a mechanism for orderly and predictable succession to the throne. There is no theoretical treatise on the issue, but practice suggests the following principles: There could be only one sovereign at a time, after his accession only his direct male descendants could claim the throne, and each of them had an equal claim to it. In the absence of a principle for determining succession—the normal situation for monarchies throughout history—it was decided by circumstance and politics. As Mughal history went on, the princes themselves became more involved in the process of succession. The leading officers of the empire enthroned Akbar without significant controversy; he was an adolescent and close to court when Humayun died suddenly. His brother Mirza Muhammad Hakim was an infant and in distant Kabul. Neither prince played an active role. In all three later cases, the issue of succession became prominent well before the incumbent ruler actually died. The future Jahangir rebelled in 1600 and claimed the throne in 1602; though formally reconciled with Akbar, he maintained a separate establishment in Allahabad until his brother Danyal died in 1604. He returned to court, apparently fearing the maneuvers of Khusraw's backers, but the vast majority of officers supported him, and he succeeded to the throne with Akbar's blessing. Khusraw challenged him only because Rajah Man Singh and Khan Azam Mirza Aziz Kukah, two of Akbar's closest confidants, supported him, hoping to ensure that they retained the prominence that their personal relationships with Akbar had brought them. Khusraw fled the court the next year, apparently because he feared that his father would exclude him from the succession. Later princes acted from similar motivations.

In the later cases, some or all the princes had become leading officers. Shah Jahan had initiated the succession war but failed to ensure his succession when he confronted the combination of Asaf Khan, Nur Jahan, and Mahabat Khan and the latter's generalship. He probably would not have revolted if Nur Jahan had not sought to ensure the succession of her son-in-law Shahryar in order to maintain her own position after her husband died. When Shah Jahan himself fell ill, his four sons became the leading officers of the empire. Nearly all the senior officers of the reign had died; the four sons were the governors of the major provinces, and Dara Shukuh dominated the central administration. There was thus no possible mechanism for resolving the dispute except war. I discuss the succession to Aurangzeb in the section on decline.

The Mughal doctrine of kingship and social order thus changed profoundly during the empire's history, and changes had equally profound political effects. The end of the doctrine of collective sovereignty and the modification of the appanage system paralleled changes in the Ottoman and Safavid empires. Without this basic alteration, none of the three empires could have avoided the fragmentation that eventually afflicted most Turko-Mongol dynasties. It was an indispensable part of Akbar's reforms, along with the suspension of the Shari restrictions on non-Muslims, so that they could become part of the ruling class of the empire, and the development of court rituals that removed the ruler from the category of Muslim. No other important Muslim ruler abandoned enforcement of the Shariah as Akbar did. His decision gave the Mughal Empire its distinctive foundation and characteristics, as well as facilitating co-optation of much the pool of Hindu military manpower.

EXPANSION AND MILITARY ORGANIZATION

Bernard Cohn's four levels of politics provide a useful framework for understanding the expansion of the Mughal Empire. The Mughals sought, and managed, to eliminate all other claimants to imperial sovereignty in South Asia and to establish a monopoly on the secondary level, meaning to make provincial rulers Mughal provincial governors. For the most part, however, the Mughals did not attempt to reorder the regional and local levels of politics but to pacify and co-opt indigenous power holders on those levels. Success on the imperial and secondary levels required victories in battles and sieges, or Mughal military superiority. Military triumphs, however, only set the preconditions for success on the regional and local levels. Some actors on the regional level, such as the major Rajput principalities, required military campaigns to subdue; however, the result of those campaigns did not eliminate the principalities but incorporated them into the empire. As expansion began with military superiority, so does this discussion.

Although Mughal military history includes no lack of combat, with numerous campaigns and sieges, there were remarkably few major battles. None took place after the victory over the Afghans at Raj Mahal in 1576, except for those between Mughal princes during the succession wars of 1658 and 1659 and from 1707 to 1708, and against the Safavids outside Qandahar and the Uzbeks north of the Hindu Kush. As Carl von Clausewitz explained nearly two centuries ago, combat is the only effective force in war even when no combat takes place, and the mere possibility of battle may have the same effect as an actual battle. The paucity of battles during a century of steady Mughal expansion indicates that their opponents avoided offering battle because they expected to lose. Only dynasties that challenged the Timuri/Mughal claim to imperial sovereignty challenged the Timurids in pitched battles: the Lodi Afghans at the first Panipat, the Sisodias at Khanwa, the Surs at Chausa and Kanauj and then the second Panipat, and the Kararani Afghans at Tukaroi and Raj Mahal. At least three factors explain this situation: The reputation of Mughal military power deterred other enemies from facing them in the field, the secondary and regional principalities that the Mughals confronted could not produce field armies capable of meeting the Mughals in the field, and the pretension to sovereignty on the imperial level required offering battle. The Mughals had clear superiority in field battles well into the eighteenth century.

Babur's great victories at Panipat in 1526 and Khanwa in 1527 began the demonstration of that superiority. They followed the same pattern as the Ottoman victories at Chaldiran, Marj Dabik, and Mohacs. Babur employed an Ottoman expert, Ustad Ali Quli, who arranged the Timurid forces in the standard Ottoman formation, a wagon fortress with the artillery and gun-armed infantry in the center and the mounted archers on the wings. The combination of firearms and cavalry defeated far larger Afghan and Rajput forces that had neither the weapons nor the tactics to respond. Although these victories did not produce a permanent Timurid domain in Hindustan, they did clearly give the Timurids enormous military prestige. That prestige did not deter Shir Shah (then Shir Khan) Sur from challenging Humayun. It did, however, deter him from challenging the Timurid forces directly in the field. At Chausa, he succeeded with a surprise attack on the Mughal camp; at Bilgram he took advantage of disarray in the Timurid forces and used a converging attack to collapse the wagon fortress. The second Panipat, which actually determined the survival of the Timurids in Hindustan, involved neither a wagon fort nor superior artillery, for the Timurid force had none there. The Suri forces under the Hindu commander Himu relied on an elephant charge to break the Mughal cavalry; the Mughal center withdrew behind a ravine, which the elephants could not cross, and the firepower of the Mughal mounted archers did the rest.

After this triumph, only the Kararani Afghans challenged the Mughals in battle, at Tukaroi in 1575 and Raj Mahal in 1576. The Mughals won both encounters without the use of a wagon fortress and with little artillery. The marshy terrain of Bengal made employing either difficult. In any case, the Mughals won these encounters with provincial armies, not the full strength of the empire. After these encounters, no Mughal opponent in South Asia challenged them in the field before the eighteenth century.

Perhaps the Mughals benefited from the prestige of Babur's great victories, but they certainly had superiority in both firearms and cavalry. Neither alone would have guaranteed superiority on the battlefield; the combination did. The Mughals neither produced nor employed firearms as well as the Europeans or the Ottomans did. Gunpowder produced in South Asia was consistently inferior, though the reason and significance are unclear. Unlike the Ottomans, the Mughals did not engage directly in the manufacture of gunpowder but purchased it on the open market. They fell behind the Europeans in military technology only in the late seventeenth and early eighteenth centuries, when flintlock muskets supplanted matchlocks and cast iron artillery became standard. The Mughals produced and employed only matchlocks and brass and bronze guns. Against the foes they faced in South Asia, these limitations made no difference; the Mughals consistently had both more and better firearms than their enemies in the subcontinent. The same proposition held for cavalry.

Mughal superiority in cavalry derived first and foremost from Mughal control of the horse trade. South Asia's environment did not favor the production of quality horses; cavalry forces had to depend on their import from the northwest, Iran and central Asia, and the west, Arabia. Once the Mughals gained control of Gujarat, they had effective control of these roots. True to their central Asian heritage, they relied primarily on mounted archers; lacking the tradition and practice of this difficult art, their rivals in the subcontinent could not field such a force. The Mughals also made effective use of heavy (shock) cavalry. Their combination of field artillery and cavalry supplanted a military system based on war elephants. The Mughals did use elephants in war, particularly in their early campaigns, but not as their primary striking force.

Unable to defeat the Mughals in battle, their opponents used time and distance against them, defending fortresses and attacking Mughal lines of communication. Mughal expansion thus depended on the ability to take fortresses. Once Akbar demonstrated that ability at Chitor, he and his successors rarely had to complete another siege until the Deccan campaigns. Completing a siege meant enormous costs, in blood and treasure. The Mughals thus had great incentives to permit their adversaries to surrender for terms. At Ranthambor in 1569, Akbar besieged Surjan Hada, the ruler of the small Rajput principality of Bundi. It took the Mughals nearly a month of enormous effort to bring guns to bear against the fort, but once in place they swiftly breached its walls. Surjan Hada then immediately opened negotiations, and Akbar accepted his surrender. Surjan became a Mughal officer and Bundi a subordinate principality of the Mughal Empire. If the Mughals had been able to take fortresses swiftly and easily, they might not have been so ready to offer terms; if their eventual victory had not been certain, their adversaries would not have so willingly accepted them. This definite, but limited, military superiority gave the Mughal polity some of its basic characteristics.

The Mughal difficulty in sieges had tactical and logistic causes. Although the Mughals neither constructed nor conquered fortresses built or adapted to defeat siege guns, such citadels as Chitor and Ranthambor had such strong natural locations that it was extremely difficult to deploy guns against them. The topographic locations of fortresses in South Asia eliminated the need to redesign them to resist siege artillery. But the logistic difficulties were more serious—and certainly more chronic. Except along the rivers of the Punjab and the Ganges and Jumna, water transportation was not available in the subcontinent. Conducting a siege in the Deccan or Rajasthan thus meant operating at the end of a long overland supply line, dragging guns—the Mughal force that besieged Ranthambor advanced at a pace of only three miles a day—and transporting large quantities of food and fodder as well. Because grain could be carried overland only by grain-eating animals, it was difficult to do so in quantity over any distance. Mughal armies thus had to depend on forage. Extended sieges thus denuded the surrounding countryside, often for miles. From a logistic perspective, Mughal forces surrounding fortresses were often as much besieged as the garrisons inside. Especially in the Deccan, opposing field forces interfered with Mughal supply lines, to which Mughal armies had to devote as much effort to protecting as offensive operations. The Mughals thus had tremendous difficulties in both maintaining and ending sieges.

The difficulty the Mughals had in taking existing fortresses thus explains why Mughal fortifications did not reflect the revolution in fortification that took place in Europe in the sixteenth century in response to siege artillery. They had tall, thin walls without bastions. This limitation on Mughal power affected the Mughal political system significantly. To avoid the costs of bringing sieges to an end, the Mughals offered terms to most adversaries in sieges. The terms were favorable; they were incentives to surrender and normally offered the opposing leaders incorporation into the Mughal system as *mansabdar*s. At Ranthambor, for example, as discussed above, Surjan Hada defended the fort until Akbar's artillery had actually made a breach in the walls before opening negotiations, at which point Akbar accepted him as a Mughal *mansabdar*, with his hereditary principality of Bundi as a *jagir*. Mughal conquests thus expanded the Mughal ruling class as well as the territory of the empire. The Mughal mechanism of conquest thus depended on the combination of palpable, but limited, military supremacy and incentives for surrender. Even Daud Khan Kararani, the Afghan ruler of Bengal who posed the greatest threat to Akbar, received terms from Munim Khan after the Mughal victory at Tukaroi in 1575, though the agreement did not last. The Mughal mechanism of conquest thus reflected the two fundamental characteristics of the situation: the nature of Mughal military superiority (unquestioned but limited and expensive to exercise) and the need for the Mughals to incorporate the military manpower of the conquered territories.

Mughal expansion often took the form of intervention in local conflicts. In 1563 and 1564, for example, Akbar supported contenders for the thrones of two principalities, the Muslim Gakkhar country in the Punjab hills and Marwar. Both contenders were successful and accepted Mughal sovereignty. The practice of allowing loyal subordinate rulers to retain their principalities made this pattern possible.

As mentioned earlier, the Mughal conquests covered the parts of South Asia suitable for agriculture or pastoral nomadism. Most of the revenue came from the former, and most of the soldiers came from the latter, though, as Dirk Kolff's vital work has demonstrated, many peasants also served as soldiers. Mughal conquest did not generally mean a change in population, except at the very top of the social pyramid. The new popu-

IMAGE 5.6
Bullocks dragging siege guns up a hill during Akbar's attack on Ranthambhor Fort, Rajasthan in 1569: folio from an *Akbarnama* manuscript. This folio formed the right side of a double-page composition of the siege. It dynamically depicts the enormous difficulty of deploying heavy cannon against Rajput hill forts. Approximately forty-nine different artists from Akbar's atelier produced the vibrant illustrations for the manuscript.

lation was transient rather than permanent, since officers' military and personal entourages traveled with them from post to post. The Mughal frontier was merely a political demarcation, not necessarily a formal one, except in Bengal. There, Mughal expansion meant the extension of rice cultivation. As Richard Eaton has explained, the constant expansion of the Ganges-Brahmaputra delta east and south moved the area suitable for cultivation with it, requiring the process of clearance to proceed as well.

Mughal conquest meant that the conquered areas paid taxes to the Mughal treasury or were assigned as *jagir*s to Mughal officials. When a local potentate became a Mughal *mansabdar*, internal administration changed very little. But in area conquered rather than absorbed, such as Gujarat and Bengal, the Mughals had to make a revenue settlement, a working agreement with the zamindars and peasants who paid revenue on how taxes were to be assessed and collected. The Mughals shared the goal of making individual peasant households the unit of assessment, in accord with Irano-Islamic statecraft, which produced the Ottoman *tahrir* system. To apply it, however, would have meant the elimination of the zamindar class, which the Mughals could hardly contemplate. Instead, they attempted to co-opt the zamindars, converting them into local officials owing their status to the imperial regime rather than local affiliations and subject to imperial regulations and audit. To do so required penetrating more deeply into the society of Hindustan than any of their predecessors could, though not nearly as deeply as the Ottomans routinely did.

The conquest of such provinces as Gujarat involved the establishment of a revenue settlement with the zamindars of the province, which took considerable time and effort. It is unclear whether such settlements involved actual measurement of the land and observation of its productivity or merely a review of existing revenue records, registration of zamindars, and establishment of a pattern of assessment and collection. It is clear, however, that Mughal conquest involved the establishment of political and financial relationships with local elites.

The process of expansion thus involved multiple competing claimants for the revenue of the conquered area: the members of the existing ruling elite who became *mansabdars*; those zamindars, usually the majority, who did not become *mansabdars* and thus competed with the imperial appointees; the central treasury, which always took a share of the land revenue; and members of the Mughal ruling class who sought advancement and enhanced revenue, especially when they participated in the campaign. For most of the history of the empire, newly conquered territories produced enough revenue to satisfy all the claimants. When conquest involved sustained operations, long sieges in particular, the resulting widespread destruction often prevented newly acquired territories from producing their normal revenue for several years and thus from satisfying the demand generated in the process of conquest. During the Maratha wars, the limitations of Mughal military superiority led to the granting of high ranks, thus salaries, to various Deccani potentates, even though the prolonged warfare severely reduced the productivity of the newly acquired territories. This failure of the expansion mechanism became a major factor in Mughal decline.

The structure of the Mughal army reflected the complex political and social circumstances that produced it. Although the distinction between central and provincial forces applies to the Mughals, it is more accurate to divide the Mughal army into the central forces, the *mansabdar* forces, and the zamindar forces. Of these, only the central army owed its allegiance directly to the emperor. Unlike its Ottoman and Safavid counterparts, the Mughal central army had little political significance. It contained all the empire's artillery, at least in theory, and had infantry and cavalry components. The artillery establishment, headed by the *mir-i atish* (normally translated "master of ordnance"), included field and siege artillery. The field guns included a substantial number of light pieces, known as the *top-khanah-yi rikab* (artillery of the stirrup), which formed a part of the imperial entourage. The Mughals used a wide variety of guns, frequently casting new weapons for use in specific campaigns. They prized expertise in gunnery, frequently hiring European and Ottoman gunners.

The cavalry and infantry components of the Mughal central army are obscure. They were comparatively unimportant, both militarily and politically, and lacked the distinctive features of their contemporaries. The central cavalry were called the *ahadi*s (single fighters) and frequently had administrative positions in the palace in addition to their military obligations. Paid directly from the imperial treasury, they were loyal only to the sovereign but had no servile status. The *ahadi*s normally accompanied the imperial court and took the field only for major campaigns and unusual situations. There is even less information on the infantry component of the central army. Akbar apparently supported a corps of 12,000 musketeers, in addition to other infantry units without firearms. There is little information on the recruitment of these forces, although some ethnic groups specialized in this service. The Mughals also maintained a variety of paramilitary groups, including the mace bearers, who acted as imperial messengers, and a corps of female guards, who guarded the sovereign and harem. The female guards did not serve away from the palace and imperial camp, but they were in no way a formal or ceremonial body. Earlier Indo-Muslim rulers had had similar units. The central army included the vast majority of infantry equipped with firearms under Mughal control.

Unlike their Ottoman and Safavid contemporaries and the vast majority of Muslim dynasties for the previous half-century, the Mughals did not employ military slaves as part of the central army. Several historians have speculated about this seeming anomaly. There are two apparent explanations. Military slavery created highly skilled, loyal armies but could not provide large numbers; the enormous military labor pool of Hindustan would have overwhelmed a slave army. The Mughals also received a continuous flow of skilled soldiers from Iran and central Asia without the mechanism of military slavery.

The *mansabdar* forces were essentially a series of private armies that the *mansabdars* were paid to maintain for imperial service. *Mansabdars* had numerical ranks that theoretically indicated their place in the imperial hierarchy, the number of troops they were required to maintain, and the amount of their pay. *Mansabdars* received advances on their pay to permit them to hire soldiers but had to present their contingents for inspection in order to receive their full pay. The precursors and evolution of the *mansabdari* system are complex and uncertain, but the system was operating in this form by 1575. The use of numerical ranks clearly reflected the Turko-Mongol practice of decimal military organization. The *mansabdars* often tried to divert money from their contingents to personal use and frequently found ways to get around the inspection system. The tying of rank and contingent size was also unnecessarily inflexible, as important positions at court required status but not large contingents. In 1596–1597, Akbar separated *zat* (personal or self) and *sawar* (cavalry) ranks. An officer might thus have rank of 1,000 but only have to support two hundred troopers. Under Shah Jahan, officers were required only to provide a fraction of their *sawar* rank. The steady loosening of regulations shows that the *mansabdars* frequently disregarded them; they were rarely punished for doing so.

The disparity between regulations and practice formed a basic part of the Mughal political compromise. The regulations corresponded with the court rituals, making *mansabdars* servants of the ruler. The reality gave them the freedom their varying self-perceptions required. Many *mansabdars* were simply exempted from the muster regulations.

Mughal *mansabdars* hired a wide variety of troops. The unique capability of mounted archers made them the core of the Mughal army; they were not the majority. *Mansabdars* normally employed a cadre of loyal retainers, whose positions were often hereditary, drawn from their kinsmen or home region. In this way, *mansabdars* connected the imperial regime to the military manpower of the provinces. They supplemented their core contingents with local soldiers hired from the region in which they were stationed, sometimes cavalry but most often infantry of peasant origin.

The importance of the *mansabdars* as recruiters of troops explains much of their status. Unlike their Ottoman and Safavid counterparts, Mughal rulers rarely executed, demoted, or even reprimanded their officers. The execution of the chief of a substantial number of troops would have deprived the regime of their service, at least temporarily, and almost inevitably led to violence. Mughal sources refer to appointments and pro-motions made in order to keep the contingents of deceased *mansabdar*s together. Although sons did not inherit their father's ranks, they did, to a degree, inherit their followings, and the imperial regime normally gave them the rank necessary to support the core contingents.

Whether the zamindars' armies were part of the Mughal army is de-batable. The Mughal regime counted them as such; Abu al-Fazl's total of 342,696 cavalry and nearly 4.4 million infantry in the Mughal army, roughly 10 percent of the male population of the empire, clearly included a large number of peasant soldiers. If the zamindars were putatively im-perial officials, their troops were putatively imperial troops. Because the zamindars actually collected and remitted much of the tax revenue, their troops did serve an imperial service. They did not, however, serve in im-perial campaigns far from the local bases. Almost all zamindars had mil-itary retainers; many had guns, war elephants, and small forts. These small peasant armies gave the zamindars considerable leverage in local af-fairs, permitting them to collect the revenue that gave substance to their status. The absence of imperial control over the zamindar armies indi-cates the real autonomy of most zamindars, who were required to pro-vide auxiliary forces for imperial operations in their areas but did not otherwise support imperial authority except insofar as their role in rev-enue collection did so.

The enormous pool of potential peasant soldiers, the limited capabili-ties of the Mughal central army, the restricted central control over *mans-abdar* contingents, and the autonomy of the zamindar forces meant that the Mughals always faced the possibility of revolt in the provinces. Za-mindar revolts—normally clashes between zamindars and imperial as-signees over revenue—were not uncommon but rarely posed more than a local problem. Indeed, the Mughal central government responded to these disorders not on principle but in order to provide the *jagirdar* with his salary. *Mansabdar* revolts, however, were extremely rare after 1582 for sev-eral reasons. Most *mansabdar*s had little incentive to revolt; they were gen-erally loyal to the sovereign, felt content with their lot and prospects, and had little to fear. There was no alternative to Mughal rule. In addition, the network of fortresses and fortified cities throughout the empire made a successful revolt unlikely. If the Mughal army itself found sieges difficult, rebels found them impossible, and the system of fortresses established by Akbar controlled strategic locations and routes throughout the empire.

Shir Shah Sur had actually begun construction of the network of roads and fortresses, which Akbar completed. In addition to the famous Agra Fort, Akbar built fortified cities at Lahore and Allahabad and fortresses at Ajmer in Rajasthan, Rohtas and Attock in the northwest, and another Rohtas in Bihar. The fortresses in the northwest secured the frontier against possible Uzbek or Safavid incursions; the others secured overland trade routes and military roads and overawed potentially rebellious zamindars. The Mughals also used small citadels in major cities, especially provincial capitals. The fortress commandants were independent of provincial governors; rebel governors would have had to begin their rebellions by besieging the citadels of their own capitals.

The brief rebellion of Sultan Khusraw in 1606 offers an excellent example. The surplus of military manpower permitted the young prince to assemble an army of 10,000 men within a few days of leaving his father's court. His improvised force could not, however, take the citadel of Lahore and, deprived of a secure base, melted in the face of the imperial forces. The Mughals never attempted to form large infantry forces with firearms. They had no need to call on additional sources of military manpower, as the Ottomans did in the late sixteenth century. Infantry armies on the European model did not appear on the subcontinent until the British and French forces arrived and local rulers imitated them.

CENTRAL ADMINISTRATION

Mughal central administration differed from that of the Ottomans and Safavids because of its mobility. Even though the Mughals built massive, fortified, capital complexes at Agra and Delhi, as well as the unique imperial city of Fatehpur Sikri, the capital of the empire was always the emperor's camp, wherever it happened to be. The Mughal rulers spent more than about 35 percent of their time traveling, on campaign, on tour, or on hunting expeditions; even when they remained sedentary for months at a time, they frequently did not reside in one of the capital cities. Emperors frequently supervised campaigns from major cities close to the frontier. Akbar and Jahangir often traveled to the hills, including Kashmir, to avoid the hot season, just as the government of British India moved to the summer capital of Simla. When the emperor and court traveled, the government did so as well. This peripatetic pattern of rule reflected the Mughals' nomad heritage; it also bore some resemblance to the *digvijaya*, the ritual military procession to the four corners of the kingdom that was a component of Hindu kingship.

Mughal government at the center continued the compound of Perso-Islamic and Turko-Mongol traditions that existed in Timurid central Asia, modified for Indian conditions. It lacked the elaborate hierarchy and organization of Ottoman administration. The imperial household included numerous slaves, but there was no *devshirme*, and slaves did not occupy important positions. There was no formal distinction between palace functionaries and imperial servants in the provinces; *mansabdar*s held both types of positions and moved back and forth between them. Most Mughal bureaucrats, including court ministers, were either bureaucrats of Iranian descent or members of Persianized Hindu castes, which carried the same administrative tradition. No Mughal minister after Bayram Khan had the immense authority of an Ottoman grand vizier. Bayram Khan and his immediate successors held the title *vakil*, with the implication of regent, as Bayram Khan was. The title lost the implication of regent with Akbar's majority but remained an honorific given to the chief officer, rather than an office, and was used into Shah Jahan's reign. The highest actual office was that of vizier, or *divan-i kul* (administrator of the whole). The vizier's responsibilities included supervision of all appointments; financial affairs, including revenue, expenditures, and auditing; and verification and signing of official documents. The viziers and other administrators were either of Iranian descent or members of Persianized Hindu castes. During the decisive period of Akbar's reforms, three officers shared the responsibility of the vizierate. The vizier's chief subordinates had responsibility for specific aspects of income, expenditure, and record keeping. The *divan-i khalisa* had charge of land revenue; lands that paid revenue to the imperial treasury were classified as *khalisa*. Other officials had charge of cash salaries, *jagir* assignments, royal workshop and religious department accounts, the management of the treasury itself, and the auditing of accounts.

The *mir bakhshi* (chief of military administration) ranked immediately below the vizier. He was responsible for the management of the *mansabdari* system, including evaluation and presentation of candidates for *mansab*s and the verification of *mansab* contingents. The *mir bakhshi* also received and collated the intelligence reports received about affairs throughout the empire. *Mir bakhshi*s occasionally acted as field commanders, as did viziers.

The *sadr* (chief of religious administration) was far less prominent than the vizier or *mir bakhshi*. His position was nonetheless important, for it involved administration of the charitable revenue grants to men of religion and appointment of religious judges. Such grants were the primary mechanism of religious and cultural patronage and encompassed considerable wealth. Ulama, Sufis, and Hindu religious teachers all received such grants, which the Mughals usually called *madad-i maash* (assistance for subsistence). The Mughal *sadr*, even under Aurangzeb, lacked the influence of the Ottoman *shaykh al-Islam* or *qazi-askar* or the Safavid *sadr* or later *mullabashi*. This situation reflected the relative unimportance of the ulama in the Mughal environment.

The *mir-i saman*, the fourth of the ministers, had charge of the royal workshops, a large and important responsibility. Palace workshops produced an astonishing variety of goods for palace and governmental consumption. Aside from such basic imperial factories as the mint, arsenal, and kitchen, others produced perfume, tents, and carpets; harnesses for elephants, horses, and camels; and mattresses and bedding. The palace also included elephant, camel, horse, and cow stables. The *mir-i saman* was actually responsible for the largest industrial enterprise in the empire. The imperial workshops also produced works of art, including paintings. Several other officials had important positions at the Mughal court. The officers of the household included the *mir-i mal* (palace treasurer), *muhrdar* (seal keeper), *mir tuzuk* (master of court ceremonies), *mir manzil* (court provisioner), *khwansalar* (imperial chef), *qushbegi* (chief falconer), and *akhtah begi* (master of horse).

The Mughal harem, known as the *zenana* (in Persian, *zan-khana*, house of women), received far less attention than its Ottoman equivalent. Like the Ottoman harem, it comprised not only the wives, concubines, and female relatives of the ruler but all of the women of the palace establishment, including the female guard unit, reportedly some 5,000 women in Akbar's time and 2,000 in Aurangzeb's. The *zenana* had its own administrative structure, but it consisted entirely of women. The chief administrator had the title *sadr-i anas* (administrator of women). Senior female relatives (including foster relatives) usually held this position. The commander of the guard corps had the title *urdubegi* (chief of the camp). Members of the guard corps often had administrative positions in addition to their security responsibilities. A small number of eunuchs provided an outer guard for the *zenana*.

The women of the ruling family—mothers, foster mothers (some, but not all, of whom were wet nurses), wives, daughters, and sisters—played similar roles to their Ottoman and Safavid counterparts. They were architectural and cultural patrons, mediators, and diplomats. In addition to Maham Anaga, Nur Jahan, and Mumtaz Mahal, mentioned in the chronology, three prominent women included Hamida Banu Begum, Akbar's mother, and Jahanara and Raushanara, daughters of Shah Jahan and Mumtaz Mahal. Jahanara, the elder, was the leading royal female after her mother's death and supported Dara Shukuh; Raushanara sided with Aurangzeb.

PROVINCIAL ADMINISTRATION

The historiographic disagreement about the nature of the Mughal polity is ultimately about provincial administration, mostly about the assessment and collection of agricultural taxes. Did the Mughal regime intrude deeply into rural economic life, imperiously imposing a steadily increasing revenue demand on an unresisting countryside until it undercut its own revenue base and drove the peaceful peasants into revolt? J. F. Richards, whose views represent the received wisdom in Mughal studies, contends that Mughal power penetrated much further into the rural society of the empire than its predecessors, that the Mughal revenue system "intruded beneath the tough defenses of rural life and reshaped the economy, culture and society of Mughal India."[9] Those "tough defenses" were primarily the zamindars; provincial administration meant the interaction between the imperial regime and indigenous, local, or regional power structures. Since most *mansabdars* were not zamindars and thus shifted assignments every few years, most of the regime had no local roots, appearing to float on top of the provincial society. Did it nonetheless reach deeply enough into rural society to transform it?

Comprehension of the system of provincial administration requires understanding of the categories into which the Mughals divided land. The central government ultimately had a share in the land revenue from 90 percent of the lands in the empire. It divided these lands into three categories: *khalisa*, land that paid taxes into the central treasury; *jagir*, land assigned to officers (*mansabdars*, known in this capacity as *jagirdars*, or *jagir* holders) as salary; and *paybaqi*, land normally assigned as *jagir* but currently unassigned. Outside these categories, the Mughals made land-revenue grants, mostly to noted men of religion, both Hindu and Muslim. Such grants had several names, including the Mongol term *soyurghal*, but the Mughals most commonly used the term *madad-i maash*, which literally means "subsistence assistance." *Vaqfs*, which supported institutions rather than individuals, occupied less territory than personal grants.

The Mughal provincial regime had three levels: the provincial (*subah*), district (*sarkar*), and subdistrict (*parganah*). At the death of Akbar, the Mughal Empire had sixteen provinces: Agra, Ajmer, Allahabad, Bengal, Berar, Bihar, Delhi, Gujarat, Kabul, Kashmir, Khandesh, Lahore, Malwa, Multan, Qandahar, and Thatta (Sind). The conquests of Shah Jahan and Aurangzeb in the Deccan led to the establishment of four more provinces: Aurangabad, Bidar, Bijapur, and Hyderabad.

The structure, function, and nomenclature of the provincial administration varied significantly across the empire; the description below reflects the most common practices and terms. The provinces had, at least on paper, an elaborate administrative structure. The provincial governor (originally *sipahsalar*, literally, "army commander"; later *nazim-i subah* or *subahdar*) had responsibility for commanding the *mansabdar* army supported by the province and maintaining order. The other principle officers were the *divan* (chief financial official); provincial *bakhshi*; *waqai-navis* (news writer); *sadr*, who was also *qazi*; *kotwal*; *mir-i adl*; and in some provinces the *mir-i bahr*. The *divan*, who was not directly subordinate to the governor, was responsible for collecting the revenue from the *khalisa* lands that paid taxes to the central treasury, supervising revenue grants, and keeping the revenue records of the province. The provincial *bakhshi* supervised inspection of the contingents of the *mansabdars* assigned to the province. The *waqai-navis* reported the events of the province to the center. The *sadr-qazi* administered revenue grants to religious figures and acted as a Shari judge, with the *mir-i adl* and *kotwal* performing police and some administrative functions. The *mir-i bahr* had jurisdiction over ports and the security of river traffic in provinces with ports or navigable rivers. In addition to the public *waqai-navis*, secret informants were assigned to report to the central government. Each of the primary officials reported to a different element of the central government: the governor to the emperor himself, the *divan* to the *divan-i kul*, the provincial *bakhshi* to the *mir bakhshi*, and the *sadr* to the imperial *sadr*. These independent reporting lines, with additional intelligence-collection measures, suggest that Mughal central government retained tight control over the provincial governments. As in other circumstances, however, the degree of central power was greater in theory than in practice. It was not uncommon for a single officer to combine the offices of governor or *divan* and *bakhshi*—and sometimes all three. The Mughal central government apparently imposed only a narrow set of demands on provincial governors: remaining loyal, not usurping the symbolism of sovereignty, transmitting the revenue due to the central treasury, supporting imperial assignees in the collection of the revenue due to them, and, in accord with the circle of justice, protecting the subjects from oppression.

Sarkar administration duplicated the outline of provincial administration. The chief officer, the *fawjdar*, had primary responsibility for maintaining order and supporting the collection of revenue. In many, perhaps most, circumstances, the *fawjdar* represented Mughal authority most prominently in the provinces, providing the military support necessary for the collection of revenue. Each *sarkar* had a *qazi* and *kotwal*.

Imperial administration extended to the *parganah* level only in *khalisa* and *paybaqi* lands. In *jagir* land, the *jagirdar* or, if he was absent, his agent dealt with the collection and assessment of taxes and other local administrative matters. In the imperial *parganah*s, the central government appointed two officials, the *shiqqdar*, responsible for maintaining order, and the *amin*, responsible for tax assessment and collection. All *parganah*s had a *qanungo*, a local clerk confirmed in office by imperial decree and responsible for keeping local revenue records. One other official, the *chaudhuri*, also played a vital role: He was a zamindar, usually the leading zamindar of the *parganah*, designated by the Mughals to serve as intermediary between the zamindars of the *parganah* and the imperial regime. The *chaudhuri* frequently collected the revenue from the other zamindars and turned it over to the designated imperial recipient. His signature on the annual revenue assessment guaranteed payment of the *parganah*'s revenue; he also distributed the loans of plows, seeds, and beasts of burden that the provincial governments made to assist with cultivation. Perhaps most importantly, the *chaudhuri* represented the zamindars in negotiation with the imperial tax collector over revenue assessment.

The divergence of theory and practice applies to the assessment and collection of revenue as well. In theory, the Mughal regime did extend deeply into the provinces, assessing revenue on the level of individual cultivators, as the Ottoman did through detailed revenue surveys. Akbar sought to put that theory into practice in the so-called *karuri* experiment, which began in 1574, another aspect of the reforms that included the foundation of the *mansabdari* system. This program underlies Richards's assertion that the Mughals penetrated deeply into rural society. Rajah Todar Mal, not a Rajput but one of the Persianized Hindu bureaucrats, undertook this program, which apparently followed the initiatives of Shir Shah Sur. The process began with the collection of land and production statistics from the *qanungo*s of the empire and standardization of weights and measures. It included a new set of definitive reforms, including the appointment of a new provincial tax official, the *karuri* (a personal noun derivative of the Hindi word for "10 million," the number of rupees that the jurisdictions of the *karuri*s theoretically yielded). The *karuri*s were to direct a measurement of the revenue-producing land and collect records on crop yields and prices for the previous ten years. From this information, they were to calculate a standard revenue assessment for the zones for which they were responsible. This assessment would become the basis of the revenue assessment system known as *zabt* (assessment by measurement of land). On the basis of information from the provinces, the central government set the annual tax rate for various categories of land. The imperial tax collector or *jagirdar*'s agent made a written assessment for his jurisdiction, which the leading zamindars accepted. How much of the empire the *karuri*s actually surveyed, like how much of the empire's *jagir* land actually became *khalisa* during this period, is unclear.

Even though the *zabt* system, through land measurement, assessed tax on individual cultivators, the Mughals and their agents most often dealt with zamindars, some of whom were simply cultivators who received a cut of their neighbors' crops. The zamindar stratum limited the Mughal penetration into rural society; the Mughals assessed not households but villages or groups of villages. The Mughals regarded the zamindars as officials, not as taxpayers, but they insulated the taxpayers from the central government in much of the empire.

The *zabt* system remained valid for most of the empire in theory but frequently gave way to a procedure called *nasaq* (order, method). In the *zabt* areas, *nasaq* meant assessment based on previous measurements rather than a new one for each year. Apparently, the central government *amin* or *jagirdar*'s agent estimated the area's production on the basis of local records and calculated his cash demand in accord with prevailing prices. If the zamindars, represented by the *chaudhuri*, objected to the assessment, the imperial representative either negotiated a compromise or collected by force or the threat it. Ottoman provincial administration had no element of negotiation until the transformations of the seventeenth century. The military capabilities of the zamindars and peasants forced the Mughals to negotiate. In addition, the Mughals rarely undertook the periodic resurveys of revenue that kept the central government informed of changes in the provinces. Later central government records on the value of lands depended primarily on local records rather than on independent surveys. Under *nasaq*, then, Mughal penetration of rural society was severely limited.

Rajput and other indigenous *mansabdar*s normally received their hereditary lands as heritable *vatan-jagir*s (homeland assignments). The Mughals classified them as zamindars, like lesser landed potentates who had no imperial *mansab*s, and did not interfere in the internal arrangements of the *vatan-jagir*s.

The provinces included, of course, cities as well as the countryside. There were no zamindars in the provincial cities, but local power structures and local elites pursued their own interests in interacting with Mughal officers. Farhat Hasan, whose *State and Locality in Mughal India* analyzes this issue, concludes,

> The success or failure of the state in specific functional and institutional contexts was determined by the participation of local power-holders and the support of the pre-existing, if still largely primeval, civil society. It was quite successful in implementing measures that served the interests of the social and political elites. . . . Where this was not the case, state initiatives were quite hamstrung.

He continues,

> The political system, based as it was on shifting alliances between the state and the local system of authority, was situated in the arena of constant change and conflict. Imperial authority was appropriated by social actors to suit their purposes, increasingly embroiling it in local conflicts for symbolic and material resources.[10]

Just as the political theory articulated in Mughal texts and court rituals did not reflect the political realities beyond the imperial court, Mughal revenue theory did not reflect the reality in the provinces.

THE MUGHAL ECONOMY

In Mughal times, India's wealth was proverbial. The affluence that funded the Mughals' military and cultural achievements stemmed from agriculture, manufacturing, and overland and maritime trade. Historians agree that, in general, the empire prospered for most of Mughal times. J. F. Richards describes the Mughal period as a time of "economic growth and vitality" during which the state interfered little with the economy.[11] Even Tapan Raychaudhuri, who speaks of "the uncomplicated desire of a small ruling class for more and more material resources" also asserts that "the unification of India under an imperial authority—however extortionate in its demands—had established a structure of systematic government and a new level of security which stimulated trade, manufactures and production of cash crops."[12] European domination of the Indian Ocean and the presence of European merchants in and around the Mughal Empire contributed to, rather than damaged, its prosperity.

Any generalization about the Mughal economy rests on scattered and incomplete information. There was never a census of the empire, and other records are fragmentary at best. As a further complication, the Mughal era coincided almost exactly with the appearance of European merchants in the subcontinent. The available data permit only a rough estimation of the Mughal population. The current best estimate postulates a population of some 150 million for the entire subcontinent in 1600, with some 115 million in Mughal territory. By 1800, the subcontinent as a whole had a population of about 200 million, suggesting slow but steady growth during the Mughal period. Urban populations are extremely difficult to assess, but the populations of Agra and Delhi exceeded 500,000 in the seventeenth century, with Agra perhaps reaching 800,000 in Aurangzeb's time. Lahore rivaled the two imperial cities, perhaps reaching 700,000. Thatta, Surat, Ahmadabad, and Patna may also have reached 200,000 in population.

The fertility of the Indo-Gangetic plain made these urban concentrations possible. The long growing season permitted most peasants to reap two harvests per year. They planted a wide variety of crops, including wheat, barley, rice, and millet. Cultivation of maize and tobacco in the subcontinent began during the seventeenth century. Many peasants also produced cash crops. In general, smaller peasants concentrated on food grains while larger proprietors grew cash crops. The lack of convenient water transportation discouraged regional specialization; both food grains and other crops were grown for local consumption even in ill-suited areas.

As always in the subcontinent, the entire agricultural system depended on the monsoon rains. When the monsoon failed, especially for more than one consecutive year, it meant famine. The worst famines, and their associated epidemics, killed more than 2 million people during the Mughal period. The cultivators employed artificial irrigation, including the use of small reservoirs (called tanks in the subcontinent), wells, and water wheels. Larger reservoirs, impounded by dams, and irrigation canals were common. The Mughal rulers made substantial investments in irrigation works to extend cultivation, though their structures were not highly sophisticated.

The Mughals wanted to extract all possible revenue from the countryside but knew that oppressive taxation would interfere with cultivation and reduce available revenue in the long run. They intended the revenue system to serve that purpose, but the frequent transfer of *jagirdars* meant that they had little stake in the lasting productivity of an area; their interest was not the same as that of the regime as a whole. Provincial administrators restrained *jagirdars*; zamindars insulated the peasants. The zamindars also frequently collected the revenue in kind and sold it at market, permitting the Mughals to collect their revenue in cash. The Mughal agrarian system thus rested on a series of tensions among the central regime, the *jagirdars*, the zamindars, and the peasants, with the last two groups overlapping.

The agrarian surplus supported a wide variety of artisans and permitted the widespread cultivation of cash crops. By far the most important commodity grown was cotton, but the empire also produced silk, wool, hemp, coir, sugar cane, betel leaf, indigo, and *chay* (a red dye). In addition, the empire's peasants grew opium, saffron, tobacco, and assorted oil seeds. Indian artisans produced a wide variety of manufactures from these and other products, including cotton textiles, processed silk products, refined sugars, processed opium, and alcoholic beverages. Mughal India was self-sufficient in iron and saltpeter and produced diamonds and small quantities of copper, gold, and silver. Its artisans did not have technology as sophisticated as their Chinese and European contemporaries, lacking water-powered textile machinery and even such basic tools as the wheelbarrow. Indian mining techniques, marine technology, and metallurgy lagged far behind Europe and China. In addition, printing had not taken root in India. Despite these handicaps, the manual skill of the artisan castes that dominated Indian manufactures permitted India to compete in international markets for both textiles and metal products. Indian artisans adapted new technologies, like European shipbuilding techniques, when exposed to them.

These manufactures, as well as specialized food production, supported a thriving internal commerce, both between cities and rural areas and between towns. Most trade traveled overland. The high cost of overland transport restricted some types of commerce. Agra and Burhanpur in the Deccan were the major centers of the overland trade. The major overland routes led across the Deccan from Goa through Bijapur and Golconda to Machhilipatnam. North from Hyderabad, the route led to Aurangabad, from which separate roads led to Burhanpur and Surat. A road north from Surat led to the manufacturing center of Ahmadabad and thence through Ajmer to Agra. Other routes connected Burhanpur to Surat and Agra. In the north, the major trade routes followed the rivers, connecting Delhi and Agra with Varanasi, Patna, Bengal, and Orissa in the east and with the Punjab in the rest. From Lahore, the major center of the Punjab, trade went down the river to Multan and Thatta and overland to Kabul and Qandahar. Coastal shipping linked ports from Thatta to Chittagong in Bengal.

These routes carried a wide variety of commodities. Bengal exported large amounts of rice both up the Ganges and the Jumna to Agra and by ship to South India; it also had huge surpluses of butter and sugar. Gujarat, the most important manufacturing region, imported grain both overland and by sea. Multan sent sugar up the Indus and Ravi to Lahore and downriver to Thatta. The diversity of this trade and the long distances it crossed did not imply that its scale was proportionately large. A specialized caste, the Banjaras, managed the transportation of grain overland, often in convoys of 20,000 bullock carts, to feed major markets, but by modern standards the volume of trade was extremely small. Overland trade moved mostly by bullock cart, but horses, camels, and elephants also played a role.

A wide variety of merchants conducted this commerce. Those of the largest markets, such as Surat, were as wealthy and sophisticated as their European contemporaries. Many of the important merchants acted as bankers. Some had close relationships with members of the Mughal ruling class. Many Mughal officers and members of the ruling family acted as merchants themselves, thus investing state revenues in commerce. Mughal officials also used their coercive power to profit from the market by declaring a monopoly in a given commodity and forcing merchants to purchase licenses to trade in it or by requiring that artisans fill their orders first.

Smaller merchants normally operated over limited areas and traded a smaller variety of commodities. Even peasants acted as merchants to a limited degree, seeking the best prices for their crops. Tax collectors likewise had to dispose of the commodities they collected and thus also formed a part of the commercial network. A complex banking and credit system supported Indian commerce. Merchants used bills of exchange in lieu of cash for many transactions in long-distance trade. Imperial officers made loans from their own resources and from imperial funds under their control, frequently using their positions to protect their profits. Usury was common, with interest rates approaching 30 percent per month.

This network of commerce and the relative order that allowed it to exist made the Mughal period a time of urban growth. Virtually all large towns, not only actual Mughal centers, grew in population. Former regional capitals, such as Ahmadabad in Gujarat and Golconda in the Deccan, kept their importance as provincial capitals and commercial centers. The Mughals deliberately sought to encourage the rehabilitation of older towns and the foundation of new ones, such as Shahajahanpur, Muzaffarnagar, and Muradabad, all founded by Mughal officers. Beginning an urban foundation required relatively little investment: constructing a wall, gates, and a market and ensuring a regular water supply. If such investments could give rise to a thriving town, the overall economy must have been thriving.

For an economic historian, the growth of trade between the subcontinent and Europe, not the evolution of the Mughal Empire, may be the major theme of the sixteenth and seventeenth centuries. The Portuguese actually arrived in the subcontinent before the Mughals did, with Vasco de Gama's expedition reaching Calicut in 1497. As explained in the Ottoman chapter, the Portuguese set out to establish a maritime empire dominating the Indian Ocean. They sought to gain control of the key choke points—the Straits of Malacca and Hormuz, which they took control of in 1511 and 1515, and Jiddah, which they failed to take in 1517—as well as to establish fortified trading posts on the coast of India and elsewhere. The Estado da Índia, as the Portuguese maritime empire came to be known, sought to establish a monopoly in pepper, to divert the traffic in that commodity to the route around Africa, and to dominate shipping. Their aims were less commercial than, as Niels Steensgaard describes it, redistributive. They sought to profit from taxes and licensing fees, not to become merchants and take trade into their own hands. Merchant ships in the Indian Ocean had to purchase licenses to trade; the superiority of Portuguese ships and weapons made this possible. Portuguese power certainly curbed the activities of the indigenous merchants of the Indian Ocean littoral, but it did not end them, especially because of Portuguese corruption and laxity. The Estado da Índia did not use its power to end trade between the Indian Ocean and the Mediterranean. Because their costs were lower, the Portuguese might have undercut the prices of the caravan merchants; instead they allowed the expenses of the caravan traders to determine their prices.

Not Portuguese power but Protestant enterprise transformed Indian Ocean trade. The English East India Company (EIC) and Dutch East Indian Company (VOC), formed in 1600 and 1602, defeated the Portuguese at sea and sought not only to take over the spice trade but to create new markets for Indian products in Europe, notably textiles. The Dutch gained control of modern Indonesia, the actual source of pepper and other spices, but established trading stations, known as factories, in the subcontinent as well. The English, cut out of the spice trade, focused on the subcontinent. In the seventeenth century, the companies primarily exported Indian finished goods, notably cotton to Europe, and purchased them with specie, ultimately from the Americas. The demand for Indian cloth in Europe grew dramatically through most of the seventeenth century. The companies also exported Indian cloth to Indonesia, exchanging it for spices, and shipped Indian indigo, raw silk, and saltpeter, among other commodities, to Europe as well.

European merchants established a presence in existing trading centers as well as created new ones. The Dutch received permission to operate factories in Masulipatnam in Golconda and Surat in Mughal Gujarat by 1616. In 1615, the English East India Company arranged for James I to send Sir Thomas Roe as ambassador to Jahangir, and the British founded trading posts at Surat, Agra, Burhanpur, Patna, and other trading centers. The Safavid-English conquest of Portuguese Hormuz in 1622 and the Mughal expulsion of the Portuguese from Hooghly in 1633 expanded the scope for English and Dutch traders. The EIC acquired Madras from a local ruler in 1639 and Mumbai, ceded by Portugal to Britain in 1661, from the English Crown in 1668. Bengal, however, became the focus of

European activity in the subcontinent. The source of both raw silk and saltpeter, as well as highly valuable finished textiles, it was also the granary of the subcontinent. The EIC opened several factories there in the 1660s. A continuing disagreement with local Mughal officials over customs dues flared into a brief war in 1687 and 1689, but the EIC finally obtained the desired customs concession in 1691 and in 1696 received imperial permission to fortify the factory at what became Calcutta. The maritime power of the EIC and VOC could substitute for fortifications because they could easily blockade any port. From the coastal factories, European trading activities spread inland and produced economic changes. The VOC went beyond purchasing the patterned cotton textiles they had obtained rights to trade for at Machhilipatnam and created a new market for plain white calico, for which they arranged production. The textile industry on the Coromandel Coast grew rapidly as a result. This example shows how European commerce stimulated industrial production in coastal regions of the subcontinent. Dutch and British involvement led to sustained economic growth in Bengal, both in the production of commodities and in the textile industry. European merchants often provided capital for Indian weavers. The Mughals derived considerable revenue from taxing both weavers and merchants, and European demand for Indian products inevitably created new jobs. Since the commerce created both positions and a net inflow of specie, it clearly did not harm the interests of the Mughals or the inhabitants of their empire. Aside from the positive effects of the growth of the European trade, assessing the changes in the economy of the subcontinent and the effects of the Mughal regime is difficult. For some years, historians have assumed that the massive influx of American silver caused a silver inflation in the subcontinent comparable to that in Europe. The most recent research, however, has called this hypothesis into question.

With the monetary history of the period uncertain, generalization about economic changes under the Mughals and the economic effects of the Mughal regime is difficult. Different sectors, regions, and groups fared differently in Mughal times. Overall, the Mughal Empire prospered during the period from Akbar to Bahadur Shah. Though the Mughals did not, and could not, establish perfect order in the provinces, they established satisfactory arrangements in most of the provinces most of the time. They at least maintained enough order for the EIC and VOC to trade in the empire in considerable volume and to make significant investments there, which in turn stimulated considerable economic growth in some provinces, like Bengal. Urban growth, including the establishment of new urban foundations, also signifies economic growth. Mughal efforts to stimulate both internal and foreign trade clearly had positive effects. The rural classes in a position to profit from increased production of cash crops probably prospered more in Mughal times than peasants who produced food. If, as some historians believe, the influx of specie into the subcontinent led to an increase in the monetization of the rural economy, this process may have produced an increased revenue demand on rural food producers because they could pay taxes in coin more conveniently than in kind. The parts of the empire affected by prolonged warfare, especially the Deccan provinces, inevitably suffered impoverishment, in some cases radical impoverishment, as a result. There is, however, insufficient data to support the argument that the Mughal regime steadily impoverished the peasantry through a constant increase in revenue demand.

Mughal economic historians have often focused on how the Mughal regime affected the empire's potential to develop a capitalist economy. Since, from a Marxist perspective, the development of capitalism in Europe, notably England, permitted imperialist exploitation of India in the eighteenth and nineteenth centuries, the question has considerable moment for Indian nationalist historians. There is little doubt that the Mughal regime interfered with the potential for the development of a capitalist economy. There is equally little reason, given the context, to expect that it should have done anything else. Like the Portuguese Estado da Índia and virtually every other government of the time, the empire was clearly a redistributive mechanism, which prospered by extracting, rather than creating, wealth. The Mughals clearly saw trade as a desirable source of revenue and sought to foster it, but they did not seek to foster the type of commercial spirit that brought the English and Dutch to the Indies. Although the regime made some investment in infrastructure, which encouraged trade, it also imposed enormous costs on the society. Much of the huge army existed primarily to ensure collection of the land revenue that supported it, producing little net economic benefit. The regime also hoarded immense amounts of specie that might otherwise have been invested. Fear of extortion or excessive tax demands inhibited the activity of merchants. But it is anachronistic, or at least unreasonable, to expect the Mughal regime to have sought to stimulate the development of capitalism.

INDIAN SOCIETY IN THE MUGHAL PERIOD

Indian society was not a timeless, unchanging entity, affected only superficially by high politics; it evolved in accord with its own internal dynamics as well as external political and economic currents. As already discussed, Indian agriculture changed considerably in Mughal times. Cultivated area expanded, the growth of cash crops increased, and new crops, such as tobacco, maize, and silk, began to be produced. The increase in market agriculture meant the proliferation of new market towns as well as new international trading centers. Such economic changes cannot have occurred without major social ramifications.

Popular religion certainly changed in Mughal times as a result of Mughal policy and patronage. Conversion to Islam continued during the Mughal period. As Richard Eaton has shown, conversion to Islam on the Bengal frontier, the most important zone of conversion in Mughal times, coincided with the expansion of organized agriculture and primarily involved groups and regions outside the social and cultural structure of caste Hinduism. Recent research by William Pinch suggests that the patronage of Rajput *mansabdar*s, who devoted significant resources to the construction of Vaishnavite temples outside Rajasthan, helped to define modern sectarian Hinduism, increasing the uniformity of religious practice and broadening the sense of connection. Among Muslims, Aurangzeb's patronage of Shari Sunni Islam altered the tone of Islam in the subcontinent. The universalist strain, represented by the Chishtis and reflected in Akbar's vision, became less prominent.

The relative stability and order of Mughal rule clearly led to increased prosperity, which must have had social consequences. Economic growth and transformation inevitably produces social change.

Mughal social history has received little attention, in part because students of Indian society—for the most part, anthropologists, rather than historians—have taken little interest in the Mughals, and Mughal historians have focused on the Mughal polity and economy rather than social change. The history of Indian society under the Mughals has not yet been written.

MUGHAL CULTURAL AND INTELLECTUAL HISTORY

The Mughal regime built the Taj Mahal; that alone would establish the period as one of enormous achievement. Yet, the Taj Mahal, breathtaking

IMAGE 5.7 *Humayun's Tomb (1562–1571), Delhi.* Humayun's tomb (the first monumental Mughal dynastic mausoleum) stands at the intersection of a four-part garden with pathways and water channels. It combines the architectural legacies of the Timurids (a radially symmetrical plan and high double dome) and the Delhi Sultanate (red sandstone and white marble) forming a symbol of Mughal rule and continuity.

and inimitable as it is, is only one of many Mughal monuments, and architecture, only one medium of Mughal artistic achievement. In painting, poetry, and prose, Mughal patronage produced enduring triumphs. Because Mughal wealth so far outstripped that of the Safavids and Uzbeks, there was a steady flow of talent into the Mughal realm. During the later sixteenth and seventeenth centuries, the center of Persian culture was in the Indo-Gangetic plain.

The Taj Mahal by itself would give Mughal architecture pride of place, but it is the most outstanding of many beautiful and powerful Mughal buildings. The emperors, their families, and their officials sponsored the construction of hundreds of notable structures. The royal tombs of Humayun in Delhi, Akbar at Sikandra outside Agra, Jahangir in Lahore, and Shah Jahan and Mumtaz Mahal in the Taj are the most notable. The grandeur of these tombs, set in gardens with running water in accord with the Muslim concept of paradise, articulated divine approval of Mughal rule; the Mughal fortifications at Agra and Delhi were statements of Mughal power in stone as well as practical fortresses. The Mughal architectural style, developed under Akbar, synthesized Timurid and South Asian elements,

IMAGE 5.8 *Taj Mahal (1632–1648): the tomb of Shah Jahan's wife Mumtaz Mahal, Agra.* A magnificent symbol of sovereignty, spirituality, and romance, the Taj Mahal is a symphony of repeated and symmetrical forms faced with white marble. Punctuating the surfaces is an inlay of vegetal and floral designs in precious and semi-precious stone and Quranic verses that refer to Paradise and Judgment Day.

with Iranian influence added in Jahangir's time. In addition to buildings, the Mughals designed outstanding gardens, especially in Kashmir.

Mughal painting involved the synthesis of the great schools of painting in the Iranian world in the fifteenth century, those of Herat and Tabriz, and the traditional Indian schools of painting. All of these traditions had already produced great works. Later in Akbar's reign, European influence became part of the Mughal tradition, and, somewhat later, vice versa.

Mughal patronage had an immense influence on literature, primarily but not exclusively in Persian. Because of Mughal cultural dominance, the predominant style of Persian poetry of the sixteenth and seventeenth centuries came to be known as the Indian style, *sabk-i Hindi*. As noted in the discussion of the Indian style in the Safavid chapter, the traditional evaluation of the style as a symptom of literary decline is an aesthetic, not an objective, judgment, and there was no consciousness of literary decline at the time. The Mughals certainly considered contemporary poets worthy of massive patronage; Akbar, Jahangir, and Shah Jahan actually appointed the equivalent of a poet laureate. The Mughal emperors preferred to speak

Persian themselves. Aurangzeb, for example, spoke both Chaghatay Turkish, the language of his ancestors, and Hindustani, but used Persian. Muzaffar Alam contends that the Mughal preference for Persian served a distinct political purpose: "The culture and ethos of Persian matched . . . their vision of a diverse yet overarching empire."[13] But the Persian literary tradition in India was an extension of that of Iran, with few distinctly South Asian features.

Mughal patronage supported literatures other than Persian. Though members of the Mughal family and some of their servants continued to speak Chaghatay, it never became a literary language in South Asia. Mughal patronage supported work in Hindi and even Sanskrit, at least as late as Shah Jahan's reign. Tulsi Das (d. 1623), whose works helped to define Hindi as a literary language, had close associates at Akbar's court. Literary and religious boundaries did not coincide; Muslim poets wrote in Hindi and Hindus in Persian. Jain poets dedicated Sanskrit verses in praise of Akbar. The literary traditions of Pashto, Sindhi, and Punjabi also developed in Mughal times. Urdu, literally meaning "language of the camp," was vernacular Hindustani, linguistically similar to Hindi but transcribed in a form of Arabic script; it became a major literary language in the eighteenth century.

The pattern of Akbar's patronage reveals his intention to establish a cultural synthesis that paralleled and supported his political synthesis. The third volume of the *Ay'in-i Akbari* includes long summaries of the ethnography, geography, and social structure of India and chapters on Hindu and Jain doctrine and philosophy. Abu al-Fazl states his aim as "establishing peace and promoting concord" and asserts that "the worship of one God and the profession of His Unity among this people [the Hindus] [are] convincingly attested."[14] Al-Biruni, the great Muslim scholar of the eleventh century, made the same argument; Abu al-Fazl, however, makes his statement as a part of the Akbari constitution and as the underlying principle of Akbar's cultural program. Although Akbar's successors continued neither the scale nor the scope of this cultural patronage, the tradition did continue into Aurangzeb's time. Dara Shukuh's writing makes his interest in, and sympathy with, Hinduism unmistakable. His most famous work, the *Majma` al-Bahrayn* (Mixture of the Two Oceans), argues that Sufism and Hindu mysticism differ only in vocabulary. Interest in Hindu culture did not die with Dara Shukuh; at least one major study was written for Aurangzeb's grandson, Muhammad Muiz al-Din, who later reigned briefly as Jahandar Shah.

MUGHAL DECLINE

Most interpretations of Mughal decline reflect the writer's political circumstances and agenda rather than the realities of the late seventeenth and early eighteenth centuries. William Irvine, the earliest writer to approach the subject systematically, focused on the degenerate character of the later emperors and their officers, thus justifying British rule in India. He and his immediate successor, Jadunath Sarkar, emphasize Aurangzeb's religious policy as the immediate cause of decline. His Muslim bigotry, they assert, caused a "Hindu reaction," consisting of a series of revolts that led to the breakdown of Mughal power.[15] Ishtiaq Husain Qureshi, the leading Pakistani historian, inverts this interpretation. He blames Akbar's inclusion of Shii Muslims and Hindus in the Mughal ruling class. Despite Akbar's efforts, the Mughal Empire could only appear as Sunni Muslim rule, and neither Hindus nor Shiis could be truly loyal to it. Akbar thus erected a house of cards that inevitably collapsed despite Aurangzeb's competence.

Irfan Habib retains the outline of Sarkar's interpretation but takes a Marxist perspective. He contends that Mughal administration inevitably produced a steadily increasing agricultural-revenue demand and thus growing privation of the peasantry. Hunger and oppression produced a series of revolts. The mere willingness of peaceful peasants to join in revolts, in his view, shows their growing desperation. The reality of the armed peasantry shows the inadequacy of this hypothesis. Sarkar and Habib represent two generations of serious scholarship, but their conclusions ultimately reflect their ideological convictions rather than their scholarship. M. Athar Ali argues that "the failure of the Mughal Empire would seem to derive essentially from a *cultural* failure [emphasis his], shared with the entire Islamic world. It was this failure that tilted the economic balance in favour of Europe, well before European armies [dominated Asia],"[16] but this thesis has similar flaws. He does not explain the mechanism by which the growing economic power of Europe actually caused the political collapse of the Mughal Empire. His argument begins with the assumption that because Ottoman, Safavid, and Mughal decline occurred at the same time, there must have been a common cause.

The work of Satish Chandra has placed the study of Mughal decline on a more empirical footing. He and most subsequent serious students of Mughal decline focus on the failure of the *mansabdari* system. Indeed, because the Mughal Empire existed as a consequence of the relationship between the emperor and the *mansabdar*s, its decline had to consist of a change in that relationship. For roughly a century after the death of Akbar, the Mughal political compromise had assured the loyalty of the vast majority of *mansabdar*s. Participation in the Mughal system had offered security of income and status, the prospect of promotion, and a fair prospect of passing one's position and establishment on to one's sons. The course of events surrounding the death of Aurangzeb and continuing through the reign of Bahadur Shah reveal a change in pattern. The two great factions of the period, that of Asad Khan and Zul Fiqar Khan and that of Ghazi al-Din Khan Firuz-i Jang and Chin Qulich Khan, were more cohesive (attached to each other) than adhesive (attached to a prince). As Muzaffar Alam describes in detail, Mughal governors began to see their provincial assignments more as opportunities to begin establishing an independent power base rather than as part of a career path in Mughal service. Clearly, the compromise no longer existed; *mansabdar*s sought to assure their status by means other than loyal service to the sovereign. Factions had always existed, but their significance had changed. Mughal decline, narrowly defined, meant the failure of the Mughal political compromise. Why did it fail?

Most historians contend that Mughal expansion into the Deccan created a *jagirdari* crisis, meaning a shortage of *jagir* lands such that the demand for *jagir*s outstripped the supply. In its simplest form, this argument begins with the Mughal method of conquest, with its reliance on incentives for surrender rather than outright military victory and the destruction of the enemy. The incentives offered in the conquests of the Bijapur and Golconda and the long war against the Marathas outstripped the revenue received from the newly conquered regions. This shortfall caused disaffection among *mansabdar*s and increasing revenue pressure on the zamindars and cultivators, causing widespread zamindar revolts. J. F. Richards draws attention to another aspect of the Mughal system of conquest, the need to develop relationships with the local notables. He contends that the new provinces of Bijapur and Golconda offered enough revenue to pay the salaries of the new *mansabdar*s, but the Mughals failed to forge the ties with the indigenous elites necessary to gain effective access to it. Aurangzeb, he contends, failed to provide the military support *jagirdar*s often needed to collect their revenue. As a result, they began to look for security beyond their status as Mughal officers, by making arrangements with their enemies. M. N. Pearson contends that Mughal defeats in the Deccan, such as Shivaji's raid on the Mughal camp in 1663 and sack of Surat in 1664, shook *mansabdar* loyalty to the Timurid dynasty, which depended on military success. The demoralized *mansabdars* performed badly in the later campaigns as a result, he asserts. Unlike other students of Mughal decline, Muzaffar Alam concentrates on north India rather than the Deccan, but his findings are similar. Mughal officers, especially those with close ties to Aurangzeb and few to Bahadur Shah, sought to establish themselves in the provinces rather than gaining advancement through imperial patronage.

This behavior suggests that the *jagirdari* crisis must have had two aspects, supply and demand. Aurangzeb's campaigns in the Deccan, both the conquests of Bijapur and Golconda and the long and painful operations against the Marathas, had a less favorable balance between carrot and stick than earlier phases of Mughal expansion. The additional incentives needed to incorporate opponents into the Mughal system translated into increasing demand for *jagirs*. Richards contends that the conquests should have brought enough revenue to cover this increased demand, but the Mughals failed to come to terms with the regional elites as they had elsewhere in India. He omits, however, the enormously destructive effects of the campaigns on these regions. Earlier Mughal campaigns had had such effects. The unsuccessful siege of Parenda in 1634 consumed, by a rough calculation, all food in the 1,256 square miles surrounding the fort and all fodder in the 5,017 square miles surrounding the fort. It lasted only four months. The final sieges of Bijapur and Golconda lasted eight and seven months, respectively, involved far larger forces, and caused widespread starvation.

The sieges of Parenda, Bijapur, and Golconda, however, were small affairs compared with the sustained efforts against Maratha forts. Operations against Jinji lasted from 1690 to 1698; operations against Panhala from 1688 to 1696. The scale and range of warfare in the Deccan must have made normal agriculture impossible and prevented the Mughals from profiting from the expansion of the empire. Simultaneously, the *mansabs* offered to the Deccani elites raised demand enormously. For example, Pam Nayak, a local chieftain in coastal Andhra, received the rank of 5,000/4,000 upon entering Mughal service, nearly as great an incentive as Ali Mardan Khan, who brought the province and fortress of Qandahar to the Mughals, and the second Mir Jumlah, who brought the Hyderabad Karnatak. The incentives for submission had gone beyond the point of diminishing returns. The Mughal mechanism of conquest, and with it the Mughal mechanism of political distribution, failed in the Deccan wars.

Aurangzeb's long reign caused another major political weakness, though it did not show clearly until after the death of Bahadur Shah. The leading officers of the empire, whatever their faction or connection, all saw themselves as Aurangzebi officers. In each previous Mughal succession, some officers who had been especially close to the previous ruler were dissatisfied with their status under the new regime and were essentially irreconcilable. Bahadur Shah, like all of his predecessors, sought to replace his father's men with his own protégés, causing resentment among the established officers. The Mughal sources and later historians refer to this issue as friction between *khanahzads*, men who had been born into Mughal service, and new officers. But it was a predictable repetition of the tensions that occurred with the previous successions—one that had, however, far severer consequences because of the changed circumstances of the empire.

Bahadur Shah's normal desire to place his own protégés in the pivotal positions of the empire threatened all of the leading officers of the empire. The situation repeated in domestic politics the systemic failure of the mechanism of conquest in the Deccan. Bahadur Shah could neither satisfy the *khanahzads* nor do without them. When Zul Fiqar Khan negotiated with the younger sons of Bahadur Shah to partition the empire among them with himself as common vizier so as to deny the throne to Azim al-Shan, the obvious choice to succeed his father, his action demonstrated how thoroughly politics had changed. Mughal officers had always sought to position themselves properly for succession. In some cases, they intervened to secure their position through a favorable succession, as Khan-i Azam and Rajah Man Singh did by supporting Khusraw and Nur Jahan did by championing Shahryar. But these efforts at intervention failed; the Mughal officers in general wanted a strong and competent ruler. Zul Fiqar Khan could not have succeeded, however, without widespread support from other nobles. Chin Qulich Khan, his major rival among the Aurangzebi nobles, did not take decisive action against Zul Fiqar Khan. Dynastic loyalty no longer restrained the desire of officers for a malleable ruler, as it had after Akbar's death. Like Mahabat Khan during Jahangir's dotage, Zul Fiqar Khan believed he could have the status he deserved only by dominating the empire. But Mahabat Khan faced a weak ruler dominated by an opposing faction. Zul Fiqar Khan confronted a prince and placed the dynasty in peril for his own and his followers' sake. Being a part of the Mughal system was no longer sufficient; an officer needed additional leverage.

Alam's work on north India reveals that developments in the Mughal heartland, as well as the Deccan, increased the pressure on the *mansabdar* class. Changes in the agrarian system in the north had political ramifications. Awadh, part of the Mughal Empire since the first half of Akbar's reign, had become a rebellious province by the end of Aurangzeb's tenure. One of the zamindar groups in the province, the Bais Rajputs, had expanded their area of control substantially since Akbar's time, prospering with the spread of cash crop cultivation. This growth in rural prosperity had shifted the balance of power between the Mughal authorities and the zamindars. The governors of Awadh in later Mughal times frequently requested additional force and authority from the center to deal with the zamindars. The additional authority eventually delegated helped Awadh become an autonomous governorship, a significant step in the devolution of Mughal power. In the Punjab, the confrontations with the Sikhs and Jats likewise forced concession of autonomous powers to the governorship, ceding effective Mughal control of the province.

The establishment of autonomous governorships satisfied the needs of the officers for secure status and income at the cost of reducing the Mughal court to a purely symbolic significance. It thus represented a new form of political compromise.

THE MUGHAL SYSTEM

How should one describe the Mughal Empire? Its wealth, victories, and monuments suggest grandeur, majesty, and solidity; close analysis of its political structure suggests a delicate balancing act, even fragility. Compared with that of the Ottoman Empire, the Mughal revenue structure was both decentralized and uncertain, far more similar to the Ottoman Empire in the era of the *ayan* than during the classical period. Indeed, one may compare the *ayan* to the zamindars; both were local elites who both cooperated and competed with the imperial authority. Akbar's brief effort to eliminate the *jagir* system would have produced one far more similar to the Ottoman system, but it failed because both the expectations of the *mansabdar*s and the societies of the provinces made it impossible. In the Middle East, the poverty of agriculture and strength of pastoral nomads had prevented centralized bureaucratic rule since Abbasid times. In India, the wealth and social complexity of the society frustrated the bureaucratic agenda.

Unlike all of their Muslim predecessors in the subcontinent, the Mughals achieved an enduring legitimacy that survived their effective power. It began with the prestige of Timurid descent, prominent in India because of Timur's great victory there in 1398. Babur's great victories at Panipat and Khanwa and Akbar's political and military success and grand court rituals solidified Mughal prestige. The nature of the rituals and *sulh-i kull* translated Timurid sovereignty into a form both comprehensible and acceptable to most Hindus. The establishment of ties with Rajputs, Indian Muslims, and, later, some Marathas and other Deccanis gave the Mughals access to both the economic and the military resources of most of the country. But India's armed peasantry, under zamindar leadership, restricted Mughal penetration into the countryside. In a sense, the Mughal court and central government floated above Indian society, anchored to it through provincial administration. The frequent transfer of officials, the constant shifting of the anchors, prevented the officers from becoming more solidly connected to the society than to the court. When the anchors could not hold, that is, when officers could not send significant revenue to the center and retain enough for themselves, the regime failed. The anchors became part of the society, autonomous principalities, and the Mughal court became a symbol of sovereignty without effective authority in the provinces.

Notes

1. Peter Jackson, *The Delhi Sultanate: A Political and Military History*. Cambridge Studies in Islamic Civilization, ed. David Morgan (Cambridge: Cambridge University Press, 1999), 322.

2. Jos Gommans, *Mughal Warfare: Indian Frontiers and High Roads to Empire*. Warfare and History, ed. Jeremy Black (London: Routledge, 2002), 33.

3. Robert Sewell, *A Forgotten Empire (Vijaynagara): A Contribution to the History of India* (London: S. Sonnenschein, 1910); multiple reprints including New Delhi: National Book Trust, 1970, 1; quoted in Richard M. Eaton, *A Social History of the Deccan, 1300–1761: Eight Indian Lives*, vol. 1–8 of *The New Cambridge History of India,* ed. Gordon Johnson et al. (Cambridge: Cambridge University Press, 2005), 94.

4. Tapan Raychaudhuri, "The State and the Economy: The Mughal Empire," in *C. 1200–1750*, vol. 1 of *The Cambridge Economic History of India*, ed. Tapan Raychaudhuri and Irfan Habib (Cambridge: Cambridge University Press, 1982), 173.

5. M. Athar Ali, "The Mughal Polity—a Critique of Revisionist Approaches," *Modern Asian Studies* 27 (1993): 710; reprinted in M. Athar Ali, *Mughal India: Studies in Polity, Ideas, Society and Culture* (New Delhi: Oxford University Press, 2006), 90–91.

6. Stephen P. Blake, "The Patrimonial-Bureaucratic Empire of the Mughals," *Journal of the Royal Asiatic Society* 39 (1979): 77–99; reprinted in *The State in India, 1000–1700*, ed.

Hermann Kulke. Oxford in India Readings, Themes in Indian History, ed. Basudev Chatterji, Neeladri Bhattacharya, and C. A. Bayly (New Delhi: Oxford University Press, 1995), 278–303.

7. Bernard S. Cohn, "Political Systems in Eighteenth-Century India," *Journal of the American Oriental Society* 82 (1962); reprinted in *The Bernard Cohn Omnibus* (New Delhi: Oxford University Press, 2004), 485.

8. Sir Thomas Roe, *The Embassy of Sir Thomas Roe to India, 1615–19*, ed. Sir William Foster (London: Humphrey Milford, 1926), 86–87.

9. J. F. Richards, *The Mughal Empire*, vol. 1–5 of *The New Cambridge History of India*, ed. Gordon Johnson (Cambridge: Cambridge University Press, 1993), 93.

10. Farhat Hasan, *State and Locality in Mughal India: Power Relations in Western India, c. 1572–1730*. University of Cambridge Oriental Publications 61 (Cambridge: Cambridge University Press, 2004), 126–127.

11. Richards, *Mughal*, 204.

12. Raychaudhuri, "State and Economy," 172, 193.

13. Muzaffar Alam, *The Language of Political Islam: 1200–1800* (Chicago: University of Chicago Press, 2004), 144.

14. Abū al-Fazl ʿAllāmī, *Āʾīn-i Akbari*, 3 vols. Vol. 1, ed. D. C. Phillott, trans. H. Blochman; vols. 2 and 3, ed. Sir Jadunath Sarkar, trans. H. S. Jarret. 2nd ed. (Calcutta: Asiatic Society of Bengal, 1927–1949; reprint, New Delhi: Oriental Books Reprint, 1977–1978), 3:1–2

15. Jadunath Sarkar, *History of Aurangzib*, 5 vols. as 4 (Delhi: Orient Longman, 1973), 3:190–199. This work first appeared in 1912; its publication history is difficult to unravel.

16. M. Athar Ali, "The Passing of Empire: The Mughal Case," *Modern Asian Studies* 9 (1975): 396; *Mughal India: Studies in Polity, Ideas, Society and Culture*, 342.

Chapter 6

CONCLUSION

The power, achievements, and lasting impacts of the Ottoman, Safavid, and Mughal empires make the impasse of post-Abbasid politics hard to recall. All three empires won a degree of durable legitimacy no Muslim dynasty had attained since the Abbasids and maintained large and coherent polities for longer than any other Muslim dynasty, including the Umayyads and Abbasids. Their endurance and coherence permitted them to have enduring impacts on society and culture and on political patterns that have lasted until the present. They carried their common political heritage into disparate environments and developed unique solutions to their common dilemma. They resembled each other far more than they did their predecessors or their lesser contemporaries, like the Uzbek principalities and the Deccan kingdoms. This resemblance justifies classifying them as a distinctive type of polity, for which the term *gunpowder empire* will serve since there is no convenient alternative.

The shared background, which resulted in similarities in political ideas, vocabularies, and institutions, led both their contemporaries and later historians to see greater alikeness among them than actually existed. Thus, the French traveler Francois Bernier identified the Mughal *jagir* with the Ottoman *timar*, and the historian Irfan Habib describes Bernier's expression as a "harmless Turkicism."[1] The *timar* and the *jagir* were both forms of salary through land-revenue assignment, distinct from cash salaries on the one hand and grants of land in return for service, as in feudalism, on the other. That similarity might satisfy a political sociologist, perhaps, but should not deceive a historian. The Ottoman *sipahi* was a private soldier who might hold the same assignment for his whole career and normally had family roots in his province and district. The Mughal *mansabdar* might have had hundreds or thousands of military retainers and normally changed assignments every few years. The three empires all used land-revenue assignments, yes, but in profoundly different ways that reflected deep differences among the three regimes.

The chronological proximity and tactical similarity of the Ottoman victories at Chaldiran, Turna Dağ, Marj Dabik, Raydaniyya, and Mohacs, the Safavid triumph at Jam, and Babur's victories at the first Panipat, Khanua, and Gogra contributed to the impression of similarity. All three empires defeated their rivals on the battlefield with a combination of ar-tillery, infantry firearms, and cavalry, employed in a wagon fortress. They all made firearms a monopoly of the central government, at least in the-ory, until the Ottomans began developing their *sekban* forces at the end of the sixteenth century. But the political significance of the firearms com-ponent of the central army varied immensely. The Janissaries became one of the most important parts of the Ottoman government and ruling class; the Mughal infantry forces had no political weight whatsoever. The Ot-tomans, Safavids, and Mughals won their decisive victories with similar armies in similar battle formations and paid their provincial armies with land-revenue assignments. But given those common features, the military organizations and provincial administrations of the three empires differed about as much as possible.

The Ottoman and Mughal empires escaped the post-Abbasid impasse in part by escaping the Arid Zone, but that circumstance did not in itself guarantee success. Muslim rulers had, after all, reigned over virtually all of the territory that the Mughal Empire ruled, but never achieved either their durable power or enduring legitimacy. The Safavids escaped temporally rather than geographically. The expansion of global trade permitted them to substitute export income from cash crops for overall agricultural pros-perity. This narrow base permitted them to overcome the ecological ad-vantage of pastoral nomads, thus of tribal power, in their territory. The disruption of patterns of nomadism, thus of tribal structures, in thir-teenth-century Anatolia meant that the Ottomans never had a tribal army or overcame the structural barriers to centralization inherent in tribal con-federations. The Timurid polities in central Asia were tribal confedera-tions, but by the time Babur invaded Hindustan, the tribal structure was no longer intact. The Ottoman and Mughal armies grew out of what would have been the war bands in tribal confederations. Allegiance to the ruler, not tribal identity, defined them. This fact, as much as the advantage of firearms, led to the greater centralization of these empires. The central-government monopolies on firearms through the sixteenth century suggest that firearms did alter the political balance in favor of the ruler and the central government, but firearms alone did not make the expansion of the empires possible.

The early expansion of the Ottoman Empire, including Bayazid I's temporary but impressive triumphs, did not depend on firearms. The Ottomans did not use the wagon fortress until after Mehmed I and Murad II had reunified and established the basic form of the empire's mature institutions. Ottoman and Mughal expansion in the sixteenth century clearly depended on their ability to use firearms effectively, first and foremost in the field but also in sieges; so did the ability of the Safavids to keep the Uzbeks from conquering Khurasan and thus to unite both halves of the Iranian plateau. But victories, on the battlefield or in the sieges, did not add up to a durable empire. Muhammad ibn Tughluq conquered more of the subcontinent than Akbar did, but his empire began to fall apart even before his death. The military power of the central regimes set the conditions for the establishment of a durable polity but did not suffice to maintain it.

Transforming military victories into enduring political power meant gaining control of the agricultural revenue and military potential, primarily manpower, of the provinces. The Ottoman *tahrir* system incorporated existing tax structures and, with the security and predictability of revenue demands associated with Ottoman rule until the end of the sixteenth century, made Ottoman government acceptable to most of the conquered populations. The Ottomans gained control of the military manpower of conquered regions through the incorporation of the military elites of their principalities and culling the best of the peasant boys through the *devshirme*. *Timar* assignments in newly conquered territories brought more of the existing Ottoman manpower pool into secure *askari* status. In contrast, the original establishment of the Safavid Empire generally meant little change in the provincial revenue structure. The military manpower in question came from nomad tribes; initial Safavid conquest sometimes involved no more than a change in tribal allegiance. The transition of provinces from *mamalik* to *khass* jurisdiction meant transferring provincial revenue from Qizilbash tribes to other recipients.

The core areas of the Mughal Empire had greater agricultural wealth, denser populations, and more complicated existing social structures than the Ottoman Balkans or Anatolia. In order to establish governance, the Mughals had to come to terms with existing indigenous elites in order to extract revenue and to exploit, or at least neutralize, the massive manpower pool. The category of zamindar permitted the Mughals to come to terms with existing elites and their military followers. Their ability to focus overwhelming military force at any given point gave them enough leverage to induce most local and regional potentates to come to terms with them; their willingness to negotiate with, and concede revenue to, these existing elites allowed them to avoid the impossible task of conquering the empire in detail. Those zamindars who became *mansabdar*s contributed the military force they controlled to the imperial service. The majority who did not at least cooperated with imperial operations and usually served as a link in the revenue system. The Mughals could not eliminate the zamindars but made use of them. Even if the Mughal Empire penetrated rural society more than its predecessors, it did not do so nearly as deeply as the Ottomans did or as the Irano-Islamic tradition of statecraft required. The dominance of pastoral nomadism on much of the Iranian plateau restricted the power of the central government there; the agricultural prosperity and dense population of the Indo-Gangetic plain had a similar but lesser effect.

The centralizing tendency of the Irano-Islamic tradition of statecraft meant that the leading bureaucrats and officials constantly sought to increase the power of the ruler, and thus the bureaucracy, to the extent that circumstances permitted. The geographic setting of the Ottoman and Mughal empires fitted that tradition far better than the Arid Zone after the decline of the Sawad. Neither situation permitted the classic model of an army paid in cash on the basis of provincial revenue; the incomplete monetarization of the two economies, together with the Mughal lack of a direct means of recruiting much of the empire's manpower and need for a provincial army of standing contingents to overawe the zamindars, made such an arrangement impractical. But the military institutions of both empires, as well as of the Safavid Empire after Abbas's reforms, came far closer to that model than tribal confederation ever could.

Institutional centralization required dynastic centralization. Although all three dynasties began with the concepts of collective sovereignty and the appanage system operating, all three evaded the results that those concepts had had in tribal confederations. They did so partly by happenstance, partly by circumstance, and partly by intention. In tribal confederations, the appanages generally coincided with regions ruled by specific tribes, and the chiefs of the tribes frequently served as guardians of the princes who held the appanages. As demonstrated by the records of every tribal confederation from the Saljuqs onward, including the Safavids, through most of the sixteenth century, this situation generated frequent internecine violence. There were no equivalents of tribal chieftains in Ottoman and Mughal provinces. The assignment of princes as provincial governors in those polities lent to conflict only when the age or health of the incumbent ruler made succession an imminent problem. The Ottomans and Safavids ended the possibility of provincial revolt by confining princes to the palace. The Mughals never did, but the succession disputes, impressive as they were, did not have the political effects they had in tribal confederations.

All three dynasties succeeded in articulating their sovereignty on an imperial rather than royal level. No Muslim dynasty since the Abbasids had such enduring legitimacy from such diverse populations. The Ottomans and Mughals succeeded in winning legitimacy from populations with non-Muslim majorities. Even though the Safavids' conquests and military power never equaled those of their contemporaries, they won tacit recognition from the Ottomans and Mughals as equals as well as lasting legitimacy in their own territory. Military success—the Ottoman conquest of Constantinople and the Mamluk sultanate, the Safavid victories over the Aqquyunlu and the Uzbeks, and Babur and Akbar's triumphs and conquests—was clearly an essential element of legitimacy, but it was not sufficient by any means. In architecture, ritual, rhetoric, and literature, the Ottomans and Mughals communicated their sovereignty so as to win acceptance from their Muslim and non-Muslim subjects. The Safavids used the imposition of Shii Islam as a means of winning recognition of their sovereignty and differentiating themselves from their competitors. The Ottomans took over their Byzantine predecessors' role as the chief sponsors and protectors of the Orthodox Church and held the loyalty and support of their Orthodox subjects well into the eighteenth century. The Ottoman transition to the sedentary sultanate, from conquering warriors to pious patrons and protectors of Sunni Islam, did not alienate their Orthodox, Armenian, or Jewish subjects.

All the empires shifted from universalist, messianic creeds to confessional, Shariah-based ideologies, the Ottomans and Safavids by the mid-sixteenth century, the Mughals more than a century later. Government patronage of the ulama establishments and, in the Ottoman and Safavid empires, suppression of Shii and Sunni Islam helped to define the pattern of popular piety in much of the Islamic world. Neither the Usuli variety of Twelver Shiism, which dominates contemporary Shii piety, nor the separatist Islam that led to the partition of British India existed before Safavid and Mughal times. The Safavids from the beginning, but especially in the Majlisi era, made the establishment of Shii, Shari Islam with piety defined by the ulama. The particularist variety of Islam in South Asia developed in reaction to Akbar's universalism and did not receive official patronage until Aurangzeb's time. Aurangzeb himself was far more flexible and less intolerant than his reputation suggests, but the image, not the reality, is his historical legacy. Not by design but as a result of providing a secure position for Rajput officers within the Mughal system, the Mughal regime helped to define the current pattern of sectarian Hinduism as well. The three empires created sharper distinctions of religious identity throughout their territories.

The centralization that the three empires achieved had distinct, though varying, limits. In much of the Ottoman Empire before the seventeenth century, the central government had a direct relationship with the individual soldiers of the provincial army and through them, in their administrative capacity, the individual peasant family. But even the individual Ottoman *sipahi* was never a mere extension of the central government. Well into the sixteenth century, the provincial military elites, the central government and its servants, and the peasants functioned in tension. The provincial elites sought to control as much of the provincial land and revenue as they could; court and central-government officials sought the security of provincial appointments and thus competed with the established provincials for land assignments. The Safavids had direct relationships with individual soldiers in the provincial army when military slaves held land-revenue assignments, but to judge from the results, the central government exercised little control.

From the perspective of world history, the simultaneous collapses of the Safavid and Mughal polities and decline of Ottoman power relative to the European empires of the time ought to have a common cause and form part of a global trend. It would be tidier and trendier that way and, if the rising European powers were to blame, politically satisfying for many observers as well. It appears, however, that the devolution of central power, a more concrete expression than imperial decline, in the three empires had different causes and different dynamics. The Safavid Empire collapsed because the regime failed to maintain enough military power to survive a threat that a few decades earlier would have been minor. The empire collapsed in the provinces when the central government suddenly fell. The unquestioned legitimacy of the regime did not translate into the ability to mobilize in the provinces an army capable breaking the siege of Isfahan. Once the central government and its revenue arrangements broke down, the balance of political power returned to the pastoral nomads.

The Mughal central regime failed as well, but differently. It consisted, ultimately, of the relationship between the secondary, regional, and local potentates of the empire and the Mughal rulers. The failure of the mechanism of expansion in the Deccan made the regime incapable of providing the security of position, status, income, and prospect for promotion that its officers had come to expect. Since being a loyal Mughal officer was no longer a sufficient guarantee, the officers began to fend for themselves. What had been provinces and districts became de facto autonomous principalities. Competition, rather than appointment and assignment, began to determine the distribution of authority and revenue. The political breakdown led to the collapse of the commercial system focused on the empire and thus created opportunities for European merchants and companies.

The Ottoman Empire survived because it adapted. It lost territory and granted European merchants extraterritorial rights; its system of provincial administration and its provincial army changed completely. Its relative power declined, but the systemic changes in the Ottoman regime, which even at the time some observers identified as decline, were adaptations necessary for survival. In 1730, the empire remained a major regional power. It had lost territory; it had lost prestige; it had lost, perhaps, self-confidence. But it had not yet become the sick man of Europe.

The period that this text covers ended nearly three hundred years ago. Most readers will come to it ultimately as a result of events in the twenty-first century. The impacts of the three remain vivid today, but there is no direct, obvious, emotionally satisfying linkage from the events of September 11, 2001. There is a great temptation to make the global war on terrorism—to use the most common of the inadequate names for the current conflict—the latest phase in the struggle between East and West, which Herodotus claims began with the rape of Europa, or the continuation of a millennium and a half of warfare between Muslims and Christians. In

this perspective, Fatih Mehmed and Qanuni Sulayman appear as the predecessors and precursors of Osama Bin Ladin and Ayman al-Zawahiri. But
the ideology of today's totalitarian Islamists descends not from that of the
Ottomans and their contemporaries but from traditions of dissent, generally directed against such power holders. The intellectual tradition that
produced both the Sunni and the Shii varieties of totalitarian Islamism
began with Jalal al-Din al-Afghani in the nineteenth century and reflects
the influence of Western totalitarian thought (primarily, but not exclusively, Leninist). Its earlier precursors, however, come not from the ruling
ideologies of the Ottomans, Safavids, and Mughals but from such dis-
senters as the Kadizelis and, despite an immense difference in ethos, the
Safavid movement. Like Shah Ismail, the leaders of al-Qaida promise a
utopian redress of concrete grievances. On the Shii side, the rise of the Shii
ulama that began with Safavid sponsorship was a necessary prerequisite for
the appearance of Khomeini and his doctrine that the ulama should rule,
but none of his predecessors in Safavid times, not even Majlisi, envisioned
such a doctrine.

Notes

1. François Bernier, *Travels in the Mogul Empire*, trans. Archibald Constable, ed. Vincent A.
Smith, 2nd rev. ed. (New Delhi: Oriental Books Reprint, 1983), 224 (original printing, London: Oxford University Press, 1934); Irfan Habib, *The Agrarian System of Mughal India, 1556–
1707*, 2nd ed. (New Delhi: Oxford University Press, 1999), 368.

Glossary

The glossary entries consist of the word as it appears in the text, the Modern Turkish spelling of Ottoman words in parentheses if it differs from the transliteration, the initial *O*, *S*, or *M* to designate which empire used the term, and the definition. If there is no initial, the term is used more broadly than in a single empire.

Agha (*ağa*) (O): master; a title of authority

Ahadi (M): single fighter; member of the cavalry component of the Mughal central army

Akche (*akçe*) (O): standard Ottoman silver coin

Akhtah begi (M): master of horse

Akinji (*akıncı*) (O): frontier raider or irregular light soldier

Alim: man of learning, specifically one learned in the Islamic religious sciences; singular of ulama

Amin (*emin*) (O): see *il yazijisi*

Amir al-muminin: commander of the faithful, the working title of the caliphs

Amir al-umara: amir of amirs, cognate to *beylerbey*; in early Safavid usage, denoted the chief officer; in later usage, a provincial governor; in Mughal usage was purely an honorific

Amir-i divan: chief of administration in a tribal confederation

Andarun (*Enderun*) (O): the Inner Service, which staffed the sultan's household, including the female establishment

Askari (*askeri*): military; designation for the entire ruling class of a military patronage state, especially the Ottoman Empire; a recipient of an imperial salary rather than a payer of taxes

Avariz-i divaniye (*avarız-ı divaniye*) (O): a capitation tax imposed on rural males, originally levied in emergency and later the basis of rural taxation

Ayan (O): provincial notables; specifically, the notables who dominated the rural Ottoman Empire in the eighteenth century

Azab (*azap*) (O): auxiliary infantry soldier

Bab-i ali (*babıâli*) (O): high gate; name of the grand vizier's staff; the French translation, Sublime Porte, became the standard European term for the Ottoman regime

Bahadur: Mongol word for hero, used as a royal title in the Timurid, Aqquyunlu, and other empires

Bakhshi (M): military administrator; manager of the *mansabdari* system

Bash (*baş*) *kadin* (O): mother of the first-born son of an Ottoman ruler

Bash daftardar (*baş defterdar*) (O): literally, "head clerk"; state treasurer and member of the Imperial Council

Bedestan (O): covered market; the mark of commercial importance in Ottoman cities

Bey: the Turkic word for chief, leader, or general, cognate to the Arabic *amir*

Beylerbey: bey of beys; title of Ottoman and Safavid provincial governors

Beylerbeylik (O, S): province

Beylik: province or principality governed or ruled by a bey; used specifically to refer to the principalities of post-Saljuq Anatolia

Birun (O): the Outer Service, the Ottoman bureaucracy outside the palace

Boluk (O): a unit of *sekban* or *sarija* infantry

Boluk-bashi (*bölük başi*) (O): the commander of a *boluk*

Boy (O): tribe; the second largest grouping of pastoral nomads recognized in Ottoman usage

Buyuk Odasi (*Büyük Odası*) (O): Large Chamber; component of the *Andarun* service responsible for training *devshirme*

Chatrpati: Sanskrit title for a universal sovereign; title taken by Shivaji

Chaudhuri (M): a prominent *zamindar*, usually the leading *zamindar* of a *parganah*, appointed to serve as an intermediary between the *zamindar*s of the district and Mughal officials

Chavush (*chavuş*) (O): imperial messenger

Chavush bashi (*çavush başi*): head of imperial messengers; one of the chief officials of the Outer Service (*agha*s of the stirrup)

Chift (O): the land a peasant family could cultivate with a single pair of oxen (the literal meaning of *chift*)

Chift bozan resmi (O): land-abandonment tax, exacted from peasants who leave their land

Chift-khanah (*çift-hane*) (O): peasant household cultivating a *chiftlik*; rural tax payer

Chiftlik (*çiftlik*) (O): a household cultivating a *chift*, the basic unit of Ottoman rural taxation

Chift-resmi (*çift-resmi*) (O): *chift* tax; tax paid by a *chift-khanah*

Daftar (*defter*): notebook or record book

Daftar kadhudasi (*defter kethüdası*) (O): provincial financial official for supervision of *zeamet* assignments

Daftardar (*defterdar*) (O): clerk; specifically the fiscal officer appointed by the central government to *salyanah* provinces

Daftar-khanah (S): imperial office responsible for financial records

Dar al-insha (S): imperial office responsible for correspondence

Dar al-saadah aghasi (*darüsaade ağası*) (O): master of the House of Felicity; administrator of the *Andarun* and thus of the Ottoman palace harem; also known as the chief white eunuch

Darbandji (*derbendçi*) (O): border guard; paramilitary force straddling the *askari*/*raya* boundary

Daulat (M): literally, "fortune"; the modern Persian word for "state"; Humayun defined officers and bureaucrats as men of *daulat*

Devshirme (*devşirme*) (O): the levy of boys; Ottoman forced recruitment of Christian boys for service in the central army and bureaucracy

Digvijaya: Sanskrit word for "conquest of the four quarters"; a ritual procession by a Hindu ruler around the frontiers of his domain

Dish Khazineh (*Dış Hazine*) (O): outer treasury; component of the *Andarun* responsible for financial records

Divan (M): chief financial officer of a province

Divan begi: chief judicial official

Divan-i ala (S): literally, "high court"; imperial bureaucracy

Divan-i khalisa (M): central government official responsible for land revenue payable to the central treasury

Divan-i kul (M): chief administrator; equivalent to grand vizier

Doganji Odasi (*Doğancı Odası*) (O): Falconry Department

Farr: Persian word for the divine charisma of the ruler

Fatwa (*fetva*): legal ruling by an authority in *fiqh*

Fawjdar (M): *sarkar* (district) governor; responsible for maintaining order and supporting revenue collection

Fiqh: Islamic jurisprudence

Fitna: literally, in Arabic, "temptation"; term for periods of trial or division within the Muslim community

Ghaza: frontier raiding

Ghazi: frontier raider

Ghulam (*gulâm*): literally, "young man"; one of the standard words for a military slave

Ghulaman-i khassay-i sharifa (S): military slave component of the Safavid army

Ghulat/ghuluww: extremist/extremism

Hadith: report of a statement or action of the Prophet, the second most important source for Shariah law after the Quran

Hazine-i âmire (*hazine âmirah*) or *Khazinah Odasi* (*Hazine Odası*) (O): Imperial Treasury

Hukumet sanjak (*Hükûmet sancak*) (O): semiautonomous tribal, usually Kurdish, district

Ich khazinah (*iç hazine*) (O): inner treasury; treasury of the *Andarun* and repository of the emperor's valuables

Ichoglani (*içoğolanı*) (O): one of the most promising of the *devshirme* boys

Ihtisab: market standards

Ijtihad: independent legal reasoning

Ilmiye (O): the religious establishment

Iltizam (O): tax farm

Il-yazicisi (*il-yazıcısı*) (O): official responsible for making period revenue surveys; tax assessor

Imaret (O): urban foundation funded by members of the imperial family and high officials to stimulate urban development

Iqta: land-revenue assignment

Ishiq-aqasi-bashi (S): chief court official; in charge of protocol and palace administration

Isnaf (*esnaf*) (O): merchant engaged in local trade in guild products

Ispenje (*ispence*) (O): see *chift-resmi*

Itimad al-Dalwah (S): grand vizier

Jagir (M): land-revenue assignment

Jagirdar (M): holder of a *jagir*; a *mansabdar* in the capacity of a recipient of land revenue

Jalali (*celâlî*) (O): Ottoman military rebel of the late sixteenth and early seventeenth centuries seeking inclusion in the *askari* elite

Janissary (O): *yeni cheri*, or new army; the infantry component of the Ottoman central army, recruited through the *devshirme*

Jariye (*cariye*) (O): female slave or concubine; member of the imperial female establishment

Jebelu (*cebelü*) (O): a cavalry soldier employed by a *sipahi*

Jharuka darshan (M): Akbar's custom of appearing daily on a small balcony (the *jharuka*) before the general public and receiving their salutes

Jizya (*cizye*): capitation tax collected from non-Muslim subject populations

Joft: the land a peasant family could cultivate with a single pair of oxen (the literal meaning of *joft*); cognate of *chift*

Kadin (*kadın*) (O): woman, a title given to four senior imperial concubines

Kadkhuda (*kethüda*): local headman

Kalantar (S): town headman, an imperial appointee

Kapudan-i darya (*kapudan-i darya*) (O): grand admiral; member of the imperial council

Karuri (M): Mughal revenue official; office created as part of Akbar's reforms and responsible for the assessment and collection of revenue for new jurisdictions that produced 10 million rupees of revenue

Katib (*kâtip*) (O): clerk and local informant who assists the *il yazijisi* in conducting *tahrir*

Khadim al-haramayn al-shairfayn (O): servitor of the two sanctuaries, Mecca and Medina; title used by the Mamluk sultans and taken by the Ottomans

Khalifa, khalifat rasulullah: caliph, caliph of the Prophet of God

Khalifat al-khulafah (S): chief subordinate of the Safavid shah in his capacity as *pir* of the Safavid Sufi order

Khalisa (M): land that paid revenue to the central treasury rather than an assignee or grantee

Khanazad (M): son of the household; man born into Mughal service

Khan-i Khanan: khan of khans; title of chief officer

Khasiki (*haseki*) (O): an imperial concubine

Khass (*has*): literally, "special" or "particular," implying "imperial"; applied, in all three empires, to land that paid revenue to the central treasury

Khass oda (*has oda*) (O): privy chamber; the emperor's personal staff

Khass oda bashi (*has oda başı*) (O): the emperor's personal bodyguard; chief of the privy chamber

Khassa (S): designation of provinces under the direct control of the central government

Khass-i humayun (*has-i humayun*) (O): land that paid revenue to the central treasury rather than an assignee

Khazinah-i amiran (*hazine-i âmire*) (O): imperial treasury

Khazine daftari (*hazine defterdar*) (O): provincial official responsible for management of *zeamet* assignments

Khutba: sermon after the Friday prayer in which the name of the sovereign is mentioned

Khwansalar (M): imperial chef

Kiler Odasi (*Kiler Odası*) (O): Imperial Commissary

Kotwal (M): provincial police official

Kucuk Odasi (*Küçük Odası*) (O): Small Chamber; part of the *Andarun* with responsibility for training *devshirme*

Madad-i maash (M): land-revenue grant

Mahmil: ceremonial palanquin sent on the pilgrimage to Mecca

Majlis-navis (S): recorder of audiences; recording and corresponding secretary of the ruler

Mamalik (S): literally, "property"; term for a province under standard provincial administration

Mamluk: literally, "owned"; the most common term for a military slave

Mansabdar (M): holder of an office (*mansab*), with numerical rank, later ranks, denoting his status in the hierarchy of officers, income, and the number of troops he was required to maintain

Mansabdari: adjective form of *mansabdar*

Marja al-taqlid: pattern for imitation; a Shii *alim* of sufficient learning to provide guidance to others

Mazhab (*mezheb*; Arab: *madhab*; pl. *madhahib*): one of the four major divisions of Sunni Islam, usually but erroneously translated as school of law

Millet (O): religious community; specifically, a non-Muslim community within the Ottoman Empire

Mir bakhshi (M): second-highest Mughal official; responsible for the administration of the *mansabdari* system

Mir manzil (M): official responsible for provisioning the court

Mir tuzuk (M): master of court ceremonies

Miri (*mîrî*) (O): taxable land; land not granted in *mulk* or *vaqf*

Mir-i adl (M): provincial official responsible, with the *sadr*/*qazi* and *kotwal*, for the administration of justice and police functions

Mir-i atish (M): master of ordnance, commander of artillery

Mir-i bahr (M): provincial official responsible for naval (riverine) operations

Mir-i mal (M): court treasurer

Mir-i saman (M): superintendent of the imperial workshop

Mudarra (*müdarra*) (O): policy of moderation in Ottoman expansion

Mufti (*müfti*) (O): jurisconsult

Muhrdar (M): keeper of the seal

Muhtasib (*muhtesib*): market inspector; responsible for supervision of prices, trade practices, and quality of goods

Muhtasib al-mamalik (S): chief accountant; director of the *daftar-khanah*

Mujadid: renewer

Mujtahid: individual qualified for independent legal reasoning

Mulk (O): in Ottoman land theory, land granted as heritable and alienable freehold

Mullabashi (S): leading Shii *alim*; position comparable to Ottoman *shaykh al-Islam*

Multezim (*mültezim*) (O): tax farmer

Munshi al-mamalik (S): chief accountant; responsible for the *daftar-khanah*

Muqataa (*mukataa*) (O): revenue source conceded to a tax farmer; also a land-revenue assignment in Ottoman Egypt

Murad (M): hope; Humayun classified artists, musicians, and poets as men of *murad*

Mustawfi (S): accountant

Mustawfi al-mamalik (S): chief accountant

Mustawfi-yi khassa (S): accountant for *khass* revenue

Muteferrika (*müteferrika*) (O): son of a subordinate ruler or important provincial governor; kept at court as a hostage and attached to the *birun*

Mutesellim (*mütesellim*) (O): local deputy of a *beylerbey* or *sanjakbey*

Nasaq (M): literally, "order" or "method"; system of tax assessment based on previous land measurements rather than remeasuring the land each year

Nazim-i subah (M): provincial governor

Nazir-i buyutat (S): superintendent of the imperial workshop

Nefer-i am (O): general mobilization to defend a town or village against the *jalalis*

Nishanji (*Nişancı*) (O): head of chancery

Oba (O): tent; smallest subdivision of nomad populations recognized by the Ottoman administration

Padishah: Iranian word for emperor

Padishah alam panah: world-sheltering emperor; implies the stance of the ruler as protector rather than conqueror

Parganah (M): subdistrict; the smallest unit of provincial administration

Pashakapisi (*paşakapısı*) (O): see *bab-i ali*

Paybaqi (M): land available for assignment as a *jagir*

Pir: leader of a Sufi order

Pish namaz: prayer leader

Pronoia: Byzantine term for a land-revenue assignment; precursor of the Ottoman *timar*

Qaisar (O): Caesar; used as an imperial title

Qaisariyyah (S): covered market; equivalent of an Ottoman *bedestan*

Qanun (*Kanun*): dynastic law

Qanungo (M): local clerk responsible for keeping the revenue records of a *parganah*

Qanunnamah (*kanunnamah*) (O): book of dynastic or administrative law; term covered provincial tax-and revenue-assignment records

Qapi aghasi (*kapı ağası*) (O): master of the gate

Qapiqullu (*kapıkulu*; pl. *qapiqullar*) (O): slaves of the Porte; the slave component of the Ottoman ruling class

Qapuchi-bashi (O, S): chief eunuch of the harem; also see *dar al-saadah aghasi*

Qazi (*kadi*): Shariah judge; in the Ottoman Empire, he had administrative as well as judicial responsibilities

Qazi-askar (*kadı asker*) (O): chief judge of Anatolia or Rumelia; member of the Imperial Council

Qazilik (*kadılık*): judicial and administrative district for which a *qazi* had jurisdiction

Qilich (*kılıç*) (O): literally, "sword"; a *timar* assignment capable of supporting one *sipahi*

Qul: military slave

Qullar (S): military slaves; specifically, the military slave component of the central army

Qullaraqasi (S): commander of the military slave component of the central army

Qurchi (S): member of the cavalry component of the central army recruited from the Qizilbash tribes

Qurchibashi (S): commander of the *qurchi*s

Qushbegi (M): chief falconer

Rais (S): head of a guild

Rais al-kuttab (*reisülküttab*) (O): chief scribe of the Imperial Council

Raya (O): herd or flock; the taxpaying class in a military patronage state; opposite of *askari*; used primarily with reference to the Ottoman Empire

Rayjabhisheka: ceremonial bath; Hindu royal ritual

Saadat (M) happiness; Humayun defined the ulama and Sufis as men of *saadat*

Sabk-i Hindi: Indian style; the style of Persian poetry popular in the Safavid/Mughal era

Sadr: religious administrator with specific responsibility for land-revenue grants

Sadr-i anas (M): administrator of the *zenana*; position generally held by senior female members of the imperial family

Sadr-i azam (*sadrazam*) (O): exalted minister; title of Ottoman grand vizier

Sadr-qazi (M): provincial official combining the functions of *sadr* and *qazi*

Sahib-i zaman: lord of the age; title given to the awaited imam and or used to imply messianic status

Sahib-qiran (*sâhib-qirân*): lord of the fortunate conjunction; title first used by Timur; used in the sixteenth century with messianic implications

Salyanah (*salyane*) (O): autonomous province, paying only an annual tribute

Sanjak (*sancak*) (O): district; basic unit of Ottoman provincial administration

Sanjakbey (*sancakbey*) (O): governor of a *sanjak*

Sarija (*sarıca*) (O): peasant infantry

Sawar (M): cavalry; second component of a *mansabdar*'s rank, denoting the number of troops he was expected and paid to maintain

Sayyid: descendent of Muhammad

Seferli Odasi (*Seferli Odası*) (O): Campaign Chamber; component of the *Andarun*

Sekban (O): peasant infantry

Shahanshah: king of kings; Iranian title for a universal sovereign

Shahisivani (S): love of the shah; principle of loyalty that superseded *sufigari*

Shahsivin (S): lover of the shah; Qizilbash soldier who chose identification with the sovereign above his tribal identity

Shaykh al-Islam (O): chief *mufti* (jurisconsult) of the empire
Shiqqdar (M): subdistrict (*parganah*) administrator
Sipahi (*sipâhî*) (O): cavalry trooper
Sipahsalar: commander in chief of the army
Soyurghal (S): land-revenue grant
Subah (M): province
Subahdar (M): provincial governor
Subashi (*subaşî*) (O): subdistrict governor; company-grade officer in the field
Sufigari (S): Sufi conduct; loyalty to the Safavid Sufi order
Sulh-i kull (M): peace with all; Akbar's policy of treating adherents of all religions equally
Sultan: unrestricted sovereign governing in accord with the Shariah
Sultan al-Rum (O): sultan of Rome; early Ottoman title
Sultan-i Azam (O): exalted sultan; early Ottoman title
Tabarray/tabarrayyan (S): literally, "disavowers"; public cursors of the enemies of Ali
Tabur jangi (*tabur cengi*) (O): wagon tactics; the use of carts to create a field fortification for use by artillery and infantry armed with firearms
Tahrir (O): provincial revenue survey
Tamlik (*temlik*) (O): grant of freehold to an Ottoman official or notable to support a *vaqf*
Tekalif (*tekâlif*) (O): cash tax imposed by provincial governors; originally an emergency levy that became a standard levy in the seventeenth century
Timar (O): land-revenue assignment to an individual cavalryman
Timar daftardar (*defterdar*) (O): provincial financial official; supervisor of *timar* assignments
Tiyul (S): land-revenue assignment
Tufangchi (S): infantryman equipped with a firearm
Tufangchibashi (S): commander of infantry; one of the highest officials of state in later Safavid history
Tujjar (*tüccar*) (O): merchant engaged in long-distance trade
Tupchi (S): gunner
Tupchibashi (S): chief of artillery or master of ordnance
Uch (*uç*) (O): frontier zone
Ulus (O): literally, "people"; the largest unit of nomad populations recognized by the Ottomans
Urdubegi (M): commander of the sovereign's female guards
Urf (*örf*) (O): Ottoman dynastic or customary law
Uymaq (*oymak*): tribe; used specifically for the component tribes of the Qizilbash confederation
Vakil (S): regent, agent, or assistant; used for the chief officer in Shah Ismail's reign
Vali (S): title of an autonomous vassal king or chieftain
Valide sultan (O): sultan's mother; not merely a situation but an official position at the Ottoman court, one of the most prominent
Vaqf (*vakf*): charitable endowment
Vatan-jagir (M): homeland assignment; the hereditary territory of a *zamindar* who is a *mansabdar*
Vazifah (S): land-revenue grant
Voyvoda (O): local agent of an Ottoman official
Waqai-navis (M): news writer; Mughal provincial official responsible for informing the central government of events in the province
Yeni cheri (*yeni çeri*) (O): see *janissary*
Yigitbashi (*yiğitbaşı*) (O): subordinate guild official
Zabt (M): tax assessment through land measurement
Zamindar (M): landholder; holder of a claim to land revenue before the Mughal conquest

Zan-khana: see *zenana*

Zat (M): literally, "self"; the numerical rank of a Mughal *mansabdar*, defining his personal salary and standing in the hierarchy but not the number of troops he was required to maintain

Zaviye (O): Sufi lodge

Zeamet (O): land-revenue assignment worth between 20,000 and 200,000 *akche* per year; given to *subashi*s

Zenana (M): house of women; standard term for the female element of the Mughal court

Zimmi: *dhimmi* in Arabic; protected person; a non-Muslim subject of a Muslim ruler

Dynastic Tables

This chart shows regnal dates, not lifetimes, of rulers. It does not show succession disputes. Brothers who reigned in succession are shown together on a single line, below their father.

OTTOMAN RULERS, 1300–1730

Osman I c. 1300–1326

Orkhan I 1326–1354

Murad I 1354–1389

Bayazid I 1389–1402

Interregnum 1402–1413

Mehmed I 1413–1421

Murad II 1421–1451

Mehmed II 1451–1481

Bayazid II 1481–1512

Selim I 1512–1520

Sulayman I 1520–1566

Selim II 1566–1574

Murad III 1574–1595

Mehmed III 1595–1603

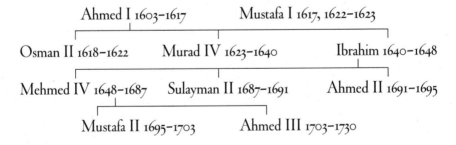

Ahmed I 1603–1617   Mustafa I 1617, 1622–1623

Osman II 1618–1622   Murad IV 1623–1640   Ibrahim 1640–1648

Mehmed IV 1648–1687   Sulayman II 1687–1691   Ahmed II 1691–1695

Mustafa II 1695–1703   Ahmed III 1703–1730

SAFAVID RULERS, 1500–1722

Ismail I 1500–1524

Tahmasp 1524–1576

Ismail II 1576–1577   Muhammad Khudabandah 1577–1588

Abbas I 1588–1629

Muhammad Baqir Mirza (executed 1615)

Safi 1629–1642

Abbas II 1642–1666

Sulayman 1666–1694

Sultan Husayn 1694–1722

TIMURID AND MUGHAL RULERS, 1494–1748

Babur 1494–1530

Humayun 1530–1556

Akbar 1556–1605

Jahangir 1605–1627

Shah Jahan 1628–1658

Aurangzeb 1658–1707

Bahadur Shah 1707–1712

Jahandar Shah 1712   Muhammad Azim al-Shan   Rafi ush-Shan   Jahan Shah

Farrukhsiyar 1712–1719   Muhammad Shah 1719–1748

Rafi al-Darajat 1719   Rafi al-Daulah 1719

Chronology

Names (and regnal years) of sovereigns are in italics.

Date	Central and Western Europe; European Expansion	The Balkans, Anatolia, and the Arab Lands	Iran and Central Asia	South Asia	East Asia
907–1123					Mongol Liao dynasty in northern China
960–1279					Song dynasty in southern and central China
1040			Saljuqs defeat Ghaznavids at Dandanqan and conquer eastern Iran		
1055		Saljuqs take Baghdad and dominate Middle East			
1066	Norman conquest of England				
1071		Saljuqs defeat Byzantines at Malazgirt			
1080–1243		Rum Saljuqs dominate Anatolia			
1085	Toledo falls to Reconquista				
1099		First Crusade takes Jerusalem			
1114–1234					Jurchen rule north China as Qin dynasty
1118			Saljuq Empire begins to fragment		
1130–1211					Qara-Khitay rule eastern Turkestan
1171–1250		Ayyubids rule Egypt and Syria			
1187		Salah al-Din Ayyubi (Saladin) defeats crusaders at Hattin and conquers Jerusalem			
1193				Muslim Ghurids take Delhi	

1204–1261 .... Latin rule in Byzantine Empire

1206–1227 .... *Chingiz Khan*

1206–1290 .... "Slave Dynasty" rules Delhi sultanate

1215 .... Magna Carta

1219 .... Mongols enter Middle East

1241 .... Mongol victory at Leignitz

1243 .... Mongols defeat Rum Saljuqs at Köse Dagh

1250–1517 .... Mamluk Kingdom in Egypt

1252–1334 .... Shaykh Safi, founder of the Safavid

1258 .... Mongols take Baghdad

1258–1335 .... Mongol Il-Khan kingdom in Iran and Iraq

1259–1294 .... *Kubilai Khan*

1260 .... Mamluks defeat Mongols at Ayn Jalut and rule Syria to 1516

1260–1368 .... Mongols rule China as Yuan dynasty

1279 .... Mongols complete conquest of Song Empire

1280–1324 .... *Osman*

1290–1320 .... Khalji dynasty rules Delhi sultanate

1291 .... Mamluks expel crusaders from Palestine

1295–1304 .... *Ghazan Khan*; Il-Khans become Muslims

Date	Central and Western Europe; European Expansion	The Balkans, Anatolia, and the Arab Lands	Iran and Central Asia	South Asia	East Asia
1301		Battle of Baphaeon			
1320–1325				Ghiyath al-Din Tughluq, Delhi sultan	
1321	Death of Dante Aligheri				
1324–1362		Orkhan			
1325–1351				Muhammad ibn Tughluq, Delhi sultan; conquers Deccan	
1326		Ottomans take Bursa			
1331–1355		Stephen Dushan rules Serbia			
1335–1370			Disorder and fragmentation in Iran and central Asia		
1338–1453	Hundred Years' War				
1346	English defeat French at Crecy				
1347–1525				Bahmani sultanate in Deccan	
1351–1398				Fragmentation of Tughluq authority	
1354		Conquests of Gallipoli and Ankara			
1356	English defeat French at Poitiers				
1360–1389		Murad I			
1361		Ottomans take Edirne			
1368					Mings expel Mongols from China
1370–1405			Timur in central Asia and Iran		
1389		Ottomans defeat Serbs at Kosovo			
1389–1402		Bayazid I			
1396		Ottomans defeat crusader coalition at Nicopolis			

1398	*Timur* sacks Delhi; Sayyid dynasty in Delhi
1400	Death of Geoffrey Chaucer
1402	*Timur* defeats Ottomans at Ankara
1402–1413	Ottoman Empire divided
1403–1421	Chinese exploration of the Indian Ocean
1405	*Mehmed I* in control of Anatolia
1407–1447	*Shah Rukh* in central Asia and eastern Iran
1413	*Mehmed* unifies Ottoman Empire
1413–1421	*Mehmed I*
1415	England defeats France at Agincourt
1416	Revolt of Shaykh Badr al-Din
1420–1431	Hussite Wars
1421–1451	*Murad II*
1430	Ottomans take Salonica
1439	Conquest of Serbia
1446	Ottomans defeat Hungarians at Varna
1447–1460	Shaykh Junayd
1451–1481	*Mehmed II*
1451–1526	Lodi dynasty in Delhi
1453	Ottomans take Constantinople
1455–1485	War of the Roses
1460–1488	Shaykh Haydar
1462–1505	*Ivan III, grand prince of Moscow*

Date	Central and Western Europe; European Expansion	The Balkans, Anatolia, and the Arab Lands	Iran and Central Asia	South Asia	East Asia
1467–1481			*Uzun Hasan Aqquyunlu* in western Iran		
1468		Ottomans conquer Karaman			
1473		Ottomans defeat Aqquyunlu at Bashkent			
1480		Ottomans take Otranto			
1481–1490			*Sultan Yaqub Aqquyunlu*		
1481–1512		*Bayazid II*			
1488			Death of Shaykh Haydar; his sons are imprisoned		
1492	Aragon and Castile conquer Granada, last Muslim principality in Spain; Jews expelled from Spain; Columbus discovers America				
1494	French invade Italy		Sultan Ali killed; Ismail in Gilan; Babur rules Fargana		
1494–1530				*Babur*	
1497	Vasco da Gama enters Indian Ocean				
1499			Ismail leaves Gilan		
1501–1524			*Shah Ismail I*		
1508			Safavids take Baghdad		
1509–1547	*Henry VIII, king of England*				
1510			Safavids defeat Uzbeks at Marv and conquer Khurasan; Babur and Safavids ally		
1512	Battle of Ravenna		Uzbeks defeat Safavids at Ghujduvan		
1512–1520		*Selim I*			

Year			
1514		Ottomans defeat Safavids at Chaldiran	Babur abandons central Asia
1515	Battle of Marignano	Ottomans defeat Zul Qadr at Turna Dağ	
1515–1547	*Francis I, king of France*		
1516		Battle of Marj Dabik; Syria conquered	
1516–1556	*Charles V, king of Spain; Holy Roman Emperor from 1519*		
1517	Reformation begins	Ottomans defeat Mamluks at Raydanniyya and conquer Egypt	
1519–1522	Ferdinand Magellan expedition around the world		
1519–1556	*Charles V, Holy Roman Emperor*		
1520–1566	*Sulayman I*		
1521		Ottomans conquer Rhodes	
1522		Ottomans take Belgrade	
1524–1576		*Shah Tahmasp I*	
1525	Battle of Pavia		Babur invades Hindustan
1525–1527			Bahmani sultanate fragments into regional kingdoms
1526		Ottomans defeat Hungary at Mohacs	Babur defeats Lodis at first Panipat
1527			Babur defeats Rana Sanga of Mewar at Khanwa
1528			Safavids defeat Uzbeks at Jam
1529	First siege of Vienna		Babur defeats Afghan coalition
1530–1556			*Humayun*
1533		Ottoman-Hapsburg truce	

Date	Central and Western Europe: European Expansion	The Balkans, Anatolia, and the Arab Lands	Iran and Central Asia	South Asia	East Asia
1534		Ottomans take Baghdad			
1538		Ottomans defeat Holy League at Preveza			
1539				Shir Khan defeats Humayun at Chausa	
1540				Shir Khan defeats Humayun at Kanauj	
1545				Shir Shah dies	
1552	Russians conquer Kazan				
1555		Treaty of Amasya; siege of Malta fails		Humayun takes Delhi	
1556	Russian conquest of Astrakhan			Humayun dies; Mughals defeat Surs at second Panipat	
1556–1558	*Phillip II, king of Spain*				
1556–1605				*Akbar*	
1558–1603	*Elizabeth I, queen of England*				
1559	Peace of Cateau-Cambresis ends Hapsburg Valois Wars				
1565				Battle of Talikota	
1566–1574		*Selim II*			
1567				Siege of Chitor	
1571		Battle of Lepanto			
1572	Massacre of St. Bartholomew				
1573				Mughals conquer Gujarat	
1574–1595		*Murad III*			
1575				Mughals defeat Karanani Afghans at Tukaroi	
1575–1576				Mughals conquer Bengal and Khandesh	
1576				Mughals defeat Karanani Afghans at Raj Mahal	

1576–1577	*Ismail II*	
1577–1588	*Muhammad Khudabandah*	
1578	Saadians of Morocco defeat Portuguese at al-Qasr al-Kabir	
1580–1583		Rebellion in Bihar and Bengal
1588	Spanish Armada	
1588–1629	*Shah Abbas I*	
1589–1610	*Henry IV, king of France*	
1590		Mughals conquer Sind
1593–1606	Ottoman–Hapsburg Long War	
1595–1603	*Mehmed III*	
1596	Ottomans defeat Hapsburgs at Mezokeresztes	
1598	Edict of Nantes	Unification of Japan under Hideyoshi
1603–1605	Safavids conquer Azerbaijan and southern Caucasus	
1603–1617	*Ahmed I*	
1603–1867		Tokugawa shogunate in Japan
1605	Safavids defeat Ottomans at Sufiyan	
1605–1627	*Jahangir*	
1606	Treaty of Sitva-Torok	
1617–1618	*Mustafa I (first reign)*	Mughals conquer Mewar
1618–1622	*Osman II*	
1621		Shah Jahan revolts
1622	Safavids and English take Hormuz	
1622–1623	*Mustafa I (second reign)*	
1623–1640	*Murad IV*	

Date	Central and Western Europe; European Expansion	The Balkans, Anatolia, and the Arab Lands	Iran and Central Asia	South Asia	East Asia
1627				Mahabat Khan's coup d'état	
1627–1658				*Shah Jahan*	
1629–1642			*Shah Safi*		
1633				Mughals take Daulatabad	
1638				Mughals take Qandahar	
1639		Treaty of Qasr-i Shirin			
1640–1648		*Ibrahim*			
1642–1649	English Civil War				
1642–1666			*Abbas II*		
1643–1715	*Louis XIV, king of France*				
1644					Manchus conquer China and establish Qing dynasty
1645–1647				Mughal expedition to central Asia	
1648			Safavids take Qandahar		
1648–1687		*Mehmed IV*			
1649				Qandahar expedition	
1652				Qandahar expedition	
1653				Qandahar expedition; Aurangzeb invades Bijapur and Golconda	
1656–1659		Köprülü Mehmed Pasha			
1658				Aurangzeb defeats Dara Shukuh at Samugarh	
1658–1707				*Aurangzeb*	
1659				Aurangzeb defeats Shah Shuja at Khajwa	
1659–1676		Fazil Ahmed Pasha			
1661–1715	*Louis XIV, king of France*				
1664		Ottomans and Hapsburgs fight to a draw at St. Gotthard			

1666–1694	*Sulayman*
1670	Maratha wars begin
1674	Coronation of Sivaji
1676–1683	Kara Mustafa Pasha
1679	Jizya reimposed
1679–1681	Crisis in Rajasthan; rebellion of Sultan Akbar
1680	Shivaji dies
1682–1707	Aurangzeb in the Deccan
1683	Second siege of Vienna
1686	Mughals conquer Bijapur
1687	Mughals conquer Golconda; Hapsburgs defeat Ottomans at Mohacs
1687–1691	*Sulayman II*
1688	Glorious Revolution
1688–1697	War of the League of Augsburg
1689	Russia and China sign Treaty of Nerchinsk
1691	Hapsburgs defeat Ottomans at Slankamen
1691–1695	*Ahmed II*
1694–1722	*Sultan Husayn*
1695–1703	*Mustafa II*
1697	Hapsburgs defeat Ottomans at Zenta
1699	Treaty of Carlowitz
1700–1721	Great Northern War
1701–1714	War of Spanish Succession
1703	Edirne Event
1703–1730	*Ahmed III*
1707–1712	*Shah Alam (Bahadur Shah)*

Date	Central and Western Europe; European Expansion	The Balkans, Anatolia, and the Arab Lands	Iran and Central Asia	South Asia	East Asia
1711		Ottomans defeat Peter the Great in Pruth campaign			
1712				*Jahandar Shah*	
1712–1719				*Farrukhsiyar*	
1716		Hapsburgs defeat Ottomans at Peterovaradin			
1718		Treaty of Passarowitz			
1718–1730		Tulip Period			
1719				*Rafi al-Darajat, Rafi al-Daulah*	
1719–1748				*Muhammad Shah*	
1722			Ghilzays take Isfahan		

Bibliographic Essay

This essay serves both as a guide to further reading and as an account of the primary authorities on which I have relied. The accompanying bibliography is a full list of works consulted. The structure of the essay does not match the book precisely. To conserve space, here I give only authors, titles, and, for specific parts of books, page numbers; the bibliography contains complete information.

General Background

Marshall G. S. Hodgson, *The Venture of Islam: Conscience and History in a World Civilization*, provides the fundamental framework for this enquiry. Book 5 of *Venture*, the first of the third volume, covers the three empires. For the concept of gunpowder empire, see *Venture*, 3:17–19; William H. McNeill, *The Pursuit of Power*, 95–98, and *The Age of Gunpowder Empires, 1450–1800*, 99–102. Kenneth Chase, *Firearms: A Global History to 1700*, is an outstanding achievement.

On Western views of the three empires, see Robert Schwoebel, *The Shadow of the Crescent: The Renaissance Image of the Turk, 1453–1517*; Norman Daniel, *Islam and the West: The Making of an Image*; Nancy Bisaha, *Creating East and West: Renaissance Humanists and the Ottoman Turks*; Lucette Valensi, *The Birth of the Despot: Venice and the Sublime Porte*; Andrew Wheatcroft, *The Ottomans: Dissolving Images*; Aslı Çırakman, *From the "Terror of the World" to the "Sick Man of Europe": European Images of the Ottoman Empire and Society from the Sixteenth Century to the Nineteenth*. Perry Anderson, *Lineages of the Absolute State*, describes the development of Western views of Asian monarchies. Despite its Marxist orientation, it is an excellent piece of intellectual history.

Common Heritage, Common Dilemma

The standard references on the Sasanians are Arthur Christensen, *L'Iran sous les Sassanides*, and the relevant chapters of Ehsan Yarshater, ed., *The Parthian and Sasanian Periods*. Touraj Daryaee, *Sasanian Iran (224–651 CE): Portrait of a Late Antique Empire*, is a new survey; there is also Ahmad Taffazoli, *Sasanian Society: Warriors, Scribes, Dehqans*.

On the Abbasid caliphate as an Irano-Islamic empire, see Hodgson, *Venture*, 1:280–284. Though dated, Gustave E. Von Grunebaum, *Medieval Islam: A Study in Cultural Orientation*, 1–64, demonstrates the fundamental symmetry of Byzantine and Abbasid political forms, showing that the Abbasids had adopted the symbolism of empire. F. E. Peters, *Allah's Commonwealth: A History of the Near East, 600–1100 AD*, 472–474, discusses the importance of the Sasanian precedent for the Abbasids. Michael G. Morony, *Iraq After the Muslim Conquest*, demonstrates irrefutably the enormous extent of continuity between Sasanian and Muslim Iraq but does not deal directly with governmental institutions. See also Douglas E. Streusand, "Sir Hamilton A. R. Gibb, Abu Yusuf, and the Concept of Islamic Civilization."

On kingship in general, A. M. Hocart's *King's and Councillors* and *Kingship*, though dated, still offer important insights. On sacral kingship in the ancient Middle East, see Henri Frankfort, *Kingship and the Gods: A Study of Ancient Near Eastern Religion As the Integration of Society and Nature*; F. W. Buckler, "The Oriental Despot"; G. Widengren, "The Sacral Kingship of Iran." John E. Woods, *The Aqquyunlu: Clan, Confederation, Empire*, 4–7, discusses the concept in the Islamic context. Patricia Crone, *God's Rule: Six Centuries of Medieval Islamic Political Thought*, argues that until the ulama defined themselves as the principal interpreters of the Prophet's revelation in the ninth century, the caliphs had religious as well as political authority, but she does not address sacral kingship. On the emergence of Islamic concepts of kingship aside from the caliphate, see *Encyclopedia of Islam*, s.v. "Sultan," by J. H. Kremers and Wilferd Madelung. For early Islamic usage and the central lands of Islam, see Madelung, "The Assumption of the Title Shahanshah by the Buyids."

Linda T. Darling is in the process of completing a systematic study of the concept of the circle of justice. Until its completion, her remarks in *Revenue-Raising and Legitimacy: Tax Collection and Finance Administration in the Ottoman Empire, 1560–1660*, 283–289, and "'Do Justice, Do Justice, for That Is Paradise': Middle Eastern Advice for Indian Muslim Rulers," will serve. See also Lewis V. Thomas, *A Study of Naima*, 78.

On the conditions that mandated fiscal decentralization and the institutional responses to it, see *Encyclopedia of Islam*, s.v. "Hawala," by Halil Inalcık; Fernand Braudel, *The Mediterranean and the Mediterranean World in the Age of Phillip II*, 1:276–295; Owen Lattimore, *The Inner Asian Frontiers of China*; Claude Cahen, "L'evolution de l'Iqta` du IX'e au XII'e siècle"; Ann K. S. Lambton, "Reflections on the Iqta`."

On pastoral nomadism, see Thomas J. Barfield, *The Nomadic Alternative*, esp. 131–179; Anatoly M. Khazanov, *Nomads and the Outside World*. On nomadism in general, see Douglas L. Johnson, *The Nature of Nomadism*. X. de Planhol, "The Geography of Settlement," and E. Sunderland, "Pastoralism, Nomadism, and Social Anthropology of Iran," discuss nomadism in Iran from the perspective of human geography. For historical perspective on this issue, see Hodgson, *Venture*, 1:483–485, 2:4–8, 69–91.

Robert L. Canfield, ed., *Turko-Persia in Historical Perspective*, especially Canfield's "Introduction: The Turko-Persian Tradition," explores the addition of the Turkic element to the Irano-Islamic synthesis. The articles collected in C. E. Bosworth, ed., *The Turks in the Early Islamic World*, provide excellent coverage of the topic. On the Saljuq Empire, see Claude Cahen, "The Turkish Invasion: The Selchukids"; Ibrahim Kafesoglu, *A History of the Seljuks: Ibrahim Kafesoglu's Interpretation and the Resulting Controversy*; C. E. Bosworth, "The Political and Dynastic History of the Iranian World (AD 1000–1217)"; A. K. S. Lambton, "Internal Structure of the Saljuq Empire." On the Turkic penetration of Anatolia and the Saljuqs of Rum, see Speros Vryonis, *The Decline of Medieval Hellenism in Asia Minor and the Process of Islamization from the Eleventh Through the Fifteenth Century*; Claude Cahen, *Pre-Ottoman Turkey: A General Survey of the Material and Spiritual Culture and History, c. 1071–1330* and *The Formation of Turkey: The Seljukid Sultanate of Rum, Eleventh to Fourteenth Centuries*; Osman Turan, "Anatolia in the Period of the Seljuks and the Beyliks." On the Battle of Malazgirt, see J. F. C. Fuller, *Decisive Battles*, 205–223.

David O. Morgan, *The Mongols*, is the best introduction to the Mongols. On the Mongols in the Middle East, Claude Cahen, "The Mongols and the Near East," offers a brief and incisive account of the Mongols in Iran. Joseph F. Fletcher, "The Mongols: Ecological and Social

Perspectives," yields important insights. J. A. Boyle, "Dynastic and Political History of the Il-Khans," I. P. Petrushevsky, "The Socio-Economic Condition of Iran Under the Il-Khans," and Bertold Spuler, *The Mongol Period*, are more detailed but less insightful. B. Vladimirtsov, *Le regime social des Mongols*, is still of fundamental importance. *The Secret History of the Mongols* is the most important primary source on the Mongols. Igor de Rachelwiltz's translation, which includes eight hundred pages of commentary, is a magnificent scholarly achievement and supersedes all other translations, including that of Francis Cleaves. Eric Voegelin, "The Mongol Orders of Submission to the European Powers," though written without access to *The Secret History*, offers the best explanation of Mongol ideology—or rather civic theology. Voegelin integrates his analysis of Mongol doctrine into his general view of the history of political ideas in *The New Science of Politics*, 52–59. On collective sovereignty and the appanage system, see Martin B. Dickson, "Uzbek Dynastic Theory in the Sixteenth Century," and Woods, *Aqquyunlu*, 12–16.

On politics and political ideas in the post-Mongol Middle East, see Woods, *Aqquyunlu*; Beatrice Forbes Manz, *The Rise and Rule of Tamerlane*, 107–127, *Power, Politics and Religion in Timurid Iran*, and "Tamerlane and the Symbolism of Sovereignty"; Anne F. Broadridge, *Kingship and Ideology in the Islamic and Mongol Worlds*; H. R. Roemer, "The Jalayrids, Muzaffarids and Sarbadārs," "Tīmūr in Iran," "The Successors of Tīmūr," and "The Türkmen Dynasties."

On Islamic jurisprudence in general, see Wael Hallaq, *A History of Islamic Legal Theories—an Introduction to Sunni Usul al-Fiqh*, and N. J. Coulson, *A History of Islamic Law*. Bernard Lewis, *The Jews of Islam*, offers an excellent, succinct discussion of the status of *zimmis*. For a general introduction to Sufism in the context of Islam in general, see Alexander Knysh, *Islamic Mysticism: A Short History*, and Hodgson, *Venture*, 2:201–254. Annemarie Schimmel, *Mystical Dimensions of Islam*, is the best general work on Sufism. J. Spencer Trimingham, *The Sufi Orders in Islam*, offers an institutional history. On Suhravardi and Ibn al-Arabi, see Schimmel, *Mystical Dimensions*, 187–227, 259–263, and Seyyed Hossein Nasr, *Three Muslim Sages: Avicenna-Suhrawardi-Ibn 'Arabi*. On the religious beliefs of the Turkic and Mongol nomads, see Jean-Paul Roux, *Les traditions des nomades de la Turquie meridionale* and "Un survivance des traditions turco-mongoles chez les Sefevides"; Claude Cahen, "Le probleme du Shi'isme dans l'Asie Mineure turque preottomane"; Irene Melikoff, "L'Islam heterodoxe en Anatolie and "Les origines centre asiatiques du Soufism anatolien."

On *ghuluww* dissent and the Baba Ishaq uprising specifically, see Turan, "Anatolia"; Kafesoglu, *History of the Seljuks*, 77; Cahen, *Pre-Ottoman*, 136–137, and *Formation*, 70, 164–165, 265–266; Cemal Kafadar, *Between Two Worlds: The Construction of the Ottoman State*, 73–75. Bernard Lewis, "The Significance of Heresy in Islam," puts religious dissent in political context but without reference to *ghuluww* or nomadism.

On jihad, see David Cook, *Understanding Jihad*; Michael Bonner, *Jihad in Islamic History: Doctrine and Practices*; Rudolph Peters, *Jihad in Classical and Modern Islam*; Douglas E. Streusand, "What Does Jihad Mean?"

The Ottoman Empire

Suraiya Faroqhi, *Approaching Ottoman History: An Introduction to the Sources*, is an excellent beginning to the study of Ottoman history. Jane Hathaway's "Rewriting Eighteenth-Century Ottoman History," is vital for its topic. Caroline Finkel, *Osman's Dream: The History of the Ottoman Empire*, is the best narrative history of the Ottoman Empire. In addition to Finkel, I drew upon Halil Inalcık, *The Ottoman Empire: The Classical Age, 1300–1600*, "The Emergence of the Ottomans," "The Rise of the Ottoman Empire," and "The Heyday and Decline of the

Ottoman Empire"; Uriel Heyd, "The Later Ottoman Empire in Rumelia and Anatolia," P. M. Holt, "The Later Ottoman Empire in Egypt and the Fertile Crescent"; V. J. Parry, "The Reigns of Bāyezīd II and Selīm I, 1481–1520," "The Reign of Sulaimān, 1520–1566," "The Successors of Sulaimān, 1566–1617," and "The Period of Murād IV"; A. N. Kurat, "The Reign of Mehmed IV, 1648–1687"; A. N. Kurat and J. S. Bromley, "The Retreat of the Turks, 1683–1730"; Dorothy Vaughan, *Europe and the Turk*; Halil Inalcık and Donald Quataert, eds., *An Economic and Social History of the Ottoman Empire*; Colin Imber, *The Ottoman Empire, 1300–1650: The Structure of Power*; Daniel Goffman, *The Ottoman Empire and Early Modern Europe*; Peter F. Sugar and Donald W. Treadgold, *Southeastern Europe Under Ottoman Rule: 1354–1804*; Donald Quataert, *The Ottoman Empire, 1700–1922*; P. M. Holt, *Egypt and the Fertile Crescent, 1516–1922*; Stanford J. Shaw, *Empire of the Ghazis*. Though convenient and complete, Shaw's work contains numerous errors, both factual and interpretive. See the reviews by V. L. Ménage and Colin Imber. The periodization also reflects the views of Darling, *Revenue-Raising and Legitimacy*, 2–16, and Baki Tezcan, "The Politics of Early Modern Ottoman Historiography."

Heath W. Lowry, *The Nature of the Early Ottoman State*, discusses the debate on the Wittek thesis on pp. 5–13 and summarizes findings on pp. 130–143. Wittek states the thesis in *The Rise of the Ottoman Empire*. See also Kafadar, *Between Two Worlds*, 29–59. Rudi Paul Lindner, *Nomads and Ottomans in Medieval Anatolia*, is best understood in the context provided by Kafadar and Lowry. Linda T. Darling, "Contested Territory: Ottoman Holy War in Comparative Context," is the best treatment of the problem of the relationship between jihad and *ghaza*.

For the frontier principality phase, see, in addition to the general works listed above, Lowry, *Nature*, and Kafadar, *Between Two Worlds*. Lowry and Kafadar have brought early Ottoman historiography to a new level of sophistication. See also Elizabeth Zachariadou, ed., *The Ottoman Emirate, 1300–1389*. Older works consulted include M. Fuad Köprülü, *The Origins of the Ottoman Empire*, and Halil Inalcık, "The Question of the Emergence of the Ottoman State." On the maritime aspect of this history, see Halil Inalcık, "The Rise of the Turcoman Maritime Principalities in Anatolia, Byzantium, and the Crusades," and Norman Houseley, *The Later Crusades from Lyons to Alcazar, 1274–1580*. On the crusade and battle of Nicoplis, see Aziz S. Atiya, "The Crusade in the Fourteenth Century." For these events from the perspective of Byzantine history, see George Ostrogorsky, *History of the Byzantine State*, 504–511, 517–533.

On the Crimean Tatars and Ottoman involvement in the territory north of the Black Sea, see Morgan, *Mongols*, 128; Alan W. Fisher, *The Crimean Tatars*; Brian L. Davies, *Warfare, State and Society on the Black Sea Steppe*. On the Northern Wars, see Robert I. Frost, *The Northern Wars, 1558–1721*.

On the maritime aspects of Ottoman strategy and expansion in both the Mediterranean and the Indian Ocean, see Palmira Brummett, *Ottoman Seapower and Levantine Diplomacy in the Age of Discovery*. On the Ottomans in the western Mediterranean, see Andrew C. Hess, "The Evolution of the Ottoman Seaborne Empire," *The Forgotten Frontier*, and "Piri Reis and the Ottoman Response to the Voyages of Discovery." Jan Glete, *Warfare at Sea, 1550–1650: Maritime Conflicts and the Transformation of Europe*, explains the transformation of naval warfare and development of the Western concept of sea power. John Francis Guilmartin, *Gunpowder and Galleys: Changing Technology and Mediterranean Warfare at Sea in the Sixteenth Century*, incisively explains the difference between maritime warfare in the Mediterranean and elsewhere.

On the Portuguese rivals of the Ottomans, see M. N. Pearson, *The Portuguese in India*, and C. R. Boxer, *The Portuguese Seaborne Empire, 1425–1825*. On the general situation in the Indian Ocean at this time, see Michael Pearson, *The Indian Ocean*, 133–157.

Colin Imber has been the most productive student of Ottoman ideology. His works on the topic include his *Ottoman Empire,* 115–127, "Frozen Legitimacy," "Ideals and Legitimation in Early Ottoman History," "The Legend of Osman Ghazi," "Ottoman Dynastic Myth," and "Sülaymân As Caliph of the Muslims: Ebû's-Su`ûd's Formulation of Ottoman Dynastic Ideology." Leslie P. Peirce, *The Imperial Harem: Women and Sovereignty in the Ottoman Empire,* is an extremely important contribution. Cornell Fleischer explains the messianic aspect of Ottoman ideology in "Shadow of Shadows: Prophecy in Politics in 1530s Istanbul," "Seer to the Sultan: Haydar-i Remmal and Sultan Süleyman," and "The Lawgiver As Messiah: The Making of the Imperial Image in the Reign of Süleymân." Other important articles include Halil Inalcık, "State, Sovereignty and Law During the Reign of Süleymân" and "State and Ideology Under Sultan Süleyman"; Fatma Müge Göçek, "The Social Construction of an Empire: Ottoman State Under Süleymân the Magnificent"; Hakan T. Karateke, "Legitimizing the Ottoman Sultanate" and "Opium for the Subjects? Religiosity As Legitimizing Factor for the Ottoman Sultan"; Gülrû Necipoğlu, "Süleymân the Magnificent and the Representation of Power in the Context of Ottoman-Hapsburg-Papal Rivalry." On Ottoman law and religious policy, see Halil Inalcık, "Sulayman the Lawgiver and Ottoman Law" and *Encyclopedia of Islam,* s.v. "Kanun: Financial and Public Administration"; Imber, *Ebu`s-Su`ud*; Madeline C. Zilfi, *The Politics of Piety: The Ottoman Ulema in the Postclassical Age, 1600–1800,* "The Kadizadelis: Discordant Revivalism in Seventeenth-Century Istanbul," and "A Medrese for the Palace: Ottoman Dynastic Legitimation in the Eighteenth Century,.."

Halil Inalcık, "Ottoman Methods of Conquest," is the fundamental study of Ottoman expansion; it has probably influenced me as much as any other single article. See also his "Timariotes chretiens en Albanie au XV siècle," and Klaus Michael Röhrborn, *Untersuchungen zur osmanischen Verwaltungsgeschichte.*

Comprehension of Ottoman military organization and warfare requires study in broader context. For this context, see Chase, *Firearms*; Bert S. Hall, *Weapons and Warfare in Renaissance Europe: Gunpowder, Technology, Tactics*; Christopher Duffy, *Siege Warfare: The Fortress in the Early Modern World, 1494–1660* and *Fire and Stone: The Science of Fortress Warfare, 1660–1860.* The phenomenally productive Jeremy Black has written one relevant book, *European Warfare in a Global Context, 1660–1815,* and edited three more: *European Warfare, 1453–1815, European Warfare, 1494–1660,* and *War in the Early Modern World, 1450 and 1815.* Sir Charles Oman's *A History of the Art of War in the Middle Ages* and *A History of the Art of War in the Sixteenth Century* are still extremely valuable for battle history despite their age.

On military organization and warfare, see Imber, *Ottoman Empire,* 252–287; Rhoads Murphey, *Ottoman Warfare, 1500–1700*; Gábor Ágoston, *Guns for the Sultan: Military Power and the Weapons Industry in the Ottoman Empire* and "Ottoman Warfare in Europe, 1453–1826"; Mark L. Stein, *Guarding the Frontier: Ottoman Border Forts and Garrisons in Europe*; Virginia Aksan, "Ottoman War and Warfare"; Rhoads Murphey, "The Ottoman Attitude Toward Western Technology: The Role of Efrenci Technicians in Civil and Military Applications." On the general subject of the acquisition of war supplies, see V. J. Parry, "Materials of War in the Ottoman Empire." Useful studies of individual battles and sieges include John Stoye, *The Siege of Vienna,* and Ernle Bradford, *The Great Siege: Malta 1565.* Guilmartin, *Gunpowder,* includes a series of detailed battle and campaign studies.

On the diffusion of firearms and the changes in the Ottoman army, see David Ayalon's classic *Gunpowder and Firearms in the Mamluk Kingdom: A Challenge to a Medieval Society*; Djurdjica Petrović, "Fire-arms in the Balkans on the Eve of and After the Ottoman Conquests of the Fourteenth and Fifteenth Centuries"; Halil Inalcık, "The Socio-Political Effects of the

Diffusion of Fire-arms in the Middle East" and most importantly, "Military and Fiscal Transformation in the Ottoman Empire." The later evolution of the Ottoman military reflects the extensive and prolonged debate over the military revolution, on which see Geoffrey Parker, *The Military Revolution: Military Innovation and the Rise of the West, 1500–1800.*

Inalcık, *Classical*, 76–103, is the basis for the treatment of the palace and central administration. See also Inalcık's "Land Problems in Turkish History," *Encyclopedia of Islam*, s.v. "Kanun: Financial and Public Administration," and "The Problem of the Relationship Between Byzantine and Ottoman Taxation." Shaw, *Empire*, 116, is a schematic diagram of the plan of Topkapi palace in Istanbul, showing the relationship of the different palace services to the ground plan of the building. On the Ottoman provinces and provincial administration, see Inalcık, *Classical*, 104–120, and Röhrborn, *Untersuchungen*. Stanford J. Shaw, *The Financial and Administrative Organization and Development of Ottoman Egypt*, covers Ottoman Egypt.

This discussion of Ottoman economy is derived primarily from Inalcık, *Classical*, 121–139, and the relevant chapters of Inalcık and Quataert, *Economic and Social History*, namely Inalcık's "The Ottoman State: Economy and Society, 1300–1600," Suraiya Faroqhi, "Crisis and Change, 1590–1699," and Bruce McGowan, "The Age of the Ayans, 1699–1812." Inalcık's "Capital Formation in the Ottoman Empire" and "The Ottoman Economic Mind and Aspects of the Ottoman Economy," are vital, as is Şevket Pamuk, *A Monetary History of the Ottoman Empire*. On English commerce, see Ralph Davis, "England and the Mediterranean." The standard history of Levantine commerce, W. Heyd, *Histoire du commerce du Levant au Moyen-Age*, is invaluable but gives the false impression that the expansion of the Ottoman Empire reduced Levantine trade. It is long overdue for replacement. On Ottoman cities, see Inalcık, *Classical*, 140–160; Edhem Eldem, Daniel Goffman, and Bruce Masters, *The Ottoman City Between East and West: Aleppo, Izmir, and Istanbul*; Halil Inalcık, "The Hub of the City: The Bedestan of Istanbul."

Suraiya Faroqhi, *Subjects of the Sultan: Culture and Daily Life in the Ottoman Empire*, Leslie Peirce, *Morality Tales: Law and Gender in the Ottoman Court of Aintab*, and Walter G. Andrew and Mehmet Kalpakli, *The Age of the Beloved: Love and the Beloved in Early-Modern Ottoman and European Culture and Society*, will serve to introduce the reader to the depth and sophistication of contemporary studies of Ottoman social history. Faroqhi's book is also the best point of access to Ottoman cultural and intellectual history. Cornell Fleischer, *Bureaucrat and Intellectual in the Ottoman Empire: The Historian Mustafa Ali*, and Thomas, *A Study of Naima*, are great contributions.

The discussion of stress and transformation, as well as the decision not to call it decline, reflects four of Inalcık's articles: "Centralization and Decentralization in Ottoman Administration," "Military and Fiscal Transformation," "Ottoman Decline and Its Effects upon the Reaya," and "The Socio-Political Effects of the Diffusion of Fire-arms in the Middle East." It also reflects Darling, *Revenue-Raising and Legitimacy*; William J. Griswold, *The Great Anatolian Rebellion, 1000–1020/1591–1611*; Karen Barkey, *Bandits and Bureaucrats: The Ottoman Route to State Centralization*; Fleischer, *Bureaucrat and Intellectual*; B. Cvetkova, "Problemes du régime ottoman dans les Balkans du seizième au dix-huitième siècle"; Metin Kunt, *The Sultan's Servants: The Transformation of Ottoman Provincial Government, 1550–1650.*

The Safavid Empire

Gene R. Garthwaite, *The Persians*, puts Safavid history in the general context of Iranian history. There are three general accounts of the Safavids: Andrew J. Newman's *Safavid Iran: Re-*

birth of a Persian Empire, Roger Savory's *Iran Under the Safavids*, and H. R. Roemer's "The Safavid Period." On early Safavid history, see Michel M. Mazzaoui, ed., *The Origins of the Safawids: Šiʿism, Sufism and the Gulat*; Zeki Velidi Togan, "Sur l'origine des Safavides"; Sayyid Ahmad Kasravi, *Shaykh Safi va Tabarash*. Said Amir Arjomand, *The Shadow of God and the Hidden Imam: Religion, Political Order, and Societal Change in Shiʿite Iran from the Beginning to 1890*, 66–84, discusses the general religious background of the Safavid movement. The extensive works of Rudi Matthee, mentioned below and in the bibliography, are among the most important recent contributions to Safavid historiography. His forthcoming work on Safavid decline and Colin P. Mitchell's *New Perspectives on Safavid Iran: Empire and Society*, which I have not seen, will form the basis of the next generation of Safavid studies.

On Shah Ismail and his reign, see Ghulam Sarwar, *History of Shah Ismaʿil Safawi*; Jean Aubin, "L'avenement des Safavides reconsideré"; A. H. Morton, "The Early Years of Shah Ismaʿil in the *Afzal al-Tavarikh*"; R. M. Savory, "The Consolidation of Safawid Power in Persia." On the situation in eastern Iran and Mawarannahr in the early sixteenth century and the Uzbek principalities, see H. R. Roemer, "The Successors of Tīmūr"; V. V. Barthold, *Ulugh Beg*; Mahin Hajianpur, "The Timuri Empire and the Uzbeg Conquest of Mawarannahr"; Gavin Hambly, "The Shaybanids"; Bertold Spuler, *The Mongols in History*; Roemer, "The Successors of Tīmūr"; Martin B. Dickson, "Shah Tahmasp and the Uzbeks: The Duel for Khurasan with ʿUbayd Khan"; R. D. McChesney, *Waqf in Central Asia* and *Encyclopedia Iranica*, s.v. "Central Asia, vi. in the 10th–12th/16th–18th Centuries." McChesney's work constitutes a renaissance in Uzbek studies. Aside from Martin Dickson's unpublished dissertation, there is no literature on Tahmasp specifically. W. Hinz, "Schah Esmaʿil: Ein Beitrag zur Geschichte der Safaviden," H. R. Roemer, *Der Niedergang Irans nach dem Tode Ismaʿils des Grausamen*, and Roger M. Savory, "The Political Significance of the Murder of Mirza Salman," cover the disordered period between the death of Tahmasp and the accession of Abbas I. There also exists no recent scholarly study on Abbas in a Western language, only Lucien Louis Bellan, *Chah ʿAbbas I, sa vie, son histoire*.

On later Safavid history, see D. M. Lang, "Georgia and the Fall of the Safavi Dynasty"; John Foran, "The Long Fall of the Safavid Dynasty"; A. K. S. Lambton, "Tribal Resurgence and the Decline of Bureaucracy in Eighteenth-Century Persia"; Laurence Lockhart, *The Fall of the Safavi Dynasty and the Afghan Occupation of Persia*. Martin Dickson's review essay, "The Fall of the Safavi Dynasty," shreds Lockhart's interpretation.

On Safavid ideology and religious policy, see Kathryn Babayan, *Mystics, Monarchs, and Messiahs: Cultural Landscapes of Modern Iran*, and Ernest Tucker's review thereof. See also V. Minorsky, "The Poetry of Shah Ismaʿil"; Erika Glassen, "Schah Ismaʿil, ein Mahdi der Anatolischen Turkmenen?" and "Schah Ismaʿil und die theologen seiner Zeit"; Arjomand, *Shadow*, 67–199; Ruli Jurdi Abisaab, *Converting Persia: Religion and Power in the Safavid Empire*; Alexander H. Morton, "The Chub-i Tariq and Qizilbash Ritual in Safavid Persia"; Jean Calmard, "Les rituels shiites et le pouvoir: L'imposition du Shiisme safavide: Eulogies et maledictions canoniques," and "Shiʿi Rituals and Power in the Consolidation of Safavid Shiʿism: Folklore and Popular Religion"; Charles Melville, "Shah ʿAbbas and the Pilgrimage to Mashhad"; Kathryn Babayan, "Sufis, Dervishes, and Mullas: The Controversy over Spiritual and Temporal Dominion in Seventeenth-Century Iran"; B. S. Amoretti, "Religion in the Timurid and Safavid Periods"; S. H. Nasr, "Spiritual Movements, Philosophy, and Theology in the Safavid Period."

On Safavid military organization, Masashi Haneda's *Le chah et les Qizilbas: Le système militaire safavid*, *Encyclopedia Iranica*, s.v. "Army: iii Safavid," and "The Evolution of the Safavid Royal Guard" supersede the early scholarship of Laurence Lockhart in "The Persian Army in the Safavid Period," which was considered standard for two generations. See also Rudi

Matthee, "Unwalled Cities and Restless Nomads: Firearms and Artillery in Safavi Iran," and Sussan Babaie et al., *Slaves of the Shah: New Elites in Safavid Iran*. Willem Floor, *Safavid Government Institutions*, is the most important work on the Safavid government. There is also Klaus Röhrborn, *Provinzen und Zentral Gewalt Persiens im 16. und 17. Jahrhundert* and "Regierung und Verwaltung Irans unter den Safawiden," as well as a series of works by Roger M. Savory: "Safavid Administrative System," "The Principal Offices of the Safawid State During the Reign of Isma`il I (907–30/1501–24)," "The Principal Offices of the Safawid State During the Reign of Tahmasp I (930–84/1524–76)," "A Secretarial Career Under Shāh Ṭahmāsp (1524–1576)," and "The Office of Khalifat al-Khulafa Under the Safawids." There are now three Safavid administrative manuals available in translation: Vladimir Minorsky, ed. and trans., *The Tadhkirat al-Muluk: A Manual of Safavid Administration*; Mohammad Rafi al-Din al Ansari, *Dastur al-Muluk*; Miza Naqi Nasiri, *Titles and Emoluments in Safavid Iran: A Third Manual of Safavid Administration*.

On the Safavid economy, see Ronald Ferrier, "Trade from the Mid-14th Century to the End of the Safavid Period"; Bert Fragner, "Social and Internal Economic Affairs"; Willem Floor, *A Fiscal History of Iran in the Safavid and Qajar Periods*; Rudolph P. Matthee, *The Politics of Trade in Safavid Iran: Silk for Silver, 1600–1730*; Amin Banani, "Reflections on the Social and Economic Structure of Safavid Persia at Its Zenith"; Ahmad Ashraf, "Historical Obstacles to the Development of a Bourgeoisie in Iran"; Hans-Joachim Kissling, "Şah Ismail Ier, la nouvelle route des Indes, et les Ottomans"; Jean-Louis Bacque-Grammont, "Études turco-safavides I: Notes sur le blocus du commerce iranien par Selim Ier"; Rudiger Klein, "Caravan Trade in Safavid Iran"; Anne Kroell, "Bandar `Abbas à la fin du regne des Safavides"; Maxime Siroux, "Les caravanserais routièrs safavids"; Rudi Matthee, "The East India Company Trade in Kerman Wool"; Linda K. Steinmann, "Shah `Abbas and the Royal Silk Trade, 1599–1629." On the broader commercial context, see Stephen Frederic Dale, *Indian Merchants and Eurasian Trade, 1600–1750*; K. N. Chaudhuri, *Trade and Civilization in the Indian Ocean from the Rise of Islam to 1750*; Niels Steensgaard, *The Asian Trade Revolution of the Seventeenth Century*.

Safavid cultural history begins with art and architecture, on which see Jon Thompson and Sheila R. Canby, eds., *Hunt for Paradise: Court Arts of Safavid Iran, 1501–1576*; Basil Gray, "The Arts in the Safavid Period"; Anthony Welch, *Shah `Abbas and the Arts of Isfahan* and *Artists for the Shah: Late Sixteenth Century Painting at the Imperial Court of Iran*; Robert Hillenbrand, "Safavid Architecture." On Safavid literature, see Z. Safa, "Persian Literature in the Safavid Period"; Ehsan Yarshater, "Persian Poetry in the Timurid and Safavid Periods" and "Safavid Literature: Progress or Decline"; Aziz Ahmad, "The Formation of the Sabk-Hindi"; Jan Rypka, "History of Persian Literature Up to the Beginning of the 20th Century"; Felix Tauer, "Persian Learned Literature from Its Beginnings Up to the End of the Eighteenth Century"; Sholeh Quinn, *Historical Writing During the Reign of Shah `Abbas: Ideology, Imitation and Legitimacy in Safavid Chronicles*. The fourth volume of E. G. Browne's *A Literary History of Persia* is no longer current but still valuable.

On developments in religious thought during the Safavid period, see, in addition to the works listed in the section on ideology and law, Fazlur Rahman, *The Philosophy of Mullā Ṣadrā*.

The Mughal Empire

John F. Richards, *Mughal Empire*, is the standard general volume on the Mughals. On the South Asian background, see Peter Jackson, *The Delhi Sultanate: A Political and Military History*, and André Wink's three-volume *Al-Hind: The Making of the Indo-Islamic World*, which includes *Early Medieval India and the Expansion of Islam, 7th to 11th Centuries, The Slave Kings and the Early Islamic Conquest, 11th to 13th Centuries,* and *Indo-Islamic Society, 14th to 15th Centuries.* Catherine B. Asher and Cynthia Talbot, *India Before Europe,* and Satish Chandra, *History of Medieval India,* are convenient surveys. Richard M. Eaton, *A Social History of the Deccan, 1300–1761: Eight Indian Lives* and *The Rise of Islam and the Bengal Frontier, 1204–1760,* are tremendously valuable. Bernard S. Cohn, "Political Systems in Eighteenth-Century India," even though it deals with the eighteenth century, is of fundamental importance in understanding politics in premodern South Asia.

The essays collected in Richard M. Eaton, ed., *India's Islamic Traditions, 711–1750,* provide excellent background on Islam in South Asia, most notably Eaton's introduction. See also Eleanor Zelliot, "A Medieval Encounter Between Hindu and Muslim: Eknath's Drama-Poem *Hindu-Turk Samvād*"; Yohanan Friedman, "Islamic Thought in Relation to the Indian Context"; Aditya Behl, "The Magic Doe: Desire and Narrative in a Hindavi Sufi Romance, Circa 1503." Richard M. Eaton, *Temple Desecration and Muslim States in Medieval India,* demonstrates that both Muslim and Hindu rulers destroyed the monumental temples of their enemies as a symbol of their triumphs; the act did not constitute religious persecution. On the Mughal polity in general, see Muzaffar Alam and Sanjay Subrahmanyam, introduction to *The Mughal State, 1526–1750*; Farhat Hasan, *State and Locality in Mughal India: Power Relations in Western India, c. 1572–1730,* 1–3; Douglas E. Streusand, *The Formation of the Mughal Empire*; Stephen P. Blake, "The Patrimonial-Bureaucratic Empire of the Mughals"; M. Athar Ali, "The Mughal Polity—a Critique of Revisionist Approaches." Jos Gommans, *Mughal Warfare: Indian Frontiers and High Roads to Empire,* offers fundamental insight into Mughal politics.

For the Timurid background, see the works of Beatrice Forbes Manz cited above and Roemer, "The Successors of Tīmūr." On Babur, see his memoirs, *The Baburnama: Memoirs of Babur, Prince and Emperor,* and Stephen Dale's biography, *The Garden of the Eight Paradises: Bābur and the Culture of Empire in Central Asia, Afghanistan, and India, 1483–1530.*

In addition to Richards, *Mughal Empire,* the narrative derives primarily from Streusand, *Formation*; Ashirabadi Lal Srivastava, *Akbar the Great*; Ishtiaq Husain Qureshi, *Akbar: The Architect of the Mughal Empire*; Beni Prasad, *Life of Jahangir*; Banarsi Prasad Saksena, *History of Shah Jahan of Dilhi*; Jadunath Sarkar, *History of Aurangzib*; Satish Chandra, *Parties and Politics at the Mughal Court, 1707–1740*; Lt. Col. Sir Wolseley Haig and Sir Richard Burn, eds., *The Mughal Period,* which contains more chronological detail than Richards.

J. S. Grewal, in *Muslim Rule in India* and *Medieval India: History and Historians,* reviews British interpretations of Mughal history. Examples of the standard Indian interpretation include K. M. Pannikar, *A Survey of Indian History*; Stanley Wolpert, *A New History of India,* 126–134; Colin Mason, *A Short History of Asia,* 152–153. Ishtiaq Husain Qureshi, *The Muslim Community of the Indian Subcontinent,* S. M. Ikram, *Muslim Civilization in India,* and Aziz Ahmad, *Studies in Islamic Culture in the Indian Environment,* 73–101, 167–218, are critical of Akbar and praise Aurangzeb, as most Pakistani scholars do.

Examples of general works covering Mughal history from a more sophisticated perspective include Richards, *Mughal Empire,* and Marc Gaborieau, "Akbar and the Construction of the Mughal Empire, 1556–1605" and "Mogul Splendor: The Successors of Akbar, 1605–1707." See also Francis Robinson, *The Mughal Emperors and the Islamic Dynasties of India, Iran and Central Asia,* and Annemarie Schimmel, *The Empire of the Great Mughals: History, Art, and Culture.* On Sufism in legitimacy in South Asia, see Eaton, *Temple Desecration,* 22–30, and "The Political and Religious Authority of the Shrine of Bābā Farīd in Pakpattan, Punjab."

My analysis of Akbar's ideology here builds, but improves, on my findings in Streusand, *Formation.* S. A. A. Rizvi, *Religious and Intellectual History of the Muslims in Akbar's Reign,* and

J. F. Richards, "The Formation of Imperial Authority Under Akbar and Jahangir," offer vital insight. See also K. A. Nizami, *Akbar and Religion*; Iqtidar Alam Khan, "Akbar's Personality Traits and World Outlook—a Critical Appraisal"; F. W. Buckler, "A New Interpretation of Akbar's Infallibility Decree of 1579"; M. Athar Ali, "Sulh-i Kul and the Religious Ideas of Akbar." Historians disagree about whether Akbar abolished the *jizya* once or twice; I agree with Nizami, *Akbar and Religion*, 107–108, and Richards, "Formation of Imperial Authority," 39. For criticism of this conclusion, and of much else I have to say, see M. Athar Ali's review of Streusand, *Formation*.

My findings on Mughal ideology after Akbar are primarily my own. I have also consulted Richards, "Formation of Imperial Authority"; Athar Ali, *The Mughal Nobility under Aurangzeb*; Yohanan Friedman, *Shaykh Ahmad Sirhindi: An Outline of His Thought and a Study of His Image in the Eyes of Posterity*; Sri Ram Sharma, *The Religious Policy of the Mughal Emperors*; Satish Chandra, "Jizya and the State in India During the Seventeenth Century"; M. Athar Ali, "Religious Environment under Shah Jahan and Aurangzeb." Qureshi, *The Muslim Community*, 166–167, and K. A. Nizami, "Naqshbandi Influence on Mughal Rulers and Politics," contend that Jahangir's enthronement meant a constitutional change. For ideological interpretations of the clash between Dara Shukuh and Aurangzeb, see Aziz Ahmad, "Dara Shikoh and Aurangzeb"; Schimmel, *Mystical Dimensions*, 360–363; M. Athar Ali, "The Religious Issue in the War of Succession." Stephen P. Blake, *Shahjahanabad: The Sovereign City in Mughal India, 1639–1739*, is important for understanding both ideology and administration. Muzaffar Alam, *The Languages of Political Islam*, is also important.

Gommans, *Mughal Warfare*, is by far the most important work on Mughal expansion and military organization. See also Streusand, *Formation*, 51–81, which is reprinted in Jos. J. L. Gommans and Dirk H. A. Kolff, *Warfare and Weaponry in South Asia*, 1000–1800, along with a series of other useful articles and excerpts, including part of Simon Digby's important *War-Horse and Elephant*. Gommans and Kolff's introduction to that volume is useful. On the use of firearms, see Iqtidar Alam Khan, *Gunpowder and Firearms: Warfare in Medieval India*. On organization and recruitment, see, in addition to Gommans, *Mughal Warfare*, and Streusand, *Formation*, see Dirk H. A. Kolff, *Naukar, Rajput and Sepoy: The Ethnohistory of the Military Labour Market in Hindustan, 1450–1850*, and R. A. Alavi, "New Light on Mughal Cavalry." On the *mansabdari* system, see Athar Ali, *Mughal Nobility*, and Shireen Moosvi, "Evolution of the Mansab System Under Akbar"; Athar Ali's *The Apparatus of Empire* lists every change in the rank and appointment of *mansabdar*s between 1574 and 1658.

On Mughal central administration and the Mughal court, see Ibn Hasan, *The Central Structure of the Mughal Empire*; I. H. Qureshi, *The Administration of the Mughal Empire*; U. N. Day, *The Mughal Government*. Ruby Lal, *Domesticity and Power in the Early Mughal World*, and Gavin R. G. Hambly, "Armed Women Retainers in the Zenanas of Indo-Muslim Rulers: The Case of Bībī Fāṭima," discuss the Mughal female establishment.

Irfan Habib, *An Atlas of the Mughal Empire*, is the most important source on Mughal geography and contains a substantial amount of economic and administrative information as well. Habib's *The Agrarian System of the Mughal Empire* is a vital source on both provincial administration, especially taxation, and the rural economy, though it suffers from his effort to impose a Marxist framework. On provincial administration, see P. Saran, *The Provincial Government of the Mughals, 1526–1658*; J. F. Richards, *Mughal Administration in Golconda*; Norman Ahmad Siddiqui, "Faujdar and Faujdari Under the Mughals"; A. Jan Qaisar, "Distribution of the Revenue Resources of the Mughal Empire Among the Nobility." Hasan, *State and Locality*, the most recent significant work on the Mughal provincial regime, emphasizes the balance between the Mughals and provincial power holders.

The first volume of *The Cambridge Economic History of India*, c. 1200–1750, edited by Tapan Raychaudhuri and Irfan Habib, is the most important source on the Mughal economy. The important chapters include Habib's "Population," "Systems of Agricultural Production,: Mughal India," "Agrarian Relations and Land Revenue: North India" and "Monetary System and Prices"; Raychaudhuri, "The State and the Economy: The Mughal Empire" and "Non-Agricultural Production: Mughal India"; Gavin Hambly, "Towns and Cities: Mughal India"; and Satish Chandra, "Standards of Living: Mughal India." See also Habib's "Potentialities of Capitalistic Development in the Economy of Mughal India," and Sanjay Subrahmanyam, "Precious Metal Flows and Prices in Western and Southwest India: Some Comparative and Conjectural Aspects."

On Mughal art and architecture, see Ebba Koch's three major books: *Mughal Architecture: An Outline of Its History and Development*, *Mughal Art and Imperial Ideology: Collected Essays*, and *The Complete Taj Mahal and the Riverfront Gardens of Agra*. There are numerous art books of Mughal paintings; Schimmel, *Empire*, 270–283, is a useful review of the Mughal painting tradition. On Mughal literature and intellectual history, see Rizvi, *Religious and Intellectual History* and *History of Sufism in India*, and Jan Marek, "Persian Literature in India,"

Though antique, William Irvine, *Later Mughals*, is still the most complete narrative of Mughal history after Aurangzeb. Sarkar, *Aurangzib*, 3:190–199, and Qureshi, *The Muslim Community*, present the standard Indian and Pakistani views of Mughal decline. Habib, *The Agrarian System*, 364–405, presents a Marxist interpretation of Mughal decline. M. Athar Ali presents his "cultural failure" hypothesis in "The Passing of Empire: The Mughal Case." For more concrete approaches, see Satish Chandra's, *Parties and Politics at the Mughal Court, 1707–1740*, "Review of the Crisis of the Jagirdari System," "Reassessing Aurangzeb," and "Aurangzeb—a Critical Review"; Muzaffar Alam, *The Crisis of Empire in Northern India: Awadh and the Punjab 1707–1748*; J. F. Richards, "The Imperial Crisis in the Deccan" and "The Hyderabad Karnatik, 1687–1707"; M. N. Pearson, "Shivaji and the Decline of the Mughal Empire." On the Marathas, see Stuart Gordon, *The Marathas, 1600–1818*, and Govind Sakaram Sardesai, *A New History of the Marathas*.

Bibliography

This bibliography represents a good-faith effort to include all the works I have consulted in the process of producing this book. There are almost certainly some omissions, notably articles in *Encyclopedia of Islam* and *The Encyclopedia Iranica*. In some cases, the bibliography entries include information on reprints without giving pages numbers. Those reprints reproduce the original pagination.

Abisaab, Ruli Jurdi. *Converting Persia: Religion and Power in the Safavid Empire*. London: I. B. Tauris, 2004.

Abū al-Fazl ʿAllāmī. *Āʾin-i Akbari*. 3 vols.: Vol. 1, ed. D. C. Phillott, trans. H. Blochman; vols. 2 and 3, ed. Sir Jadunath Sarkar, trans. H. S. Jarret. 2nd ed. Calcutta: Asiatic Society of Bengal, 1927–1949. Reprint, New Delhi: Oriental Books Reprint, 1977–1978.

———. *Akbar-nama*, trans. Henry Beveridge. 3 vols. Calcutta: Asiatic Society of Bengal, 1897–1921. Reprint, New Delhi: Ess Ess Publications, 1979.

Ágoston, Gábor. *Guns for the Sultan: Military Power and the Weapons Industry in the Ottoman Empire*. Cambridge Studies in Islamic Civilization, gen. ed. David Morgan. Cambridge: Cambridge University Press, 2005.

———. "Ottoman Warfare in Europe, 1453–1826." In *European Warfare, 1453–1815*, ed. Jeremy Black, 118–144. New York: St. Martin's Press, 1999.

Ahmad, Aziz. "Dara Shikoh and Aurangzeb." In *Studies in Islamic Cultures in the Indian Environment*, 191–200. Oxford: Clarendon Press, 1964.

———. "Epic and Counter-Epic in Medieval India." *Journal of the American Oriental Society* 83 (1963): 470–476. Reprinted in *India's Islamic Traditions, 711–1750*, ed. Richard M. Eaton, 37–49. Oxford India Readings: Themes in Indian History. New Delhi: Oxford University Press, 2003.

———. *Studies in Islamic Culture in the Indian Environment*. Oxford: Clarendon Press, 1964.

———. "The Formation of the Sabk-Hindi." In *Iran and Islam: In Memory of the Late Vladimir Minorsky*, ed. C. E. Bosworth, 1–10. Edinburgh: Edinburgh University Press, 1971.

Ahmed, Tariq. *Religio-Political Ferment in the North West Frontier During the Mughal Period: The Raushaniya Movement*. Delhi: Idarah-i Adabiyyat Delli, 1983.

Aksan, Virginia H. "Ottoman War and Warfare." In *War in the Early Modern World, 1450 and 1815*, ed. Jeremy Black, 147–176. Boulder, CO: Westview 1999.

al Ansari, Mohammad Rafi al-Din. *Dastur al-Muluk*, trans. Willem Floor and Mohammad H. Faghfoory. Costa Mesa, CA: Mazda, 2007.

Alam, Muzaffar. *The Crisis of Empire in Northern India: Awadh and the Punjab, 1707–1748*. New Delhi: Oxford University Press, 1983.

————. *The Languages of Political Islam: India, 1200–1800.* Chicago: University of Chicago Press, 2004.

Alam, Muzaffar, and Sanjay Subrahmanyam, eds. *Indo-Persian Travels in the Age of Discoveries, 1400–1800.* Cambridge: Cambridge University Press, 2007.

————, eds. *The Mughal State, 1526–1750.* Oxford in India Readings: Themes in Indian History. New Delhi: Oxford University Press, 2001.

Alavi, R. A. "New Light on Mughal Cavalry." *Medieval India: A Miscellany* 2 (1972): 70–99.

Allouche, Adel. *The Origins and Development of the Ottoman-Safavid Conflict: 902–962/1550–1555.* Islamkundliche Untersuchungen, gen. ed. Klaus Schwarz Verlag 91. Berlin: Klaus Schwarz Verlag, 1983.

Amoretti, B. S. "Religion in the Timurid and Safavid Periods." In *The Timurid and Safavid Periods,* ed. Peter Jackson and Laurence Lockhart, 610–655. Vol. 6 of *The Cambridge History of Iran,* gen. ed. Harold Bailey Cambridge: Cambridge University Press, 1986.

Anderson, Perry. *Lineages of the Absolute State.* London: N. L. B., 1974.

Andrew, Walter G., and Mehmet Kalpakli. *The Age of the Beloved: Love and the Beloved in Early-Modern Ottoman and European Culture and Society.* Durham, NC: Duke University Press, 2005.

Ansâri, Mohammad Rafi` al-Din. *Dastur al-Moluk: A Safavid State Manual,* trans. Willem Floor and Mohammad H. Faghfoory, with commentary by Willem Floor. Costa Mesa, CA: Mazda, 2007.

Anwar, Firdos. *Nobility Under the Mughals, 1628–1658.* New Delhi: Manohar, 2001.

Arjomand, Said Amir. *The Shadow of God and the Hidden Imam: Religion, Political Order, and Societal Change in Shi`ite Iran from the Beginning to 1890.* Chicago: University of Chicago Press, 1984.

Asher, Catherine B. *Architecture of Mughal India.* Part 1, Vol. 4 of *The New Cambridge History of India,* gen. ed. Gordon Johnson. Cambridge: Cambridge University Press, 1992.

Asher, Catherine B., and Cynthia Talbot. *India Before Europe.* New York: Cambridge University Press, 2006.

Ashraf, Ahmad. "Historical Obstacles to the Development of a Bourgeoisie in Iran." In *Studies in the Economic History of the Middle East,* ed. M. A. Cook, 308–332. London: Oxford University Press, 1970.

Ashtor, Eliyahu. *Levant Trade in the Later Middle Ages.* Princeton, NJ: Princeton University Press, 1983.

Athar Ali, M. *Mughal India: Studies in Polity, Ideas, Society, and Culture.* New Delhi: Oxford University Press, 2006.

————. "Religious Environment under Shah Jahan and Aurangzeb." In *Mughal India: Studies in Polity, Ideas, Society and Culture,* 200–209. Oxford: Oxford University Press India, 2006.

————. Review of Douglas E. Streusand, *The Formation of the Mughal Empire.* *Medieval India* 1 (1992): 216–217.

————. "Sulh-i Kul and the Religious Ideas of Akbar." In *Mughal India: Studies in Polity, Ideas, Society and Culture,* 158–159. New Delhi: Oxford University Press, 2006.

————. *The Apparatus of Empire: Awards of Ranks, Offices and Titles to the Mughal Nobility, 1573–1658.* New Delhi: Oxford University Press, 1985.

————. *The Mughal Nobility Under Aurangzeb.* Rev. ed. New Delhi: Oxford University Press, 2002.

————. "The Mughal Polity—a Critique of Revisionist Approaches." *Modern Asian Studies* 7 (1993): 669–710. Reprint in *Mughal India: Studies in Polity, Ideas, Society and Culture.* New Delhi: Oxford University Press, 2001, 82–93.

————. "The Passing of Empire: The Mughal Case." *Modern Asian Studies* 9 (1975): 385–396.

————. "The Religious Issue in the War of Succession." In *Mughal India: Studies in Polity, Ideas, Society and Culture*, 158–173. Oxford: Oxford University Press India, 2006.

Atiya, Aziz S. "The Crusade in the Fourteenth Century." In *The Fourteenth and Fifteenth Centuries*, ed. Harry W. Hazzard, 3–26. Vol. 3 of *A History of the Crusades*, gen. ed. Kenneth M. Setton. 2nd ed. Madison: University of Wisconsin Press, 1975.

Aubin, Jean. "L'avenement des Safavides reconsideré." *Moyen Orient et Ocean Indien* 5 (1988): 1–130.

————. "La politique religieuse des Safavides." In *Le Shi`isme Imamite*, 115–129. Travaux du Centre d'Études Superieures Speciale d'Histoire des Religions de Strasbourg. Paris: Presses Universitaires de France, 1970.

Ayalon, David. *Gunpowder and Firearms in the Mamluk Kingdom: A Challenge to a Medieval Society*. 2nd ed. London: Frank Cass, 1978.

Aziz, Abdul. "Thrones, Chairs and Seats Used by Indian Mughals." *Journal of Indian History* 16 (1937): 186–225.

Azmeh, Ali. *Muslim Kingship: Power and the Sacred in Muslim, Christian, and Pagan Polities*. London: I. B. Tauris, 1997.

Babaie, Sussan, et al. *Slaves of the Shah: New Elites in Safavid Iran*. London: I. B. Tauris, 2004.

Babayan, Kathryn. *Mystics, Monarchs, and Messiahs: Cultural Landscapes of Modern Iran*. Harvard Middle Eastern Monographs 35. Cambridge, MA: Harvard University Press for the Center for Middle East Studies, Harvard University, 2002.

————. "Sufis, Dervishes, and Mullas: The Controversy over Spiritual and Temporal Dominion in Seventeenth-Century Iran." In *Safavid Persia: The History and Politics of an Islamic Society*, ed. Charles Melville, 117–138. London: I. B. Tauris, 1993.

————. "The "Aqa'id al-Nisā": A Glimpse of Ṣafavid Women in Local Isfahani Culture." In *Women in the Medieval Islamic World*, ed. Gavin R. G. Hambly, 429–468. Vol. 6 of *The New Middle Ages*, gen. ed. Bonnie Wheeler. New York: St. Martin's Press, 1998.

Babinger, Franz. *Mehmed the Conqueror and His Time*, ed. William C. Hickman, trans. Ralph Manheim. Bollingen 96. Princeton, NJ: Princeton University Press, 1978.

Babur Padishah Ghazi, Zahir al-Din Muhammad. *Babur-Nama*, trans. Annette Susannah Beveridge. 2 vols. London: Author, 1922. Reprint, 2 vols. as 1, New Delhi: Oriental Books Reprint, 1979.

————. *The Baburnama: Memoirs of Babur, Prince and Emperor*, ed. and trans. Wheeler M. Thackston. New York: Oxford University Press, 1996.

Bacque-Grammont, Jean Louis. "Études turco-safavides I: Notes sur le blocus du commerce iranien par Selim Ier." *Turcica* 6 (1975): 66–88.

Baer, Marc David. *Honored by the Glory of Islam: Conversion and Conquest in Ottoman Europe*. New York: Oxford University Press, 2008.

Baldwin, Marshall W., ed. *The First Hundred Years*. Vol. 1 of *A History of the Crusades*, gen. ed. Kenneth M. Setton. 2nd ed. Madison: University of Wisconsin Press, 1969.

Banani, Amin. "Reflections on the Social and Economic Structure of Safavid Persia at Its Zenith." *Iranian Studies* 11 (1978): 83–116.

Barfield, Thomas J. *The Nomadic Alternative*. Upper Saddle River, NJ: Prentice Hall, 1993.

Barkan, Omer Lufti. "The Price Revolution of the Sixteenth Century: A Turning Point in the Economic History of the Near East," trans. Justin McCarthy. *International Journal of Middle East Studies* 6 (1975): 3–28.

Barkey, Karen. *Bandits and Bureaucrats: The Ottoman Route to State Centralization*. Ithaca, NY: Cornell University Press, 1994.

Barthold (Bartold), V. V. *Ulugh Beg.* Vol. 2 of *Four Studies on the History of Central Asia*, trans. V. and T. Minorsky. Leiden, Netherlands: E. J. Brill, 1968.

Bartold, Vasilii Vladimirovitch. *Mussulman Culture*, trans. Shahib Suhrawardy. Foreword by Sir Hassan Suhrawardy. Calcutta: University of Calcutta Press, 1934. Reprint, with introduction by Gariele Marranci. New York: Oxford University Press, 2010.

Barzegar, Karim Najafi. *Intellectual Movements During the Timuri and Safavid Period.* Delhi: Indian Bibliographies Bureau, 2005.

Bashir, Shahzad. "After the Messiah: The Nūrbakhshiyyeh in Late Timurid and Early Safavid Times." In *Society and Culture in the Early Modern Middle East: Studies on Iran in the Safavid Period*, ed. Andrew J. Newman, 295–314. Leiden: E. J. Brill, 1998.

———. *Messianic Hopes and Mystical Visions: The Nūrbakhshīya Between Medieval and Modern Islam.* Studies in Comparative Religion, ed. Frederick M. Denny. Columbia: University of South Carolina Press, 2003.

Behl, Aditya. "The Magic Doe: Desire and Narrative in a Hindavi Sufi Romance, Circa 1503." In *Indian Islamic Traditions, 711–1750*, ed. Richard M. Eaton, 180–208. Themes in Indian History. Delhi: Oxford University Press, 2003.

Bellan, Lucien Louis. *Chah `Abbas I, sa vie, son histoire.* Paris: Paul Geuthner, 1932.

Berkey, Jonathan P. *The Formation of Islam: Religion and Society in the Near East, 600–1800.* Themes in Islamic History, ed. Patricia Crone. New York: Cambridge University, 2003.

Bernier, François. *Travels in the Mughal Empire*, ed. Vincent Smith, trans. Archibald Constable. 2nd rev. ed. London: Oxford University Press, 1934. Reprint, New Delhi: Oriental Books Reprint, 1983.

Biruni, Muhammad ibn Ahmad. *Al-Beruni's India: An Account of the Religions, Philosophy, Literature, Geography, Chronology, Astronomy, Customs, Law and Astrology of India About AD 1030.* London: Kegan, Paul, Trench, Trubner & Co., 1910. Reprint, New Delhi: Oriental Reprint, 1983.

Bisaha, Nancy. *Creating East and West: Renaissance Humanists and the Ottoman Turks.* Philadelphia: University of Pennsylvania Press, 2004.

Black, Anthony. *The History of Islamic Political Thought.* New York: Routledge, 2001.

Black, Jeremy, ed. *European Warfare, 1453–1815.* New York: St. Martin's Press, 1999.

———, ed. *European Warfare, 1494–1660.* Warfare and History, gen. ed. Jeremy Black. London: Routledge, 2002.

———. *European Warfare in a Global Context, 1660–1815.* Warfare and History, gen. ed. Jeremy Black. London: Routledge, 2007.

———. *Rethinking Military History.* London: Routledge, 2004.

———. *War in the Early Modern World, 1450 and 1815.* Boulder, CO: Westview 1999.

Blake, Stephen P. *Half the World: The Social Architecture of Safavid Isfahan, 1590–1722.* Islamic Art and Architecture Series 9, gen. ed. Abbas Daneshvari. Costa Mesa, CA: Mazda Press, 1999.

———. "Shah `Abbas and the Transfer of the Safavid Capital from Qazvin to Isfahan." In *Society and Culture in the Early Modern Middle East: Studies on Iran in the Safavid Period*, ed. Andrew J. Newman, 145–164. Leiden: E. J. Brill, 1998.

———. *Shahjahanabad: The Sovereign City in Mughal India, 1639–1739.* Cambridge: Cambridge University Press, 1990.

———. "The Patrimonial-Bureaucratic Empire of the Mughals." *Journal of Asian Studies* 39 (1971): 77–99. Reprinted in *The State in India, 1000–1700*, ed. Hermann Kulke, 278–303. Oxford in India Readings: Themes in Indian History, gen. ed. Basudev Chatterji, Neeladri Bhattacharya, and C. A. Bayly. New Delhi: Oxford University Press, 1995.

Blunt, Wilfrid. *Isfahan: Pearl of Persia*. New York: Stein & Day, 1966. Reprint, London: Pallas Athene, 2009.

Boettcher, Susan R. "Confessionalization: Reformation, Religion, Absolutism, and Modernity." *History Compass* 2 (2004):1–10.

Bonner, Michael. *Jihad in Islamic History: Doctrine and Practices*. Princeton, NJ: Princeton University Press, 2006.

Bosworth, C. E. "The Political and Dynastic History of the Iranian World (AD 1000–1217)." In *The Saljuq and Mongol Periods*, ed. J. A. Boyle, 1–202. Vol. 5 of *The Cambridge History of Iran*, gen. ed. Harold Bailey. Cambridge: Cambridge University Press, 1968.

———, ed. *The Turks in the Early Islamic World*. The Formation of the Classical Islamic World 9, ed. Lawrence I. Conrad. Aldershot, UK: Ashgate, 2007.

Boxer, C. R. *The Dutch Seaborne Empire, 1600–1800*. History of Human Society, ed. J. H. Plumb. New York: Alfred A. Knopf, 1970.

———. *The Portuguese Seaborne Empire, 1415–1825*. History of Human Society, ed. J. H. Plumb. New York: Alfred A. Knopf, 1969.

Boyle, J. A. "Dynastic and Political History of the Il-Khans." In *The Saljuq and Mongol Periods*, ed. J. A. Boyle, 303–421. Vol. 5 of *The Cambridge History of Iran*, gen. ed. Harold Bailey. Cambridge: Cambridge University Press, 1968.

Bradford, Ernle. *The Great Siege: Malta 1565*. London: Hodder & Stoughton, 1961.

Brand, Michael, and Glenn D. Lowry, eds. *Fatehpur Sikri: A Source Book*. Cambridge, MA: The Aga Khan Program for Islamic Architecture at Harvard University and the Massachusetts Institute of Technology, 1985.

Braudel, Fernand. *The Mediterranean and the Mediterranean World in the Age of Phillip II*, trans. Sian Reynolds. 2 vols. New York: Harper & Row, 1972.

Braun, Hellmut. "Iran Under the Safavids and in the Eighteenth Century," trans. F. R. C. Bagley. In *The Last Great Muslim Empires*, ed. Hans J. Kissling et al. Princeton, NJ: Markus Weiner, 1996. Original publication, 1969.

Broadridge, Anne F. *Kingship and Ideology in the Islamic and Mongol Worlds*. Cambridge Studies in Islamic Civilization, gen. ed. David O. Morgan. Cambridge: Cambridge University Press, 2008.

Brockelmann, Carl. *History of the Islamic Peoples*, trans. Joel Carmichael and Moshe Perlmann. New York: Capricorn Books, 1960.

Browne, E. G. *A Literary History of Persia*. Cambridge: Cambridge University Press, 1925–1928.

Brummett, Palmira. *Ottoman Seapower and Levantine Diplomacy in the Age of Discovery*. Studies in the Social and Economic History of the Middle East, ed. Donald Quataert. Albany: State University of New York Press, 1994.

Buckler, F. W. "A New Interpretation of Akbar's Infallibility Decree of 1579." *Journal of the Royal Asiatic Society* (1924): 590–608.

———. "The Oriental Despot." *Anglican Theological Review* 10 (1927–1928): 238–249.

Bulliet, Richard W. *Islam: The View from the Edge*. New York: Columbia University Press, 1994.

Burn, Richard, Sir. "Humayun." In *The Mughal Period*. Vol. 4 of *The Cambridge History of India* 4, ed. Lt. Col. Sir Wolseley Haig and Sir Richard Burn, 21–44. Cambridge: Cambridge University Press, 1937.

Burton-Page, J. "The Sultanates of the Deccan." In *The Cambridge History of Islam*, ed. P. M. Holt, Ann K. S. Lambton, and Bernard Lewis, 2:63–66. 2 vols. Cambridge: Cambridge University Press, 1970.

Cahen, Claude. "L'évolution de l'Iqta` du IX'e au XII'e siècle." *Annales* 8 (1953): 25–52.

———. "Le probleme du Shi`isme dans l'Asie Mineure turque preottomane." In *Le Shi`isme imamate*, 115–129. Travaux du Centre d'Études Superieures Speciale d'Histoire des Religions de Strasbourg. Paris: Presses Universitaires de France, 1970.

———. *Pre-Ottoman Turkey: A General Survey of the Material and Spiritual Culture and History, c. 1071–1330*. London: Sidgwick & Jackson, 1968.

———. *The Formation of Turkey: The Seljukid Sultanate of Rum, Eleventh to Fourteenth Centuries*, ed. and trans. P. M. Holt. Harlow, UK: Longman, 2001.

———. "The Mongols and the Near East." In *The Later Crusades, 1189–1311*, ed. Robert Lee Wolff and Harry W. Hazard, 735–758. Vol. 2 of *A History of the Crusades*, gen. ed. Kenneth M. Setton. 2nd ed. Madison: University of Wisconsin Press, 1969.

———. "The Turkish Invasion: The Selchukids." In *The First Hundred Years*, ed. Marshall W. Baldwin, 135–176. Vol. 1 of *A History of the Crusades*, gen. ed. Kenneth M. Setton. 2nd ed. Madison: University of Wisconsin Press, 1969.

———. "The Turks in Iran and Anatolia Before the Mongol Invasions." In *The Later Crusades, 1189–1311*, ed. Robert Lee Wolff and Harry W. Hazard, 693–714. Vol. 2 of *A History of the Crusades*, gen. ed. Kenneth M. Setton. 2nd ed. Madison: University of Wisconsin Press, 1969.

———. "Y a-t-il eu des corporations professionelles dans le monde musulman classique." In *The Islamic City: A Colloquium*, ed. A. H. Hourani and S. M. Stern, 51–64. Papers on Islamic History 1. Philadelphia: University of Pennsylvania Press, 1970.

Calmard, Jean, ed. *Études safavides*. Paris: Institut Français de Recherche en Iran. Louvain, Belgium: Diffusion, Peeters, 1993.

———. "Les rituels shiites et le pouvoir: L'imposition du Shiisme safavide: Eulogies et maledictions canoniques." In *Études safavides*, ed. Jean Calmard, 109–150. Paris: Institut Français de Recherche en Iran. Louvain, Belgium: Diffusion, Peeters, 1993.

———. "Shi`i Rituals and Power in the Consolidation of Safavid Shi`ism: Folklore and Popular Religion." In *Safavid Persia: The History and Politics of an Islamic Society*, ed. Charles Melville, 139–191. London: I. B. Tauris, 1993.

Canby, Sheila R., ed. *Safavid Art and Architecture*. London: British Museum, 2002.

Canfield, Robert L, ed. *Turko-Persia in Historical Perspective*. School of American Research Advanced Seminar Series, gen. ed. Douglas W. Schwartz. Cambridge: Cambridge University Press, 1991.

Caroe, Olaf, Sir. *The Pathans, 550 BC–AD 1957, with an Epilogue on Russia*. Oxford in Asia Historical Reprints from Pakistan Modern Series, ed. Percival Spear. Oxford: Oxford University Press, 1983.

Casale, Giancarlo. "An Ottoman Intelligence Report from the Mid-Sixteenth Century Indian Ocean." *Journal of Turkish Studies* 31 (2007): 181–188.

———. "Global Politics in the 1580s: One Canal, Twenty Thousand Cannibals and an Ottoman Plot to Rule the World." *Journal of World History* 18 (2007): 267–296.

———. "Ottoman *Guerre de Course* and the Indian Ocean Spice Trade." *Itinerario* 23 (2008): 59–79.

———. "The Ottoman Administration of the Spice Trade in the Sixteenth-Century Red Sea and Persian Gulf." *Journal of the Economic and Social History of the Orient* 49 (2006): 170–198.

Chandler, David. *The Campaigns of Napoleon*. New York: Macmillan, 1966.

Chandra, Satish. "Aurangzeb—a Critical Review." In *Essays on Medieval Indian History*. Oxford: Oxford University Press, 2006.

———. *Essays on Medieval Indian History.* New Delhi: Oxford University Press, 2003.

———. *Historiography, Religion and State in Medieval India.* New Delhi: Har Anand, 1996.

———. *History of Medieval India.* New Delhi: Orient Longman, 2007.

———. "Jizyah and the State in India During the Seventeenth Century." *Journal of the Economic and Social History of the Orient* 12 (1969): 322–340. Reprinted in *Essays on Medieval Indian History,* 305–325. New Delhi: Oxford University Press, 2003.

———. *Parties and Politics at the Mughal Court, 1707–1740.* 3rd ed. New Delhi: Asia Publishing, 1979.

———. "Reassessing Aurangzeb." *Seminar,* no. 364, (1989): 22–46.

———. "Review of the Crisis of the Jagirdari System." In *Medieval India: Society, the Jagirdari Crisis and the Village.* New Delhi: Macmillan Publishers India, 2000.

———. *Social Change and Development in Medieval Indian History.* New Delhi: Har-Anand, 2008.

———. "Standards of Living: Mughal India." In *Circa 1200–1750,* ed. Tapan Raychaudhuri and Irfan Habib. Vol. 1 of *The Cambridge Economic History of India,* ed. Dharma Kumar and Tapan Raychaudhuri. Cambridge: Cambridge University Press, 1982.

———. *State, Pluralism, and the Indian Historical Tradition.* Oxford Collected Essays. New Delhi: Oxford University Press, 2008.

Chardin, Jean. *Voyages du Chevalier Chardin en Perse, et autres lieux de l'Orient,* ed. L. Langles. New. ed. 11 vols. Paris: Le Normant, 1811.

Chase, Kenneth. *Firearms: A Global History to 1700.* New York: Cambridge University Press, 2003.

Chaudhuri, K. N. *Asia Before Europe: Economy and Civilization of the Indian Ocean from the Rise of Islam to 1750.* Cambridge: Cambridge University Press, 1990.

———. "Foreign Trade: European Trade with India." In *Circa 1200–1750,* ed. Tapan Raychaudhuri and Irfan Habib, 382–406. Vol. 1 of *The Cambridge Economic History of India,* ed. Dharma Kumar and Tapan Raychaudhuri. Cambridge: Cambridge University Press, 1982.

———. *The Trading World of Asia and the English East India Company: 1660–1760.* Cambridge: Cambridge University Press, 1978.

———. *Trade and Civilization in the Indian Ocean from the Rise of Islam to 1750.* Cambridge: Cambridge University Press, 1985.

Christensen, Arthur. *L'Iran sous les Sassanides.* 2nd. ed. Osnabruck: O. Zeller, 1971.

Christian, David. *Maps of Time: An Introduction to Big History.* Berkeley: University of California Press, 2004.

Cipolla, Carlo M. *Guns, Sails and Empires: Technological Innovation and the Early Phase of European Expansion, 1400–1700.* Cambridge Studies in Early Modern History. Cambridge: Cambridge University Press, 1974.

Çırakman, Aslı. *From the "Terror of the World" to the "Sick Man of Europe": European Images of the Ottoman Empire and Society from the Sixteenth Century to the Nineteenth.* New York: Peter Lang, 2005.

Clausewitz, Carl von. *On War,* ed. and trans. Michael Howard and Peter Paret. Princeton, NJ: Princeton University Press, 1976.

Cleaves, Francis, trans. *The Secret History of the Mongols.* Cambridge, MA: Harvard University Press, 1982.

Cohn, Bernard S. "African Models and Indian Histories." In *Realm and Region in Traditional India,* ed. Richard G. Fox, 90–113. Duke University Comparative Studies on Southern Asia Monograph and Occasional Papers 14. Durham, NC: Duke University Press, 1977.

Reprinted in *An Anthropologist Among the Historians*, with an introduction by Ranajit Guha. New Delhi: Oxford University Press, 1987, 200–223, itself reprinted in *The Bernard Cohn Omnibus*, with an introduction by Dipesh Chakrabarty. New Delhi: Oxford University Press, 2004.

———. *An Anthropologist Among the Historians*, with an introduction by Ranajit Guha. New Delhi: Oxford University Press, 1987.

———. *India: The Social Anthropology of Civilization*. Englewood Cliffs, NJ: Prentice Hall, 1971. Reprinted in *The Bernard Cohn Omnibus*, with an introduction by Dipesh Chakrabarty. New Delhi: Oxford University Press, 2004.

———. "Political Systems in Eighteenth-Century India." *Journal of the American Oriental Society* 82 (1962): 312–320. Reprinted in *The Bernard Cohn Omnibus*, 483–499. New Delhi: Oxford University Press, 2004.

———. *The Bernard Cohn Omnibus*. New Delhi: Oxford University Press, 2004.

Cook, David. *Understanding Jihad*. Berkeley: University of California Press, 2005.

Cook, M. A., ed. *A History of the Ottoman Empire to 1730: Chapters from the Cambridge History of Islam and the New Cambridge Modern History*, gen. ed. M. A. Cook. Cambridge: Cambridge University Press, 1976.

———. *Population Pressure in Rural Anatolia*. London: Oxford University Press, 1972.

———, ed. *Studies in the Economic History of the Middle East*. London: Oxford University Press, 1970.

Corbin, Henry. *Avicenna and the Visionary Recital*, trans. Willard R. Trask. New York: Pantheon Books, 1960.

Coulson, N. J. *A History of Islamic Law*. Islamic Surveys 2. Edinburgh: Edinburgh University Press, 1964.

Crone, Patricia. "Did al-Ghazālī Write a Mirror for Princes?" *Jerusalem Studies in Arabic and Islam* 10 (1987): 167–191.

———. *God's Rule: Six Centuries of Medieval Islamic Political Thought*. New York: Columbia University Press, 2004.

Cvetkova, B. "Problemes du régime ottoman dan les Balkans du seizième au dix-huitième siècle." In *Studies in Eighteenth Century Islamic History*, eds.Thomas Naff and Roger Owen, 165–183. Papers on Islamic History 4. Carbondale: Southern Illinois University Press, 1977.

Dadvar, Abolghasem. *Iranians in Mughal Politics and Society: 1606–1658*. New Delhi: Gyan, 2000.

Dale, Stephen Frederick. *Indian Merchants and Eurasian Trade, 1600–1750*. Cambridge Studies in Islamic Civilization, gen. ed. David Morgan. Cambridge: Cambridge University Press, 1994.

———. "Steppe Humanism: The Autobiographical Writings of Zahir al-Din Muhammad Babur, 1483–1530." *International Journal of Middle East Studies* 22 (1990): 37–58.

———. *The Garden of the Eight Paradises: Bābur and the Culture of Empire in Central Asia, Afghanistan, and India, 1483–1530*. Brill's Inner Asian Library 10. Leiden, Netherlands: E. J. Brill, 2004.

———. "The Poetry and Autobiography in the *Bâbur-Nâma*." *Journal of Asian Studies* 55 (1986): 635–664.

Daniel, Norman. *Islam and the West: The Making of an Image*. Rev. ed. Oxford: One World, 1993.

Darling, Linda T. "Contested Territory: Ottoman Holy War in Comparative Context." *Studia Islamica* 91 (2001): 133–163.

———. "'Do Justice, Do Justice, for That Is Paradise': Middle Eastern Advice for Indian Muslim Rulers." *Comparative Studies of South Asia, Africa and the Middle East* 22 (2002): 3–19.

———. "Persianate Sources on Anatolia and the Early History of the Ottomans." *Studies on Persianate Societies* 2 (2004): 126–144.

———. "Political Change and Political Discourse in the Early Modern Mediterranean World." *Journal of Interdisciplinary History* 38 (2008): 505–531.

———. *Revenue-Raising and Legitimacy: Tax Collection and Finance Administration in the Ottoman Empire, 1560–1660.* The Ottoman Empire and Its Heritage: Politics, Society, Economy. Leiden, Netherlands: E. J. Brill, 1996.

———. "Social Cohesion (`Asabiyya) and Justice in the Late Medieval Period." *Comparative Studies in Society and History* 49 (2007): 329–357.

Daryaee, Touraj. *Sasanian Iran, 224–651 CE: Portrait of a Late Antique Empire.* Costa Mesa, CA: Mazda Publishers, 2008.

Davies, Brian L. *Warfare, State and Society on the Black Sea Steppe.* Warfare and History, gen. ed. Jeremy Black. London: Routledge, 2007.

Davis, Ralph. "England and the Mediterranean." In *Essays in the Economic and Social History of Tudor and Stuart England*, ed. F. J. Fischer, 117–137. Cambridge: Cambridge University Press, 1961.

Day, U. N. *The Mughal Government.* New Delhi: Munshiram Manoharlal, 1970.

De Planhol, X. "The Geography of Settlement." In *The Land of Iran*, ed. W. B. Fisher, 409–432. Vol. 1 of *The Cambridge History of Iran*, gen. ed. Harold Bailey. Cambridge: Cambridge University Press, 1968.

De Rachelwiltz, Igor, trans. *The Secret History of the Mongols.* 2 vols. Leiden, Netherlands: E. J. Brill, 2006.

Denison-Ross, E., Sir. "Babur." In *The Mughal Period.* Vol. 4 of *The Cambridge History of India*, ed. Lt. Col. Sir Wolseley Haig and Sir Richard Burn, 1–20. Cambridge: Cambridge University Press, 1937.

DeWeese, Devin. *Islamization and Native Religion in the Golden Horde: Baba Tükles and Conversion to Islam in Historical and Epic Tradition.* University Park: Pennsylvania State University Press, 1994.

———, ed. *Studies on Central Asian History of Yuri Bregel.* Indiana University Uralic and Altaic Series 167, ed. Denis Sinor. Bloomington: Indiana University Research Institute for Inner Asian Studies, 2001.

Dickson, Martin B. "Shah Tahmasp and the Uzbeks: The Duel for Khurasan with `Ubayd Khan." PhD diss., Princeton University, 1958.

———. "The Fall of the Safavid Dynasty." *Journal of the American Oriental Society* 82 (1962): 503–517.

———. "Uzbek Dynastic Theory in the Sixteenth Century." In *Proceedings of the 25th International Congress of Orientalists*, 3:208–216. 4 vols. Moscow: n.p., 1963.

Digby, Simon. *War-Horse and Elephant in the Delhi Sultanate: A Study of Military Supplies.* Oxford: Oxford University Press, 1971. Reprint, 2005.

Duffy, Christopher. *Fire and Stone: The Science of Fortress Warfare, 1660–1860.* London: Peters, Fraser & Dunlop, 1975. Reprint, Edison, NJ: Castle Books, 2006.

———. *Siege Warfare: The Fortress in the Early Modern World, 1494–1660.* London: Routledge & Kegan Paul, 1979. Reprint, London: Routledge, 2000.

Dughlat, Mirza Muhammad Haidar. *Tarikh-i Rashidi*, ed. N. Elias, trans. Sir E. Denison Ross, as *A History of the Moghuls of Central Asia.* 2nd ed. London: Curzon Press, 1898. Reprint, New York: Barnes & Noble, 1972.

Eaton, Richard M. *A Social History of the Deccan, 1300–1761: Eight Indian Lives*. Vol. 1:8 of *The New Cambridge History of India*, gen. ed. Gordon Johnson. Cambridge: Cambridge University Press, 2005.

———. *Essays on Islam and Indian History*. New Delhi: Oxford University Press, 2000.

———, ed. *India's Islamic Traditions, 711–1750*. Oxford India Readings: Themes in Indian History. New Delhi: Oxford University Press, 2003.

———. *Temple Desecration and Muslim States in Medieval India*. Gurgaon: Hope India, 2004.

———. "The Political and Religious Authority of the Shrine of Bābā Farīd in Pakpattan, Punjab." In *Moral Conduct and Authority: The Place of Adab in South Asian Islam*, ed. Barbara Metcalf, 333–356. Berkeley: University of California Press, 1984.

———. *The Rise of Islam and the Bengal Frontier: 1204–1760*. Berkeley: University of California Press, 1993.

Echraqi, Ehsan. "Le *Dar al-Saltana* de Qazvin, deuxième capitale des Safavides." In *Safavid Persia: The History and Politics of an Islamic Society*, ed. Charles Melville, 105–116. London: I. B. Tauris, 1993.

Efendiev, Oktaj. "Le rôle des tribus de langue turque dans la creation de l'état safavide." *Turcica* 6 (1974): 24–33.

Eldem, Edhem, Daniel Goffman, and Bruce Masters, *The Ottoman City Between East and West: Aleppo, Izmir, and Istanbul*. Cambridge Studies in Islamic Civilization, ed. David Morgan et al. Cambridge: Cambridge University Press, 1999.

Elliot, H. M. *The History of India As Told by Its Own Historians*, ed. S. Dowson. 8 vols. London: Trubner, 1866–1877. Multiple reprints.

Encyclopedia Iranica, s.v. "Alqas Mirza." By Cornell Fleischer.

Encyclopedia Iranica, s.v. "Central Asia, vi. In the 10th-12th/16th-18th Centuries." By R. D. McChesney.

Encyclopedia Islamica, s.v. "Army, iii. Safavid." By Masashi Haneda.

Encyclopedia of Islam, 2nd ed., s.v. "Hawala," "Kanun: Financial and Public Administration," and "Kanunname." By Halil Inalcık.

Encyclopedia of Islam, 2nd ed., s.v. "Shah-sevan." By Vladimir Minorsky.

Encyclopedia of Islam, s.v. "Sultan." By J. H. Kremers and Wilferd Madelung.

Eraly, Abraham. *The Mughal Throne: The Sage of India's Great Emperors*. London: Weidenfeld and Nicholson, 2003.

Esper, Thomas. "The Replacement of the Longbow by Firearms in the English Army." *Technology and Culture* 61 (1965): 382–393.

Falsafi, Nasr Allah. *Zindigani-yi Shah `Abbas I Avval*. 4 vols. Tehran: Danishgah-i Tehran, 1955–1961.

Faroqhi, Suraiya. *Approaching Ottoman History: An Introduction to the Sources*. Cambridge: Cambridge University Press, 1999.

———. "Crisis and Change, 1590–1699." In *An Economic and Social History of the Ottoman Empire*, ed. Halil Inalcık and Donald Quataert, 411–636. Cambridge: Cambridge University Press, 1994.

———. *Pilgrims and Sultans: The Hajj Under the Ottomans, 1517–1683*. London: I. B. Tauris, 1994.

———. *Subjects of the Sultan: Culture and Daily Life in the Ottoman Empire*, trans. Martin Bott. London: I. B. Tauris, 2005.

Ferrier, Ronald. "Trade from the Mid-14th Century to the End of the Safavid Period." In *The Timurid and Safavid Periods*, ed. Peter Jackson and Laurence Lockhart, 412–490. Vol. 6 of

The Cambridge History of Iran, gen. ed. Harold Bailey Cambridge: Cambridge University Press, 1986.

———. "Women in Safavid Iran: The Evidence of European Travelers." In *Women in the Medieval Islamic World*, ed. Gavin R. G. Hambly, 383–406. Vol. 6 of *The New Middle Ages*, gen. ed. Bonnie Wheeler. New York: St. Martin's Press, 1998.

Findley, Carter Vaughn. *The Turks in World History*. New York: Oxford University Press, 2003.

Finkel, Caroline. *Osman's Dream: The History of the Ottoman Empire*. New York: Basic Books, 2005.

———. *The Administration of Warfare: The Ottoman Military Campaigns in Hungary, 1593–1606*. Wiener Zeitschrift für die Kunde des Morenlandes Supplement 14. Vienna: Verlag des Verbandes der Wissenschaftlichen Gesellschaften Österreichs, 1988.

Fisher, Alan W. *The Crimean Tatars*. Studies of Nationalities in the USSR Series, ed. Wayne Vucinich. Stanford, CA: Hoover Institution Press, 1978.

Fisher, Michael H., ed. *Visions of Mughal India: An Anthology of European Travel Writing*. London: I. B. Tauris, 2007.

Fleischer, Cornell H. *Bureaucrat and Intellectual in the Ottoman Empire: The Historian Mustafa Ali*. Princeton, NJ: Princeton University Press, 1986.

———. "Seer to the Sultan: Haydar-i Remmal and Sultan Süleyman." In *Cultural Horizons: A Festschrift in Honor of Talat S. Halman*, ed. Jayne L. Warner, 290–299. Syracuse, NY: Syracuse University Press, 2001.

———. "Shadow of Shadows: Prophecy in Politics in 1530s Istanbul." *International Journal of Turkish Studies* 13 (2007): 51–62.

———. "The Lawgiver As Messiah: The Making of the Imperial Image in the Reign of Sülaymân." In *Sülaymân the Magnificent and His Time*, ed. Gilles Veinstein (Paris: La Documentation Français, 1992).

Fletcher, Joseph F. "The Mongols: Ecological and Social Perspectives." *Harvard Journal of Asiatic Studies* 46 (1968): 11–50.

Floor, Willem. *A Fiscal History of Iran in the Safavid and Qajar Periods*. Persian Studies Series 17, ed. Ehsan Yarshater. New York: Bibliotheca Persica Press, 1998.

———. *Safavid Government Institutions*. Costa Mesa, CA: Mazda Press, 2001.

Folz, Richard C. *Mughal India and Central Asia*. Oxford Pakistan Paperbacks. Karachi, Pakistan: Oxford University Press, 1998.

Foran, John. "The Long Fall of the Safavid Dynasty." *International Journal of Middle East Studies* 24 (1992): 281–304.

Fragner, Bert. "Social and Internal Economic Affairs." In *The Timurid and Safavid Periods*, ed. Peter Jackson and Laurence Lockhart, 491–567. Vol. 6 of *The Cambridge History of Iran*, gen. ed. Harold Bailey Cambridge: Cambridge University Press, 1986.

Frankfort, Henri. *Kingship and the Gods: A Study of Ancient Near Eastern Religion As the Integration of Society and Nature*. Chicago: University of Chicago Press, 1948.

Friedman, Yohanan. "Islamic Thought in Relation to the Indian Context." In *Islam et société en Asie du Sud*, ed. Marc Gaborieau, 79–91. Paris: École des Hautes Études en Sciences Sociales, 1986. Reprinted in *India's Islamic Traditions, 711–1750*, ed. Richard M. Eaton, 50–63. Oxford India Readings: Themes in Indian History. New Delhi: Oxford University Press, 2003.

———. *Shaykh Ahmad Sirhindi: An Outline of His Thought and a Study of His Image in the Eyes of Posterity*. McGill Islam Studies 2. Montreal: McGill-Queen's University Press, 1971.

Frost, Robert I. *The Northern Wars, 1558–1721*. Modern Wars in Perspective, ed. H. M. Scott and B. W. Collins. New York: Longman, 2000.

Fuller, J. F. C. *Decisive Battles*. New York: Charles Scribner's Sons, 1940.

Gaborieau, Marc. "Akbar and the Construction of the Mughal Empire, 1556–1605." In *A History of Modern India, 1480–1950*, ed. Claude Markovits, trans. Nisha George and Maggy Hendry, 81–95. London: Anthem Press, 2002.

———. "Mogul Splendor: The Successors of Akbar, 1605–1707." In *A History of Modern India, 1480–1950*, ed. Claude Markovits, trans. Nisha George and Maggy Hendry, 96–110. London: Anthem Press, 2002.

Garthwaite, Gene R. *The Persians*. The Peoples of Asia, ed. Morris Rossabi. Oxford: Blackwell Publishing, 2005.

Gerber, Haim. *Islamic Law and Culture, 1600–1840*. Studies in Islamic Law and Society 9, eds. Ruud Peterrs and Bernard Weiss. Leiden, Netherlands: E. J. Brill, 1999.

Al-Ghazali, Abu Hamid Muhammad. *Naṣīhat al-Mulūk*, trans. F. R. C. Bagley as *Ghazali's Book of Rules for Kings*. London: Oxford University Press, 1964.

Gibb, E. J. W. *History of Ottoman Poetry*. 6 vols. London: Luzac, 1900–1909.

Gibb, H. A. R. "Lufti Pasha and the Ottoman Caliphate." *Oriens* 15 (1962): 287–295.

———. "The Social Significance of the Shuubiya." In *Studia Orientalia Ioanni Pedersen septuagenario A.D. VII id. Nov. anno MCMLIII a colleges discipulis amicis dictate*, 105–114. Hauniae [Copenhagen]: E. Munksgaard, 1953. Reprinted in *Studies on the Civilization of Islam*, ed. Stanford J. Shaw and William R. Polk, 62–74. Boston: Beacon, 1962.

Gibbons, Herbert Adams. *The Foundation of the Ottoman Empire*. New York: Century, 1916. Reprint, London: Frank Cass, 1968.

Gilmartin, David, and Bruce B. Lawrence, eds. *Beyond Turk and Hindu: Rethinking Religious Identities in Islamicate South Asia*. Gainesville: University Press of Florida, 2000.

Glassen, Erika. "Schah Isma`il, ein Mahdi der Anatolischen Turkmenen?" *Zeitschrift der deutschen morgenlandischen Gesellschaft* 121 (1971): 69.

———. "Schah Isma`il und die theologen seiner Zeit." *Der Islam* 48 (1971–1972): 254–268.

Glete, Jan. *Warfare at Sea, 1550–1650: Maritime Conflicts and the Transformation of Europe*. Warfare and History, gen. ed. Jeremy Black. London: Routledge, 2000.

Goçek, Fatma Müge. "The Social Construction of an Empire: Ottoman State Under Sülaymân the Magnificent." In *Sülaymân the Second and His Time*, ed. Halil Inalcık and Cemal Kafadar, 103–120. Istanbul: Isis Press, 1993.

Goffman, Daniel. *The Ottoman Empire and Early Modern Europe*. New Approaches to European History, gen. ed. William Beik and T. C. Blanning. Cambridge: Cambridge University Press, 2002.

Goldstone, Jack A. *Revolution and Rebellion in the Early Modern World*. Berkeley: University of California Press, 1991.

Gommans, Jos. *Mughal Warfare: Indian Frontiers and High Roads to Empire*. Warfare and History, gen. ed. Jeremy Black. London: Routledge, 2002.

Gommans, Jos. J. L., and Dirk H. A. Kolff. *Warfare and Weaponry in South Asia*. Oxford India Readings: Themes in Indian History, gen. ed. Muzaffar Alam et al. New Delhi: Oxford University Press, 2001.

Gordon, Stewart. *The Marathas, 1600–1818*. Vol. 2:4 of *The New Cambridge History of India*, gen. ed. Gordon Johnson. Cambridge: Cambridge University Press, 1998.

———. *When Asia Was the World*. Philadelphia: Da Capo Press, 2008.

Graham, Terry. "The Ni'matu'llāhī Order Under Safavid Suppression and in Indian Exile." In *Late Classical Persianate Sufism*, ed. Leonard Lewisohn and David Morgan, 165–200. Vol. 3 of *The Heritage of Sufism*. Oxford: Oneworld, 1999.

Gray, Basil. "The Arts in the Safavid Period." In *The Timurid and Safavid Periods*, ed. Peter Jackson and Laurence Lockhart, 877–912. Vol. 6 of *The Cambridge History of Iran*, gen. ed. Harold Bailey. Cambridge: Cambridge University Press, 1986.

Grewal, J. S. *Medieval India: History and Historians*. Amritsar, India: Guru Nanak University, 1975.

———. *Muslim Rule in India*. London: Oxford University Press, 1970.

———. *The Sikhs of the Punjab*. Vol. 2:3 of *The New Cambridge History of India*, gen. ed. Gordon Johnson. Rev. ed. Cambridge: Cambridge University Press, 1999.

Griswold, William J. *The Great Anatolian Rebellion, 1000–1020/1591–1611*. Islamkundliche Untersuchungen 83. Berlin: Klaus Schwarz Verlag, 1983.

Grousset, Rene. *The Empire of the Steppes: A History of Central Asia*, trans. Naomi Walford. New Brunswick, NJ: Rutgers University Press, 1970.

Guilmartin, John Francis, Jr. *Gunpowder and Galleys: Changing Technology and Mediterranean Warfare at Sea in the Sixteenth Century*. Rev. ed. London: Conway Maritime Press, 2003.

Habib, Irfan. ed. "Agrarian Relations and Land Revenue: North India." In *Circa 1200–1750*, ed. Tapan Raychaudhuri and Irfan Habib. Vol. 1 of *The Cambridge Economic History of India*, ed. Dharma Kumar and Tapan Raychaudhuri. Cambridge: Cambridge University Press, 1982.

———. *Akbar and His India*. New Delhi: Oxford University Press, 1997.

———. *An Atlas of the Mughal Empire*. New Delhi: Oxford University Press, 1982.

———. "Monetary System and Prices." In *Circa 1200–1750*, ed. Tapan Raychaudhuri and Irfan Habib, 360–381. Vol. 1 of *The Cambridge Economic History of India*, ed. Dharma Kumar and Tapan Raychaudhuri. Cambridge: Cambridge University Press, 1982.

———. "Population." In *Circa 1200–1750*, ed. Tapan Raychaudhuri and Irfan Habib. Vol. 1 of *The Cambridge Economic History of India*, ed. Dharma Kumar and Tapan Raychaudhuri. Cambridge: Cambridge University Press, 1982.

———. "Potentialities of Capitalistic Development in the Economy of Mughal India." *Journal of Economic History* 29 (1961): 32–78.

———. "Systems of Agricultural Production: Mughal India." In *Circa 1200–1750*, ed. Tapan Raychaudhuri and Irfan Habib. Vol. 1 of *The Cambridge Economic History of India*, ed. Dharma Kumar and Tapan Raychaudhuri. Cambridge: Cambridge University Press, 1982.

———. *The Agrarian System of Mughal India, 1556–1707*. 2nd ed. New Delhi: Oxford University Press, 1999.

Haig, Wolseley, Sir. "Sher Shah and the Sur Dynasty: The Return of Humayun." In *The Mughal Period*. Vol. 4 of *The Cambridge History of India*, ed. Lt. Col. Sir Wolseley Haig and Sir Richard Burn, 45–69. Cambridge: Cambridge University Press, 1937.

Haig, Wolseley, Lt. Col. Sir, and Sir Richard Burn, eds. *The Mughal Period*. Vol. 4 of *The Cambridge History of India*. Cambridge: Cambridge University Press, 1937.

Hajianpur, Mahin. "The Timuri Empire and the Uzbeg Conquest of Mawarannahr." In *Central Asia*, ed. Gavin Hambly, 150–162. New York: Dell Publishing, 1969.

Haldon, John. *Warfare, State, and Society in the Byzantine World, 565–1204*. Warfare and History, gen. ed. Jeremy Black. London: UCL Press, 1999.

Hall, Bert S. *Weapons and Warfare in Renaissance Europe: Gunpowder, Technology, Tactics*. Baltimore: Johns Hopkins University Press, 1997.

Hallaq, Wael. *A History of Islamic Legal Theories—an Introduction to Sunni Usul al Fiqh*. Cambridge: Cambridge University Press, 1997.

Hallissey, Robert C. *The Rajput Rebellion Against Aurangzib*. Columbia: University of Missouri Press, 1977.

Hambly, Gavin R. G. "Armed Women Retainers in the Zenanas of Indo-Muslim Rulers: The Case of Bībī Fāṭima." In *Women in the Medieval Islamic World*, ed. Gavin R. G. Hambly, 429–468. Vol. 6 of *The New Middle Ages*, gen. ed. Bonnie Wheeler. New York: St. Martin's Press, 1998.

———. "The Shaybanids." In *Central Asia*, ed. Gavin Hambly, 163–174. New York: Dell Publishing, 1969.

———. "Towns and Cities: Mughal India." In *Circa 1200–1750*, ed. Tapan Raychaudhuri and Irfan Habib. Vol. 1 of *The Cambridge Economic History of India*, ed. Dharma Kumar and Tapan Raychaudhuri. Cambridge: Cambridge University Press, 1982.

———, ed. *Women in the Medieval Islamic World*. Vol. 6 of *The New Middle Ages*, gen. ed. Bonnie Wheeler. New York: St. Martin's Press, 1998.

Haneda, Masashi. *Le chah et les Qizilbas: Le système militaire safavid*. Islamkundliche Untersuchungen 119. Berlin: Klaus Schwarz Verlag, 1987.

———. "The Evolution of the Safavid Royal Guard." *Iranian Studies* 22 (1989): 57–85.

Harrington, Joel F., and Helmut Walser Smith. "Confessionalization, Community, and State Building in Germany, 1555–1870." *Journal of Modern History* 69 (1997): 77–101.

Hasan, Farhat. *State and Locality in Mughal India: Power Relations in Western India, c. 1572–1730*. University of Cambridge Oriental Publications 61. Cambridge: Cambridge University Press, 2004.

Hasan, S. Nurul. *Religion, State and Society in Medieval India*, ed. Satish Chandra. Oxford India Paperbacks. New Delhi: Oxford University Press, 2005.

Hathaway, Jane. "Rewriting Eighteenth-Century Ottoman History." *Mediterranean Historical Review* 19 (2004): 29–53.

———. *The Arab Lands Under Ottoman Rule, 1516–1800*. Harlow, UK: Pearson Longman, 2008.

Hattox, Ralph S. *Coffee and Coffee Houses: The Origins of a Social Beverage in the Medieval Middle East*. Seattle: University of Washington Press, 1985.

Hazard, Harry W., ed. *The Fourteenth and Fifteenth Centuries*. Vol. 3 of *A History of the Crusades*, gen. ed. Kenneth M. Setton. Madison: University of Wisconsin, 1975.

Hazard, Harry W., and Norman P. Zacouer, eds. *The Impact of the Crusades on Europe*. Vol. 6 of *A History of the Crusades*, gen. ed. Kenneth M. Setton. Madison: University of Wisconsin Press, 1989.

Headley, John M., Hans J. Hillerbrand, and Anthony J. Papadas, eds. *Confessionalization in Europe, 1555–1700: Essays in Honor and Memory of Bodo Nischan*. Aldershot, UK: Ashgate, 2004.

Herrmann, Gottfried. *Persiche Urkunden der Mongolenzeit: Text-und Bildteil*. Documenta Iranica et Islamica 2, ed. Monika Gronke. Weisbaden, Germany: Harrassowitz, Verlag, 2004.

Hess, Andrew C. "Piri Reis and the Ottoman Response to the Voyages of Discovery." *Terrae Incognitae* 6 (1974): 19–37.

———. "The Evolution of the Ottoman Seaborne Empire." *American Historical Review* 75 (1970): 1892–1919.

———. *The Forgotten Frontier*. Publications of the Center for Middle Eastern Studies 10. Chicago: University of Chicago Press, 1978.

———. "The Moriscos: An Ottoman Fifth Column in Sixteenth-Century Spain." *American Historical Review* 74 (1968): 1–25.

Hexter, J. H. *Reappraisals in History: New Views on History and Society in Early Modern Europe*. With a foreword by Peter Laslett. Evanston: IL: Northwestern University Press, 1961. Multiple reprints.

Heyd, Uriel. "The Later Ottoman Empire in Rumelia and Anatolia." In *The Cambridge History of Islam*, ed. P. M. Holt, Bernard Lewis, and Ann K. S Lambton, 1: 354–73. (Cambridge: Cambridge University Press, 1970).

Heyd, W. *Histoire du commerce du Levant au Moyen-Age.* 2 vols. Leipzig, Germany: Otto Harrassowitz, 1885.

Hillenbrand, Robert. "Safavid Architecture." In *The Timurid and Safavid Periods*, ed. Peter Jackson and Laurence Lockhart, 759–843. Vol. 6 of *The Cambridge History of Iran*, gen. ed. Harold Bailey. Cambridge: Cambridge University Press, 1986.

Hinz, Walter. *Irans Aufstieg Nationalstaat im fünzehnetn Jahrhundert.* Berlin and Leipzig, Germany: Walter de Gruyter, 1936.

———. "Schah Esma`il: Ein Beitrag zur Geschichte der Safaviden." *Mitteilungen des Seminars fur Orientalische Sprachen* 36 (1933): 19–100.

Hocart, A. M. *Kings and Councillors: An Essay in the Comparative Anatomy of Human Society*, ed. Rodney Needham. Foreword by E. E. Evans-Pritchard. Classics in Anthropology, ed. Rodney Needham. Chicago: University of Chicago Press, 1970. Original publication, Cairo: Printing Office Paul Barbey, 1936.

———. *Kingship.* Oxford: Oxford University Press, 1927. Reprint, 1969.

Hodgson, Marshall G. S. *The Secret Order of the Assassins: The Struggle of the Early Nizari Isma`ilis Against the Islamic World.* The Hague: Mouton, 1955. Reprint, Philadelphia: University of Pennsylvania Press, 2005.

———. *The Venture of Islam: Conscience and History in a World Civilization.* 3 vols. Chicago: University of Chicago Press, 1974.

Holt, P. M. *Egypt and the Fertile Crescent, 1516–1922.* Ithaca, NY: Cornell University Press, 1966.

———. "The Later Ottoman Empire in Egypt and the Fertile Crescent." In *The Cambridge History of Islam*, ed. P. M. Holt, Bernard Lewis, and Ann K. S Lambton, 1:263–393. 2 vols. (Cambridge: Cambridge University Press, 1970).

Houseley, Norman. *The Later Crusades from Lyons to Alcazar, 1274–1580.* Oxford: Oxford University Press, 1992.

Husain, Afzal. *The Nobility Under Akbar and Jahangir: A Study of Family Groups.* New Delhi: Manohar, 1999.

Husain, Yusuf. *Indo-Muslim Polity: Turko-Afghan Period.* Simla, India: Indian Institute of Advanced Study, 1971.

Ibn Asad Davani, Jalal al-Din Muhammad. *Lavami al-Ishraq fi Makarim al-Akhlaq.* Lahore, Pakistan: Nawal Kishore, 1866–1867.

Ibn Hasan. *The Central Structure of the Mughal Empire.* London: Oxford University Press, 1936. Reprint, New Delhi: Munshiram Manoharlal, 1980.

Ikram, S. M. *Muslim Civilization in India*, ed. Ainslie T. Embree. New York: Columbia University Press, 1964.

Imber, Colin. *Ebu`s-Su`ud: The Islamic Legal Tradition.* Jurists: Profiles in Legal Theory, ed. William Twining and Neil MacCormick. Stanford, CA: Stanford University Press, 1997.

———. "Frozen Legitimacy." In *Legitimizing the Order: The Ottoman Rhetoric of State Power*, ed. Hasan Karateke and Maurus Reinkowski, 99–110. The Ottoman Empire and Its Heritage: Politics, Economy and Society, gen. ed. Suraiya Faroqhi and Halil Inalcık. Leiden, Netherlands: E. J. Brill, 2005.

———. "Ideals and Legitimation in Early Ottoman History." In *Sülaymân the Magnificent and His Age: The Ottoman Empire in the Early Modern World*, ed. Metin Kunt and Christine Woodhead, 149–150. New York: Longman, 1995.

———. "Ottoman Dynastic Myth." *Turcica* 19 (1987): 16–20.

———. Review of *History of the Ottoman Empire and Modern Turkey*, by Stanford J. Shaw and Ezel Kural Shaw. *English Historical Review* 93 (1978): 393–395.

———. *The Crusade of Varna, 1443–1445*. Crusader Texts in Translation 14, ed. Malcom Barber et al. Aldershot, UK: Ashgate, 2006.

———. "The Legend of Osman Ghazi." In *The Ottoman Emirate*, ed. Elizabeth Zachariadou, 67–76. Rethymnon, Greece: Crete University Press, 1993.

———. "The Navy of Sulayman the Magnificent." *Archivum Ottomanicum* 6 (1980): 211–282.

———. *The Ottoman Empire: 1300–1650: The Structure of Power*. New York: Palgrave Macmillan, 2002.

———. "The Persecution of Ottoman Shi`ites According to the *Muhimme Defterleri*, 1565–1585." *Der Islam* 56 (1979): 245–273.

———. "Süleymân As Caliph of the Muslims: Ebû`s-Su`ud's Formulation of Ottoman Dynastic Ideology." In *Sülaymân the Magnificent and His Time*, ed. Gilles Veinstein, 179–184. Paris: La Documentation Française, 1992.

Inalcık, Halil. "Capital Formation in the Ottoman Empire." *Journal of Economic History* 29 (1969): 97–140.

———. "Centralization and Decentralization in Ottoman Administration." In *Studies in Eighteenth-Century Islamic History*, ed. Thomas Naff and Roger Owen, 27–52. Papers on Islamic History 4 (Carbondale: Southern Illinois University Press, 1977).

———. *Fâthi Devri Üzerinde Tetkikler ve Vesikalar*. Ankara: Türk Tarih Kurumu, 1954.

———. "Land Problems in Turkish History." *The Muslim World* 45 (1958): 221–224.

———. "Mehmed the Conqueror (1432–1481) and His Time." *Speculum* 35 (1960): 408–427.

———. "Military and Fiscal Transformation in the Ottoman Empire." *Archivum Ottomanicum* 6 (1980): 283–337. Reprinted in *Studies in the Social and Economic History of the Ottoman Empire*. London: Variorum, 1985.

———. "Ottoman Decline and Its Effects upon the Reaya." In *Aspects of the Balkans: Continuity and Change*, ed. Henrik Birnbaum and Speros Vryonis, 338–354. The Hague: Mouton, 1972. Reprint, Halil Inalcık. *The Ottoman Empire: Conquest, Organization and Economy*. London: Variorum, 1978.

———. "Ottoman Methods of Conquest." *Studia Islamica* 2 (1954): 103–129.

———. "Rice Cultivation and Celtukcireaya System in the Ottoman Empire." *Turcica* 14 (1982): 77.

———. "State and Ideology under Sultan Süleyman." In *The Middle East and the Balkans Under the Ottoman Empire: Essays on Economy and Society*, ed. İlhan Başgöz, 70–96. Indiana University Turkish Studies and Turkish Ministry of Culture 9. Bloomington: Indiana University Turkish Studies, 1993.

———. "State, Sovereignty and Law During the Reign of Sülaymân." In *Sülaymân the Second and His Time*, ed. Halil Inalcık and Cemal Kafadar, 69–102. Istanbul: Isis Press, 1993.

———. *Studies in Ottoman Social and Economic History*. London: Variorum, 1985.

———. "Sulayman the Lawgiver and Ottoman Law." *Archivum Ottomanicum* 1 (1969): 105–138.

———. "The Emergence of the Ottomans." In *The Cambridge History of Islam*, ed. P. M. Holt, A. K. S. Lambton, and Bernard Lewis, 1:263–294. 2 vols. Cambridge: Cambridge University Press.

———. "The Heyday and Decline of the Ottoman Empire." In *The Cambridge History of Islam*, ed. P. M. Holt, A. K. S. Lambton, and Bernard Lewis, 1:324–353. 2 vols. Cambridge: Cambridge University Press.

———. "The Hub of the City: The Bedestan of Istanbul." *International Journal of Turkish Studies* 1 (1980): 1–17.

———. "The Impact of the Annales School on Ottoman Studies and New Findings." *Review* 1 (1978): 90–96. Reprinted in *Studies in Ottoman Social and Economic History*. London: Variorum, 1985.

———. *The Middle East and the Balkans Under the Ottoman Empire: Essays on Economy and Society.* Indiana University Turkish Studies and Turkish Ministry of Culture Joint Series 9, gen. ed. İlhan Başgöz. Bloomington: Indiana University Turkish Studies, 1993.

———. "The Ottoman Economic Mind and Aspects of the Ottoman Economy." In *Studies in the Economic History of the Middle East from the Rise of Islam to the Present Day*, ed. M. A. Cook, 207–218. London: Oxford University Press, 1970.

———. *The Ottoman Empire: Conquest, Organization and Economy.* London: Variorum, 1978.

———. *The Ottoman Empire: The Classical Age, 1300–1660*, trans. Norman Itzkowitz and Colin Imber. London: Weidenfeld and Nicholson, 1973.

———. "The Ottoman State: Economy and Society, 1300–1600." In *An Economic and Social History of the Ottoman Empire*, ed. Halil Inalcık and Donald Quataert, 9–379. Cambridge: Cambridge University Press, 1994.

———. "The Ottoman Succession and Its Relation to the Turkish Concept of Sovereignty." In *The Middle East and the Balkans Under the Ottoman Empire: Essays on Economy and Society*, 37–69. Indiana University Turkish Studies and Turkish Ministry of Culture Joint Series 9, gen. ed. İlhan Başgöz. Bloomington: Indiana University of Turkish Studies, 1993.

———. "The Ottoman Turks and the Crusades, 1329–1451." In *The Impact of the Crusades on Europe*, ed. Harry W. Hazard and Norman P. Zacour, 222–275. Vol. 6 of *A History of the Crusades*, gen. ed. Kenneth M. Setton. Madison: University of Wisconsin Press, 1989.

———. "The Ottoman Turks and the Crusades, 1451–1522." In *The Impact of the Crusades on Europe*, ed. Harry W. Hazard and Norman P. Zacour, 311–353. Vol. 6 of *A History of the Crusades*, gen. ed. Kenneth M. Setton. Madison: University of Wisconsin Press, 1989.

———. "The Problem of the Relationship Between Byzantine and Ottoman Taxation." Aktendes 40 Internationalen-Kongresses 1958, Munich, 237–242. 1960. Reprint, Halil Inalcık, *The Ottoman Empire: Conquest, Organization and Economy* (London: Variorum, 1978), 237–242.

———. "The Question of the Emergence of the Ottoman State." *International Journal of Turkish Studies* 2 (1980): 71–79. Reprinted in *Studies in Ottoman Social and Economic History*. London: Variorum, 1985.

———. "The Rise of Ottoman Historiography." In *Historians of the Middle East*, ed. Bernard Lewis and Peter M. Holt, 152–168. London: Oxford University Press, 1962.

———. "The Rise of the Ottoman Empire," In *The Cambridge History of Islam*, ed. P. M. Holt, A. K. S. Lambton, and Bernard Lewis, 1:295–323. 2 vols. Cambridge: Cambridge University Press.

———. "The Rise of the Turcoman Maritime Principalities in Anatolia, Byzantium, and the Crusades." *Byzantinische Forschungen* 9 (1985): 179–217. Reprinted in *The Middle East and the Balkans Under the Ottoman Empire: Essays on Economy and Society*, 309–341. Indiana University Turkish Studies and Turkish Ministry of Culture Joint Series 9, gen. ed. İlhan Başgöz. Bloomington: Indiana University of Turkish Studies, 1993.

———. "The Socio-Political Effects of the Diffusion of Fire-Arms in the Middle East." In *War, Technology, and Society in the Middle East*, ed. V. J. Parry and M. E. Yapp, 195–217. London: Oxford University Press, 1975.

————. "Timariotes chretiens en Albanie au XV siècle." *Mitteilungen des Osterreiches Staat-sarchivs* 4 (1951): 118–138.

Inalcık, Halil, and Donald Quataert, eds. *An Economic and Social History of the Ottoman Empire.* Cambridge: Cambridge University Press, 1994.

Inan, Afet. *The Oldest Map of America, Drawn by Piri Reis*, trans. Leman Yolac. Ankara: Türk Tarih Kurumu Basimevi, 1954.

Inden, Ronald. *Imagining India.* Cambridge, MA: Basil Blackwell, 1990.

————. "Ritual, Authority and Cyclic Time in Hindu Kingship." In *Kingship and Authority in South Asia*, ed. J. F. Richards, 28–73. South Asian Studies 3. Madison: University of Wisconsin, Madison, South Asian Studies, 1978.

Irvine, William. *Later Mughals*, ed. Jadunath Sarkar. 2 vols. Calcutta: M. C. Sarkar, 1921–1922. Reprint, 2 vols. as 1, with *The History of Nadir Shah's Invasion*, by Jandunath Sarkar. New Delhi: Munshiram Manoharlal, 1996.

————. *The Army of the Indian Moghuls.* London: Luzac, 1903. Reprint, Delhi: Asia, 1962.

Islam, Riazul. *Indo-Persian Relations: A Study of the Political and Diplomatic Relations Between the Mughal Empire and Iran.* Studies of the History and Geography of Iran 32. Tehran: Iranian Culture Foundation, 1970.

İslamoğlu-İnan, Huri. *The Ottoman Empire and the World-Economy.* Studies in Modern Capitalism. Cambridge: Cambridge University Press, 1987.

Jackson, Peter. *The Delhi Sultanate: A Political and Military History.* Cambridge Studies in Islamic Civilization, gen. ed. David Morgan. Cambridge: Cambridge University Press, 1999.

Jennings, R. C. "Firearms, Bandits, and Gun Control." *Archivum Ottomanicum* 6 (1980): 339–358.

Johnson, Douglas L. *The Nature of Nomadism.* University of Chicago Department of Geography Research Papers 118. Chicago: University of Chicago, Department of Geography, 1969.

Johnson, Rosemary Stanfield. "Sunni Survival in Safavid Iran: Anti-Sunni Activities During the Reign of Tahmasp I." *Iranian Studies* 27 (1994): 123–133.

Kafadar, Cemal. *Between Two Worlds: The Construction of the Ottoman State.* Berkeley: University of California Press, 1995.

Kafesoglu, Ibrahim. *A History of the Seljuks: Ibrahim Kafesoglu's Interpretation and the Resulting Controversy*, ed. and trans. Gary Leiser. Carbondale: Southern Illinois University Press, 1988.

Kaiser, David. *Politics and War: European Conflict from Philip II to Hitler.* Cambridge, MA: Harvard University Press, 1990.

Kaplan, Robert D. *Balkan Ghosts: A Journey Through History.* New York: St. Martin's, 1993.

Karateke, Hakan. "Legitimizing the Ottoman Sultanate." In *Legitimizing the Order: The Ottoman Rhetoric of State Power*, ed. Hasan Karateke and Maurus Reinkowski, 13–54. The Ottoman Empire and Its Heritage: Politics, Society, Economy, gen. ed. Suraiya Faroqhi and Halil Inalcık. Leiden, Netherlands: E. J. Brill, 2005.

————. "Opium for the Subjects? Religiosity As Legitimizing Factor for the Ottoman Sultan." In *Legitimizing the Order: The Ottoman Rhetoric of State Power*, ed. Hasan Karateke and Maurus Reinkowski, 111–130. The Ottoman Empire and Its Heritage: Politics, Society, Economy, gen. ed. Suraiya Faroqhi and Halil Inalcık. Leiden, Netherlands: E. J. Brill, 2005.

Kasravi, Sayyid Ahmad. *Shaykh Safi va Tabarash.* Tehran: Payman, 1944.

Kelly, Majorie, ed. *Islam: The Religious and Political Life of a World Community.* New York: Praeger, 1984.

Kennedy, Hugh. *The Armies of the Caliphs: Military and Society in the Early Islamic State.* Warfare and History, ed. Jeremy Black. London: Routledge, 2001.

———. *The Prophet and the Age of the Caliphates: The Islamic Near East from the Sixth to the Eleventh Century.* A History of the Middle East, ed. P. M. Holt. London: Longman, 1986.

———. *When Baghdad Rules the Muslim World: The Rise and Fall of Islam's Greatest Dynasty.* Cambridge, MA: Da Capo Press, 2004.

Khan, Iqtidar Alam. "Akbar's Personality Traits and World Outlook—a Critical Appraisal." In *Akbar and His India*, ed. Irfan Habib, 79–96. New Delhi: Oxford University Press, 1997.

———. *Gunpowder and Firearms: Warfare in Medieval India.* Aligarh Historian Society Series, ed. Irfan Habib. New Delhi: Oxford University Press, 2004.

———. *Mirza Kamran.* New York: Asia, 1964.

———. "Mughal Court Politics During Bairam Khan's Regency." *Medieval India: A Miscellany* 1 (1969): 21–38.

———. *The Political Biography of a Mughal Noble: Mun'im Khan Khan-i Khanan, 1497–1575.* New Delhi: Orient Longman, 1973.

Khazanov, Anatoly M. *Nomads and the Outside World*, trans. Julia Crookenden. 2nd ed. Madison: University of Wisconsin Press, 1994.

Khoury, Dina Rizk. *State and Provincial Society in the Ottoman Empire: Mosul, 1540–1834.* Cambridge Studies in Islamic Civilization, gen. ed. David Morgan. Cambridge: Cambridge University Press, 1997.

Kissling, Hans-Joachim. "Şah Ismail Ier, la nouvelle route des Indes, et les Ottomans." *Turcica* 6 (1975): 89–102.

Klausner, Carla L. "The Seljuk Vizierate: A Study of Civil Administration." Harvard Middle East Monographs. Cambridge, MA: Harvard University Press, 1973.

Klein, Rudiger. "Caravan Trade in Safavid Iran." In *Études safavides*, ed. Jean Calmard, 305–318. Paris: Institut Français de Recherche en Iran, 1993.

Knysh, Alexander. *Islamic Mysticism: A Short History.* Themes in Islamic Studies 1. Leiden: Brill 2000.

Koch, Ebba. *Mughal Architecture: An Outline of Its History and Development, 1526–1858.* Munich: Prestel, 2001.

———. *Mughal Art and Imperial Ideology: Collected Essays.* New Delhi: Oxford University Press, 2001.

———. *The Complete Taj Mahal and the Riverfront Gardens of Agra.* London: Thames & Hudson, 2006.

Kolff, Dirk H. A. *Naukar, Rajput and Sepoy: The Military Labor Market in Hindustan, 1450–1850.* Cambridge: Cambridge University Press, 1990.

Köprülü, M. Fuad. *The Origins of the Ottoman Empire*, ed. and trans. Gary Leiser. Albany: State University of New York Press, 1992. Original publication, in French in 1935.

Kortpeter, C. Max. *Ottoman Imperialism During the Reformation: Europe and the Caucasus.* New York University Studies in Near Eastern Civilization 5. New York: New York University Press, 1972.

Kozlowski, Gregory C. "Private Lives and Public Piety: Women and the Practice of Islam in Mughal India." In *Women in the Medieval Islamic World*, ed. Gavin R. G. Hambly, 469–488. Vol. 6 of *The New Middle Ages*, gen. ed. Bonnie Wheeler. New York: St. Martin's Press, 1998.

Kroell, Anne. "Bandar `Abbas à la fin du regne des Safavides." In *Études safavides*, ed. Jean Calmard, 319–340. Paris: Institut Français de Recherche en Iran, 1993.

Kulke, Hermann, ed. *The State in India, 1000–1700.* Oxford in India Readings: Themes in Indian History, gen. ed. Basudev Chatterji, Neeladri Bhattacharya, and C. A. Bayly. New Delhi: Oxford University Press, 1995.

Kumar, Raj, ed. *Military System of the Mughals.* New Delhi: Commonwealth Publishers, 2004.

Kunt, I. Metin. "The Later Muslim Empires: Ottomans, Safavids, Mughals." In *Islam: The Religious and Political Life of a World Community,* ed. Marjorie Kelly, 113–136. New York: Praeger, 1984.

———. *The Sultan's Servants: The Transformation of Ottoman Provincial Government, 1550–1650.* The Modern Middle East Series 14. New York: Columbia University Press, 1983.

Kurat, A. N. "The Reign of Mehmed IV, 1648–1687." In *A History of the Ottoman Empire to 1730: Chapters from the Cambridge History of Islam and the New Cambridge Modern History,* ed. M. A. Cook, 157–177. Cambridge: Cambridge University Press, 1976.

Kurat, A. N., and J. S. Bromley, "The Retreat of the Turks, 1683–1730." In *A History of the Ottoman Empire to 1730: Chapters from the Cambridge History of Islam and the New Cambridge Modern History,* ed. M. A. Cook, 178–220. Cambridge: Cambridge University Press, 1976.

Labib, Subhi. "The Era of Suleyman the Magnificent: Crisis of Orientation." *International Journal of Middle East Studies* 10 (1979): 435–451.

Laine, James W. *Shivaji: Hindu King in Islamic India.* Oxford: Oxford University Press, 2003.

Lal, K. S. "Timur's Visitation of Delhi." *Proceedings of the Indian Historical Congress* 20 (1958): 197–203.

Lal, Ruby. *Domesticity and Power in the Early Mughal World.* Cambridge Studies in Islamic Civilization, gen. ed. David Morgan. Cambridge: Cambridge University Press, 2005.

Lambton, A. K. S. "Internal Structure of the Saljuq Empire." In Vol. 5 of *The Cambridge History of Iran,* gen. ed. Harold Bailey. *The Saljuq and Mongol Periods,* ed. J. A. Boyle, 203–282. Cambridge: Cambridge University Press, 1968.

———. "Islamic Political Thought." In *The Legacy of Islam.* 2nd ed., ed. Joseph Schacht with C. E. Bosworth, 404–424. Oxford: Oxford University Press, 1974.

———. *Landlord and Peasant in Persia.* Oxford: Oxford University Press, 1953.

———. "Quis Custodiet Custodes: Some Reflections on the Persian Theory of Government." *Studia Islamica* 5 (1956): 125–148, and 6 (1956): 125–146.

———. "Reflections on the Iqta`." In *Arabic and Islamic Studies in Honor of Hamilton A.R. Gibb,* ed. George Makdisi, 358–376. Leiden: E. J. Brill, 1965.

———. "Tribal Resurgence and the Decline of Bureaucracy in Eighteenth-Century Persia." In *Studies of Eighteenth Century Islamic History,* gen. ed. Thomass Naff and Roger Owen, 108–132. Carbondale: Southern Illinois University Press, 1977.

Lane, Frederick C. *Venice: A Maritime Republic.* Baltimore: Johns Hopkins University Press, 1973.

Lang, D. M. "Georgia and the Fall of the Safavi Dynasty." *Bulletin of the School of Oriental and African Studies* 14 (1952): 523–532.

Lattimore, Owen. *The Inner Asian Frontiers of China.* New York: American Geographical Society, 1940.

Lemercier-Quelquejay, Chantal. "The Kazakhs and the Kirghiz." In *Central Asia,* ed. Gavin Hambly, 140–149. Weidenfeld and Nicholson Universal History. London: Weidenfeld and Nicholson, 1969.

Leonard, Karen. "The 'Great Firm' Theory of the Decline of the Mughal Empire." *Comparative Studies in Society and History* 21 (1979): 151–167. Reprinted in *The Mughal State,* eds. Muzaffar Alam and Sanjay Subrahmanyam, 398–420. Oxford in India Readings: Themes in Indian History. New Delhi: Oxford University Press, 2001.

Lewis, Bernard. *Cultures in Conflict: Christians, Muslims, and Jews in the Age of Discovery.* New York: Oxford University Press, 1995.

———. *Istanbul and the Civilization of the Ottoman Empire.* The Centers of Civilization Series 9. Norman: University of Oklahoma, 1963.

———. "Ottoman Observers of Ottoman Decline." *Islamic Studies* 1 (1962): 71–87. Reprinted in *Islam and Histor,* 209–222. New York: Library Press, 1973.

———. *The Jews of Islam.* Princeton, NJ: Princeton University Press, 1984.

———. "The Significance of Heresy in Islam." *Studia Islamica* 1 (1953): 43–63. Reprinted in *Islam and History: Ideas, Men, and Events in the Middle East.* 2nd ed. exp. Chicago: Open Court, 2001, 217–236.

Lewisohn, Leonard. "Sufism and the School of Isfahan." In *Late Classical Persianate Sufism,* ed. Leonard Lewisohn and David Morgan, 63–134. Vol. 3 of *The Heritage of Sufism.* Oneworld, 1999.

Lewisohn, Leonard, and David Morgan, eds. *Late Classical Persianate Sufism.* Vol. 3 of *The Heritage of Sufism.* Oxford: Oneworld, 1999.

Lindner, Rudi Paul. *Nomads and Ottomans in Medieval Anatolia.* Bloomington: Indiana University Press, 1983.

Lockhart, Laurence. *The Fall of the Safavi Dynasty and the Afghan Occupation of Persia.* Cambridge: Cambridge University Press, 1958.

———. "The Persian Army in the Safavid Period." *Der Islam* 34 (1959): 89–98.

Lowry, Heath W. *The Nature of the Early Ottoman State.* Albany: State University of New York Press, 2003.

Madelung, Wilferd. "The Assumption of the Title Shahanshah by the Buyids." *Journal of Near Eastern Studies* 28 (1969): 84–105, 168–183.

———. *The Succession to Muhammad: A Study of the Early Caliphate.* Cambridge: Cambridge University Press, 1997.

Manz, Beatrice Forbes. "Family and Ruler in Timurid Historiography." In *Studies on Central Asian History in Honor of Yuri Bregel,* ed. Devin DeWeese, 57–78. Indiana University Uralic and Altaic Series 167, ed. Denis Sinor. Bloomington: Indiana University Research Institute for Inner Asian Studies, 2001.

———. *Power, Politics and Religion in Timurid Iran.* Cambridge Studies in Islamic Civilization, gen. ed. David Morgan. Cambridge: Cambridge University Press, 2007.

———. "Tamerlane and the Symbolism of Sovereignty." *Iranian Studies* 28 (1988): 105–122.

———. "The Development and Meaning of Chaghatay Identity." In *Muslims in Central Asia,* ed. Jo-Ann Gross, 27–45. Durham, NC: Duke University Press, 1992.

———. *The Rise and Rule of Tamerlane.* Cambridge Studies in Islamic Civilization. Cambridge: Cambridge University Press, 1989.

Marek, Jan. "Persian Literature in India." In Jan Rypka et al., *History of Iranian Literature,* ed. Karl Jahn, 711–734. Dordrecht, Netherlands: D. Reidel, 1968.

Markovits, Claude, ed. *A History of Modern India, 1480–1950,* trans. Nisha George and Maggy Hendry. London: Anthem Press, 1994.

Mason, Colin. *A Short History of Asia.* New York: Palgrave, 2000.

Matthee, Rudi. "Administrative Stability and Change in Late Seventeenth-Century Iran: The Case of Shaykh ʿAli Khan Zanganah, 1669–1689." *International Journal of Middle East Studies* 26 (1994): 77–98.

———. "Between Aloofness and Fascination: Safavid Views of the West." *Iranian Studies* 31 (1998): 219–246.

———. "Coffee in Safavid Iran: Commerce and Consumption." *Journal of the Economic and Social History of the Orient* 37 (1994): 1–32.

———. "Introduction to 'Historiography and Representation in Safavid and Afsharid Iran.'" *Iranian Studies* 31 (1998): 143–147.

———. "Mint Consolidation and the Worsening of the Late Safavid Coinage: The Mint of Huwayza." *Journal of the Economic and Social History of the Orient* 44 (2001): 505–539.

———. "The Career of Mohammad Beg, Grand Vizier of Shah 'Abbas II (r. 1642–1666)." *Iranian Studies* 24 (1991): 17–36.

———. "The East India Company Trade in Kerman Wool." In *Études safavides*, ed. Jean Calmard, 343–360. Paris: Institut Français de Recherche en Iran, 1993.

———. *The Pursuit of Pleasure: Drugs and Stimulants in Iranian History, 1500–1900*. Princeton, NJ: Princeton University Press, 2005.

———. "The Safavid Mint of Huwayza. In *Society and Culture in the Early Modern Middle East: Studies on Iran in the Safavid Period*, ed. Andrew J. Newman, 265–294. Leiden: E. J. Brill, 1998.

———. "Unwalled Cities and Restless Nomads: Firearms and Artillery in Safavi Iran." In *Safavid Persia: The History and Politics of an Islamic Society*, ed. Charles Melville, 389–416. London: I. B. Tauris, 1993.

Matthee, Rudolph P. *The Politics of Trade in Safavid Iran: Silk for Silver, 1600–1730*. Cambridge Studies in Islamic Civilization, gen. ed. David O. Morgan. Cambridge: Cambridge University Press, 1999.

May, Timothy. *The Mongol Art of War: Chinggis Khan and the Mongol Military System*. Yardley, PA: Westholme, 2007.

Mazzaoui, Michel M., ed. *Safavid Iran and Her Neighbors*. Salt Lake City: University of Utah Press, 2003.

———, ed. *The Origins of the Safavids: Šiʿism, Sufism and the Gulat*. Freiberger Islamstudien 3. Weisbaden, Germany: Franz Steiner Verlag, 1972.

McCarthy, Justin. *The Ottoman Turks: An Introductory History to 1923*. London: Longman, 1997.

McChesney, R. D. "A Note on Iskandar Beg's Chronology." *Journal of Near Eastern Studies* 39 (1980): 53–63.

———. "'Barrier of Heterodoxy'? Rethinking the Ties Between Iran and Central Asia in the Seventeenth Century." In *Safavid Persia*, ed. Charles Melville, 232–269. Pembroke Persian Papers 4, ed. Charles Melville. London: I. B. Tauris, 1996.

———. "Comments on 'The Qajar Uymaq in the Safavid Period, 1500–1722.'" *Iranian Studies* 14 (1981): 87–105.

———. "The Central Asian Hajj-Pilgrimage in the Time of the Early Modern Empires." In *Safavid Iran and Her Neighbors*, ed. Michel Mazzaoui, 129–156. Salt Lake City: University of Utah Press, 2003.

———. "The Conquest of Herat, 995–6/1587/8: Sources for the Study of Safavid/Qizilbash Shibanid Relations." In *Études safavides*, ed. Jean Calmard, 69–108. Paris: Institut Français de Recherche en Iran, 1993.

———. *Waqf in Central Asia*. Princeton, NJ: Princeton University Press, 1991.

McGowan, Bruce. "The Age of the Ayans, 1699–1812." In *An Economic and Social History of the Ottoman Empire*, ed. Halil Inalcık and Donald Quataert, 637–758. Cambridge: Cambridge University Press, 1994.

McNeill, J. R., and William H. McNeill. *The Human Web: A Bird's-eye View of World History*. New York: Norton, 2003.

McNeill, William H. *Age of Gunpowder Empires, 1450–1800.* Essays on Global and Comparative History. American Historical Association, 1990.

———. *Europe's Steppe Frontier, 1500–1800.* Chicago, University of Chicago Press, 1964.

———. *The Pursuit of Power.* Chicago: University of Chicago Press, 1982.

———. *The Rise of the West: A History of the Human Community, with a Retrospective Essay.* Chicago: University of Chicago Press, 1991.

Melikoff, Irene. "L'Islam heterodoxe en Anatolie." *Turcica* 14 (1982): 142–154.

———. "Le probleme kizilbaş." *Turcica* 6 (1975): 65–67.

———. "Les origines centre asiatiques du Soufism anatolien." *Turcica* 20 (1988): 7–19.

Melville, Charles. "New Light on the Reign of Shah ʿAbbās: Volume III of the *Afḍal al-Tavārīkh*." In *Society and Culture in the Early Modern Middle East: Studies on Iran in the Safavid Period,* ed. Andrew J. Newman, 63–96. Leiden: E. J. Brill, 1998.

———, ed. *Safavid Persia: The History and Politics of an Islamic Society.* London: I. B. Tauris, 1993.

———. "Shah ʿAbbas and the Pilgrimage to Mashhad." In *Safavid Persia: The History and Politics of an Islamic Society,* ed. Charles Melville, 191–229. London: I. B. Tauris, 1993.

Ménage, Victor L. Review of *Empire of the Ghazis: The Rise and Decline of the Ottoman Empire.* Vol. 1 of *History of the Ottoman Empire and Modern Turkey,* by Stanford J. Shaw. *Bulletin of the School of Oriental and African Studies* 41, no. 1 (1978): 160–162.

———. "The Beginnings of Ottoman Historiography." In *Historians of the Middle East,* ed. Bernard Lewis and Peter M. Holt, 168–179. London: Oxford University Press, 1962.

Meskoob, Shahrokh. *Iranian Nationality and the Persian Language,* ed. John R. Perry, trans. Michael C. Hillman. Washington, DC: Mage Publishers, 1992.

Michell, George. *The Majesty of Mughal Decoration: The Art and Architecture of Islamic India.* London: Thames & Hudson, 2007.

Minorsky, Vladimir. Introduction and appendixes to *The Tadhkirat al-Muluk: A Manual of Safavid Administration,* ed. and trans. Vladimir Minorsky. Gibb Memorial Series, n.s. 14. London: E. J. W. Gibb Memorial Trust, 1943. Reprint, Cambridge: E. J. W. Gibb Memorial Trust, 1980.

———. "The Poetry of Shah Ismaʿil." *Bulletin of the School of Oriental and African Studies* 10 (1942): 1006–1053.

Misra, Neeru. *Succession and Imperial Leadership Among the Mughals, 1526–1707.* Delhi: Konark Publishers, 1992.

Mitchell, Colin P. "Provincial Chancelleries and Local Lines of Authority in 16th-Century Safavid Iran." *Oriente Moderno* 88 (2008): 483–507.

———. *Sir Thomas Roe and the Mughal Empire.* Karachi, Pakistan: Area Study Centre for Europe, 2000.

Momen, Moojan. *An Introduction to Shiʿi Islam.* New Haven, CT: Yale University Press, 1985.

Monshi, Eskandar Beg. *History of Shah ʿAbbas the Great,* trans. Roger M. Savory. Persian Heritage Series 28. Boulder, CO: Westview Press, 1978.

Moosa, Matti. *Extremist Shiites: The Ghulat Sects.* Syracuse, NY: Syracuse University Press, 1988.

Moosvi, Shireen. "Evolution of the Mansab System Under Akbar." *Journal of the Royal Asiatic Society* (1978): 171–183.

Moreen, Vera Basch. *Iranian Jewry's Hour of Peril and Heroism: A Study of Babai Ibn Lutf's Chronicle, 1617–1622.* New York: Columbia University Press, 1987.

———. "The Persecution of Iranian Jews During the Reign of Shah ʿAbbas II, 1642–1666." *Hebrew Union College Annual* 52 (1981): 275–309.

Morgan, David. "Re-thinking Safavid Shi`ism." In *Late Classical Persianate Sufism, 1500–1730*, ed. Leonard Lewisohn and David Morgan, 19–27. Vol. 3 of *The Heritage of Sufism*. Oxford: Oneword, 1999.

———. *The Mongols*. The Peoples of Europe, ed. James Campbell and Barry Cunliffe, 2nd ed. Oxford: Blackwell, 2007.

Morony, Michael G. *Iraq After the Muslim Conquest*. 2nd ed. Piscataway, NJ: Gorgias Press, 2005.

Morton, Alexander H. "The Chub-i Tariq and Qizilbash Ritual in Safavid Persia." In *Études safavides*, ed. Jean Calmard, 225–245. Paris: L'Institut Français de Recherche en Iran, 1993.

———. "The Early Years of Shah Isma`il in the *Afzal al-Tavarikh*." In *Safavid Persia: The History and Politics of an Islamic Society*, ed. Charles Melville, 27–52. London: I. B. Tauris, 1996.

Mukhia, Harbans. *The Mughals of India*. The Peoples of Asia, gen. ed. Morris Rossabi. Oxford: Blackwell, 2004.

Murphey, Rhoads. *Ottoman Warfare, 1500–1700*. New Brunswick, NJ: Rutgers University Press, 1999.

———. "The Ottoman Attitude Toward Western Technology: The Role of Efrenci Technicians in Civil and Military Applications." In *Contributions a l'histoire economique et sociale de l'Empire Ottoman*, ed. Jean-Louis Bacque-Grammont and Paul Dumont, 287–294. Leuven, Belgium: Edition Peters, 1983.

Mushtaqui [*sic*], Shaikh Rizq Ullah. *Waqi`at-e-Mushtaqui*, ed. and trans. Iqitdar Hussain Siddiqui. New Delhi: Indian Council of Historical Research, 1993.

Naff, Thomas, and Roger Owen, eds. *Studies in Eighteenth-Century Islamic History*. Papers on Islamic History 4. Carbondale: Southern Illinois University Press, 1977.

Namier, Lewis Bernstein, Sir. *The Structure of Politics at the Accession of George III*. 2nd ed. London, Macmillan, 1957.

Naqvi, H. K. *Urbanization and Urban Centres Under the Great Mughals*. Simla, India: Indian Institute of Advanced Study, 1971.

Nasiri, Mirza Naqi. *Titles and Emoluments in Safavid Iran: A Third Manual of Safavid Administration*, trans. Willem Floor. Washington, DC: Mage Publishers, 2008.

Nasr, Seyyed Hosain. "Spiritual Movements, Philosophy and Theology in the Safavid Period." In *The Timurid and Safavid Period*, ed. Peter Jackson and Laurence Lockhart, 656–697. Vol. 6 of *The Cambridge History of Iran*, gen. ed. Harold Bailey, 656–697. Cambridge: Cambridge University Press, 1986.

———. "The Place of the School of Isfahan in Islamic Philosophy and Sufism." In *Late Classical Persianate Sufism, 1500–1730*, ed. Leonard Lewisohn and David Morgan, 3–18. Vol. 3 of *The Heritage of Sufism*. Oxford: Oneword, 1999.

———. *Three Muslim Sages: Avicenna-Suhrawardi-Ibn `Arabi*. Delmar, NY: Caravan Books, 1976.

Necipoğlu, Gülrû. "Sülaymân the Magnificent and the Representation of Power in the Context of Ottoman-Hapsburg-Papal Rivalry." In *Sülaymân the Second and His Time*, ed. by Halil Inalcık and Cemal Kafadar, 175–224. Istanbul: Isis Press, 1993.

Newman, Andrew J. *Safavid Iran: Rebirth of a Persian Empire*. London: I. B. Tauris, 2006.

———, ed. *Society and Culture in the Early Modern Period: Studies on Iran in the Safavid Period*. Islamic History and Civilization 46, ed. Wadad Kadi and Rotraud Wielandt. Leiden, Netherlands: E. J. Brill, 2003.

———. "The Myth of Clerical Migration to Safavid Iran." *Die Welt des Islams* 33 (1993): 66–112.

Nizam al-Mulk. *The Book of Government or Rules for Kings*, trans. Hubert Darke. 2nd ed. Persian Heritage Series 32. London: Routledge & Kegan Paul, 1978.

Nizami, Khaliq Ahmad. *Akbar and Religion*. New Delhi: Idarah-i Adabiyyat Delli, 1989.

————. "Naqshbandi Influence on Mughal Rulers and Politics." *Islamic Culture* 39 (1965): 46–47.

————. *On History and Historians of Medieval India.* New Delhi: Munshiram Manoharlal, 1983.

Nurbakhsh, Javad. "Forward: The Evolution of Sufism." *Late Classical Persianate Sufism,* ed. Leonard Lewisohn and David Morgan, xxv–xxviii. Vol. 3 of *The Heritage of Sufism.* Oxford: Oneworld, 1999.

Oman, Charles, Sir. *A History of the Art of War in the Middle Ages.* 2 vols. London: Methuen, 1924. Reprint, London: Greenhill, 1991.

————. *A History of the Art of War in the Sixteenth Century.* New York: E. P. Dutton, 1937. Reprint, New York: AMS Press, 1979.

Ostrogorsky, George. *History of the Byzantine State,* trans. Joan Hussey. Rev. ed. New Brunswick, NJ: Rutgers University Press, 1969.

Özbaran, Salih. "Ottoman Naval Policy in the South." In *Sülaymân the Magnificent and His Age,* ed. Metin Kunt and Christine Woodhead, 55–71. London: Longman, 1995.

Özel, Oktay. "Limits of the Almighty: Mehmed II's 'Land Reform' Revisited." *Journal of the Economic and Social History of the Orient* 42 (1999): 226–246.

Pamuk, Şevket. *A Monetary History of the Ottoman Empire.* Cambridge Studies in Islamic Civilization, gen. ed. David O. Morgan. Cambridge: Cambridge University Press, 2000.

Pannikar, K. M. *A Survey of Indian History.* 4th ed. New York: Asia, 1964.

Pant, Chandra. *Nur Jahan and Her Family.* Allahabad, India: Dandewal, 1979.

Parker, Geoffrey. *Success Is Never Final: Empire, War, and Faith in Early Modern Europe.* New York: Basic Books, 2002.

————. *The Army of Flanders and the Spanish Road.* 2nd ed. Cambridge: Cambridge University Press, 2004.

————. *The Military Revolution: Military Innovation and the Rise of the West, 1500–1800.* 2nd ed. Cambridge: Cambridge University Press, 1996.

Parry, V. J. "Materials of War in the Ottoman Empire." In *Studies in the Economic History of the Middle East,* ed. M. A. Cook, 219–229. London: Oxford University Press, 1970.

————. "The Period of Murād IV, 1617–48." In *A History of the Ottoman Empire to 1730: Chapters from the Cambridge History of Islam and the New Cambridge Modern History,* ed. M. A. Cook, 133–156. Cambridge: Cambridge University Press, 1976.

————. "The Reign of Sulaimān, 1520–1566." In *A History of the Ottoman Empire to 1730: Chapters from the Cambridge History of Islam and the New Cambridge Modern History,* ed. M. A. Cook, 79–102. Cambridge: Cambridge University Press, 1976.

————. "The Reigns of Bāyezīd II and Selīm I, 1481–1520." In *A History of the Ottoman Empire to 1730: Chapters from the Cambridge History of Islam and the New Cambridge Modern History,* ed. M. A. Cook, 54–78. Cambridge: Cambridge University Press, 1976.

————. "The Successors of Sulaimān, 1566–1617." In *A History of the Ottoman Empire to 1730: Chapters from the Cambridge History of Islam and the New Cambridge Modern History,* ed. M. A. Cook, 103–132. Cambridge: Cambridge University Press, 1976.

Parry, V. J., and M. E. Yapp, eds. *War, Technology, and Society in the Middle East.* London: Oxford University Press, 1975.

Paterson, W. P. "The Archers of Islam." *Journal of the Economic and Social History of the Orient* 9 (1966): 69–87.

Pearson, M. N. "Merchants and States." In *The Political Economy of Merchant Empires: State Power and World Trade, 1350–1750,* ed. James D. Tracy, 41–116. Cambridge: Cambridge University Press, 1991.

———. "Shivaji and the Decline of the Mughal Empire." *Journal of Asian Studies* 35 (1976): 221–235.

———. *The Portuguese in India*. Vol. 1:1 of *The New Cambridge History of India*, gen. ed. Gordon Johnson. Cambridge: Cambridge University Press, 1987.

Pearson, Michael. *The Indian Ocean*. Seas in History, gen. ed. Geoffrey Scammel. London: Routledge, 2003.

Peirce, Leslie P. *Morality Tales: Law and Gender in the Ottoman Court of Aintab*. Berkeley: University of California Press, 2003.

———. "The Family As Faction: Dynastic Politics in the Reign of Sülaymân." In *Sülaymân the Magnificent and His Time*, ed. Gilles Veinstein, 105–116. Paris: La Documentation Française, 1992.

———. *The Imperial Harem: Women and Sovereignty in the Ottoman Empire*. Studies in Middle Eastern History, gen. ed. Bernard Lewis, Itamar Rabinovich, and Roger Savory. New York: Oxford University Press, 1993.

Perry, John R. "Forced Migration in Iran During the Seventeenth and Eighteenth Centuries." *Iranian Studies* 8 (1975): 199–215.

———. "Justice for the Underprivileged: The Ombudsman Tradition." *Journal of Near Eastern Studies* 37 (1978): 203–215.

Peters, F. E. *Allah's Commonwealth: A History of the Near East, 600–1100 AD*. New York: Simon and Schuster, 1973.

Peters, Rudolph. *Jihad in Classical and Modern Islam*. Princeton Series on the Middle East, ed. Bernard Lewis and Heath Lowry. Princeton, NJ: Markus Weiner Publishers, 1996.

Petrovic, Djurdjica. "Fire-arms in the Balkans on the Eve of and After the Ottoman Conquests of the Fourteenth and Fifteenth Centuries." In *War, Technology, and Society in the Middle East*, ed. V. J. Parry and M. E. Yapp, 164–194. London: Oxford University Press, 1975.

Petrushevsky, I. P. "The Socio-Economic Condition of Iran Under the Il-Khans." In *The Saljuq and Mongol Periods*, ed. J. A. Boyle, 483–537. Vol. 5 of *The Cambridge History of Iran*, gen. ed. Harold Bailey. Cambridge: Cambridge University Press, 1968.

Petry, Carl F., ed. *Islamic Egypt, 640–1517*. Vol. 1 of *The Cambridge History of Egypt*. Cambridge: Cambridge University Press, 1998.

———. *Twilight of Majesty: The Reigns of the Mamlūk Sultans al-Ashraf Qāyitbāy and Qānṣūh al-Ghawrī*. Middle East Center, Jackson School of International Studies Occasional Papers 4. Seattle: University of Washington Press, 1993.

Philipp, Thomas, and Ulrich Haarmann, eds. *The Mamluks in Egyptian Politics and Society*. Cambridge Studies in Islamic Civilization, gen. ed. David Morgan. Cambridge: Cambridge University Press, 1998.

Phul, Raj Kumar. *Armies of the Great Mughals*. New Delhi: Oriental Publishers and Distributors, 1978.

Pinch, William R. *Warrior Ascetics and Indian Empires*. Cambridge Studies in Indian History and Society. Cambridge: Cambridge University Press, 2006.

Pipes, Daniel. *Slave Soldiers and Islam: The Genesis of a Military System*. New Haven, CT: Yale University Press, 1981.

Piterberg, Gabriel. *An Ottoman Tragedy: History and Historiography at Play*. Studies on the History of Society and Culture, ed. Victoria E. Bonnell and Lynn Hunt. Berkeley: University of California Press, 2003.

Prasad, Beni. *Life of Jahangir*. 5th ed. Allahabad, India: Indian Press, 1973.

Preston, Diana, and Michael Preston. *The Taj Mahal: Passion and Genius at the Heart of the Mughal Empire*. New York: Walker, 2007.

Qaisar, Ahsan Jan. "Distribution of the Revenue Resources of the Mughal Empire Among the Nobility." In *The Mughal State, 1526–1750,* ed. Muzaffar Alam and Sanjay Subrahmanyam. Oxford in India Readings: Themes in Indian History. New Delhi: Oxford University Press, 2001.

———. *The Indian Response to European Technology and Culture, 1498–1707.* Delhi: Oxford University Press, 1982.

Quataert, Donald. *The Ottoman Empire, 1700–1922.* New Approaches to European History, gen. ed. William Beik and T. C. W. Blanding. 2nd ed. Cambridge: Cambridge University Press, 2005.

Quinn, Sholeh A. *Historical Writing During the Reign of Shah ʿAbbas: Ideology, Imitation and Legitimacy in Safavid Chronicles.* Salt Lake City: University of Utah Press, 2000.

———. "Rewriting Niʾmatuʾllāhī History in Safavid Chronicles." In *Late Classical Persianate Sufism,* ed. Leonard Lewisohn and David Morgan, 204–224. Vol. 3 of *The Heritage of Sufism.* Oxford: Oneword, 1999.

———. "The Timurid Historiographical Legacy: A Comparative Study of Historiographical Writing." In *Society and Culture in the Early Modern Middle East: Studies on Iran in the Safavid Period,* ed. Andrew J. Newman, 19–32. Leiden: E. J. Brill, 1998.

Quiring-Zoche, Rosemarie. *Isfahan im 15. und 16. Jahrhundert: Eing Beitrag zur persichen Stadtgeschichte.* Islamkundliche Untersuchungen 54. Freiburg, Germany: Klaus Schwarz, 1980.

Qureshi, Ishtiaq Husain. *Akbar: The Architect of the Mughal Empire.* Karachi, Pakistan: Maaref, 1978.

———. "India Under the Mughals." In *The Cambridge History of Islam,* ed. P. M. Holt, Ann K. S. Lambton, and Bernard Lewis, 2:35–62. 2 vols. Cambridge: Cambridge University Press, 1985.

———. "Muslim India Before the Mughals." In *The Cambridge History of Islam,* ed. P. M. Holt, Ann K. S. Lambton, and Bernard Lewis, 2:3–34. 2 vols. Cambridge: Cambridge University Press, 1970.

———. *The Administration of the Mughal Empire.* Patna, India: N. V. Publications, n.d.

———. *The Muslim Community of the Indian Subcontinent.* 2nd ed. Karachi, Pakistan: Maaref, 1971.

———. *The Muslim Community of the Indo-Pakistan Subcontinent.* 2nd ed. Karachi, Pakistan: Maaref, 1977.

Rabie, H. *The Fiscal System of Egypt.* London: Oxford University Press, 1972.

Rahman, Fazlur. *Islam.* 2nd ed. Chicago: University of Chicago Press, 1979.

———. *The Philosophy of Mullā Ṣadrā.* Albany: State University of New York Press, 1975.

Ramazani, Rouhollah K. *The Foreign Policy of Iran, 1500–1941.* Charlottesville, VA: University Press of Virginia, 1966.

Ray, Sukumar. *Bairam Khan,* ed. M. H. A. Beg. Karachi, Pakistan: Institute of Central and West Asian Studies, 1992.

———. *Humāyūn in Persia.* Calcutta: Royal Asiatic Society of Bengal, 1948. Reprint, Asiatic Society Monograph Series 6. Kolkata: Asiatic Society, 2002.

Raychaudhuri, Tapan. "Non-Agricultural Production: Mughal India." In *Circa 1200–1750,* ed. Tapan Raychaudhuri and Irfan Habib, 261–307. Vol. 1 of *The Cambridge Economic History of India,* ed. Dharma Kumar and Tapan Raychaudhuri. Cambridge: Cambridge University Press, 1982.

———. "The State and the Economy: The Mughal Empire." In *Circa 1200–1750,* ed. Tapan Raychaudhuri and Irfan Habib, 172–192. Vol. 1 of *The Cambridge Economic History of*

India, ed. Dharma Kumar and Tapan Raychaudhuri. Cambridge: Cambridge University Press, 1982.

Raychaudhuri, Tapan, and Irfan Habib, eds. *Circa 1200–1750*. Vol. 1 of *The Cambridge Economic History of India*, ed. Dharma Kumar and Tapan Raychaudhuri. Cambridge: Cambridge University Press, 1982.

Reid, James J. "Comments on Tribalism As a Socioeconomic Formation." *Iranian Studies* 12 (1979): 275–281.

———. *Studies in Safavid Mind, Society, and Cultures*. Costa Mesa, CA: Mazda Press, 2000.

———. "The Qajar Uymaq in the Safavid Period, 1500–1722." *Iranian Studies* 11 (1978): 117–143.

———. *Tribalism and Society in Islamic Iran, 1500–1629*. Studies in Near Eastern Culture and Society 4. Malibu, CA: Undena Publications, 1983.

Reis, Piri. *Kitab-i Bahriye*, ed. Ertugrul Zekai Okte, trans. Robert Bragner. 2 vols. Ankara: Ministry of Culture and Tourism, 1988.

Reis, Sidi Ali. *Mir'at al-Mamalik*, trans. Robert Bragner as *The Travels of a Turkish Admiral*. London: Luzac, 1899. Reprint, Lahore, Pakistan: Al-Biruni, 1975.

Richards, J. F. *Mughal Administration in Golconda*. Oxford: Clarendon Press, 1975.

———. "Norms of Comportment Among Imperial Mughal Officers." In *Moral Conduct and Authority: The Place of Adab in South Asian Islam*, ed. Barbara Daly Metcalf, 255–289. Berkeley: University of California Press, 1984.

———. "The Formation of Imperial Authority Under Akbar and Jahangir." In *Kingship and Authority in South Asia*, ed. J. F. Richards, 256–258. Madison: University of Wisconsin South Asia Studies, 1978. Reprint in *The Mughal State, 1526–1750*, ed. Muzaffar Alam and Sanjay Subrahmanyam, 126–167. Oxford in India Readings: Themes in Indian History. New Delhi: Oxford University Press, 2001.

———. "The Hyderabad Karnatik, 1687–1707." *Modern Asian Studies* 9, no. 2 (1975): 241–260.

———. "The Imperial Crisis in the Deccan." *Journal of Asian Studies* 35 (1976): 237–256.

———. *The Mughal Empire*. Vol. 1:5 of *The New Cambridge History of India*, gen. ed. Gordon Johnson. Cambridge: Cambridge University Press, 1993.

Rizvi, S. A. A. *A History of Sufism in India*. 2 vols. New Delhi: Munshiram Manoharlal, 1975–1983.

———. *Muslim Revivalist Movements in Northern India in the Sixteenth and Seventeenth Centuries*. Agra, India: Agra University, 1965.

———. *Religious and Intellectual History of the Muslims in Akbar's Reign*. New Delhi: Munshiram Manoharlal, 1975.

Roberts, Michael. *Essays in Swedish History*. London: Weidenfeld and Nicholson, 1967.

———. *The Military Revolution: 1560–1660*. Belfast: M. Boyd, 1956.

Robinson, Francis. *The Mughal Emperors and the Islamic Dynasties of India, Iran and Central Asia*. London: Thames & Hudson, 2007.

Roe, Thomas, Sir. *The Embassy of Sir Thomas Roe to India, 1615–19*, ed. Sir William Foster. London: Humphrey Milford, 1926.

Roemer, H. R. *Der Niedergang Irans nach dem Tode Isma`ils des Grausamen*. Wurzburg: K. Triltsch, 1939.

———. "The Jalayrids, Muzaffarids and Sarbadārs." In *The Timurid and Safavid Periods*, ed. Peter Jackson and Laurence Lockhart, 1–41. Vol. 6 of *The Cambridge History of Iran*, gen. ed. Harold Bailey Cambridge: Cambridge University Press, 1986.

———. "The Qizilbash Turcomans: Founders and Victims of the Safavi Theocracy." In *Intellectual Studies on Islam: Essays Written in Honor of Martin B. Dickson*, ed. Michel M. Mazzaoui and Vera B. Moreen, 27–40. Salt Lake City: University of Utah Press, 1990.

———. "The Safavid Period." In *The Timuri and Safavi Periods*, ed. Peter Jackson and Laurence Lockhart, 189–350. Vol. 6 of *The Cambridge History of Iran*, gen. ed. Harold Bailey. Cambridge: Cambridge University Press, 1986.

———. "The Successors of Tīmūr." In *The Timurid and Safavid Periods*, ed. Peter Jackson and Laurence Lockhart, 98–146. Vol. 6 of *The Cambridge History of Iran*, gen. ed. Harold Bailey. Cambridge: Cambridge University Press, 1986.

———. "The Türkmen Dynasties." In *The Timurid and Safavid Periods*, ed. Peter Jackson and Laurence Lockhart, 147–188. Vol. 6 of *The Cambridge History of Iran*, gen. ed. Harold Bailey. Cambridge: Cambridge University Press, 1986.

———. "Timur in Iran." In *The Timurid and Safavid Periods*, ed. Peter Jackson and Laurence Lockhart, 42–97. Vol. 6 of *The Cambridge History of Iran*, gen. ed. Harold Bailey. Cambridge: Cambridge University Press, 1986.

Rogers, Clifford J., ed. *The Military Revolution Debate: Readings on the Military Transformation of Early Modern Europe*. Boulder, CO: Westview Press, 1995.

Rohrborn, Klaus Michael. *Provinzen und Zentral Gewalt Persiens im 16. und 17. Jahrhundert*. Studien zur Sprache, Geschichte und Kultur des islamichen Orients, n.s. 2. Berlin: Walter de Gruyter, 1966.

———. "Regierung und Verwaltung Irans unter den Safawiden." In *Regierung und Verwaltung des Vorderen Orients in Islamischen Zeit*, ed. H. R. Idris and K. M. Rohrborn, 17–50. *Handbuch der Orientalistik*, ed. B. Spuler, *Erste Abteilung: Der Nahe Mittelere Osten*, Bd. 6, Abschnitt 5, Teil 1. Leiden, Netherlands: E. J. Brill, 1979.

———. *Untersuchungen zur osmanischen Verwaltungsgeschichte*. Studien zur Sprache, Geschichte und Kultur des islamischen Orients, n.s. 5. Berlin: Walter de Gruyter, 1973.

Ross, E. Denison, Sir. "Babur." In *The Mughal Period*. Vol. 4 of *The Cambridge History of India*, ed. Lt. Col. Sir Wolseley Haig and Sir Richard Burn, 1–20. Cambridge: Cambridge University Press, 1937.

Roux, Jean-Paul. *Les traditiones des nomads de la Turquie meridionale*. Bibliotheque Archeologique et Historique de l'Institut Français d'Archeologie d'Istanbul 24. Istanbul: Institut Français d'Archeologie, 1970.

———. "Un survivance des traditions turco-mongoles chez les Sefevides." *Revue de l'Histoire des Religions* 153 (1973): 11–18.

Runciman, Steven. *Byzantine Style and Civilization*. Harmondsworth, UK: Penguin, 1975.

Rypka, Jan. "History of Persian Literature Up to the Beginning of the 20th Century." In Jan Rypka et al., *History of Iranian Literature*, ed. Karl Jahn, 291–304. Dordrecht, Netherlands: D. Reidel, 1968.

Sabahuddin, Abdul, and Rajshree Shukla. *The Mughal Strategy of War*. Delhi: Global Vision Publishing House, 2003.

Sachau, Edward C. *Alberuni's India*, trans. Edward C. Sachau. London: Kegan Paul, Trench, Trubner, 1910. Reprint, New Delhi: Oriental Books Reprint Corporation, 1983.

Safa, Z. "Persian Literature in the Safavid Period." In *The Timurid and Safavid Periods*, ed. Peter Jackson and Laurence Lockhart, 948–964. Vol. 6 of *The Cambridge History of Iran*, gen. ed. Harold Bailey Cambridge: Cambridge University Press, 1986.

Saksena, Banarsi Prasad. *History of Shah Jahan of Dilhi*. Allahabad: Central Book Depot 1962. Original publication, 1932

Saran, P. *The Provincial Government of the Mughals, 1526–1658*. 2nd ed. Bombay: Asia, 1973.

Sardesai, Govid Sakaram. *A New History of the Marathas*. Rev. ed. 3 vols. Bombay: Phoenix, 1957.

Sarkar, Jadunath. *History of Aurangzib*. 5 vols. Calcutta: M. C. Sarkar, 1912–1924. Reprint, Bombay: Orient Longman, 1974.

———. *Military History of India*. Bombay: Orient Longman, 1960.

———. *The Fall of the Mughal Empire*. 4 vols. Calcutta: 1932–1950.

———. *The Life of Mir Jumla: The General of Aurangzeb*. 2nd ed. New Delhi: Rajesh Publications, 1979.

Sarwar, Ghulam. *History of Shah Isma`il Safawi*. Aligarh, India: Author, 1939. Reprint, New York: AMS Press, 1975.

Sastri, K. A. Nilakanta. *A History of South India*. 4th ed. Madras, India: Oxford University Press, 1966.

Savory, Roger M. "A Secretarial Career Under Shāh Ṭahmāsp (1524–1576)." *Islamic Studies* 2 (1963): 343–350.

———. *Iran Under the Safavids*. Cambridge: Cambridge University Press, 1981.

———. "Safavid Persia." In *The Cambridge History of Islam*, ed. P. M. Holt, Ann K. S. Lambton, and Bernard Lewis, 1:394–429. 2 vols. Cambridge: Cambridge University Press, 1970.

———. "The Consolidation of Safawid Power in Persia." *Der Islam* 41 (1965): 71–94.

———. "The Office of Khalifat al-Khulafa Under the Safawids." *Journal of the American Oriental Society* 85 (1965): 497–502.

———. "The Political Significance of the Murder of Mirza Salman." *Islamic Studies* 3 (1964): 181–191. Reprinted in *Studies on the History of Safawid Iran*. London: Variorum, 1987.

———. "The Principal Offices of the Safawid State During the Reign of Isma`il I (907–30/1501–24)." *Bulletin of the School of Oriental and African Studies* 23 (1960): 93–99.

———. "The Principal Offices of the Safawid State During the Reign of Tahmasp I (930–84/1524–76)." *Bulletin of the School of Oriental and African Studies* 24 (1961): 65–85.

———. "The Safavid Administrative System." In *The Timurid and Safavid Periods*, ed. Peter Jackson and Laurence Lockhart, 351–372. Vol. 6 of *The Cambridge History of Iran*, gen. ed. Harold Bailey. Cambridge: Cambridge University Press, 1986.

———. "Very Dull and Arduous Reading: A Reappraisal of the History of Shāh `Abbās the Great." *Hamdard Islamicus* 3 (1980): 19–37.

Schacht, Joseph, with C. E. Bosworth, eds. *The Legacy of Islam*. 2nd ed. Oxford: Oxford University Press, 1974.

Schimmel, Annemarie. *Mystical Dimensions of Islam*. Chapel Hill: University of North Carolina Press, 1975.

———. *The Empire of the Great Mughals: History, Art, and Culture*, ed. Burzine K. Waghmar, trans. Corinne Attwood. London: Reaktion Books, 2004.

Schuster-Walser, Sibylla. *Das Safawidsche Persien im Spiegel Europaischer Reiseberichte, 1502–1722*. Baden Baden, Germany: Bruno Grimm, 1970.

Schwoebel, Robert. *The Shadow of the Crescent: The Renaissance Image of the Turk, 1453–1517*. New York: St. Martin's Press, 1967.

Sefatgol, Mansur. "Rethinking the [sic] Safavid Iran (907–1148/1501–1736)." *Journal of Asian and African Studies* 72 (2006): 5–16.

Setton, Kenneth M., ed. *A History of the Crusades*. 6 vols. Madison: University of Wisconsin Press, 1969–1989.

Sharma, G. N. *Mewar and the Mughal Emperors*. Agra, India: Shiva Lal Agarwala, 1954.

Sharma, Sri Ram. *The Religious Policy of the Mughal Emperors*. 3rd ed. New York: Asia House, 1972.

Shaw, Stanford J. *Empire of the Ghazis.* Vol. 1 of *History of the Ottoman Empire and Modern Turkey.* Cambridge: Cambridge University Press, 1976.

———. *The Financial and Administrative Organization and Development of Ottoman Egypt.* Princeton, NJ: Princeton University Press, 1962.

Shivram, Balkrishan. *Jagirdars in the Mughal Empire During the Reign of Akbar.* New Delhi: Manohar, 2008.

Siddiqui, Iqtidar Husain. *History of Shir Shah Sur.* Aligarh, India: P. C. Dwadash Shreni, 1971.

———. *Mughal Relations with the Indian Ruling Elite.* New Delhi: Munshiram Manoharlal, 1983.

———. *Some Aspects of Afghan Despotism in India.* Aligarh, India: Three Men Publication, 1969.

Siddiqui, N. A. "Faujdar and Faujdari Under the Mughals." *Medieval India Quarterly* 4 (1961): 22–35.

Simidchievea, M. "*Siyāsat-Nāme* Revisited: The Question of Authenticity." *Proceedings of the Second European Conference of Iranian Studies,* ed. B. G. Fragner et al. Rome: n.p., 1995.

Siroux, Maxime. "Les caravanserais routiers safavids." *Iranian Studies* 7 (1974): 348–375.

Sivan, Emmanuel. *Islam et la Croisade: Idéologie et propagande dans réactions musulmanes aux Croisades.* Paris: Adrien Maissonneuve, 1968.

Smail, D. C. *Crusading Warfare, 1097–1193, with a New Bibliographical Introduction by Christopher Marshall.* Cambridge Studies in Medieval Life and Thought. 2nd ed. Cambridge: Cambridge University Press, 1995.

Smith, John Masson, Jr. *The History of the Sarbadar Dynasty 1336–1381* AD *and Its Sources.* The Hague: Mouton, 1970.

Smith, Vincent A. *Akbar the Great Mogul.* 2nd rev. ed. New Delhi: S. Chand, 1962.

Sohrweide, Hanna. "Der Sieg der Safaviden in Persien und seine Ruckwirkungen auf die Schiiten Anatoliens im 16. Jahrhundert." *Der Islam* 41 (1965): 95–223.

Sonbol, Amira El Azhry. *Women, the Family, and Divorce Laws in Islamic History.* Contemporary Issues in the Middle East. Syracuse, NY: Syracuse University Press, 1996.

Soucek, Svat. *A History of Inner Asia.* Cambridge: Cambridge University Press, 2000.

Soudavar, Abolala. *The Aura of Kings: Legitimacy and Divine Sanction and Iranian Kingship.* Bibliotheca Iranica Intellectual Traditions Series 10, ed. Hossein Ziai. Costa Mesa, CA: Mazda Press, 2003.

Sourdel, Dominique. *Le vizirat `abbaside de 749 à 936.* 2 vols. Damascus: Institute Français de Damas, 1959–1960.

Spear, Percival. *A History of India.* Vol. 2. Harmondsworth, UK: Penguin, 1970.

Spicehandler, Ezra. "The Persecution of the Jews of Isfahan Under Shah `Abbas II, 1642–1666." *Hebrew Union College Annual* 46 (1975): 331–347.

Spuler, Bertold. *The Mongol Period.* Vol. 2 of *The Muslim World,* trans. F. R. C. Bagley. Leiden, Netherlands: E. J. Brill, 1968.

———. *The Mongols in History,* trans. Geoffrey Wheeler. New York: Praeger, 1971.

Srivastava, Ashirabadi Lal. *Akbar the Great.* 2nd ed. 3 vols. Agra, India: Shiva Lal Agarwala, 1972–1973.

Steensgaard, Niels. *The Asian Trade Revolution of the Seventeenth Century.* Chicago: University of Chicago Press, 1974. Original publication, as *Carracks, Caravans, and Companies.* Scandinavian Institute of Asian Studies Monograph Series 17. Copenhagen: Scandinavian Institute of Asian Studies, 1973.

Stein, Burton. *Vijaynagara.* Vol. 1:2 of *The New Cambridge History of India,* gen. ed. Gordon Johnson. Cambridge: Cambridge University Press, 1989.

Stein, Mark L. *Guarding the Frontier: Ottoman Border Forts and Garrisons in Europe.* New York: Tauris Academic Studies, 2007.

Steinmann, Linda K. "Shah ʿAbbas and the Royal Silk Trade, 1599–1629." *British Society for Middle East Studies Bulletin* 14 (1988): 68–74.

Stoye, John. *The Siege of Vienna.* New York: Holt, Rinehart and Winston, 1965.

Streusand, Douglas E. "Sir Hamilton A. R. Gibb, Abu Yusuf, and the Concept of Islamic Civilization." In *History and Historiography of Post-Mongol Central Asia: Studies in Honor of Professor John E. Woods,* ed. Judith Pfeiffer and Sholeh Quinn, with Ernest Tucker, 542–544. Berlin: Otto Harrasowitz, 2006.

———. *The Formation of the Mughal Empire.* Delhi: Oxford University, 1989.

———. "What Does Jihad Mean?" *Middle East Quarterly* 4 (1997): 9–17.

Subrahmanyam, Sanjay. "A Tale of Three Empires: Mughals, Ottomans, and Hapsburgs in a Comparative Context." *Common Knowledge* 12 (2006): 66–92.

———. "Connected Histories: Notes Towards a Reconfiguration of Early Modern Eurasia." *Modern Asian Studies* 31 (1997): 735–762.

———. Introduction to *Money and the Market in India,* ed. Sanjay Subrahmanyam, 1–56. Oxford India Readings: Themes in Indian History. Delhi: Oxford University Press, 1998.

———. "Precious Metal Flows and Prices in Western and Southwest Asia: Some Comparative and Conjectural Aspects." *Studies in History* 7 (1991): 79–105.

———. *The Political Economy of Commerce: Southern India.* Cambridge: Cambridge University Press, 1990.

Sugar, Peter F., and Donald W. Treadgold. *Southeastern Europe Under Ottoman Rule: 1354–1804.* Vol. 5 of *A History of East Central Europe.* Seattle: University of Washington Press, 1977.

Sunderland, E. "Pastoralism, Nomadism, and Social Anthropology of Iran." In *The Land of Iran,* ed. W. B. Fisher, 611–683. Vol. 1 of *The Cambridge History of Iran,* gen. ed. Harold Bailey. Cambridge: Cambridge University Press, 1968.

Szuppe, Maria. "The 'Jewels of Wonder': Learned Ladies and Princess Politicians in the Provinces of Early Safavid Iran." In *Women in the Medieval Islamic World,* ed. Gavin R. G. Hambly, 325–348. Vol. 6 of *The New Middle Ages,* gen. ed. Bonnie Wheeler. New York: St. Martin's Press, 1998.

Taffazoli, Ahmad. *Sasanian Society: Warriors, Scribes, Dehqans.* Ehsan Yarshater Distinguished Lecture Series in Iranian Studies 1. New York: Bibliotheca Persica, 2000.

Talbot, Cynthia. "Inscribing the Other, Inscribing the Self: Hindu-Muslim Identities in Precolonial India." *Comparative Studies in Society and History* 37 (1995): 692–722.

Tapper, Richard. "Shahsevan." In *Muslim Peoples: A World Ethnographic Survey,* ed. Richard V. Weekes, 2:670–674. 2nd ed. 2 vols. Westport, CT: Greenwood Press, 1984.

———. "Shahsevan in Safavid Persian." *Bulletin of the School of Oriental and African Studies* 37 (1974): 321–354.

Tauer, Felix. "Persian Learned Literature from Its Beginnings Up to the End of the Eighteenth Century." In Jan Rypka et al., *History of Iranian Literature,* ed. Karl Jahn, 419–482. Dordrecht, Netherlands: D. Reidel, 1968.

Tezcan, Baki. "The Politics of Early Modern Ottoman Historiography." In *The Early Modern Ottomans: Remapping the Empire,* ed. Virginia H. Aksan and Daniel Goffman, 167–198. Cambridge: Cambridge University Press, 2007.

Thapar, Romila. *A History of India.* Vol. 1. Harmondsworth, UK: Penguin, 1966.

Thomas, Lewis V. *A Study of Naima,* ed. Norman Itzkowitz. New York University Studies in Near Eastern Civilization 4. New York: New York University Press, 1972.

Thompson, Edward, and G. T. Garratt. *Rise and Fulfillment of British Rule in India*. London: Macmillan, 1934. Reprint, Allahabad, India: Central Book Depot, 1976.

Thompson, Jon, and Sheila R. Canby. *Hunt for Paradise: Court Arts of Safavid Iran: 1501–1576*. Milan, Italy: Skira, 2003.

Tietze, Andreas, ed. *Mustafa Ali's Counsel for Sultans*, trans. Andreas Tietze. 2 vols. Vienna: Österreichische Akademie der Wissenshaften, 1978–1982.

Tod, James. *Annals and Antiques of Rajasthan, with a Foreword by Douglas Sladen*. 2 vols. London: George Routledge & Sons, 1914. Reprint, New Delhi: M. N. Publishers, 1978.

Togan, Zeki Velidi. "Sur l'origine des Safavides." In *Melanges Massignon III*, 345–357. Damascus: Institut Français de Damas, 1957.

Tracy, James D. *The Political Economy of Merchant Empires: State Power and World Trade, 1350–1750*. Studies in Comparative Early Modern History, gen. ed. James D. Tracy. Cambridge: Cambridge University Press, 1991.

Trimingham, J. Spencer. *The Sufi Orders of Islam*. London: Oxford University Press, 1971.

Tucker, Ernest. Review of *Mystics, Monarchs, and Messiahs: Cultural Landscapes of Early Modern Iran* by Kathryn Babayan. *Journal of Near Eastern Studies* 67 (2008): 230–232.

Turan, Osman. "Anatolia in the Period of the Seljuks and the Beyliks." In *The Cambridge History of Islam*, ed. P. M. Holt, A. K. S. Lambton, and Bernard Lewis, 1:231–262. 2 vols. Cambridge: Cambridge University Press, 1970.

Tursun Bey. *History of Mehmed the Conqueror*, trans. Halil Inalcık and Rhoads Murphey. Chicago: Bibliotheca Islamica, 1978.

Valensi, Lucette. *The Birth of the Despot: Venice and the Sublime Porte*, trans. Arthur Denner. Ithaca: Cornell University Press, 1993.

Vaughan, Dorothy. *Europe and the Turk*. Liverpool, UK: University Press, 1954. Reprint, New York: AMS Press, 1954.

Veinstein, Gilles, ed. *Sülaymân the Magnificent and His Time*. Acts of the Parisian Conference Galeries Nationales du Grand Palais, March 7–10, 1990. Paris: La Documentation Française, 1992.

Vladimirtsov, B. *Le regime social des Mongols*, with a preface by Rene Grousset, trans. Michel Carsow. Paris: Adrien-Maisonneuve, 1948.

Voegelin, Eric. "The Mongol Orders of Submission to the European Powers." *Byzantion* 15 (1940–1941): 378–413.

———. *The New Science of Politics*. With Foreword by Dante Germino. Chicago: University of Chicago Press, 1987.

Von Grunebaum, Gustave E. *Medieval Islam: A Study in Cultural Orientation*. 2nd ed. Chicago: University of Chicago Press, 1953.

Vryonis, Speros. *The Decline of Medieval Hellenism in Asia Minor and the Process of Islamization from the Eleventh Through the Fifteenth Century*. Berkeley: University of California, 1971.

Wallerstein, Immanuel. *The Modern World System*. 3 vols. New York: Academic Press, 1975–1988.

———. *World Systems Analysis: An Introduction*. Durham, NC: Duke University Press, 2004.

Walsh, J. R. "The Revolt of Alqas Mirza." *Weiner Zeitschrift fur die Kunde des Morgenlandes* 68 (1976): 61–78.

Watt, W. Montgomery. "God's Caliph: Qur'ānic Interpretations and Umayyad Claims." In *Iran and Islam: In Memory of the Late Vladimir Minorsky*, ed. C. E. Bosworth, 565–574. Edinburgh: Edinburgh University Press, 1971.

Welch, Anthony. *Artists for the Shah: Late Sixteenth Century Painting at the Imperial Court of Iran*. New Haven, CT: Yale University Press, 1976.

———. *Shah `Abbas and the Arts of Isfahan*. New York: Asia Society, 1973.

Welch, Stuart Cary. *A King's Book of Kings: The Shah-nameh of Shah Tahmasp*. New York: Metropolitan Museum of Art, 1972.

———. *Persian Painting: Five Royal Manuscripts of the Sixteenth Century*. New York: George Braziller, 1976.

Wheatcroft, Andrew. *The Ottomans: Dissolving Images*. London: Penguin, 1993.

Widengren, G. "The Sacral Kingship of Iran." In *The Sacral Kingship*, 242–257. Studies in the History of Religions, supplement to *Numen* 4. Leiden, Netherlands: E. J. Brill, 1959.

Wiesner-Hanks, Merry E. *Religious Transformations in the Early Modern World: A Brief History with Documents*. New York: Bedford-St. Martin's, 2009.

Wink, André. *Early Medieval India and the Expansion of Islam, 7th to 11th Centuries*. Vol. 1 of *Al-Hind: The Making of the Indo-Islamic World*. Leiden, Netherlands: E. J. Brill, 1993.

———. *Indo-Islamic Society, 14th to 15th Centuries*. Vol. 3 of *Al-Hind: The Making of the Indo-Islamic World*. Leiden, Netherlands: E. J. Brill, 2004.

———. *Land and Sovereignty in India: Society Under the Eighteenth-Century Maratha Svarajya*. Cambridge: Cambridge University Press, 1986.

———. *The Slave Kings and the Early Islamic Conquest, 11th to 13th Centuries*. Vol. 2 of *Al-Hind: The Making of the Indo-Islamic World*. Leiden, Netherlands: E. J. Bill, 1997.

Winter, Michael W. "Ottoman Egypt, 1525–1569." In *Egypt from 1517 to the End of the Twentieth Century*, ed. M. W. Daly, 1–33. Vol. 2 of *The Cambridge History of Egypt*. Cambridge: Cambridge University Press, 1998.

Wittek, Paul. *The Rise of the Ottoman Empire*. London: Royal Asiatic Society, 1938.

Wolff, Robert Lee, and Harry W. Hazard. *The Later Crusades, 1189–1311*. Vol. 2 of *A History of the Crusades*, gen. ed. Kenneth M. Setton. 2nd ed. Madison: University of Wisconsin Press, 1969.

Wolpert, Stanley. *A New History of India*. London: Oxford University Press, 1977.

Woods, John E. *The Aqquyunlu: Clan, Confederation, Empire*. Rev. ed. Salt Lake City: University of Utah Press, 1999.

———. *The Timurid Dynasty*. Bloomington: Indiana University Research Institute for Inner Asian Studies, 1990.

———. "Timur's Genealogy." In *Intellectual Studies on Islam: Essays Written in Honor of Martin B. Dickson*, ed. Michel M. Mazzaoui and Vera B. Moreen, 85–126. Salt Lake City: University of Utah Press, 1990.

Yarshater, Ehsan. "Persian Poetry in the Timurid and Safavid Periods." In *The Timurid and Safavid Periods*, ed. Peter Jackson and Laurence Lockhart, 965–994. Vol. 6 of *The Cambridge History of Iran*, gen. ed. Harold Bailey Cambridge: Cambridge University Press, 1986.

———. "Safavid Literature: Progress or Decline." *Iranian Studies* 7 (1974): 217–270.

———, ed. *The Parthian and Sasanian Periods*. Vol. 3 of *The Cambridge History of Iran*, gen. ed. Harold Bailey. 2 vols. Cambridge: Cambridge University Press, 1983.

Yūsuf, Khāṣṣ Ḥājib. *Wisdom of Royal Glory (Kutadgu Bilig): A Turko-Islamic Mirror for Princes*, trans. Robert Dankoff. Publications of the Center for Middle East Studies 16, ed. Richard L. Chambers. Chicago: University of Chicago Press, 1983.

Zachariadou, Elizabeth, ed. *The Ottoman Emirate, 1300–1389*. Rethymnon, Greece: Crete University Press, 1993.

Zelliot, Eleanor. "A Medieval Encounter Between Hindu and Muslim: Eknath's Drama-Poem *Hindu-Turk Samvād*." In *Images of Man: Religion and Historical Process in South Asia*, ed.

Fred W. Clothey, 171–195. Madras, India: New Era Publications, 1982. Reprint, *India's Is-lamic Traditions, 711–1750*, ed. Richard M. Eaton. Oxford India Readings: Themes in In-dian History. New Delhi: Oxford University Press, 2003.

Zilfı, Madeline C. "A Medrese for the Palace: Ottoman Dynastic Legitimation in the Eigh-teenth Century." *Journal of the American Oriental Society* 113 (1993): 184–191.

———. "The Kadizadelis: Discordant Revivalism in Seventeenth-Century Istanbul." *Journal of Near Eastern Studies* 45 (1986): 251–269.

———. *The Politics of Piety: The Ottoman Ulema in the Postclassical Age, 1600–1800*. Studies in Middle Eastern History 8. Minneapolis, MN: Bibliotheca Islamica, 1988.

———. "Women and Society in the Tulip Period, 1718–1730." In *Women, the Family, and Divorce Laws in Islamic History*, gen. ed. Amira El Azhary Sonbol, 290–303. Contemporary Issues in the Middle East. Syracuse, NY: Syracuse University Press, 1996.

Illustration Credits

Image 3.1 *Portrait of (Fatih) Mehmed II Smelling a Rose*, attributed to Shiblizade Ahmed, ca. 1480, Turkey, opaque watercolor on paper. *Source:* Collection of the Topkapı Sarayı Müzesi, Istanbul (H. 2153, fol. 10r).

Image 3.2 *Sulayman at the Battle of Rhodes in 1522*: folio from the *Süleymanname* (Story of Sulayman) of Arifi, artist unknown, ca. 1558, Turkey, opaque watercolor and gold on paper. *Source:* Collection of the Topkapı Sarayı Müzesi, Istanbul (Inv. H. 1517, fol. 143a).

Image 3.3 *Sultan Sulayman I*, by Melchior Lorck, dated 1559, engraving. *Source:* Collection of the Austrian National Library, Vienna, Picture Archive (PORT 00034083_01).

Image 3.4 *Selim II receiving gifts from the Safavid Ambassador Shah Quli at Edirne in 1568*: folio from a manuscript of the *Nüzhet el-Esrar el-Ahbar der Sefer-i Szigetvar* (chronicle of the Szigetvar campaign of Ahmed Feridun Pasha), attributed to Nakkash Osman, 1568–1569, Turkey, opaque watercolor and gold on paper. *Source:* Collection of the Topkapı Sarayı Müzesi, Istanbul (Inv. H. 1524, fol. 257b).

Image 3.5 *Sultan Ahmed III*: folio from the *Kebir Musavver Silsilename* (Great Illustrated Genealogy [of the Sultans]), by Levni Abdulcelil Celebi, 1703–1730, Turkey, opaque watercolor and gold on paper. *Source:* Collection of the Topkapı Sarayı Müzesi, Istanbul (Inv. A. 3109, fol. 22v).

Image 3.6 *Fatih Jami, Sultan Mehmet II Mosque Complex (1463–1471), Istanbul*, photographic studio Sébah & Joaillier, ca. 1870, albumen print photograph (number 125). *Source:* Courtesy of Special Collections, Fine Arts Library, Harvard College Library.

Image 3.7 *Selimiye Jami, Sultan Selim II Mosque Complex (1568–1574), Edirne*, photograph by Chris Heller, ca. 1990–1996. *Source:* © Chris Hellier/CORBIS.

Image 3.8 *Interior view of the Sultan Ahmet Jami, Ahmet I Mosque Complex (1609–1617), Istanbul*, photographic studio of Sébah & Joaillier, ca. 1870, albumen print photograph (number 290). *Source:* Courtesy of Special Collections, Fine Arts Library, Harvard College Library.

Image 4.1 *The battle between Shah Ismail I and Muhammad Shaybani Khan in 1510*: folio from the *Tarikh-i alam-aray-i Shah Ismail* (The World Adorning History of Shah Ismail), by Mu'in Musavvir, Iran, Isfahan, ca. 1688, opaque watercolor, gold, and ink on paper, Freer Gallery of Art, Smithsonian Institution, Washington, D.C., Gift of Martha Mayor Smith and Alfred Mayor in memory of A. Hyatt Mayor, F2000.3. *Source:* Freer Gallery of Art, Smithsonian Institution, Washington, D.C.

Image 4.2 *Portrait of Shah Abbas I*, by Bishn Das, India, ca. 1618, opaque watercolor and gold on paper, Inv.: ME 1920,0917,013.2, British Museum, London. *Source:* © The Trustees of the British Museum / Art Resource, NY.

Image 4.3 *Caravanserai at the Ganj `Ali Khan Complex, (1598–1619) Kerman*, photographed by Dr. Khosrow Bozorgi, July, 2006. *Source:* Courtesy of Dr. Khosrow Bozorgi, Ph.D. Arch. The University of Oklahoma.

Image 4.4 *Feast of Sada*: folio from the Shah Tahmasp *Shahnama* (The Book of Kings) of Firdawsi, attributed to Sultan Muhammad, Iran, Tabriz, c. 1520–1522, opaque watercolor, gold, silver, and ink, on paper, Gift of Arthur A. Houghton Jr., 1970 (1970.301.2), The Metropolitan Museum of Art. *Source:* Image copyright © The Metropolitan Museum of Art / Art Resource, NY.

Image 4.5 *Firdawsi's Parable of the Ship of Shiism*: folio from the Tahmasp *Shahnama* (The Book of Kings), attributed to Mirza Ali, Iran, Tabriz, ca. 1530–1539, opaque watercolor, gold, silver, and ink on paper, Gift of Arthur A. Houghton Jr., 1970 (1970.301.1), The Metropolitan Museum of Art. *Source:* Image copyright © The Metropolitan Museum of Art / Art Resource, NY.

Image 4.6 *Aerial view of the Maydan-i Shah (1590–1595), Isfahan*, photograph by Roger Wood, May 21, 1968. *Source:* © Roger Wood/CORBIS.

Image 4.7 *View of the Shah Mosque (1611–ca. 1638) and Ali Qapu (early 17th century), Isfahan*, titled "Meidân-i-Châh ou Place Royale, Ispahan" from *Voyage en Perse, de MM. Eugène Flandin, peintre, et Pascal Coste, architecte, attachés à l'ambassade de France en Perse, pendant les années 1840 et 1841*, by Eugène Flandin, lithograph. *Source:* Asian and Middle Eastern Division, The New York Public Library, Astor, Lenox and Tilden Foundations.

Image 4.8 *Masjid-i Shaykh Lutfullah (1617), Isfahan*, photograph by Paule Seux. *Source:* © Paule Seux/Hemis/Corbis.

Image 5.1 *Buland Darwaza (1521–1522 to 1574) at Fatehpur Sikri, Uttar Pradesh*, photograph by Namit Arora. *Source:* © Namit Arora, shunya.net.

Image 5.2 *Akbar Giving Thanks on Hearing of the 1579 Victory in Bengal*: folio from an *Akbarnama* (Story of Akbar) manuscript, by La'l and Nand, India or Pakistan, 1590–1595, opaque watercolor, silver, and gold on paper (Inv.: IS.2:101–1896), Victoria and Albert Museum, London. *Source:* Copyright © V&A Images–All rights reserved.

Image 5.3 *Jahangir and Shah Abbas (Jahangir's Dream)*: folio from the St. Petersburg Album, by Abu'l Hasan, India, ca. 1618, opaque watercolor, gold, silver, and ink on paper, Freer Gallery of Art, Smithsonian Institution, Washington, D.C.: Purchase, F45.9. *Source:* Freer Gallery of Art, Smithsonian Institution, Washington, D.C.

Image 5.4 *Equestrian portrait of Shah Jahan*: folio from the Shah Jahan Album, attributed to Payag, ca. 1627, India, opaque watercolor and gold on paper, Purchase, Rogers Fund and The Kevorkian Foundation Gift, 1955 (55.121.10.21), The Metropolitan Museum of Art, New York. *Source:* Image copyright © The Metropolitan Museum of Art / Art Resource, NY.

Image 5.5 *Darbar of Aurangzeb*, attributed to Hashim, India, c. 1660, opaque watercolor and gold on paper, Museum of Islamic Art, Doha-Qatar (MS.54). *Source:* Museum of Islamic Art, Doha-Qatar.

Image 5.6 *Bullocks dragging siege guns up a hill during Akbar's attack on Ranthambhor Fort, Rajasthan in 1569*: folio from an *Akbarnama* (Story of Akbar) manuscript, by Miskina (composition) and Bhura (colors, details), India or Pakistan, ca. 1590–1595, opaque watercolor and gold on paper, Victoria and Albert Museum, London (Inv.: IS.2–1896 72/117). *Source:* © V&A Images, London / Art Resource, NY.

Image 5.7 *Humayun's Tomb (1562–1571), Delhi*, photograph by Namit Arora. *Source:* © Namit Arora, shunya.net.

Image 5.8 *Taj Mahal (1632–1648): the tomb of Shah Jahan's wife Mumtaz Mahal, Agra*, photograph by Aftab Jalia. *Source:* Image courtesy of Aftab Jalia.

Index